CW01664166

Workman Unashamed

The Testimony of a Christian Freemason

Christopher Haffner

Lewis Masonic

First published 1989
Revised and enlarged hardback edition 2005
This paperback edition first published 2020

ISBN 978 0 85318 589 5

All rights reserved. No part of this book may be reproduced or transmitted in any form or by any means, electronic or mechanical, including photocopying, recording, scanning or by any information storage and retrieval system, on the internet or elsewhere, without permission from the Publisher in writing.

© Christopher Haffner 2005 / 2020

Published by Lewis Masonic
an imprint of Ian Allan Publishing Ltd, Shepperton, Middx TW17 8AS.

Printed in England.

Visit the Lewis Masonic website at www.lewismasonic.co.uk

Copyright
Illegal copying and selling of publications deprives authors, publishers and booksellers of income, without which there would be no investment in new publications. Unauthorised versions of publications are also likely to be inferior in quality and contain incorrect information. You can help by reporting copyright infringements and acts of piracy to the Publisher or the UK Copyright Service.

CONTENTS

DEDICATION

I dedicate this book to those Christian teachers who have been influential in my life and have widened my understanding of the Faith, so as to create what is becoming slowly and with God's help,

> 'a workman who has no need to be ashamed,
> rightly handling the word of truth'
> (2 *Tim* 2:15 RSV).

To the Revd Matthew Morgan Griffiths, Chaplain of Emanuel School, who taught me the elements of Biblical criticism and Old Testament history. To Dr D. Martyn Lloyd Jones, Minister of Westminster Chapel, who taught me that Christianity is trust in Jesus Christ. To the Revd W. M. F. Scott, Principal of St Aidan's College, who carefully prepared me for confirmation. To the Revd Canon Robert Nelson, Rector of Liverpool, who taught me that Catholicism is both Biblical and evangelistic. To the Revd David A. Edwards, Chaplain to Liverpool University, who introduced me to Neo-orthodoxy and Biblical Theology. To the Very Revd F. W. Dillistone, Dean of Liverpool, who showed me that symbolism is a means to understanding. To the Revd Stephen F. Sidebotham, Vicar of Christ Church Kowloon Tong, who taught me that leadership is caring for people. To Dr Philip Chan, Elder of Alliance Church, Kowloon Tong, who showed me that evangelical faith is not necessarily exclusive. To Father Raymond E. Brown, whose books have taught me that Roman Catholicism may indeed be becoming catholic. And to the Very Revd Dr Paul Clasper, Dean of Hong Kong, who taught me that the practice and communication of the Faith can be an enjoyable experience.

ALSO BY CHRISTOPHER HAFFNER

Masonic Books

The Craft in the East
Amoy: the Port and the Lodge
Regularity of Origin

Published Articles

Women in the Craft?
Black and Blue
Freemasonry in Eighteenth Century Canton
A Brief History of District Grand Lodge (Hong Kong and the Far East)
Things Chinese
Masonry Universal: a Geographical Study
Father Noah
Freemasonry in the Last Unknown (New Guinea)
Congratulations on Becoming a Master Mason
Notes on Prince Hall Masonry in the Far East
A Visit to Emulation Lodge of Improvement
Lodge Harry S. Truman No 1725 (Osan, Korea)
Paul Chater: Keystone of Hong Kong Masonry
Oration – Brother Samuel Moses Perry
Democracy and Dictatorship
Structure in Freemasonry
Three Masons of Deshima (Japan)
Scottish Ritual in the Orient
British and American Masonry in the Far East
Oration-Brother Alec Hutton Potts
Masonic Research
Freemasonry in Hong Kong
The Antient Landmarks Revisited
With Frank van Ginkel: The First Japanese Freemasons
With Jan Huysman: French Lodges in Hong Kong and Shanghai
Progress in the Science
Freemasonry and Islam: a Problem Area
Oration – Brother Richard Charles Lee
The Antient Charges Reconsidered
Freemasonry—Towards Informed Discussion (in St John's Cathedral, Hong Kong)
The Five Gifts of the Genies (The Jubilee Chapter No 2013)

Non-Masonic

Biblical Buildings
A Meditation on Toleration
Insurance and Construction Contracts
Architecture and the Law
Powers and Duties of an Arbitrator
Commencement, Completion and Delays
Principles of Arbitration
The Last One Hundred and Fifty Years of Architecture

ABOUT THE AUTHOR

Christopher Haffner, known as Kit, was born in 1936 in Tolworth, Surrey. The original Haffners were nineteenth century German immigrants to Lancashire, and both his parents were born in the Burnley area. He was educated at Emanuel School, London, and the Liverpool School of Architecture.

Kit's first significant religious experience was a commitment made at Westminster Chapel under the ministry of Dr Martyn Lloyd-Jones at the age of thirteen. Whilst his churchmanship has changed over the years, this basic fact has remained a pillar to his faith. He has held various lay offices in the Anglican Church including membership of the diocesan synod whilst in Hong Kong. He preached in church on several occasions and was the first layperson invited to give Bible expositions in St John's Cathedral on topics such as 'Biblical Buildings'.

From his early years, Kit wished to be an architect (with an occasional sideways glance at ordination), and this wish was fulfilled as he graduated with first class honours from Liverpool University. He then travelled by Jeep overland to Calcutta, and thence made his way to Hong Kong, where he signed a four-year contract in 1959 but worked thereafter until 1993. For most of that time he was senior partner of a firm of architects, structural engineers and interior designers. He became President of the Hong Kong Institute of Architects, Chairman of the local branch of the Institute of Arbitrators, and first Chairman of the Architects' Registration Board. He lectured on legal aspects of architectural practice at Hong Kong University, tutored a master's degree in arbitration at the Hong Kong City Polytechnic and was invited on several occasions to lecture in mainland Chinese universities.

Kit married Maureen in 1965 and they have three children. Now that he is retired and they live in England, all three visit the family home to sample their mother's cooking once a week, with spouses or spouses-to-be.

He was initiated into Freemasonry in the Corinthian Lodge of Amoy in 1962 and became its master in 1971. He subsequently went through the chairs of lodges and 'higher degree' bodies in the English, Irish and Scottish constitutions. He was patented by the Grand Master of England as District Grand Master of Hong Kong and the Far East, and held Grand Rank on a substantive or honorary basis under several jurisdictions including China (Taiwan). He held the thirtieth degree.

His first full book, *The Craft in the East*, was published in 1975. He belonged to lodges of research in Ireland, Maine, California, Texas and New York. He had been one of the 14,000 members of the correspondence circle of the Quatuor Coronati Lodge of London for some years when in 1984 he received the honour of election to full membership, attending at least two meetings a year from Hong Kong, and was elected its master for 1990-91, during which he attended all meetings. In 1982 he was awarded the Ira S. Holder Certificate of Literature for an article on 'Prince Hall Masonry in the Far East'. In 1987 he received Fellowship of the Philalethes Society of

Prince Hall masonry which is restricted to forty, the only holder outside America, and the Takashi Komatsu Distinguished Service Award of the Grand Lodge of Japan.

The story of Kit's subsequent retirement from Freemasonry is given in the Preface to the second edition of this book, which follows. He stressed at the time and subsequently that this did not involve repudiation of any positive views about Freemasonry which he had expressed over many previous years.

ACKNOWLEDGEMENTS

I acknowledge with grateful thanks the enthusiastic support given to me in the final production of this book by VW the Revd Neville Barker Cryer, Grand Chaplain, and W Bro Roy Wells, Past Junior Grand Deacon, my colleagues in the Quatuor Coronati Lodge No 2076, and the present and former editors of its Transactions, *Ars Quatuor Coronatorum*.

I wish to express my thanks to the authors and publishers of various books quated in the text. In each case, I hope that adequate reference has been made to enable the interested reader to locate full details in the Bibliography, and to further research topics of specific interest to him.

I would also like to express my thanks to John Hamill of the United Grand Lodge of England for making available various church reports on Freemasonry issued at around the time of and after the publication of the first edition of this book. These have formed the basis of much of Part Five.

The Revd Neville Barker Cryer has been constant in his encouragement, and for this I continue to be grateful. He made available to me the first chapter of his forthcoming book *Did you know this too?* which is on 'The Churches' Concern with Freemasonry'.

I have been grateful for discussion with Douglas Burford on the reasoning behind the changes made in the English Royal Arch degree, as well as copies of relevant documentation.

I am grateful too for correspondence with Caroline Windsor in connection with her forthcoming anthology on 'Attitudes to and Experiences of Freemasonry within the Church.'

PREFACE TO THE SECOND EDITION

When Lewis Masonic asked me for permission to reprint *Workman Unashamed* I had to think very seriously before saying Yes. The reason for the slow response was that when I wrote the book I was District Grand Master of Hong Kong and the Far East, but when the request came, I had retired both from my work and my lodges. I regarded myself as no longer a Freemason, and wondered what use re-publication could possibly serve when the obvious riposte to the evidence of the book would be that it had all become meaningless. How could the views of a man who had resigned his lodge memberships for reasons connected with his faith be used to support lodge membership for others? Unfortunately the answer can only be given by placing my heart on my sleeve, and revealing a period in my life which has previously only been known to a few close friends.

I had felt a call to the ministry of the church since my twenties as a student, but was persuaded by both family and clergy friends that I should continue my studies and go into practice as an architect. Soon the call was obscured by work pressures and then family commitments, and I was happy feeling that I was serving God in my work, especially as I specialised in projects with a humanitarian function such as rehabilitation centres, schools including those for children with disabilities, and even the occasional church. Eventually the call to ministry began to come to the fore again and I discussed it with the Bishop of Hong Kong and Macau, but he offered the same advice, that I should stay as I was. He also advised that since I was an expatriate he would not consider an application from me to be ordained, but would happily ordain me if asked to do so by a bishop in my country of origin.

Suffice it to say that the Bishop of Kensington put me forward to a Selection Conference of the Church of England's Advisory Board on Ministry in April 1992. At this I made no secret of my role in Freemasonry, and as a result had a painful interview with the Bishop of Plymouth who argued that many in every congregation would be unhappy to seek the counsel of a mason, and might even reject my ministry outright. I countered that all in my present congregation knew of my lodge membership and that even as a layperson some families of masons came because of it. I was 'not recommended,' but in the letter explaining this to the Director of Ordinands (which I was not supposed to have seen; secrecy is not a masonic prerogative) so far as I was aware there was little or no mention of Freemasonry, but a series of other reasons were given, which included presumptions on matters that had not been discussed with me (such as our presumed reasons for leaving Hong Kong, at that stage not even decided), and others that were contrary to what I had said (such as a supposed disinterest in academic study, about which I had actually expressed enthusiasm). A few of them were good. Nevertheless, I asked my vicar not to write to the Bishop of Kensington putting these objections, feeling that he should make his decision without being pestered. Eventually, after a wait of about six months after the conference, he said No.

Meantime my wife and I had reviewed our finances and decided to take the bull by the horns. I retired from my work and started living in Kensington. We looked for a local church and soon chose a 'plant' of Holy Trinity Brompton, the church that originated the Alpha Course. Needless to say, we were quickly involved in attending such a course. Not long after, the bishop gave his blessing to my starting theological studies 'at my own risk' and, because it was commutable, I enrolled at Oak Hill, an Evangelical Anglican college in North London. In the main I found the experience thoroughly enjoyable. Whilst I was there we had 'placements' for the nine months of a full academic year in a variety of parishes, and because I was relatively new to it I was able to arrange for one of these to be in the church that we had started attending.

During this year I was asked to lead one small Alpha group with a woman in the congregation, and my wife happened to 'share' with her the fact that I was a Freemason. She was extremely distressed and at once went to the vicar and stated that she could not work with me in any circumstances. The vicar, who already knew of my lodge membership, nevertheless adopted the 'weaker brethren' argument, that I should not cause my brother or sister to stumble because of anything that I did. I must resign from Freemasonry or give up my placement altogether.

I spent two months on this problem and then resigned from my lodges. I did so with a letter explaining that I withdrew nothing that I had written in favour of the Craft, by implication this book. My resignation was purely the result of the situation in which I had found myself and the conclusion must not be reached that I had found masonic membership to be incompatible with my faith. The reaction of the lodges was universally one of great regret, a belief that what I had done was in their view unnecessary, but also of sad understanding. But many of my former masonic brethren are still my good friends.

The woman in the church who had objected to sharing a course with me could not accept this as adequate. She stated that I must burn my regalia in public and go through an exorcism. It transpired eventually that she believed herself to be under a curse because her grandfather had been a Freemason. The vicar agreed with my view that, since I considered that I had not sinned by masonic membership (other than a little pride, and perhaps overeating on festive occasions), no such extreme measures were necessary. He asked me to go ahead leading the Alpha group meetings with his wife in her place.

Some of the church members were also in an organisation which rejoices in the name of Full Gospel Business Man's Fellowship International and I attended some of its meetings, including one in which an ex-mason spoke of his good and bad impressions of Freemasonry, the bad eventually heavily predominating. I was told that I must give similar testimony to the evils of masonry, and when I refused was told that my ministry could not be blessed by God. It did not take me long to realise that if the blessing of God depended on having to speak of imaginary evils in a largely good organisation, those who asked me to do so must have a very different view of God from the Supreme Being whom I worship.

So I attended a second selection conference, this time being put forward by the Bishop of London as the Bishop of Kensington had died. Masonry again was on the agenda, and I was grilled unpleasantly by an Anglican nun about my inconsistency and lack of fidelity to the Craft, suggesting that these defects of character would come out if I were ordained. I explained that I was dealing with priorities, that for myself it had been a traumatic exercise, and that my priority, even as a Freemason, had to be my faith. I was again 'not recommended'. This time the secret letter explaining the rejection to the Director of Ordinands did not so far as I know mention the Craft. Instead it stressed my presumed heavy leadership style because I had been boss of my firm in Hong Kong. This was put forward as the main reason despite my arguments at the conference that my firm had been a private professional firm serving its clients in much the same way that a ministerial team serves its parishioners, and that I had been the modestly successful chair of several voluntary organisations. However, the selection conference concluded that I would inevitably be pastorally insensitive. With exemplary sensitivity, the Director opened his debriefing by quoting from the letter, that I was 'a hopeless case' and that I should be discouraged from trying again. I took the advice, mainly because I had no residual faith in the selection system.

This meant that I was free to extend the two-year diploma course into a three-year degree. I then was licensed as a Reader, which I have found to be a very enabling role without the full responsibilities of the ordained. I had time to do a further degree at Heythrop College and became a Master of Theology, the study for which I found to be even more enjoyable than Oak Hill. My wife and I moved out of London and I am happy to say that my activity in the local church has been thoroughly fulfilling, and both of us feel that we have been blessed.

I have the weekly fellowship of a local church and the more intimate fellowship of Bible studies held in my home. I have the fellowship of Readers as they meet locally and in national conferences, and that of a few other Christian organisations to which I belong. Of course I miss the regular and unquestioning fellowship that Freemasonry offers. But I do not think that my resignation was unnecessary, because at that time it was important for me to confront the priorities in my life. Regrettably this writing of further text to bring *Workman Unashamed* up to date has been traumatic, bringing to the surface wounds that I thought I had succeeded in forgetting.

But at least with the reissue of *Workman Unashamed*, I can look back over a decade with an open mind at the pleasure that masonry gave me, and see even more clearly how unjustified are the attacks made on it by my Christian brothers and sisters.

Christopher Haffner
Feast of the Four Crowned Martyrs, 2004

PART ONE

Introduction

1
Reasons

INNOCENT AMUSEMENTS

I acknowledge that there are certain Christians to whom the whole of this book will be meaningless. They have not only made up their minds about Freemasonry, but about a whole series of activities which they regard as improper in a Christian.

A friend loaned me a book written by the early nineteenth-century evangelist, Charles G. Finney. This had recently been reprinted, no doubt because it was considered to be relevant to this generation. This is what the author says in a chapter on 'Innocent Amusements':

> Whatever is lawful in a moral agent or according to the law of God is right. If anyone, therefore, engages lawfully in any employment or in any amusement, he must do so from a supreme love to God and equal love to his neighbor; and is, therefore, not an impenitent sinner but a Christian. It is simply absurd and a contradiction to say that an impenitent soul does, or says, or omits anything with a right heart. If impenitent, his ultimate motive must necessarily be wrong; and consequently, nothing in him is innocent, but all must be sinful. What then is innocent amusement? It must be that and only that which is not only right but actually is engaged in with a single eye to God's glory and the interests of His kingdom. If this be not the ultimate and supreme design, it is not an innocent but a sinful amusement. . . . No act or course of action should, therefore, be adjudged as either innocent or sinful without ascertaining the supreme motive of the person who acts.
>
> Parents should remember this in regard to the amusements of their unconverted children. Sunday School teachers and superintendents who are planning amusements for their Sunday Schools, preachers who spend their time in planning amusements for the young, who lead their flocks to picnics, in pleasure excursions, and justify various games, should certainly remember that unless they are in a holy state of heart, and do all this from supreme love to God and a design in the highest degree to glorify God thereby, these ways of spending time are by no means innocent but highly criminal, and those who teach people to walk in these ways are simply directing the channels in which their depravity shall run.
>
> The question often arises: 'Are we never to seek such amusements?' . . . Surely a Christian must be fallen from his first love, he must have turned back into the world, before he can feel the necessity or have the desire of seeking enjoyment in worldly sports and pastimes. A spiritual mind cannot seek enjoyment in worldly society . . . To a mind in communion with God their worldly spirit and ways, conversation and folly is repulsive and painful, as it is so strongly

> suggestive of the downward tendency of their souls and of the destiny that awaits them. (Finney pp78–82)

Whilst nothing will convince the likes of Charles Finney that Freemasonry might be of any value to a Christian, it is proper to examine the question which he poses. Is there such a thing as innocent amusement outside the tiny sphere which he has described? Does Freemasonry lie potentially within any larger definition? May it even be a force for good in the life of a Christian? The whole of this book is an attempt to examine these questions, and to give a positive answer.

MASONIC RESPONSE

Surprisingly, the teachings of Freemasonry have much in common with Charles Finney's views. Laying aside the reticence of the average mason, and acknowledging that the so-called 'secrets' of masonic ceremonial have been exposed with a fair degree of accuracy many times over, it is possible—without a breach of any obligation to keep silent—to quote from the modern exposures written by men like the Revd Walton Hannah and James Dewar, in order to give the outsider a balanced picture of 'the Craft'.

Finney suggests that all a Christian does must have a supreme objective. A new mason is taught immediately after he is initiated:

> As a Freemason let me recommend . . . such a prudent and well regulated course of discipline as may best conduce to the preservation of your corporeal and mental faculties in their fullest energy, thereby enabling you to exert those talents wherewith God has blessed you, as well to His glory as to the welfare of your fellow-creatures. (Hannah: *Darkness Visible* ppl07–108. Later references to 'Hannah' are to this book.)

Even before that, he is taught the proper use of time in terms of priorities which do not apparently differ too far from those of Charles Finney:

> The 24 inch Gauge represents the twenty-four hours of the day, part to be spent in prayer to Almighty God; part in labour and refreshment; and part in serving a friend or Brother in time of need. . . . (ibid p106)

But the fact that Freemasons are men of all religious beliefs means that Christians like Charles Finney would have a great deal to say about the 'impenitent' and the 'unconverted' within the masonic fold. His basic presupposition is missing. Within their lodges, Freemasons are not concerned with salvation and conversion, but with taking men as they are and pointing them in the direction of brotherhood and moral improvement. In so far as the Order is successful in this aim, it is content, and leaves the member to devote himself to his own religious faith to receive the grace of salvation.

Charles Finney writes of the 'ultimate and supreme design' of 'God's glory and the interests of His kingdom'. By contrast, Freemasonry has a much more earthly ambition. After the installation of a new Master, the brethren of the lodge are exhorted:

> that we shall have but one aim in view, to please each other and to unite in the grand design of being happy and communicating happiness. (*Emulation Ritual* pp203–204)

Is there a category of 'innocent amusements' into which such a grand design can be fitted?

When we look at the New Testament, we can see in the lives of the Apostles a dedication and singleness of purpose which is difficult to challenge. When St Paul made tents, he did it for the Lord's sake. When he studied the pagan temples of Athens, he did so to assemble background material for his famous Areopagus speech.

But surely there is a case to be made out for enjoyment of something for its own sake. We are not told that Jesus gritted His teeth in desperation during his thirty years as a growing boy and a carpenter, before the time came for the start of His ministry. We are left to presume that He of all people thoroughly enjoyed His preparatory years. When water is made into 'the best wine' at the start of that ministry, it is a private matter to aid the assembled company in their enjoyment of a wedding. In His parables, He offers us many examples of enjoyment of something for its own sake: it is good to rejoice with one's neighbours when a lost sheep is found, or to kill a fatted calf for the whole household when a prodigal son returns. The New Testament message is not one of rejection of every source of enjoyment—it is a message of a balanced existence where direct service to God and our fellow men is balanced with proper enjoyment of those things in life with which we have been blessed.

There nevertheless remains a basic problem in a Christian approach to Freemasonry. It has some of the characteristics of a religion, yet it is of itself incomplete. Whilst it sets moral standards which are—certainly when taken as a whole—a challenge to any man, they fall short of the ultimate standards demanded by most faiths, especially those of the true faith revealed in the person and teaching of Jesus Christ.

THE READER

It is my sincere wish that this book may be of value to several groups of people who find Freemasonry perplexing, and even to those who are already committed one way or the other.

The first and main group is those Christians who are not masons, and are not already wholly of the view that Freemasonry is evil. It is not aimed at making masons of them—recruitment is far from my ambition, but at enabling them to better understand the masons that they meet. Within this group could well be the wives of keen masons who find it hard to talk about masonry at home. Equally, there will I hope be clergy who have difficulty relating to Freemasons who play roles, often of some importance, in the organisation of their churches.

The second group is those Freemasons who are still trying to piece together a meaningful understanding of the relationship of their religious duties to those apparently superimposed by masonic membership. The problems of Christian existence in the currents of early twenty-first century life are such that no mason could possibly claim to know all the answers. I certainly do not expect to answer all such questions, but perhaps I may set the minds of searching Freemasons off on paths which prove fruitful.

There may be a small third group, very similar to the second, but consisting of non-Christians who are sufficiently interested in the relationship of Freemasonry to religion that they find this book to be of value. Again, this book does not intend to seek converts to the Christian faith, but to provide a balanced justification for the overall attitude of the Craft to all religions. It would be a matter of great delight to me if Freemasons committed to Islam, to Judaism, to the Noble Eightfold Path of Buddhism, and so on, were to write similar books from the standpoint of their own faiths.

A fourth group which I envisage consists of those Freemasons who, far from entertaining doubts, are wholeheartedly in favour of Freemasonry. I have in mind the mason who says, 'Freemasonry is good enough as a religion for me', or 'There is nothing unChristian about a man who follows the principles of masonry'. To these masons I suggest that my book may prove the inadequacy of the Craft without a deep faith in Jesus Christ, with all that this implies in terms of human existence. At the most, his masonic activity should be seen as but a part of this higher commitment.

A final group will of course be those Christians who are seeking for ammunition to use in their warfare against the Craft. No doubt I will have provided much for them to use. It is my hope that this book will however filter out those irrelevant arguments based on inaccurate presuppositions about masonry which exist in all anti-masonic literature. If Freemasonry is to be attacked, then let the enemy attack something which exists, and not a caricature.

MUCH ADO ABOUT NOTHING

Apart from being the title of a Shakespearian play, 'Much Ado' is the title of a chapter in a well-known attack on Freemasonry, implying that the organisation of Freemasonry takes up a lot of time and effort to no real effect. I am not now concerned about this argument as such—the majority of men who are not masons waste far more time in pursuits which have far less benefit to society than the modest efforts of the lodges and their members. A fuller answer is given in the chapter on Priorities.

I am concerned to point out that many of the attacks which have recently taken place on masonry are to an even greater extent 'much ado about nothing'. Some time ago my wife showed me a pamphlet by an evangelical Christian author who gave seven reasons why a Christian cannot be a mason, clearly thought to be clinching arguments against which no answer is possible. Only two of them I acknowledge to be possibly relevant. These are alleged references in the writings of a long dead but famous American masonic leader, Albert Pike, on the subject of Lucifer, and to a masonic god in the rituals. These and related accusations are considered in separate chapters in this book.

However, in the five other arguments I happily join with the author of the pamphlet. He does Freemasonry the honour of equating it with the Christian faith, and then makes a comparison of the two. But this type of argument cannot even be equated with 'comparing an apple with an orange'. He is comparing a revelation from the Son of God with a private men's club which requires faith in a Supreme Being as a minimum qualification for membership. I agree wholeheartedly with the author of the pamphlet on the issue of the superiority of the Christian faith. But then I would agree—were he to put such an argument—that full time ministry in the church is superior to my former mundane job as an architect, even though I believe that I was serving the Lord in my work. Such an argument does not automatically make every Christian wish to be a full time minister, nor does it make it wrong for a Christian to be an architect.

Not only do I agree with the author of the pamphlet about the self evident superiority of Christianity, but so does Freemasonry at an official level. A recent pamphlet published by the United Grand Lodge of England says:

> Freemasonry is far from indifferent to religion. Without interfering in religious practice it expects each member to follow his own faith, and *to place above all other duties his duty to God* by whatever name He is known. *(Freemasonry and Religion)*

Comparing a divine revelation with a club with a view to proving one to be superior, when the club already acknowledges the superiority of the other, is truly 'Much Ado about Nothing'.

Another example arises from the tendency of anti-masonic writers to create artificial scenarios which they believe parallel the Craft, and because they do not like the result, they condemn Freemasonry. Let me give you some examples from John Lawrence's *Freemasonry—a religion?*:

> He says on page 117 that in order to sell phoney Chanel No 5 on Oxford Street, you would make it look like the real thing. Freemasonry has chaplains, prayers, ceremony, candles, and all the 'trappings' of religion. Because selling phoney Chanel No 5 is wrong, so is Freemasonry.

He tells a tale on page 79, of a man who was authorised by a local government to issue cheques on its behalf. He received an appeal for famine relief, and without authorisation made out a large cheque in its support. Because this is wrong, he concludes by amazing sleight-of-hand that it is wrong for Freemasons to invoke the name of God.

Book after book could be written at this level. The result would be nothing other than 'Much Ado about Nothing'.

STRUCTURE

I have divided this book into four parts.

In this introductory part, I will give enough information about masonry in general, and about some of the terminology involved to prepare for the rest of the book. It must be remembered that there have been books about religion in general since mankind first learned to write, and about the Christian faith for close on two thousand years. Perhaps less well known to the outsider is the vast expanse of literature about Freemasonry which members of the Order have produced. A classic bibliography, called 'Wolfsteig' after its author, contains a listing of eighty thousand volumes for Europe alone, and American contributions would bring this to over a hundred thousand (*Coil's Encyclopedia* p376). This introduction must therefore be taken for what it is worth—a mere survey of the important issues.

The second part deals with those criticisms of Freemasonry which have been made by its detractors on a general basis, not specifically concerned with the accusations of heresy which Christians have made over the last fifty years. These are the subject of the third part. Much the same pressure of space applies to both these sections—the reader will readily imagine how much has been published on each of the heresies, let alone the more general subjects. And the final part will deal with some conclusions as to what, if anything, the churches have failed to learn from Freemasonry, and what Freemasonry is being taught by the criticisms of the churches.

Most Christians who are Freemasons find little incompatibility between the two. It was a matter of surprise to them that the Methodist Church in England should have issued *Guidance* on 3 July 1986, suggesting that Methodists should not become members of the Craft. The document acknowledges that:

> There are many loyal and sincere Methodists who are Freemasons, whose commitment to Christ is unquestionable and who see no incompatibility in their membership of the Methodist Church and of Freemasonry.

It seems strange to the writer and other Christians that such an acknowledgement can be made in a document providing 'guidance' in the opposite direction. My text will examine possible reasons for this as expressed in the ever increasing number of books on the subject, and see if they are based on reality or on an unbalanced selection of data and a fertile imagination.

It is my hope that this book will provide a background of sanity for future discussion of the real nature of the fraternity, in which I held a position of responsibility of which I was proud, and of which I am unashamed.

2
Meanings

CHRISTIAN

Much useless discussion results from failing to define what is being discussed, until too late in the day it is realised that the difference was not one of real opinion but of use of words. In this book it is therefore of paramount importance that we look at the meaning of words like 'religion' and 'Christian'.

We can find the origin of the word Christian in the Bible, and that is a good place to start. In *Acts* 11:26, we read 'It was in Antioch that the disciples first got the name of Christians'. A disciple is someone who follows the teaching of another person, so a Christian is someone who follows the teaching of Jesus Christ. We should not confuse disciple with apostle—whilst all Christians are disciples, only those disciples who witnessed Jesus' life and were selected for leadership came to be labelled apostles.

The concept of a Christian as a person who follows the teaching of Jesus is good for our purposes. It does not presuppose any entrenched theological position like that of an evangelical or Catholic. An evangelical would probably wish to say that a Christian is someone who has placed his personal trust in Jesus Christ for eternal life. A Catholic would lay emphasis in his definition on someone who has been baptised and participates in the sacraments administered by the leaders of the church, given authority in succession to the apostles. I do not wish to write exclusively for either of these, or any other Christian group, but for all Christians.

I think that you are entitled to know something of my own presuppositions, since no matter how I may attempt to disguise them, they will come out in the following pages. I am an Anglican, and attend my local church because I enjoy it and find it fulfilling. I attend practically every Sunday.

As an infant I was baptised in the Methodist Church where my mother had taught Sunday School. I attended a school with a chapel and an Anglican chaplain. I started my life as a convinced Christian in a Congregational Church in London, and since it was far from my home, moved in turn to the nearby Baptist Church, an Assembly of Plymouth Brethren and an evangelical Anglican Church. During my University years I was prepared for confirmation by the Principal of an Anglican theological college, and despite his misgivings attended a parish church thereafter which described itself as 'Prayer Book Catholic', a position which I largely retain. I was also active in the Student Christian Movement and the Anglican Chaplaincy. My wife's family are largely Roman Catholic, and I have frequently worshipped with them. In my last years in Hong Kong, I started attending Bible studies run by evangelical friends and a charismatic businessman's group, and thoroughly enjoyed their fellowship. I have benefited from all my relationships within this spectrum of worship and Christian experience.

Does this make me a Christian? Yes, it does—not only under my own wide definition, but also under the two narrower definitions that I have proposed for evangelicals and Catholics. Of course, it does not necessarily make me a good Christian, and I suspect that at the end of a lifetime of effort, prayer and even inspiration, I will be but a poor shadow of my Master.

RELIGION

Much of the debate about Freemasonry has centred on the question, Is Freemasonry a religion? A sensible definition of religion is absolutely crucial to a consideration of the issue. Those who wish to accuse Freemasonry of being a religion—or a substitute for it have defined the word in such a way as to prove their point, and the official pronouncements of Grand Lodges have done the reverse.

I have heard evangelical preachers denying that Christianity is a religion, stating that it is simply trust in Jesus Christ, and that you can be as religious as is humanly possible without having a personal relationship with the living Christ, and therefore not be a Christian. Whilst I also accept that view in its context, even the church in which this was being said had an organised form, a membership roll, a set time of worship on Sundays, a body of 'sound' doctrine, and at least the majority of the trappings of 'religion'. But amongst evangelicals this distinction between Christianity and religion is a not uncommon view: Radio Bible Class's *Our Daily Bread* concludes each day's notes with an aphorism, and for 2 June 1987 this was, 'Christianity begins where religion ends, with the resurrection'.

But most people accept that Christianity is a religion. An encyclopedia definition of religion runs:

> A set of rulings and beliefs, regarded as instituted in some manner by a supreme authority beyond the challenge of man. The practical pursuits involved in obeying a religion are often organised through institutions and rites. The basic principles of a religion may be observed merely as part of a ritual routine, or they may be specifically expressed as a declaration of faith. ... In founded religions, announced by a prophet or master, where faith is expressed, a conscious commitment is required; in its subtler forms this involves a definite belief concerning the ultimate nature of things, the authorship and destiny of the world. ...
>
> Most religions are practiced through certain formal rites carried out by priests in special holy places or shrines. By enjoining certain forms of behaviour on men, religion constitutes a force making for social cohesion. Such basic injunctions of many religions as those, for example, that forbid killing, stealing and lying are in

> fact preconditions for any viable human society. (*New Caxton Encyclopedia* pp5041–42)

The last part of this quotation emphasises the relationship of religion to everyday life—the majority of the ten commandments are about a man's relationship to his fellow man.

THE SECULAR

Freemasons have tended to draw a distinction between 'religion' and 'religious', by saying that their Order is not a religion but it is religious. This is probably an attempt to put into simple words the fact that masons are required as such to believe in a Supreme Being and to say prayers, but have no theology, no meetings for worship, no 'evangelism' in the form of membership drives, and so on.

This emphasises the difficulty that all Christians have in deciding what is a religious and what a secular activity. For the irreligious person this is easy—religion is what goes on in places of worship and when religious people say their prayers. For a person of faith, however, this is totally unsatisfactory, and the tendency is for them to say that every human act is religious. Many of us have admired the spiritual struggles shown in the film *Chariots of Fire*. In this, winning a race became a religious activity. The Christian follows St Paul's exhortation in *Colossians* 3:23, 'Whatever you are doing, put your whole heart into it, as if you were doing it for the Lord and not for men'. If he is unable to say this about something he is doing, he should not be doing it.

I read a book recently about modern Christians and the Arts, and found that the author—an evangelical Christian—was equally uneasy about any tendency to compartmentalise life:

> In the nineteenth century . . . spirituality was seen [for the first time] as something separate from the rest of real life. It was above ordinary things; it was cut off and not part of the everyday working out of our lives. Spirituality became something religious and had a great deal less to do with truth, daily life, applying Christian principles through that life. . . . Thus certain things were regarded as spiritual and other things as secular.
>
> The true division in the Christian life between one group of activities . . . and another is that line we call sin. . . . Either Christ has redeemed the whole man, including every part of him (except those things that are sinful), or he has redeemed none of them. Either our whole life comes under the Lordship of Christ or no part can effectively come under it. (Schaeffer p27)

I agree wholly with this view; a Christian who is a Freemason must be able to see his lodge membership within the Lordship of Christ.

CHRISTIAN OPINION

Much use will be made by me of the opinions of other Christians. Indeed, I have tried to give a balance of such viewpoints throughout, so as to make the book as relevant as possible. It seems clear that a defence of Freemasonry written solely for evangelicals would be very different from one written exclusively for Roman Catholics. Yet I am neither, and so must perforce rely on what others tell me of their views.

I am looking at Christian opinion from two angles. First, what have a wide range of Christians said against the Craft, especially during the latter part of this century? Secondly, what beliefs do present day Christians of all schools of thought have on topics which seem to relate to the theme of this book, such as comparative religion, the authority of the Bible, heresy, formality in worship, and so on?

My Christian upbringing has been very biblical. I started my pilgrimage under a minister who preached solely about its words, and soon found myself leading schoolboy Bible studies. I was prepared for confirmation by an evangelical Anglican grounded in the Scriptures. I have for many years attended a church where three separate lessons are read each Sunday in accordance with a lectionary designed to give a proper balance of Old and New Testament teaching, and I retain a distinct preference for preachers who expound the Scriptures and spare the congregation their personal social commentary. I attend studies or expositions of the Bible regularly, and read it daily at home.

This means that I intend to quote from the Bible a lot, although I will take great care with the context. All Christians accept the authority of God's written word, even if they may debate its value relative to reason and tradition. I believe that the supreme authority in making Christian value judgements must be the overall balance given by the Scriptures, interpreted in the light of reason and tradition whilst the heart is prayerfully guided by the Paraclete. I shall be quoting from the *New English Bible* almost exclusively, because I have grown to know it as the pew Bible of my former church, though not my personal favourite. Occasionally I shall use the Authorised or King James version, because that is the version usually used in masonic ritual.

For sources of present day Christian opinion, I have found great benefit from Richard McBrien's *Catholicism*, which seems to give a very concise, clear and up-to-date overview of the doctrines of his church. I have also found value in looking at a number of books produced by the Evangelical Alliance and the Inter Varsity Fellowship. As would be expected within Anglicanism, apart from the Thirty-Nine Articles of 1562, nothing of any real authority has been produced. I have subscribed to *Theology* for a few years, and found what I presume is intelligent Anglican opinion of the present day enshrined in its pages. In addition, I have looked with interest at a few extreme fundamentalist and old fashioned Roman Catholic books on relevant subjects.

This book was written largely before the publication of the report of the Working Group established by the Standing Committee of the General

Synod of the Church of England entitled *Christianity and Freemasonry—Are They Compatible?—a contribution to discussion*. The importance of the last phrase in this title cannot be overstressed. The report was prepared after merely five meetings, under a limited budget, and admits that a proper report should be, 'by a larger group, working for a longer time, equipped with research assistants, armed with legal advisors and furnished with more substantial evidence'. The acceptance by Synod of its incomplete contents was as 'a contribution to discussion', and it was on that basis that the resolution recommended it to consideration by the parishes.

The draft text of this book covered in essence all the issues but one raised by the report—the exception being the two letters from former masons published as an appendix in support of an allegation that Freemasonry causes psychic disturbance—but references to the report have been added where it seems appropriate. The contribution of the two Freemason members of the Working Group is not made explicit, except in the last paragraph where, despite 'differences of opinion', they 'agree that there are clear difficulties'. I have assumed that their contribution was largely one of steering the rest of the committee clear of total misapprehensions about the Craft, and perhaps in this they were partly successful. It would seem that the bulk of the text is the product of the non-mason members.

Canon R. Lewis, himself not a mason, referred to the problems of taking ill-informed Christian opinion seriously in his speech to the Synod:

> I am appalled, I am bound to say, by the unsolicited material that has been sent to me . . . prior to this debate. What beggars my imagination is the way in which anyone, for whatever sort of malicious or neurotic reason, who writes anything denouncing freemasonry is assumed by some to be telling the truth. They are not. We have seen it in public life and we have seen it here. The Church should be different. Denials are of no avail, and I quote from one letter. 'I have come across the following quotes from Albert Pike' and he goes on to quote what Albert Pike says. My researches tell me that Albert Pike never has, never had, any connection with England, and that what he writes is almost, if not all, rubbish; and yet it is he who is believed. I am ashamed when fellow Christians are so gullible and so uncharitable, and that is putting it charitably. (Synod Proceedings p248)

Like Canon Lewis, I am appalled by what I have read and heard on tapes produced by evangelical and charismatic preachers, when what is stated as fact and condemned as unspeakably wrong bears no relationship to the Freemasonry of my own experience. Surprisingly, the errors seem to be all the greater when the preacher prefixes his condemnation with an indication of his own involvement in the Craft in his earlier, misguided years. For example, David Pawson's tape about Freemasonry, in which he expresses his ignorance but shows that he has tried hard to get to the truth, is fairer than many comments by former masons. His errors are mainly that he deals with an out of date form of the obligation, and that he places too much reliance on the opinion of Walton Hannah about the Royal Arch word.

But I have tried in this book to give a balanced view of extreme opinions, and even of Albert Pike where he is quoted by Christians against the Craft.

Whilst I expect to satisfy no one wholly with this *pot pourri* of Christian viewpoints, I hope equally that no one will feel that the opinion of his branch of the divided church has been ignored!

FREEMASONRY

Every Freemason has to learn a short catechism after his initiation, and one couplet goes:

> What is Freemasonry?
> A peculiar [meaning unique] system of morality, veiled in allegory and illustrated by symbols.

Perhaps it is a good enough definition for a beginner, but it does not take us far.

In a talk which I gave to a lodge of instruction, I did my best to expand it by saying that Freemasonry is a series of independent societies which trace their descent, directly or indirectly, from the operative masons of medieval Europe, consisting of good men and true of any religious faith. They meet privately to perform ceremonies which have a symbolism based upon the art of building in general and upon legends connected with structures whose erection is recorded in the Old Testament in particular. This is done with a view to inculcating moral attitudes and creating a brotherhood based upon a common belief in the Fatherhood of the Creator of the Universe. (Haffner, *Structure in Freemasonry* p21)

I do not now retract this definition in any way, but must admit that it excludes Orders which are restricted in membership to masons who believe in the Holy Trinity and whose ceremonies are generally based on legends connected with the Crusades. These Orders will be discussed later in this book.

The United Grand Lodge of England has not been notable for the frequency of its issue of official explanations, but in a welcome break with this tradition, in 1984 it published a pamphlet called *What is Freemasonry?* Whilst this is well worth reading in full, the following extracts are particularly appropriate:

> Freemasonry is one of the world's oldest secular fraternal societies. . . . [It] is a society of men concerned with moral and spiritual values. Its members are taught its precepts by a series of ritual dramas, which follow ancient forms and use stonemasons' customs and tools as allegorical guides.
>
> The essential qualification for admission into and continuing membership is belief in a Supreme Being. Membership is open to men of any race or religion who can fulfil this essential qualification and are of good repute.
>
> Freemasonry is not a religion, nor is it a substitute for religion. Its essential qualification opens it to men of many religions and it expects them to continue to follow their own faith. It does not allow religion to be discussed at its meetings.
>
> A Freemason is encouraged to do his duty first to his God (by whatever name he is known) through his faith and religious practice; and then, without detriment to his family and those dependent on him, to his neighbour through charity and service.

It can immediately be seen that the field of Freemasonry impinges on the field of religion somewhat more than the Liverpool Football Club, and somewhat less than the British and Foreign Bible Society. Since it will be readily conceded that the latter is neither a religion nor the property of any one church, even if religious, cannot the same distinction be made for the Craft?

MASONIC AUTHORITY

The final consideration of this introductory chapter is the question of authority in Freemasonry, especially in its official pronouncements.

It is an extremely elusive matter. First, there is no international masonic organisation which can make a pronouncement for the whole masonic world. The largest Grand Lodge is the United Grand Lodge of England with 350,000 members in eight thousand lodges, in England and Wales and in Districts overseas. The smallest is the Grand Lodge of Luxembourg, with four lodges and perhaps two hundred members. The greatest concentration of masons lies in the United States of America, with some two million masons in eighty separate Grand Lodges. Even though the American Grand Masters meet every three years for a conference, this has no executive role, and there is clearly no one to speak authoritatively for them all, let alone for the other sovereign jurisdictions of the world.

The Grand Lodge of England has published three books—apart from its minutes and the *Constitutions* (rules for its own government and that of its lodges)—during almost two hundred and ninety years of existence. So there is very little that is official or authoritative, and almost all the tens of thousands of books published about masonry in this country and overseas merely represent the personal views of individual Freemasons. Those that venture into print usually have an axe to grind, and may even at times seem to represent the lunatic fringe of the Craft.

Whilst I sympathise with the late Stephen Knight (author of the anti-Masonic best seller, *The Brotherhood*) in his search for official authority, I cannot but object when he refers to a badly written answer to an exposé of masonry as 'this official view propounded . . . for public digestion' (Knight p234). The book—*Light Invisible*—possesses no trace of official sanction.

In a similar way, 'Anglo-Catholic'—the author of *Reflections on Freemasonry* of 1930—goes to great lengths to prove that the woolly ramblings of W. L. Wilmshurst are 'official' by examining the manner in which they were recommended by the publishers of masonic books at that time, and by the fact that the author received the rank of Past Assistant Grand Director of Ceremonies. Masonic publishers are not essentially different from other publishers: there is a certain element of idealism, well larded with the need to keep solvent. I have no wish to belittle the rank conferred on Wilmshurst, but a glance at a current *Masonic Year Book* will indicate that this is annually conferred on some 130 senior masons. Generally this is on the recommendation of their Provincial Grand Masters for service to the Province and its lodges, and to masonry as a whole. It was quite clearly not a specific recognition of Wilmshurst's writings. 'Anglo-

Catholic' was so concerned to prove Wilmshurst 'official' that he contrived a method of getting him to deny a rumour that his writings were officially disapproved of (pp35–37). Neither argument proves the point: individual books by masons, no matter how popular, are not the official viewpoint of a Grand Lodge.

RITUAL

It must be even more difficult for the non-mason to understand the official position of the ceremonial of masonry, often published in booklets called 'Rituals' or 'Workings', frequently with parts somewhat disguised by abbreviation or code. In many jurisdictions—such as Massachusetts— they are officially published, whilst in others like California, publication is prohibited. In the British Isles, the situation is as follows:

> In England, the last demonstrations of an official ritual followed the Union of two rival Grand Lodges in 1813, but nothing was published. Since then, all workings and the published ritual books, though based on what probably took place to a varying degree, are unofficial. Certainly, detailed phraseology cannot be regarded as official.
>
> In Ireland, a Grand Lodge of Instruction demonstrates an official ritual, but it is not published. Brethren are expected to attend to learn how the ceremonies are to be properly performed. Nothing that is printed is therefore 'official', and even the printed booklets allowed for the officers of lodges outside Ireland are strictly unofficial.
>
> In Scotland, no attempt to harmonise the many unofficial workings of individual lodges and of those who choose the more widely used published rituals has ever been made, but the ceremony of placing a new Master in his chair, handing over the charter and investing new office-bearers is published by the Grand Lodge. That, at least, can be said to be official.

But in all these workings, it can be fairly assumed that something which is known to the Grand Lodge and not in accordance with its overall policy would have been objected to, and—subject to the democratic rights of the individual lodge—excised. In general terms, the published ritual books of the Grand Lodges of the British Isles are more or less 'official'; the words to be spoken more so than the descriptive rubrics.

There has been a recent change of policy in England, in that the omission of the penalties from the obligations was made obligatory by a democratic vote in both Grand Lodge and Grand Chapter, and one senior London lodge was afterwards suspended for not implementing the change in due time. The specific points agreed by the governing bodies are obligatory, and only minor changes are permitted as lodges and chapters of instruction and ritual associations fit them into the wording of the existing unofficial rituals.

In the 'higher' degrees, the governing bodies for England and Wales and for Scotland generally publish an agreed official booklet of the ritual—

which can thus be assumed to be official. In Ireland, the situation for these degrees remains as for the Craft.

Throughout this book, I will attempt to explain the extent to which each quotation may be regarded as official. However, it must be admitted that my book as a whole is bound to be subject to exactly the same failings as those of anti-masonic writers like Stephen Knight, as I am in no sense an official spokesman for the Craft. I was a normal Freemason belonging to lodges under the English, Irish and Scottish jurisdictions, and to 'research' lodges in London, California, New York and Maine. My initiation took place over forty years ago. I belonged to several of the so-called 'higher' degrees. I had certain responsibilities in Freemasonry in my local region, which means that I have official tasks to perform. My frequent contact with masons from other jurisdictions in the Philippines and Japan, as well as those from the west coast of the States and Canada, Australia and New Zealand, means that I have a breadth of experience that few can emulate. Whilst I hope that my opinions may be regarded as of value, they still cannot be treated as official.

3
Organisation

THE LODGE

The basic unit of masonic organisation is the lodge. Operative masons worked, dined, discussed and slept in workshops attached to the building on which they were working, and for as long as there is any tradition on the subject the workshop was called the lodge. Eventually, despite the retention of usage in the profane world, the masons stopped calling the building in which they met by this name, but referred to themselves—an association of men—as a 'lodge'.

Such a lodge was formed when a group of masons started working together on a new project, and they disbanded on its completion. There was no central organisation, yet somehow a common code of conduct and historical tradition grew up and assumed written form as the 'Old Charges', which applied to all masons throughout the land of England, and wherever in Wales, Scotland and Ireland English influence was felt. Parallel organisations existed in Germany (which died out in the eighteenth century) and France (which still exist as the Compannionage, separate from modern Freemasonry). The masons were sometimes impressed by the Crown to work in out-of-the-way castles, or selected in a slightly more kindly manner to work on remote monasteries. Even when they were formed in towns, their commitment to a single project meant that they had an impermanence which discouraged their forming a part of the civic structure. Except for a few places, notably London and the larger burghs of Scotland, masonic lodges were quite distinct from the guilds of the towns, which had a permanent existence so as to govern the trades within the town.

Some of these characteristics still exist to this day. The lodge remains the basic organisational unit. It is still formed when a number of masons get together to form one. It still has certain inherent rights of self government and propagation, and the detail of the manner of conducting its meetings is to some extent a matter of the democratic choice of its members.

By the beginning of the eighteenth century, different trends were evident north and south of Hadrian's Wall. In Scotland, the lodges had become a part of the civic organisation, like other guilds, and they were still endeavouring to control the mason trade within specific geographical areas. In England, the trade was generally without any formal control, and those 'lodges' which existed were convivial clubs which met with no concern for the operative masonry, except for the occasional gentleman's discussion on the latest theory of architecture, then very much the classical style of Palladio. But the traditions of the operative lodges were not altogether lost, and the document giving the common code of behaviour which had bound their operative forebears was still very much in evidence as a part of the ceremony of making new members.

THE MEN'S CLUB

The nature of a lodge is wholly mundane, and it has no mystical significance as has the Christian church. It was simply a trade organisation which evolved into a private men's club. It may induce a deep sense of loyalty to the organisation and to other members, but then so does a trade union or a football club. The Grand Lodge of Scotland states categorically:

> Masonic Lodges, Grand, Provincial and Daughter, are voluntary associations of individuals in no sense legally distinguishable from Clubs, and have accordingly no legal personality. (*Digest of Rulings* p12)

The masonic ritual itself abounds with references of this type, using a veritable thesaurus of terms for club:

> In a *society* so widely extended as Freemasonry . . . it cannot be denied that we have many members of rank and opulence; neither can it be concealed that . . . there are some who . . . are reduced to the lowest ebb of poverty and distress. (Hannah p105)
>
> As you have passed through the ceremony of your initiation, let me congratulate you on being admitted a member of our ancient and honourable *institution*. (ibid p107)
>
> And as this *association* has been formed and perfected with so much unanimity and concord, long may it continue. May brotherly love and affection ever distinguish us as men and as masons. (*Emulation Ritual* p204)

GRAND LODGES

In 1717, four of these lodges in London formed the first Grand Lodge in the world. By doing so, they gave up a part of their inherent right to govern themselves, and subjected their organisation to central control. It may be a matter of conjecture whether they realised this, as it appears that they merely wished to dine together somewhat more sumptuously than they each did alone. But with the appointment of central officials, and the designation of one of them to write a very much modified version of the 'Old Charges' as the new *Constitutions*, a central government began to enforce its rulings with reprimands, suspensions and expulsions, just as does any such governing body.

This premier Grand Lodge initially confined its jurisdiction to the cities of London and Westminster, but applications for authorisation to meet as regular lodges began to come in from all parts of England, and the jurisdiction soon expanded to the whole of the country. Ireland, France and

Scotland soon copied England in forming their own Grand Lodges, whilst the American Colonies, India and the rest of Europe received an intermediate organisational unit, the Provincial Grand Lodge, to govern clusters of lodges within the overall jurisdiction of England. Old independent lodges continued to exist, rival Grand Lodges sprang up from various sources, but through it all and to this day, the central control of the regular Grand Lodges within each country or state has been predominant.

One of the major rights which the Grand Lodges took away from the individual lodges which formed them was that of free propagation. Whilst a minimum number of masons could always get together and form a permanent or temporary lodge—subject to any state control such as that provided by the Schaw Statutes of 1598 and 1599 in Scotland—with the development of Grand Lodges the group then had to petition for a warrant to meet, and their formal organisation was a matter for the elected Grand Master or Grand Lodge as a whole. Since each Grand Lodge defined its own geographical jurisdiction, it could logically only warrant lodges in its own territory, though in fact Grand Lodges have always reserved the right to form lodges where no other Grand Lodge claims jurisdiction. Thus it has always been possible for lodges of several jurisdictions to exist in 'open territory', and then to form a Grand Lodge of their own.

Sometimes only a bare majority of the existing lodges do so, leaving the minority under their old jurisdiction. For example, in Japan today there are old lodges governed from England, Scotland, Massachusetts and the Philippines, as well as a majority of lodges under the young Grand Lodge of Japan. Needless to say, this separation according to masonic jurisdiction does not reflect the national origin of the members of each lodge, or their political viewpoints; it is a matter of historical accident and the democratic rights of the members. This variety of tradition within one country is often appreciated as widening the horizons of the fraternity as to the essentials and accidents of true Freemasonry.

Today, a hundred and fifty-nine regular Grand Lodges control the vast majority of masonic activity throughout the world. Each is a sovereign body, owing no allegiance to any other Grand Lodge. Their allegiance is to the concept of masonry established by the *Constitutions* written for the premier Grand Lodge in 1721. None of them actually uses that book in an unamended form, and the international fraternity controls itself by a system of mutual recognitions that the others practise true Freemasonry. It is thus virtually impossible for any one Grand Lodge to alter the nature of masonry by its own enactment, as the other regular bodies would withdraw recognition. Great pressure would then be exercised by members travelling to other places, who found that they could not continue to meet with their former brethren, to restore the lost essence of the Craft.

To some extent, each Grand Lodge treasures a lineal descent from those which were formed in the early eighteenth century in the British Isles. In the case of Scotland, there is a clear connection with those lodges which controlled the trade. Lodges still exist which can trace their origin back to the fifteenth century, and a few have minutes dating to the end of the sixteenth. English and Irish lodges were in a more advanced state of evolution when they formed their Grand Lodges and their records were very much poorer, but the intention to continue social aspects of the mason trade as a convivial institution was still there. (A paper presented to the Quatuor Coronati Lodge has suggested that patronage was the motivating force.)

HIGHER DEGREES

It will always be a matter of debate as to how many degree ceremonies there were in operative masonry, but it is clear that the Craft entered its speculative era with but two. There is evidence that between 1725 and 1730, a degree called Master Mason came into existence, probably by a rearrangement or expansion of the material within the two which already existed rather than as a totally new ceremony. There is further evidence that in the 1740s, two new degrees or Orders evolved: the Royal Arch to provide a solution to the loss of masonic secrets which was postulated in the third degree, and the Royal Order of Scotland to 'correct' the betrayal of Christianity which some masons saw in the First Charge in the *Constitutions*.

In France, the masons of the mid-eighteenth century then took over the field, and invented 'masonic' degrees by the thousand, mostly taking a theme that existed in the Royal Arch which concerned Zerubbabel's part in the rebuilding of the Temple following the return from Babylon. This was somehow combined with the idea of knighthood and—for a reason which still eludes the research of masonic scholars but may refer to a legendary continuation of Templars in Scotland—this theme was referred to as 'Ecossais' or Scottish. These degrees were frequently rejected by the established Grand Lodges as spurious masonry, but soon the situation existed where, despite this, senior masons of the establishment were at the same time active in the new 'higher' degrees.

By the end of the eighteenth century, the situation began to correct itself. Many of the degrees were ephemeral and ceased to be a problem. Others were recognised to a varying extent by official masonry as part of the overall fabric of Freemasonry. Yet others formed governing bodies of their own, controlling a series of several degrees, the most exotic being the Rite of Memphis and Misraim with ninety-six degrees (which still has a small following in France) and the best known being the Ancient and Accepted (or Scottish) Rite of thirty-three degrees, which to this day is the most extensive throughout the world after Grand Lodge Freemasonry.

All the 'higher' degree bodies regard the degree of Master Mason conferred in a Craft lodge as an essential qualification for membership. For example, the Ancient and Accepted Rite treats the first three of its thirty-three degrees as the equivalent of Craft masonry, and does not confer them itself. It is on this basis that its existence is tolerated, if not encouraged, in places with a regular Grand Lodge. However, when members of the Rite have found themselves in a country without a regular Grand Lodge, they have conferred the first three degrees within their own organisation. The status of such conferrals becomes a problem when a regular Grand Lodge is established later by the normal procedure.

Within the British Isles today, the structure of the 'higher' degrees is relatively simple in essence, if complex in detail. All accept Master Masons from Craft lodges as qualified for membership (sometimes with further qualifications). All are governed by central organisations which parallel the Grand Lodges in general structure and democratic participation (with the exception of the Ancient and Accepted Rite, which is more autocratic). Generally their headquarters are in the same capital for each country, and major meetings are held in the largest convenient masonic meeting place: the headquarters of the Grand Lodge. Grand Officers overlap, and even where this is not so, the most cordial of relations exists between the Grand Lodges and the governing bodies of the 'higher' degrees.

4
Division

CONTRADICTION

The First Charge in the *Constitutions* of 1723 refers to Freemasonry as 'the *Center* of *Union*, and the Means of conciliating true Friendship among Persons that must have remain'd at a perpetual Distance'. I would see in this the very essence of masonry. Any disunity in an organisation which is designed to promote friendship is therefore a contradiction of this very essence.

A comparison with the Christian church is inevitable. Of course, Freemasons in their lodges are not concerned with such vital matters as the means by which eternal life is to be achieved, even if they are very much concerned as individuals. But neither is there such extensive division as tears the seamless garment of Christ's bride: from the largest group of Catholics who give allegiance to His Holiness the Pope to the smallest sect of fundamentalists recently divided from their former brethren over a difference in interpretation of a biblical verse.

Nevertheless, division in Freemasonry must be admitted. The numbers are very roughly:

Regular Freemasonry:	5,500,000
Prince Hall Masonry:	250,000
Grand Orient 'Masonry':	90,000

I will try to give the reader some understanding of the divisions, but must premise that my knowledge is inevitably hearsay. Not only can I not speak for irregular masonry, but I cannot regard it as genuine Freemasonry at all.

PRINCE HALL MASONRY

The saddest of these divisions from the regular Craft is one made on racial grounds which exists in the United States of America and nearby countries.

A group of fifteen Blacks received a warrant dated 1784 from the Premier Grand Lodge of England, to form a lodge to be known as African Lodge, numbered 459. It was not invited to take part with lodges consisting of Caucasians in the new Grand Lodge of Massachusetts in 1792, and continued in existence owing a nominal allegiance to England. Under the leadership of a preacher called Prince Hall, it assumed the role of a Grand Lodge, and chartered lodges of Blacks elsewhere in the east of the States. However, along with all lodges in the new United States under England, it was erased from the rolls following the union of 1813 (Haffner, *Regularity of Origin* p125).

From this has evolved Prince Hall Masonry, a completely independent masonic organisation with Grand Lodges in each of the United States, in Canada, the West Indies and Liberia, as well as individual lodges overseas in places like England and Scotland, wherever there are American military bases. There are many separate, clandestine Negro lodges and Grand Lodges, but the Prince Hall Affiliation Grand Lodges are generally accepted as exhibiting all the characteristics of regularity apart from the technical difficulty of their separate existence in places where another Grand Lodge is already recognised.

It must be acknowledged that there are many racists in American masonry. Their position has been strengthened in recent years by four writers, humorously called 'the Gang of Four' by the prominent Prince Hall writer, Joseph Walkes, Jr. They have emphasised all the points in the history of Prince Hall Masonry which would by present day standards be treated as 'irregular', even though no American jurisdiction—regular or otherwise—could stand up to the same scrutiny applied to the early period of its existence. By this emphasis, they seek to cast doubt on the regular origin and continued existence of the Prince Hall fraternity.

There have always been masons in both camps who have felt strongly about the hypocrisy of this division, and have done their best to mitigate its effects. There are, of course, many Blacks in regular masonry around the world, including some in America. There are also whites in Prince Hall Masonry. Many regular white masons in America have supported Prince Hall Masonry in court cases against spurious imitations. Several masonic homes for the aged in the United States are shared, and foundation stones have been jointly laid. Some 'Caucasian' Grand Lodges have made their premises available for Prince Hall Affiliation Grand Lodges to meet. Above all, when they meet in their everyday lives, most American masons of both camps with any degree of sensitivity treat each other as true brethren.

My friend Joseph Walkes has reminded his readers of the division on racial grounds between two Roman Catholic organisations which closely parallel Freemasonry, the Knights of Columbus and Knights of Peter Claver, and warned the (US) National Catholic Conference of Bishops that 'those who throw stones cannot live in glass houses'. (Walkes: *A Word* p2)

The fact is, that after two hundred years of separate existence, the Prince Hall Masons have developed traditions and characteristics of their own which they feel would be lost if unity were to be sought. Many would prefer to be recognised as separate but equal (Walkes: *Black Square* passim). The problem at once becomes one of masonic legality: how can two Grand Lodges professing a proper concern for unity be recognised as authentic within the same territory.

The way out of this impasse has often been to accept a lesser standard of mutual recognition for intervisitation purposes within each State. As soon as this happened, the United Grand Lodge of England, unwilling to make the same distinction, has without exception granted full recognition to the Prince Hall Grand Lodge, and at the end of 2004 twenty-eight recognitions had been made.

RACE AND CLASS

Generally speaking, Freemasonry has a good record of openness to all races and creeds throughout its quarter millennium of history. Jews were admitted to lodges from the very beginning of the Grand Lodge era. John Pine, the engraver of the frontispiece of the first *Constitutions* of 1723 and a Grand Officer, was almost certainly Black. The fact that the premier Grand Lodge of England gave a warrant to fifteen Blacks in Massachusetts shows that it had no colour prejudice—whilst detractors claim that the officers of Grand Lodge had no way of knowing that they were Black, the very name petitioned for, 'The African Lodge', indicates no intention to hide their race.

As masonry spread around the world, lodges were partly affected by the colonial mores of the day, but seemed to manage to retain a practical vision of the human equality inculcated in their 'working'. G. E. Walker recounts the skirmishes that went on in India regarding the initiation of Indians, eventually leading in 1843 to the formation of a lodge 'especially for the admission of natives into the Craft' (p19). By the time of Rudyard Kipling, he could write:

> We'd Bola Nath, Accountant,
> An' Saul, the Aden Jew,
> An' Din Mohammed, draftsman
> Of the Survey Office, too;
> There was Babu Chuckerbutty,
> An' Amir Singh the Sikh,
> An' Castro from the fittin'-sheds,
> The Roman Catholick.
>
> We 'adn't good regalia,
> An' our Lodge was old and bare,
> But we knew the Ancient Landmarks,
> An' we kept them to a hair;
> An' lookin' on it backwards
> It often strikes me thus,
> There ain't such things as infidels,
> Excep', perhaps, it's us. (quoted in Glick p135)

Further east, the same problems and solutions occurred in the Netherlands Indies, Japan and China. The first, in 1844, was a Muslim, Abdul Rachman, son of the Sultan of Pontianak on the massive island of Borneo (Van der Veur p14). The first Japanese masons were two students initiated in Leyden in 1864 (van Ginkel and Haffner, p69). A year later, the first Chinese was rejected by a lodge in Shanghai, but in 1873 a Chinese was initiated in Massachusetts, in 1882 another in New South Wales, and finally in 1889 the first of many in China. (Haffner, *The Craft in the East* pp39, 70–72)

Outside North America, Freemasonry's record in terms of race relations certainly moved ahead of general acceptance by society at large, and almost kept pace with the more advanced of the churches, especially bearing in mind that Freemasonry is a men's club with no missionary driving force.

The same thing applies by and large to the crossing of class barriers in British society. But the general impression of masonry as an expensive hobby of the upper middle class, as expressed by Denis Bagley in a BBC Radio 4 phone-in programme, holds good for most non-masons:

> I read some time ago that it was necessary to have a considerable amount of money to be a Freemason, would you say this is correct? Would you say that you meet any ordinary working people among the masons, anyone a little down at heel, very many unemployed among the masons, or are they from the top echelons, the big businessmen, the top ranks of the police and such? *(Tuesday Call)*

The Grand Secretary replied:

> There's no idea that Freemasonry is only for the powerful and rich . . . I would mention to you a lot of professions or occupations which [are evident in masonry but] do not normally get themselves associated with richness or power. Engine drivers—I suppose they're fairly powerful!—stage hands, there's one lodge I certainly know has got porters in a building in it.

And even Stephen Knight agreed:

> I feel exactly the same as Commander Higham, and it's open to everybody, and there's no-one better to explain that than the man who's actually inside.

In his book *The Brotherhood*, Knight spun a yarn about a lodge consisting of Transport House and Labour Party officials having fixed the election of Clem Attlee as Prime Minister, and quotes from Hugh Dalton's *The Fateful Years* in proof of this (pp207–208). This would make it appear that, at least in the late thirties and forties, British socialism was heavily influenced by masonic membership. Knight does not see this as a bad thing:

> Freemasons getting together in secret to decide whom they as a group want to have as a leader seems no different from the Tribunites, the Manifesto Group or any other sub group within a party doing the same thing.

Knight's picture is true in one respect at least—there are lodges which are intended for the association of individuals who have something in common besides masonry. This is frequently evident in the name selected by the founders, such as Cyclist No 2246, Round Table Lodge of Sussex No 7965, City of London Red Cross No 3831 and Chartered Architects No 3244. It is unlikely that a school teacher would be an acceptable candidate for the Commercial Travellers Lodge No 2795 unless he were a relative of a member. But a rejection would not mean that he was not suitable for another lodge, simply that he had been ill advised by his proposer. The existence of such 'class lodges' is bound to result in exclusivism of a sort, but Grand Lodge sets a stand against such potential snobbery becoming official by refusing to sanction by-laws that do more than state a general objective of creating fellowship amongst cyclists, ex-Tablers, Red Cross supporters living in London, and the like. I would expect to be rejected if I applied for membership of a 'class' lodge whose objectives I do not share, yet on the other hand I used to be a proud member of a lodge restricted to forty 'scholars' who have written books and papers on masonic subjects. But of course intervisitation with more ordinary lodges is completely unrestricted.

Whilst I think that Lawrence is definitely overstating his case, he says:

> It would seem that in recent years freemasonry has largely recruited from the so-called working classes. A more widespread affluence has enabled a wider populace to join the craft. Some within freemasonry regard this as a lowering of standards and are highly critical and suspicious. Freemasonry has increasingly broken down cultural barriers, probably more successfully than the church has done. To its shame the church in the last 150 years has made little more than token gestures to welcome the poor and needy into Christ's kingdom, remaining middle class and remote. (p132)

In fact, Freemasonry must to some extent remain an elitist group, as the requirement for a proposer and seconder, followed by a ballot for membership helps to ensure that those who become members are 'good and true men, free born, and of mature and discreet age and sound judgement . . . no immoral or scandalous men, but of good report' ('Antient Charge' III). Fortunately, throughout the centuries masons have seen this not in terms of race, creed, class or political membership, but of personal integrity.

THE GRAND ORIENTS

Another separation within the ranks of masonry is one which came into existence in the latter part of the nineteenth century in France.

Until 1877, the first two clauses of the *Constitutions* of the Grand Orient of France were:

> 1. Its principles are the existence of God, the immortality of the soul and human solidarity.
> 2. It regards liberty of conscience as the common right of every man, and excludes no person on account of his belief.

These were changed in that year to:

> 1. Its principles are absolute liberty of conscience and human solidarity.
> 2. It excludes no person on account of his belief.

In March 1878, the United Grand Lodge of England passed the following resolutions:

> That this Grand Lodge views with profound regret the step taken by the Grand Orient of France in thus removing from its Constitutions those paragraphs which assert a belief in the existence of T.G.A.O.T.U. [the Great Architect of the Universe], because such an alteration is opposed to the traditions, practice, and

> feelings of all 'true and genuine' Freemasons from the earliest to the present time. That this Grand Lodge, whilst always anxious to receive in the most fraternal spirit the Brethren of any Foreign Grand Lodge whose proceedings are conducted according to the Ancient Landmarks of the Order, of which a belief in T.G.A.O.T.U. is the first and most important, cannot recognize as 'true and genuine' Brethren any who have been initiated in Lodges which either deny or ignore that belief.
>
> That in view of the foregoing Resolutions the W. Masters of all Lodges holding under the Grand Lodge of England be directed not to admit any foreign Brother as a Visitor unless:
>
> 1st. He is duly vouched for or unless his Certificate shows he has been initiated according to the Antient Rites and Ceremonies in a Lodge professing belief in T.G.A.O.T.U., and
>
> 2nd. Not unless he himself shall acknowledge that this belief is an essential Landmark of the Order.
>
> (quoted in Gratton and Ivy pp197–98)

This situation remains unchanged to this day—a small group of some ninety thousand 'masons' under various Grand Orients, Grand Lodges and the like in France, Belgium and to a lesser extent in Switzerland and South America remain isolated from the world of regular Freemasonry by their denial of this essential Landmark of true and genuine Freemasonry. No masonic intercourse has existed with such so-called masons to this day, and the *Constitutions* of England still contains Rule 125(b), which reads:

> No Brother . . . shall be admitted unless his certificate shows that he has been initiated according to the antient rites and ceremonies in a Lodge belonging to a Grand Lodge professing belief in T.G.A.O.T.U. . . . nor unless he himself shall acknowledge that this belief is an essential Landmark of the Order.

POLITICAL ACTIVITY

The political position of regular masonry has also been transgressed by this group. A BBC Overseas Broadcast a few years ago, called *Freemasonry—an Investigation*, put together by Paul Wade, contained an interview with a French Grand Orient member, who said:

> 'You can't have a society such as the freemasonry which does not take an interest in the current affairs. We have to. We have two meetings a month, ten months of the year. But the main work is questions, which are prepared in Paris and sent to every lodge; humanitarian questions, even moralist political questions. For instance, how to prevent vandalism spreading, and this and that, and everyone within the lodge has to discuss it.' And the fruits of the discussions are offered up to the Paris headquarters, who get on to senior freemasons in the Government. That's how French national health and social security services were evolved, and even the League of Nations. (Wade p100)

Contrast this with the official and regular position:

> English Freemasonry . . . inculcates in each of its members the duties of loyalty and citizenship, [but] it reserves to the individual the right to hold his own opinion with regard to public affairs. But neither in any Lodge, nor at any time in his

> capacity as a Freemason, is he permitted to discuss or to advance his views on theological or political questions.
> The Grand Lodge has always consistently refused to express any opinion on questions of foreign or domestic state policy either at home or abroad, and it will not allow its name to be associated with any action, however humanitarian it may appear to be, which infringes its unalterable policy of standing aloof from every question affecting the relations between one government and another, or between political parties, or questions as to rival theories of government. *(Aims and Relationships of the Craft)*

The perils of getting mixed with the pseudo-masonry of the Grand Orient type is emphasised in a booklet with the cumbersome title of *Information for the Guidance of Members of the Craft* which is handed to every new member. A paragraph on 'Attendance at Lodges Overseas' includes:

> The best method of combatting [this danger] is for Lodges to impress on their members that they should not make any Masonic contacts overseas with members of other Jurisdictions without having ascertained by application to the Grand Secretary . . . the address to which Masonic inquiries in that country should be directed. The Board recommends not only that this warning be given in Lodge verbally . . ., but that it should be printed at least once a year on Lodge Summonses.

It is evident that between the atheistic and political so-called masonry of the Grand Orient type and the regular Craft 'there is a great gulf fixed' which can only be crossed, as has happened frequently in France, by individual masons, and indeed whole lodges, transferring their allegiance to the regular Grande Loge Nationale Française.

The author's knowledge of this type of masonry can be but hearsay, and no attempt at its justification need be made. In plain words, it is not Freemasonry, and has merely retained the vestiges of a name. This view is not my own, but that of the United Grand Lodge of England:

> The Grand Lodge is aware that there do exist Bodies, styling themselves Freemasons, which do not adhere to these principles, and while that attitude exists the Grand Lodge of England refuses absolutely to have any relation with such Bodies, or to regard them as Freemasons. *(Aims and Relationships)*

In other words, it is impossible to define 'Freemasonry' in such a way as to include both types, as irregular masonry is *not* Freemasonry at all.

This view is not held by some anti-masonic writers. Vicomte Leon de Poncins' *Freemasonry and the Vatican* takes the view that all Freemasonry is the same. This is useful for the purpose of his book, as it enables him to examine the writings of irregular masons to prove that all Freemasons are gnostics, occultists, naturalists and satanists, and therefore deserving of a single condemnation. His first chapter attempts to justify this. We can ignore the first part, which simply quotes Albert Lantoine's *Lettre au Souvrain Pontife* of 1937 as favouring some sort of reconciliation between progressive Roman Catholics and irregular Freemasonry. He then goes on to quote Alec Mellor, a Parisian lawyer and a practising Roman Catholic, in favour of a reconciliation of the Roman Church with regular Freemasonry, again seeing hope in progressive Catholicism. Merely because Mellor's list of acknowledgements in *La Franc-Maçonnerie à l'Heure du Choix* contains the names of some irregular masons, he believes that he has proved that no difference exists.

I believe that any reasonable reader will accept that an official statement made in concert by three Grand Lodges has substantially greater authority than the accident of a list of acknowledgements in a book expressing the personal opinions of a single mason.

However, a warning should be carefully noted. The name 'Grand Orient' is just as legitimate as 'Grand Lodge', and a few recognised bodies use the title. Hence the Grand Orient (or Grand East) of the Netherlands has always been regarded as fully regular since its formation in 1756. The list of Grand Lodges recognised by England also includes the Grand Orient of Brazil. It is thus false to assume, as some anti-masonic writers have done, that all bodies called Grand Orient are the same in masonic doctrine as the Grand Orient of France, and that their recognition by England indicates equivocation on England's part. Indeed, the history of the Grand Orient of Italy after the 'P2' affair shows just how clear the procedures of recognition and de-recognition are.

Equally, there are further irregular bodies in France and Belgium called 'Grand Lodge'. The fact that an opinion is expressed by such a body or one of its members does not make it that of regular masonry. The name of the 'Grand Lodge' must be carefully compared with the lists issued by the three regular Grand Lodges of the British Isles.

THE EFFECT OF THE 'P2' AFFAIR

'Propaganda Massonica' was a lodge under the Grand Orient of Italy established in 1877, eventually numbered 2. By 1907 it was accused of being the Grand Master's fiefdom since its membership consisted entirely of his own influential friends, mostly made masons 'at sight' under a provision existing in American masonry and expropriated to Italy, that the Grand Master can simply declare a man to be a mason, without going through the normal ceremonies. Such a situation, when this procedure was the rule and not the exception, was regarded as improper, but the lodge surmounted the accusation and lasted until masonry was closed down by Mussolini in 1926. When masonry was revived, P2 was also revived and continued in the same general manner.

In 1970, Licio Gelli became the lodge's secretary and he virtually ran it on his own, using its influential members in improper ways. This was sufficiently evident to the Grand Orient for it to vote 400 to 6 to erase the lodge in 1974. But Gelli had a stock of official certificates and continued the lodge in a clandestine existance. Eventually in 1981, Gelli came under police surveillance for fraudulent activities and a search of his house revealed 950 names of prominent members of the so-called lodge. Several ministers resigned and the government fell. Freemasonry came under a thick black cloud in Italy and internationally.

But the Grand Orient of Italy survived largely through the self-sacrificial service of Armando Corona, a former Prime Minister of Sardinia, who gave up his political career on being elected Grand Master in 1982. Under his careful controlling hand masonry regained the respect that it had lost due to the 'P2 Affair' and international masonic recognition of the Grand Master was maintained.

Regrettably subsequent Grand Masters led the Grand Orient down the path trodden long previously by the Grand Orient of France, entering into political and religious debate. Recognition by the United Grand Lodge of England and other regular Grand Lodges was withdrawn, so a number of lodges decided to leave the Grand Orient and formed the Regular Grand Lodge of Italy, which was quickly recognised around the world, and is thriving.

That this new body represents the genuine form of masonry is having its effect on the Roman Catholic Church. At the meeting of the Grand Lodge held in June 2005, the Grand Master Fabbio Venzi appointed a new Grand Chaplain who is a Catholic priest. He had been initiated a few years previously after discussing the possibility with his bishop and receiving approval for membership of 'Anglo-Saxon Fremasonry' which is not guilty of *Machinatur contra ecclesiam*. The situation is subject to further discussion.

OTHER UNRECOGNISED 'MASONRY'

There are a number of smaller groupings which are not recognised for various reasons.

Some are just different, like those Orders of masonry which are open to women, or which have mixed membership. The Working Party of the Church of England Synod attempted to examine the ladies' Order in England, and received no replies to its queries (Working Party p2). Much has been made of the fact that a husband's permission has to be obtained for his wife to become a member, but the same applies informally in reverse; lodge committees invariably ask a candidate if he has told his wife of his intention and if she has any objection. This does not imply agreement that the Order is regular Freemasonry. The existence of such organisations permits the regular Freemason to continue in his all-male club without being too concerned that he is altogether chauvinistically male or sexist, or whatever the latest fashion sets for an appropriate adjective.

Some so-called Freemasons have a totally different origin, like the 'Chinese Freemasons' of the United States, which are the legal offshoot of the subversive triad societies of China, specifically of the Yee Hing Society, set up to support Dr Sun Yat Sen and the establishment of a Chinese republic (Tan p153).

Some Grand Lodges are not recognised, simply as a result of an incomplete tying up of loose ends. There are some hundred and sixty recognised Grand Lodges in the world, and this means that, for them all to recognise each other, some twenty thousand separate acts of recognition after due enquiry are required. It is hardly surprising that the minor differences of opinion in the minds of investigation committees result in marginally different lists in different jurisdictions. Although masonry is not concerned with political opinion, the existence or not of diplomatic relations between two countries also makes for practical differences in recognition. It is thus the case that, whilst all regular Grand Lodge have a similar lists of a hundred and eighty or so names, differences exist in a field of some twenty or so marginal Grand Lodges. The list of recognised, regular Grand Lodges has expanded over the last twenty years, first by recognition of Prince Hall Grand Lodges in the US, and secondly by the formation of new Grand Lodges in countries where Freemasonry was until recently prohibited, such as Spain and Portugal and in the countries of eastern Europe. Some of the former French colonies in Africa have also formed Grand Lodges with the encouragement of the Grande Lodge Nationale Francaise.

The background information set out above should be sufficient to prevent the non-masonic reader falling into the pitfalls which are the— hardly surprising—result of the fostering of excessive privacy by the Order. I hope that I have sufficiently emphasised the strong unity which forms the basis of the regular Craft, and its contrast with those small divisions which disfigure the name and purpose of the Order. This book is solely about the regular Craft, seen from the viewpoint of a member of the three jurisdictions which exist in the British Isles.

PART TWO

General Criticisms

5
Belief

THEOLOGY

The critics of Freemasonry are determined to convince outsiders that it is a religion, but that it has an inadequate theology. The officials of the Order are equally determined that it is not a religion, and because the discussion of religion is prohibited, it cannot develop any theology. Perhaps we should examine what belief is enshrined and inculcated in masonic ceremonial, and whether this constitutes a theology at all, adequate or not.

Theology is not the same as belief. Perhaps the difference is like the difference between organic chemistry and cooking. Theology is much more complicated and abstract, but less necessary for existence. Theology is the science of religion: the study of God's nature, His attributes, and His dealings with man *(OED)*.

Freemasons need not be upset if they are accused of having an inadequate theology. This is what a modern theologian says about a section of his church (and mine):

> It has been suggested that the real conflict of the fundamentalist faith is not with critical biblical scholarship but with theology. . . . In a certain sense fundamentalism could be described as a theology-less movement. . . . What is intended by the theologian as an attempt to restate the gospel in categories that can be understood by the modern world is perceived by the fundamentalist as a quite gratuitous attempt to foist upon the church and the world the personal and professional fashions of a theological caste. . . .
>
> I suggest that a better picture is given if we say that fundamentalism has doctrines. . . . There are certain things that are taught, doctrinal structures that are extremely important; but it is not necessary to talk of these as theology. (Barr, *Fundamentalism* pp160–62)

The picture given by Freemasonry is much simpler than this: there are not even *doctrines* in the Craft, but a few simple beliefs. The assumption made by those masons of the past who participated in the evolution of the ceremonial was that these beliefs were held by all men who had a basic belief in a Supreme Being. They could not therefore be the subject of controversy within a lodge.

The official pamphlet on *Freemasonry and Religion* expresses the view of regular Freemasonry:

> Freemasonry lacks the basic elements of religion: it has no theological doctrine, and by forbidding religious discussion at its meetings will not allow Masonic theological doctrine to develop.

THE GREAT ARCHITECT

The official position of the Grand Lodges of the British Isles is:

> The first condition of admission into, and membership of, the Order is the belief in a Supreme Being. This is essential and admits of no compromise. (*Information* p1)

A fundamental document in American Freemasonry is Mackey's list of 'Ancient Landmarks'. These are principles which are so fundamental that to remove them would compromise the structure of the Craft, and which have existed since the beginning of masonic history. One of these is:

> A Belief in the Existence of God as the Grand Architect of the Universe, is one of the most Important Landmarks of the Order. It has always been deemed essential that a denial of the existence of a Supreme and Superintending Power, is an absolute disqualification for initiation. (*Jurisprudence* p15)

Modern commentaries on the 'Landmarks', such as that of a former Dean of Harvard Law School, Roscoe Pound, maintain this as crucial, even when abandoning many others from the twenty-five of Mackey's list.

The new mason is quickly taught to address God as the 'Great Architect'. The first Charge as promulgated by the United Grand Lodge of England since 1815 contains the words:

> Let a man's religion or mode of worship be what it may, he is not excluded from the order, provided he believes in the glorious architect of heaven and earth.

At the opening of the lodge, the Master says, 'Let us invoke the assistance of the Great Architect of the Universe in all our undertakings.' He then declares the lodge to be open, 'in the Name of the Great Architect of the Universe'. (Hannah p86)

It has been suggested that 'The Great Architect of the Universe is not the Triune God of Christianity' ('Why ban masonry?'). But to a Christian Freemason, these expressions involve the Holy Trinity. When I read the first verses of the Bible, I find that it says this about the Great Architect:

> In the beginning of creation, when God made heaven and earth, the earth was without form and void, with darkness over the face of the abyss, and a mighty wind that swept over the surface of the waters. God said 'Let there be light', and there was light. (*Gen* 1:1–3)

God is the Father, the 'mighty wind' is the Holy Spirit, and the word which God spoke is Jesus Christ, who is Himself the Word through whom 'all things came to be' (*John* 1:2) and 'The real light which enlightens every man'. (*John* 1:9)

A former Bishop of Woolwich has said that Freemasonry has a 'lowest common denominator view of God, emptied of all meaning' (quoted in

Lawrence p17). In actuality, the masonic concept was created in the early eighteenth century when little was known of comparative religion except in relation to Judaism and perhaps Islam. To include all the complex strands of Buddhism in a lowest common denominator would make the task all but impossible, and Freemasons still have great difficulty with Buddhist membership in the Far East. I would say rather that the masonic concept of God is the highest common factor between Christianity, Judaism and Islam, to which is added the meaningful didactic tool of the usages of the medieval operative masons applied to explain spiritual reality in non-sectarian terms.

John Lawrence considers that the term is inadequate:

> Freemasonry does not define its god [sic] in Christian terms. He is described as an architect or geometrician rather than a creator. This is not mere playing with words. A creator is a person who creates something out of nothing, others use something already there. . . . Now the god of Freemasonry bears little relationship to the Christian idea of God. Were we to ask why it is, assuming that the craft has no intention of excluding the Christian understanding of God, that in freemasonry God is so emptied and debased that he falls far short of the biblical understanding, the answer would be that this is deliberate. (p124)

Lawrence gives no evidence that Freemasonry has deliberately attempted to debase the idea of God. I have elsewhere shown that James Anderson— the author of the concept of 'Great Architect'—was innocent of any such intention. Lawrence is condemning his own distortion.

The point surely is that the reverse is true. An architect does not *build* a building from existing bricks and mortar; he *creates* the idea of a building in his mind, and communicates it by drawings and specifications to the builder. The geometrician too works with abstract ideas, and his diagrams on paper are merely a means of communication of these to others. The concept implies that God created the laws of planetary motion and the form of a seashell as abstract geometry before He gave them physical existence. But God also uses bricks and mortar:

> This *creatio ex nihil* has important theological implications, for among other things it precludes the idea that matter is eternal . . . or that there can be any kind of dualism in the universe. . . . At the same time, however, it is clear that the idea of primary creation contained in the formula *creatio ex nihil* does not exhaust the biblical teaching on the subject. Man was not created *ex nihil* but out of the dust of the ground (*Gen* 2:7) and the beasts of the field and the fowls of the air were formed out of the ground. (*Gen* 2:19) (Douglas p245)

The term 'Great Architect' expresses what is of course an incomplete idea of God: it is not the full Nicene Creed or the Quicunque Vult. Bishop Stockwood was improperly comparing the membership qualification of a men's club with the plenitude of the church's teaching. A Christian Freemason can add any credal statement and spirituality he chooses to the concept of the Great Architect when praying. So can the follower of Islam or the noble eightfold path. But having said that, far from being an empty symbol, the idea of the Great Architect is also one from which much spiritual insight can be derived, by anyone, Freemason or not.

THE DEFINITE ARTICLE

The Church of England's Working Group has seen fit to make a distinction between '*a* Supreme Being' and '*the* Supreme Being', and maintains that the use of both terms is an evident inconsistency in Freemasonry:

> It is curious that . . . reference is made by the United Grand Lodge to the essential requirement of Freemasons that they believe in *a* Supreme Being. In the course of the present century, the United Grand Lodge has felt it desirable to issue public statements clarifying the aims and relationships of the Craft. In all three, 1920, 1938 and 1949, reference is made not to belief in *a* but *the* Supreme Being, and it is belief in *the* Supreme Being that is required in the second of those 'Basic Principles of Freemasonry for which the Grand Lodge of England has stood throughout its history'. . . .
>
> The legitimacy of the apparent assumption that the God of each and all religions can be encapsulated in the all embracing concept of the Great Architect will be discussed later in this Report. (Working Group p10)

The later discussion says:

> It has been noted earlier that the evidence of the Grand Lodge to the Working Group introduces a confusion here by speaking in one place of belief in 'a' Supreme Being and in another of belief in 'the' Supreme Being, and revealing any organisation, secular or ecclesiastical, which attempts to join men of any religion in a single organisation at the heart of which is a common ritual.
>
> It needs to be said that Freemasonry has been trying for more than two hundred years to find a solution to a problem not always candidly faced by Christian Churches of the present day when they attempt to organise or participate in 'inter-faith' services. How is this to be accomplished without testifying to the pre-eminence of Christ as God's revelation of himself to the world? How is 'offence' to other faiths to be avoided without minimalising the claims of Christianity.
>
> This having been said, Freemasonry itself has no obligation to support the claims of traditional Christianity. It is not and does not claim to be a Christian, even a religious organisation: all it asks is that any and all its members believe in 'a' or 'the' Supreme Being. It is up to the members to face the fact that although *they* understand the nature of the God to which the prayers are addressed, although *they* may be conscious of addressing *their* God and their Brother addressing *his* in the course of the rituals, the simultaneous worship [sic] of the Great Architect at least implies, if it does not actually convey, indifferentism to the claims of distinct religions.
>
> Freemasons may understand themselves either to be addressing the God of their own religion or to be addressing the God of different religions under one neutral name. Each position has its own theological problems. (pp25–26)

Now, is seems to me that the Working Group has got itself into two inextricable tangles of its own. The first is the fuss made of the definite article in what is possibly the only situation where it is irrelevant. In talking of Supreme Being, it cannot possibly matter whether He is prefixed by 'a' or 'the'. A person who can give a positive answer to, 'Do you believe in *a* Supreme Being?' must also believe that He is *the* Supreme Being, or He would not be supreme. There is no alternative position.

And the second and even stranger tangle of the Working Group is that its members apparently believe that there are several Gods (or gods) and each religion has its own. The Report talks of *their* God and *his* God. Thus to the members of the Working Party there are as many Gods as there are religions. It matters not that the members worship only the Holy Trinity themselves, they acknowledge the existence of other 'Gods'. This it seems to me is a reversion to the Hebrew faith before the revelation through Amos that all nations stood under the judgement of the one true God, and of Isaiah that even the pagan King of Persia could be Yahweh's anointed.

Christians are monotheists, believing in one God. In so far as human beings outside Christianity have a glimpse of the Truth, the God they worship is the Christian God. I am not alone in this belief:

> There are elements of truth in all religions. These truths are the fruit of a revelatory gift of God. Evangelicals often identify their source in terms of general revelation, common grace or the remnant image of God in humankind. Roman Catholics more frequently associate them with the work of the Logos, the true light, coming into the world and giving light to every man (*John* 1:9), and with the work of the Holy Spirit. (Meeking and Stott p34)

This is not the opinion of a single Christian, but the considered opinion of thirty-one evangelicals and Roman Catholics gathered to discuss a common attitude to their mission. The Working Group should perhaps first consider if it believes in one God or many. If the latter, perhaps even the all enveloping arms of Anglicanism might prove too tight to hold its members! If the former, then its condemnation of the Craft is based on a false premise.

Now imagine me standing in lodge with my head bowed in prayer between Brother Mohammed Bokhary and Brother Arjun Melwani. To neither of them is the Great Architect of the Universe perceived as the Holy Trinity. To Brother Bokhary He has been revealed as Allah; to Brother Melwani He is probably perceived as Vishnu. Since I believe that there is only one God, I am confronted with three possibilities:

They are praying to the *devil* whilst I am praying to God;
They are praying to *nothing*, as their gods do not exist;
They are praying to the *same God* as I, yet their understanding of His nature is partly incomplete (as indeed is mine—1 *Cor* 13:12).

It is without hesitation that I accept the third possibility.

It is the genius of Freemasonry that a Presbyterian minister charged with the task of rewriting the 'Old Charges' in 1723 used the expression 'Great Architect' in a masonic context, so that I can stand in prayer in this way. I do so without any compromise of my Christian faith; I do not have to justify my faith to my brethren, and they are not permitted to force their beliefs on me.

OTHER DESIGNATIONS

This name (or is it a description?) for God as the 'Great Architect' is not used consistently and exclusively. Thus the prayer at the admission of the candidate is to, 'Almighty Father and Supreme Governor of the Universe' (Hannah p96). For opening in the second degree the prayer starts, 'Let us supplicate the Grand Geometrician of the Universe' (ibid p88). In the Mark degree He is referred to as 'The Great Overseer of the Universe'. To a Master Mason, He is simply 'The Most High'. In the Royal Arch degree, the candidate is asked:

Z: Bro. A.B., in all cases of difficulty and danger, in whom do you put your trust?
Can: In the True and Living God Most High. (Hannah p160)

Inherent in these expressions are a number of beliefs about God which are fully Christian:

He made the Universe;
He did so in accordance with a system of laws;
He is our Father;
He is actively involved in governing and overseeing the Universe;
He is the Truth;
He is alive;
He is supreme.

Compare these statements with what St Paul said of the pagan Athenians:

The God who created the world and everything in it . . . is the universal giver of life and breath and all else. He created every race of men of one stock. . . . They were to seek God, and, it might be, touch and find him; though he is not far from each one of us, for in him we live and move, in him we exist; as some of your poets have said, 'We are also his offspring'. (*Acts* 17:24–29)

Far from being deistic or even relativistic, the masonic terminology used for God reflects every basic Christian concept of Him used in this quotation of St Paul.

THE MYSTICAL LECTURE

In this book our basic consideration is the ceremonial of the three degrees which consistute 'Craft masonry' together with its logical offshoots of the Royal Arch and Mark degrees. In the Royal Arch, there is a 'Mystical Lecture' which not only contains the Royal Arch Word, about which I have written in a separate chapter, but also appears to expand upon the ideas of God which I have outlined above. For example, a paragraph of the latter reads:

JEHOVAH, that great, awful, tremendous and incomprehensible Name of the Most High. It signifies I Am that I Am, the Alpha and Omega, the beginning and

> the end, the first and the last, who was and is and is to come, the Almighty. It is the name of the actual, future, eternal, unchangeable and all-sufficient God, who alone has His being in and from Himself, and gives to all others their being so that He is what He was, was what He is and will remain both what He was and what He is, from everlasting to everlasting, all creatures being dependent on His mighty will and power. (Ibid p180–81)

Does this passage extend beyond belief into theology? It takes a belief in the eternal unchangeable nature of God, and expresses it in several ways. It expands this by introducing the idea that God alone is uncreated, and reiterates man's dependence. But it remains well outside the 'science of religion'.

PRAYER

Inherent in what has just been said is a belief in prayer. The reason that masons pray together is given in the first masonic prayer of all, that with which every English lodge is opened in the first degree:

> The Lodge being duly formed, before I declare it open, let us invoke the assistance of the Great Architect of the Universe in all our undertakings. May our labours, thus begun in order, be continued in peace and closed in harmony. (Hannah p86)

It is for the same reason that every day in the House of Commons starts with prayer; that the Bishop of my Diocese starts a purely routine committee meeting about a Diocesan school with prayer. It is appropriate to start any human activity with an acknowledgement of dependence on God.

It is hard to understand the Church of England Working Group's view that opening a lodge meeting with intercessory prayer makes it an act of worship. The report says:

> Of course there is nothing unusual in attaching different meanings to the same word, but on any definition 'worship' is clearly taken to mean homage or honour paid to God. There is something very confusing, and indeed confused, about the insistence that Masonic ritual does not contain any element of worship: 'prayers in Masonic context are not acts of worship but the simple asking for a blessing at the beginning of work and returning thanks at its successful conclusion.' But prayers in Freemasonry are integral to the Rituals; is this therefore not rather a Humpty Dumpty use of language? In ordinary usage, can such prayer be distinguished from worship? (Working Group p24)

It should be noted that the Working Group did not decide that the ceremonies of initiation and the like are worship *per se*, but that they may become so because prayer is involved.

Taken to its logical conclusion, singing God Save the Queen would be improper except in church. Where does the Humpty Dumpty use of language lie? Surely, the ordinary Briton understands that saying grace before meals is not the start of an act of worship. There is a clear practical distinction between a simple prayer and worship. In the case of a lodge it is simply the start of an evening of fellowship. If it is more than that, perhaps we Freemasons should admit our guilt—we have inadvertently worshipped God!

There is a suggestion at the start of the Royal Arch ceremony, that it may constitute worship. The collect for purity from the Anglican Communion Service is used, with the last phrase chopped off (we will consider the significance of that soon). The petition is:

> Omnipotent, Omniscient, Omnipresent God, unto whom all hearts are open, all desires known, and from whom no secrets are hid, cleanse the thoughts of our hearts by the inspiration of Thy Holy Spirit, that we may perfectly love Thee and worthily magnify Thy Holy Name. (Hannah p155)

However, the prayer is not specifically for the ceremony, and it could be regarded as a prayer for the whole life of each person present; I so regard it. It is fully consistent with Christian belief that every part of a well lived life is praise. It follows that any single act—including attending a Royal Arch convocation—ought to be magnifying God's Name in this broad sense, without its claiming to constitute a formal act of worship. Charles Wesley wrote:

> In all my works Thy presence find,
> And prove Thy good and perfect will

Prayer used in masonic lodges is petition for the meeting, the life of the lodge members, and intercession for the candidate. It is not a formal act of praise or adoration. Lodge meetings are not acts of worship, set up in competition with the church next door.

SHUTTING JESUS OUT

The fact that the name of Jesus Christ does not occur in the prayers of those parts of the Freemasonry with which we are dealing has been the cause of deep concern by Christians. Here is a not untypical passage:

> It is a well known fact that at least in the lower [sic] degrees, the name of Christ is strictly excluded. When clergymen are called on to lead the religious exercises of the lodge, they are frequently instructed not to use the name of Jesus in their prayers, lest a Mohammedan or Jew be offended . . .
>
> But does the Scripture not say, 'Other foundation can no man lay than that is laid, which is Jesus Christ.' This being so, have we any right to bind ourselves by oath to an order from which His sacred name is excluded? If we truly love Him, will we frequent any place where we must leave Him outside the door? (Sanders p151)

A person for whom I have a deep respect, General William Booth, wrote to his officers in 1925:

> No language of mine could be too strong in condemning any Officer's affiliation with any Society which shuts Him outside its temples; and which in its religious ceremonies gives neither Him nor his Name any place. . . . The place where Jesus Christ is not allowed is no place for any Salvation Army Officer. (quoted in Dewar p179)

These attitudes are very persuasive to Christians who are not Freemasons; but they are based upon four misconceptions:

The first misconception is that the ceremonies of Freemasonry are those of a religion. One of the themes of this book is support for the official statement of United Grand Lodge of England, 'that Masonry is neither a religion nor a substitute for religion' and 'is not a competitor with religion'.

Since the prayers of Freemasonry are formally set out in its books of ceremonial, the quotation from Sanders about the place of masonic clergy seems to be based upon a second misunderstanding.

However, the third misunderstanding is the implicit assumption that, whilst Christians are free to join any organisation which *de facto* excludes the Name of Jesus, like a suburban golf club and the Royal Institute of British Architects, including signing promises to uphold their rules and codes of conduct, the moment the organisation says that religion is important (which Freemasonry does) and presumes to pray, it becomes prohibited. This is separating Freemasonry from all other human organisations in a way which can only start from biased presuppositions.

The fourth misconception is that the omission of the specific Name of Jesus from masonic prayer means that He is excluded from masonic meeting places. Nothing could be further from the truth. I have just explained how a Christian who is a Freemason interprets 'Great Architect of the Universe' in a Trinitarian sense. At the risk of confusing the Persons of the Trinity, I would also be prepared to interpret the 'Great Architect' as actually being Jesus. St John the Evangelist taught, 'through him all things came to be; no single thing was created without him. All that came to be was alive with his life' (*John* 1:3). Every Sunday before Communion I repeat the Nicene Creed: 'We believe in one Lord, Jesus Christ. . . . Through him all things were made.'

Masons have pointed out that, if the omission of Jesus' name from a prayer is wrong, that the Lord's prayer—'Our Father'—should not be used in Christian worship! This could extend to the excision from the lectionary readings from the *Third Letter of John* (which does not mention Christ) and, even if the whole of the Old Testament is not excluded, then at least the Protestant version of the *Book of Esther* (which does not mention God).

The truth is that it is impossible for our Lord to be shut out of a lodge meeting. The last words of *Matthew's Gospel* are, 'And be assured, I am with you always, to the end of time.' The Christian Freemason believes those words of Jesus, just as much as any other Christian.

As an aside, it is intriguing that one of the complainants whom I have quoted was the founder of the Salvation Army. This he did with the aim of supporting the work of churches which already existed, as a Christian society with no sacraments and conventional religious trappings, creating for this purpose rituals of its own based on military precedents, and which in the end became a 'denomination' in its own right. Freemasonry has steadfastly refused to follow such a path, because it would defeat its object of becoming a 'Center of Union'.

WITNESS

It would be a reasonable criticism of a Christian in Freemasonry that he is prohibited from witnessing to the saving power of our Lord. The prohibition of discussion of religion apparently eliminates this.

There are a number of important aspects of witness which should be considered. The first is that witness is not necessarily by words. In the chapter on Pelagianism I have quoted from Saints James and Paul about the relative value of faith and works, and also the teaching of Jesus in *Matthew* 25. I will simply summarise His teaching by quoting two verses:

> 'Lord, when was it that we saw you hungry and fed you, or thirsty and gave you a drink. . . .'
> 'Anything you did for my brothers here, however humble, you did for me.'

The passage then goes on to describe the hellfire reserved for those who fail this test.

Compare this with the witness described in the fundamental document of masonry known as the 'Antient Charges':

> Masons unite with the virtuous of every persuasion in the firm and pleasing bond of fraternal love; they are taught to view the errors of mankind with compassion, and to strive, by the purity of their own conduct, to *demonstrate the superior excellence of the faith they may profess*. (*Constitutions* p3, emphasis mine)

Christian and other Freemasons are specifically invited to take part in a contest: to prove by their conduct that their religious faith is effective in producing good works. Masonic teaching on witness parallels that of Jesus: 'Shed light among your fellows, so that, when they see the good you do, they may give praise to your Father in heaven'. (*Mat* 5:16)

Again, the prohibition against discussion of religion is not absolute. The official *Aims and Relationships of the Craft* says that such discussion is permitted, 'neither in any Lodge, nor in any time in his capacity as a Freemason', which effectively means that friendships made in masonic company could well be used to lead to opportunities to discuss the fullness of life available in Jesus Christ in other places.

This is exactly what may happen. The Church of England Working Group received several letters, summarised as:

> Among the evidence received by the Group were letters from Freemasons, indicating an alternative view of the consequences of Lodge meetings; that the social relationships established by meeting in Lodge actually made it possible outside its formal business to discuss and explain the peculiar claims of Christianity over any other religion. One (clerical) Freemason in fact referred to bringing men to be confirmed in the Church of England as a result of meeting them as members of his Lodge. (p38)

The position of a Freemason is, by choice, exactly the same as that of any modern Christian in our present day, multi-faith society. This is what a recent book by the Evangelical Alliance says about evangelism by school teachers:

> Supremely, the Christian teacher must demonstrate his faith in the quality of his teaching. When Christianity is seen not just as an extra-curricular activity but as something which transforms the whole of life, the Christian teacher will be marked by a concern for truth and integrity in his work, a view of colleagues and pupils as people with value, rights and dignity, and a recognition of his task as a God-given responsibility.
>
> It need hardly be said that in the multi-faith context evangelism of a captive audience in the classroom is morally indefensible. Outside the classroom activities aimed directly or indirectly at evangelism should be undertaken thoughtfully, and with the full awareness of the social and cultural consequences of conversion to Christianity. (Evangelical Alliance pp42–43)

The teaching of present day evangelicals about witness is what Freemasons have been saying for the better part of three hundred years.

IMMORTALITY

Mackey's twentieth 'landmark' follows from belief in God. He wrote:

> Subsidiary to this belief in God, as a Landmark of the Order, is the Belief in a Resurrection to a Future Life. This Landmark is taught by very plain implication, and runs through the whole symbolism of the Order. (op cit p15)

Dean Rosco Pound expresses this in similar terms in his comments on Mackey's landmarks, as 'belief in the persistence of personality'.

The Grand Lodges of the British Isles do not specifically refer to this belief in their official documents, but the ritual refers to it frequently:

> The covering of a Freemason's Lodge is a celestial canopy . . . even the Heavens. The way by which we, as Masons, hope to arrive there is by the assistance of a ladder, in Scripture called Jacob's ladder. It is composed of many staves or rounds, which point out many moral virtues, but three principal ones, which are Faith, Hope and Charity. (Hannah p112)

> The Skirret points out that straight and undeviating line of conduct laid down for our pursuit in the Volume of the Sacred Law. The Pencil teaches us that our words and actions are observed and recorded by the Almighty Architect, to whom we must give an account of our conduct through life. The compasses remind us of His unerring and impartial justice, who, having defined for our instruction the limit of good and evil, will reward or punish as we have obeyed or disregarded His Divine commands. Thus the working tools of a Master Mason teaches us to bear in mind, and act according to, the laws of our Divine Creator, that when we shall be summoned from this sublunary abode, we may ascend to the Grand Lodge above, where the world's Great Architect lives and reigns for ever. (ibid p148)

Implicit in the passages cited are a number of beliefs which flow from a belief of immortality. Some of these are recognised by the landmark lawyers of United States masonry as forming part of their definitions. The list adopted by Minnesota in 1856 added to belief in a Supreme Being, that He 'will punish vice and reward virtue'. There is no implication that masonry goes any further and provides a means of salvation. This aspect is discussed in my chapter on Pelagianism, and from that chapter it is apparent that there is the same balance between faith and works in Freemasonry as there is in the Christian church and in the Bible.

SIN

The Mystical Lecture in the Royal Arch also contains an explanation which defines man's relationship with his Creator more specifically than elsewhere in the ceremonials under consideration, or perhaps even in the whole fabric of Freemasonry. As exposed by Hannah, this says:

> The Royal Arch signs mark in a peculiar manner the relation we bear to the Most High, as creatures offending against His mighty will and power, yet still the adopted children of His mercy. (ibid p178)

The lecture is thus concerned with the contrast between God's glory and fallen man.

The Principal giving the lecture then proceeds to demonstrate each of the signs, explains its meaning, and in three cases relates it to an action by Adam, in one case extending it to Moses. The reason for introducing Adam is clear—irrespective of whether he is believed to be a historial person—as he represents the contrast between the perfect state which God wills for man, and the sinful state in which we actually exist. Introducing Moses is equally logical, as he had a revelation of God's glory and demonstrated a reaction to it. This is what the lecture says:

> The Penal sign . . . alludes to the fall of Adam, and the dreadful penalty entailed thereby on his sinful posterity, no less than death.
>
> To avert which, we are taught by the Reverential or Hailing sign to bend with humility and resignation beneath the chastening hand of the Almighty, at the same time to engraft His law in our hearts.
>
> The Penitential or Supplicatory sign . . . truly denotes that frame of heart and mind without which our prayers and oblations of praise cannot find acceptance at the throne of grace, before which how should a frail and erring creature of the dust present himself but on bended knees and with uplifted hands, at once betokening his humility and contrition?
>
> By this outward form of faith and dependence, the Fiducial sign, we show that we would prostrate ourselves with our faces to the dust. Thus must we throw ourselves on the mercy of our Divine Creator and Judge, looking forward with holy but humble confidence to His blessed promises, by which means alone we hope to pass through the ark of redemption into the presence of Him who is the great I AM. . . . (ibid pp78–79)

Far from being a developed theology, these explanations repeat the basic relationship of man to God. No offer of salvation is made, and although the last sign expresses hope, it is in undefined 'blessed promises' which a Freemason can only find by reverting to his own creed. The Christian Freemason of course sees the object of these promises made available in the redeeming work of Jesus Christ.

It should be obvious to every person going through the ceremony that no one could possibly know what gesture Adam used when confronted with his 'Divine Creator and Judge', and that the signs symbolise the 'frame of heart and mind' which it is supposed he must have felt.

There remains, however, one disconcerting phrase which introduces the last sign: 'After the manner of our holy ancestors, the atoning priests, by this outward form of faith and dependence, the Fiducial sign, we show. . . .' (ibid p178). It surely refers to the Aaronic priesthood of the Old Testament, but the Royal Arch members symbolically represent not the priestly line but workmen from the tribe of Judah. It is true that all three Principals of the chapter have passed through one of the chairs which symbolises 'Joshua, the son of Josedech, the High Priest' (Hannah p174), but the lecturer is addressing a new member. It remains a mystery to me, which I see as being of no significance to the meaning of the ceremony, and which I would happily see omitted! But, to revert to the theme of this chapter, it does not represent a theological concept.

In any case, the wording has been omitted in a recently introduced, optional explanation of the sign, which hopefully will gain wide acceptance.

NO THEOLOGY

There remains one fundamental belief enshrined within masonry which I have not mentioned: that a divine revelation exists in the form of a Sacred Volume for every religion, the Bible of course for Christians. This is the topic of my next chapter.

No other beliefs are regarded as sufficiently fundamental to Freemasonry to be included in its official statements, and I believe that I have covered all significant aspects of belief expressed in the ceremonials which we are considering. They are *basic* beliefs which merely form a common ground for fellowship. I have shown that these beliefs, held by the greater part of humankind, are not sufficient to form the foundation for a new religion, let alone for the development of any theology.

6
The Bible

THE SACRED VOLUME

The third belief that is implicit in Freemasonry is in what Freemasons called the 'Volume of the Sacred Law'. In the majority of English-speaking lodge meetings, this is the 'Authorized' or 'King James' version of the Bible. It is not necessarily the only sacred book, but others may be added, as item 3 of the *Basic Principles for Grand Lodge Recognition* makes clear:

> All initiates shall take their Obligation on or in full view of the open Volume of the Sacred Law, by which is meant the revelation from above which is binding on the conscience of the particular individual being initiated. (p3)

Hence, the Sacred Volume is the Koran to a Muslim, the Vedas to a Hindu, and so on.

Let us note in passing that the Grand Lodges of the British Isles have seen fit to describe all these books as a 'revelation from above'. God is a self-revealing God, and this involves the record of this revelation in the form of a book, whether it be what the Archangel Gabriel dictated to Mohammed, what the bronze figure showed Ezekiel, or what the Lord Buddha discovered under the sacred Bo tree.

Freemasonry does not decide between these: it is the candidate who fixes what book is binding on his conscience. There is no inconsistency here: the Christian obligates himself with his hand on the Bible, and that is binding upon him; the Muslim does so using the Koran (leaving aside the issue as to whether it should be a copy in Arabic which has not been touched by an infidel, held closed in his right hand and wrapped in a silken cloth). The question is not whether Freemasons accept these books as of equal value—they obviously do not, or all would take their obligation upon a library—but whether it is binding on the conscience of the particular individual.

PRECEDENCE

However, the situation is not quite so simple, as the Bible retains a degree of precedence. Item 4 of the *Aims and Relationships* states:

> The Bible referred to by Freemasons as the Volume of the Sacred Law, is always open in the Lodges. Every Candidate is required to take his Obligation on that book or on the Volume which is held by his particular creed to impart sanctity to an oath or promise taken upon it.

The Bible is *always* open when a lodge is open. In addition, the Volume specifically selected for the candidate is present, for him to take his obligation upon. In some more pedantic lodges, a member of the same faith is present, by invitation if necessary, to ensure that this is properly done.

The normal method of so doing is for the lodge to have only the Bible on the Master's pedestal, but to remove it elsewhere and replace it with another Volume when the candidate is not a Christian. There are alternatives, especially in the East; the Grand Lodge of India always has several Volumes open at its meetings, as does Lodge Singapore No 7178. Although the latter operates under the United Grand Lodge of England, it fulfils the requirement quoted above by always having the Bible open, but strips it of any precedence by also having open those other Volumes held sacred by its members. Needless to say, the candidate makes his promise on his own creed's volume alone.

The reason for special treatment normally reserved for the Bible is not given. I believe, however, that it is wholly logical, because, in addition to the need for a Sacred Volume upon which to take an obligation, the Bible is the specific source of much masonic ceremonial. The Bible fulfils a unique double role. But again, it must be emphasised that this does not make the Bible superior, as each candidate may choose as his Volume the revelation of his own creed.

RITUAL

Apart from its place in official statements, the Sacred Volume is referred to in masonic ritual on several occasions. Immediately after his initiation, the new mason is told:

> As a Freemason, let me recommend to your most serious contemplation the Volume of the Sacred Law, charging you to consider it as the unerring standard of truth and justice, and to regulate your actions by the divine precepts it contains. Therein you will be taught the important duties you owe to God, your neighbour and yourself. To God, by never mentioning His name but with that awe and reverence which are due from the creature to his Creator, by imploring His aid in all your lawful undertakings, and by looking up to Him in every emergency for comfort and support. To your neighbour, by acting with him on the square. . . . (Hannah, *Darkness Visible* pp107–08)

This is not the place to discuss the inerrancy of the Bible or any other Sacred Volume. Suffice it to say that, when the candidate is a Christian, he is being addressed by the Master about his own Sacred Volume, the Bible. There is no question of the Koran being commended to a Christian, or the Vedas to a Muslim. Once again, the Sacred Volumes are not being treated as of equal value, because to the new mason, his own creed's Volume is being consistently used.

There is another use of the Sacred Volume in the Royal Arch. In the address from which I have just quoted, it is referred to as *literally* a guide to life and actions, but in the Royal Arch it has become an *emblem*, albeit with similar significance.

> The Bible, Square and Compasses are the appropriate emblems of the three Grand Masters who presided at the building of the former Temple; the Bible denotes the Wisdom of King Solomon . . . but the truly speculative Mason regards them as the unerring standards of the wisdom, truth and justice of the Most High. His wisdom is amply exemplified in the Volume of the Sacred Law, which contains the record of His mighty acts, and is the register of His revealed will. . . . (ibid pp176–77)

This passage also exhibits a residual Christian belief that the Bible is the only Sacred Volume, which somehow escaped the reform of 1823, and should of course be amended. Disconcerting as its retention may be to the non-Christian, to the Christian mason the Bible remains central to his church and his lodge.

QUOTATION

In addition to referring to the Volume of the Sacred Law, which means the Bible for Christian masons, the Bible is also used as a source for masonic teaching, in three ways.

First, it is often quoted directly. In the Royal Arch ceremony, two quite long passages are read: the ode to wisdom given in *Proverbs* 2:19 and 3:13–20, and the encouragement to rebuild Jerusalem from *Haggai* 2:1–9. The latter is particularly relevant to the legend of the Royal Arch degree. Likewise, in the Mark degree, there is a series of short readings related to the communication of the signs of that degree. There are no such readings in the Craft ceremonial as exposed by Hannah, but some workings do have readings inserted immediately after the lodge is opened, and immediately after the candidate takes his obligation.

Secondly, it is often quoted within the wording of the ceremonial without actual acknowledgement. Thus 2 *Cor* 5:1 (AV) reads:

> For we know that if our earthly house of this tabernacle were dissolved, we have a building of God, an house not made with hands, eternal in the heavens.

Hannah's exposé of the Mark degree shows how this is quoted within the ritual:

> . . . we may hereafter be found worthy to receive the approving mark of the Great Overseer of the Universe, as fitted to form part of that spiritual edifice, 'that house not made with hands, eternal in the heavens'. (Hannah, *Christian By Degrees* p94)

Elsewhere, I have drawn attention to the wording within the third degree working which refers to 'that bright morning star' which has obvious reference to:

> I Jesus have sent my angel to testify to these things in the churches. I am the root and the offspring of David and the bright and morning star. (*Rev* 22:16 AV)

Examples of this kind could be multiplied at length. Masonic ritual breathes the air of the Authorized or King James version of the Bible—and in some cases that of the Geneva Bible—to an extent that many masons in this post-Christian era do not realise.

Some of the critics of the Craft do not realise it either; John Lawrence, referring to the master craftsman of King Soloman, says:

> No character in Scripture is called Hiram Abiff. There is a character called Hiram who was involved in the construction of the temple (see 1 *Kings 7*) and this is the only one to whom any link with the masonic Hiram Abiff can be drawn. . . . In 2 *Chronicles 2* this man is identified as Huram-abi. (p90)

The Hebrew name in 2 *Chronicles* 2:13 is *Le-Huram Avi* and in 2 *Chronicles* 4:16 it is *Huram Aviv*. Translators have always had difficulty about whether the second half is a name or a description (the problem with the Royal Arch word in chapter 25 is hardly new!) and early Protestant translators chose to regard it as a name. Martin Luther used Huram Abif (from 2 *Chronicles* 4:16) in *both* places, and early English translations followed this lead. But by the time of the Authorised Version, it was treated as a description—'his father's'—even if rather meaningless. Modern translators have reverted to the name concept, and in both places 'Huram-abi' is used (from 2 *Chronicles* 2:13) in the *New American Standard* which Lawrence uses, as well as the *Revised Standard Version*, *Jerusalem Bible*, etc.

The details which I have given above are from Harry Carr's *The Freemason at Work* (pp214–15), which heads the list of books recommended by Lawrence. It can only therefore be with wilful prejudice that Lawrence makes his criticism.

In masonic rituals his name is abbreviated to 'H.A.' or 'H.A.B.', and any modern detailed spelling is unknown and irrelevant. 'Huram-abi' is as good as the more conventional 'Hiram Abif'! Both editions of Anderson's *Constitutions* had extensive footnotes on the variants of Hiram's name, with 'Churam Abbif' as a transliteration of the Hebrew of 2 *Chronicles* 4:6. In the second edition of 1738 'Hiram Abbif' is used in the main text. Perhaps this part of the traditional history, obviously based on earlier translations, antedates the Authorised Version of 1611, but it is more likely that it reflects the initial unpopularity of thc AV.

A further complaint about quotation has arisen in America, concerned with the theophany to Moses from *Exodus* 3. Harmon R. Taylor, for example, in the June 1986 issue of *The Evangelist*, writes:

> The Master of the Lodge claims to be the God of Abraham, Isaac and Jacob. How awfully profane and blasphemous this is! (p47)

He precedes this statement by listing his detailed involvement in Freemasonry, including winning an award for the greatest increase in lodge attendance during his Mastership. He claims to know what he is writing about.

I was so concerned on reading this terrible accusation that I rushed to my bookshelf to find Ronayne's exposure of the American Royal Arch, *Chapter Masonry*, and searched in vain for Taylor's source. The relevant passage would appear to be:

> Candidates rise to their feet and are conducted the third time around the Chapter by the Principal Sojourner, and as they move on slowly he repeats from memory, or reads from the Monitor, *Exodus* iii:l–6, as follows:
>
> 'Now Moses kept the flock of Jethro. . . . And when the Lord saw that he turned aside to see, God called unto him. . . . Moreover He said, I am the God of thy fathers, the God of Abraham, the God of Isaac and the God of Jacob. And Moses hid his face for he was afraid to look upon God.' (p222)

Need I point out that, far from claiming to be God, the officer—who is the Principal Sojourner of a Chapter, not the Master of a lodge—is simply reading or reciting *Exodus* 3.

I checked in a second book, *Duncan's Ritual*, probably more applicable to New York where Taylor claims to have obtained his masonic experience, and there is a second passage in which a member of the chapter also quotes or reads *Exodus* 3:4b–6, in response to which the candidate kneels in reverence (p232). Far from committing an act of blasphemy, the chapter officers are using the exact words of the Authorised Version to reverently re-create something of the atmosphere of the theophany.

Taylor is relying on the ignorance of his non-masonic readers to convince them that Freemasonry is blasphemous. Is this the way of the One who taught, 'You shall know the truth, and the truth will set you free'? (*John* 8:32)

LEGEND

Thirdly, there is use of the Bible as a basis for masonic ritual. Sometimes the biblical story is told accurately but in different words. Not surprisingly, an example of this is the use of a password in *Judges* 12:6. In other cases, however, a legend has been added, referred to by masons as a 'Traditional History'. There are two major cases of this usage:

During the building of King Solomon's Temple, the skilled designer and worker to whom I have just referred was sent by the pagan King of Tyre to organise the building work. This character has fascinated masons since the early eighteenth century (possibly much earlier under a pseudonym 'Aynon') and they have evolved legends connected with his death and burial which are recounted as part of the ceremonial, but do not any have biblical basis. (See Hannah pp137–45)

During the repair of the Temple under King Josiah, the lost law of Moses was found (thought to be the basis of Deuteronomy). Following the return from Babylonian exile, the Temple was rebuilt under Zerubbabel. Royal Arch Freemasons have managed to confuse these two facts (except in Ireland, where they have stuck faithfully by King Josiah) and have added a legend of the discovery by three workmen of a vault in which the Law had been stored, again with no specific biblical basis. (See ibid pp166–70)

Whilst these legends are not found in the Bible, they are not contrary to it. Even the confusion in the Royal Arch is not disguised to the intelligent mason, and virtually any of the books available which explain masonic ceremonial and history, such as Bernard Jones' *Freemason's Book of the Royal Arch*, go into this in detail. In the Irish working, the discrepancy is specifically explained. Far from being harmful, it is my experience that the interest of a new mason in his Bible is quickened by an effort to distinguish the Biblical record from the masonic legend.

Is it wrong to add the two together? Of course, the fundamentalist will say so—he will quote the last few words of the Bible, 'I give this warning to anyone who is listening to the words of prophesy in this book; should anyone add to them, God will add to Him the plagues described in this book. . . .' (*Rev* 22:18). But then, St John the Divine was referring to the *Book of Revelation*, which was written long before the canon of the Bible as we now know it was settled.

Even the most ardent fundamentalist will sing Christmas hymns and carols about our Lord being born at *midnight*, and being visited by *three* wise men. He may even know their names—all pure legend. The Catholic on Good Friday will happily pray in front of the Stations of the Cross, one of which is devoted to St Veronica—again pure legend. Where would we be without the chapter and verse divisions added to the original text of the Bible? Or the legendary ascriptions of many of the books? For example, not one of the Gospels tells us who wrote it, but the legendary authorships have been added because they serve better than none at all.

All that must be ascertained is whether the added legend is edifying; and masons believe that theirs are.

ALLEGED MISUSE

The fourth way in which the Bible is used is where it might be claimed that it is *mis*used. Examples are those where the New Testament is used, but the name of Christ is omitted. Oswald Sanders gives as examples:

> Ye also, as lively stones, are built up as a spiritual house, an holy priesthood, to offer up spiritual sacrifices, acceptable to God [by Jesus Christ]. (1 *Peter* 2:5 AV)

> Now we command you, brethren, [in the name of our Lord Jesus Christ] that you withdraw yourselves from every brother that walketh disorderly, and not after the tradition which he received of us. (2 *Thes* 3:6 AV)

> Now them that are such we command and exhort [by our Lord Jesus Christ], that with quietness they work, and eat their own bread. (2 *Thes* 3:12 AV) (Sanders p151)

The words which Sanders claims are omitted are in square brackets. Unfortunately, Sanders does not say from which masonic ritual he is quoting, but the passages are not in any of the basic ceremonies of the Craft, Royal Arch and Mark which we are considering. Where they are included—for example the first one, used in the Tabernacles of a 'higher' degree—the name of our Lord is included with the quotation. (*Grand College . . . Ritual I*, p7)

But in general terms Sanders is not wrong, but his correctness lies not so much in relation to omitting the Name of Jesus, but in taking the text out of its context to suit masonic usage. Consider the (optional) Royal Arch charge after closing:

> . . . the world may observe and feel how truly Masons love one another. These generous principles ought to extend beyond the limited area of our own society, for every human being has a claim upon your kind offices, so much we enjoin you to do good to all, but more especially to the household of the faithful. (Hannah, *Darkness* p158)

The mason hearing this will consider that he has a duty first to other zealous masons—the household of the faithful—and thereafter to others. But when St Paul wrote, 'as we have therefore opportunity, let us do good to all men, especially unto them who are of the household of faith' (*Gal* 6:10 AV), he clearly did not mean to give preference to zealous masons. He meant fellow Christians.

Similarly, the Mark mason repeatedly hears a quotation from *Psalm* 118:22: 'The stone which the builders rejected is become the head stone of the corner' (Hannah: *Christian* p93). So important is this, that it is the Latin motto of the Order; but it is used purely in a literal sense. In the masonic legend, the overseers of the Temple under construction reject a specially cut stone out of their own ignorance as to its purpose. However, in the New Testament, this is quoted by our Lord in *Mark* 12:10 and in the other Synoptics as applying to Himself, and in *Acts* 4:11 by St Peter to the same effect. Is it wrong for a Christian Freemason to accept this non-messianic interpretation of the Psalmist's words?

Perhaps more of a problem than this is the use of words taken from *Rev* 2:17 as an explanation of the Mark sign and the small stone which each member wears. The words in brackets are omitted:

> He that hath an ear, let him hear [what the Spirit saith unto the churches]; To him that overcometh will I give to eat of the hidden manna, and will give him a white stone, and in the stone a new name written, which no man knoweth save he that receiveth it.

BIBLICAL PRECEDENTS

It is only in the last century that it has become obligatory to get quotations right every time, or to apply them strictly within the original context. Fortunately, the plethora of modern translations is such that it is not quite as important to use the exact King James wording as it was fifty years ago, but writers still expect to check their quotes carefully.

It is evident that differences exist between quotations from the Old Testament used in the New, and the original version. This is sometimes just caused by the difference between a translation from Hebrew and Greek;

more often it is the difference between the Greek Old Testament (the Septuagint) used by Greek-speaking Christians in the first century, and the original Hebrew text. These we all accept. But let me give you two examples from St Paul which fall outside this category and would be taken as misquotations by modern standards.

In *1 Cor* 2:9 he says:

> In the words of Scripture, 'Things beyond our seeing, things beyond our hearing, things beyond our imagining, all prepared by God for those who love him', these it is that God has revealed to us through the Spirit.

My Bible gives a cross reference to the nearest equivalent, *Isaiah* 64:4, which reads, 'Never has ear heard or eye seen any other god taking the part of those who wait for him'. Comparing this with St Paul's quotation, even allowing for differences in language, we find that ear and eye are reversed, and that Isaiah has no 'imagination'. The reference to 'any other god taking the part' bears no relationship to 'prepared by God for those. . . .' There is in fact a passage in the *Apocalypse of Elijah* which more closely resembles what St Paul said, but that book is not part of the Bible or even the Apocrypha, so if St Paul was quoting from that, it was not actually 'Scripture'.

Just a little further on in the same letter, St Paul says, 'For the wisdom of this world is folly in God's sight. Scripture says, "He traps the wise in their own cunning".' (1 *Cor* 3:19). *Job* 5:13 does indeed say: 'he traps the cunning in their craftiness', close enough when allowing for differing languages. But chapter 4 starts a long speech to Job by Eliphaz, and at the end of the book, 'When the LORD had finished speaking to Job, he said to Eliphaz the Temanite, "I am angry with you and your two friends, because you have not spoken as you ought about me, as my servant Job has done".' (*Job* 42:7). St Paul was quoting—as if it were valuable teaching—something which is specifically condemned at its source.

Examples could be multiplied at length of relatively minor discrepancies between Old Testament sources and New Testament quotations. Christians cannot justifiably demand an inflexible use of the Scriptures by Freemasons.

MASONIC MEANING

However, we must remember that the ceremonials of Freemasonry require the Hindu and the Buddhist—who have no prior knowledge of the Bible, nor any reason to accept its authority even on a nominal basis—to listen and learn from the quotations and legends from that book. To understand this, I must revert to the two distinct usages of the Bible which I outlined at the beginning of this chapter.

The authority of the Bible when used in masonic ceremonial is quite different from its use as the Sacred Volume upon which Christians and Jews take their obligations. It is not the authority given by a Council of the undivided Church or the Thirty-Nine Articles. It is not even used because it is believed to be inspired or infallible. The passages which are used are taken from the Bible simply because that is how Freemasonry developed, but they have to be self authenticating. A Hindu or Buddhist, hearing a passage from the Bible, treats it as any other passage, and accepts the inevitable logic of its teaching of ethical truth.

Thus the specific use of the Bible has no theological significance. It cannot become a basis for religious controversy; but it does become a means of ethical enlightenment to men of all faiths.

Christian Freemasons have found the masonic treatment of the Bible useful. Dr I. N. McCash, an Oklahoma University President wrote, 'you'll find the degrees of Masonry provide you with a most comprehensive and excellent education in Biblical literature and interpretation. One that you are apt to find nowhere else'. A Methodist minister, Wesley E. McKelvey, wrote in a similar vein:

> I have never felt even the slightest conflict between my own personal faith and practice and Freemasonry. Travelling the various Masonic roads I have been thrilled by the presentation of Biblical history and teaching. The application of both Old and New Testament history and teaching has encouraged me greatly in my own Christian experience. (quoted in Haggard p135)

7
History

A BAD NAME

Masonic history has always had a bad name. As early as 1686, Dr Robert Plot wrote in his *Natural History of Staffordshire* of 'this *History* of the craft it self; than which there is nothing I ever met with, more false and incoherent.' (quoted in Poole vol ii p21)

He was followed, amongst others, by Ambrose Bierce, who in the 1880s defined 'Freemasons' as:

> An order [sic] . . . which, originating in the reign of Charles II, among the working artisans of London, has now been joined successively by the dead of past centuries in unbroken retrogression until it now embraces all the generations on the hither side of Adam and is drumming up distinguished recruits among the pre-Creational inhabitants of the Formless Void. The order was founded at different times by Charlemagne, Julius Caesar, Cyrus, Solomon, Zoroaster, Confucius, Thothmes, and Buddha. Its emblems and symbols have been found in the Catacombs of Paris and Rome, on the stones of the Parthenon and the Chinese Great Wall, among the temples of Karnak and Palmyra and in the Egyptian Pyramids—always by a Freemason. (Bierce p134)

This definition is sufficiently close to the truth to hurt!

Nevertheless, some time ago I was asked by a senior and very intelligent ecclesiastic, who is not a Freemason but ought to have known better, whether it is true that Freemasonry sees its origins in the builders of King Solomon's Temple. He was most surprised when I said that it certainly did not!

This question is of vital importance to the theme of this book, as many of the issues between the Craft and the Christian faith can be simply resolved as a matter of history. How, for example, can Freemasonry possibly be the continuation of the Ancient Mysteries, if the earliest traces of modern masonic ceremonial dating back to the seventeenth century show no evidence of such an inheritance? If its history proves to have a start innocent of any such influence, or of Rosicrucianism, of Alchemy, and the like, then any assumption of such influence must either be a figment of the imagination of those who suggest that it exists, or it must have been added by enthusiasts during the late eighteenth or early nineteenth centuries.

The erroneous history of Freemasonry has four sources, although there is much interplay between them.

THE OLD CHARGES

The first lies in the Old Charges; their view of history is the source of Dr Plot's adverse comment. These are the basic internal document of English and Scottish operative masonry, and its possession by each separate lodge was a means of establishing its legitimacy within the loose organisation which existed in the days before the Grand Lodges were formed. It was probably read whenever new masons were admitted or made progress to the second grade of fellow.

The earliest of these are the Regius MS of about 1390 and the Cooke MS of 1425, the latter probably being a copy of something written about 1350. The Regius MS is a long poem with no later counterpart, and all other versions—of which there are over a hundred in existence—spring from the Cooke MS. The Grand Lodge No I MS of 1585 appears closer to all subsequent manuscripts than the two earliest, and recent research has re-created a possible common source of about 1530 (McLeod, both bibliographical entries, passim), in much the same way that scholars have identified an imaginary 'Q' (from *Quelle* meaning source) for those parts of the synoptic Gospels common only to Matthew and Luke.

Each of the Old Charges consists of three main parts, which follow a dedicatory prayer to the Holy Trinity: an explanation of the seven liberal arts and sciences, an account of the history of masonry, and a set of rules for behaviour. It is probable that the original text was written by a medieval cleric who based his 'history' on what was available in 1350 in books like the Polychronicon as well as the Bible. His task was to write a story which would prove to the new member that his craft had dignity and honour, based upon its antiquity and its royal patronage in many lands. We cannot grumble about what this first writer did; for example, the history of glass making commissioned by Pilkingtons goes back to glass jewellery found in Egyptian tombs, but this does not imply that Pilkingtons used Egyptian religious myths as the basis for their invention of float glass, or that Pilkingtons is a continuation of an Egyptian glass making guild.

This is how one of the Old Charges starts in its historical section:

> How this science was first begun I shall tell you; before Noes flood was a man called Lameth as it is written in ye 4 Chaptr of Gene. and this Lameth has two wives, ye one was called Adar, ye other Sella; and by the first wife Adar hee begott 2 sonnes. The one was called Jabell and ye other Juball; and by ye other wife hee had a sonne & a daughter; and these foure children found ye beginning of all Craft in ye world; this Jabell was ye elder sone; and hee found ye Craft of Geometry; and he depted flockes of Sheep & lambes in ye field, And he first wrought house of stone & tree . . . and these children did knowe that god would take vengence for sinne either by fire or water; wherefore they writ ye Sciences wch weare found in 2 pillers of stone; yt ye might bee found after ye flood. . . . (Hughan p47)

The story then meanders from Abraham and Euclid by way of King David and Solomon to Charles Martel and St Alban. Having thus started masonic history before the Flood, the writer continues in England with Prince Edwin ('Ladrian'):

> And hee got of his Father ye King a Charter, and a commission to hold every year an Assembly where they would wthin ye Realme; and to correcte wth ymselves statutes and trespasses; if it weare done wthin ye crafte; and hee held himself assembly at York and there hee made Masons, and gave ym Charges and taught them the manners of Masons. . . . (ibid pp49–50)

The problem can at once be seen: what was good 'history' in the context of 1350, having been more or less slavishly copied for over three centuries, was pretty poor stuff to Dr Plot. Nevertheless, its effect can still be seen, for example, in the American title 'York' rite, apparently claiming antecedents back to Prince Edwin's mythical charter.

ANDERSON'S CONSTITUTIONS

With the decision of the fledgling Grand Lodge to create a new set of *Constitutions*, the opportunity could have been taken to set things right, but the new history written by the historian and Presbyterian minister, Dr James Anderson, only made matters worse. This is how he treated masonic history, 'to be read At the Admission of a New Brother':

> ADAM, our first Parent, created after the Image of God, *the great Architect of the Universe*, must have had the Liberal Sciences, particularly *Geometry* written on his Heart; for even since the Fall, we find the Principles in the Hearts of his Offspring, and which, in process of time, have been drawn forth into a convenient Method of *Propositions*, by observing the Laws of *Proportion* taken from *Mechanism:* So that as the *Mechanical Arts* gave Occasion to the Learned to reduce the Elements of *Geometry* into Method, this noble Science thus reduc'd, is the Foundation of all those Arts, (particularly of *Masonry* and *Architecture*) and the Rule by which they are conducted and perform'd.
>
> No doubt *Adam* taught his Sons *Geometry*, and the use of it, in the several *Arts* and *Crafts* convenient, at least, for those early Times; for CAIN we find, built a City, which he call'd CONSECRATED, or DEDICATED, after the Name of his eldest Son ENOCH. . . . Nor can we suppose that SETH was less instructed, who . . . would take equal Care to teach *Geometry* and *Masonry* to his Offspring, who had also the mighty Advantage of *Adam's* living among them. (Anderson's *Constitutions* of 1723 pp1–3, original emphasis)

In forty-eight such pages, Anderson brings us to 'our present worthy *Grand Master*, the most noble PRINCE John Duke of MONTAGUE'. This version of masonic 'history' was expanded to 139 pages of smaller type in the second edition of the *Constitutions*—he says for example that Adam's 'Sons grew up to form a *Lodge*' and that Noah and his sons were 'four *Grand Officers*'. This was copied in all subsequent editions, until all 'history' was omitted, apparently but fortuitously by default, in that published in 1815, following the Union of the two English Grand Lodges.

CEREMONIAL

It is not in the least surprising to find that Anderson's ideas of history were solidly ingrained in the rites of modern Freemasonry, which developed their present form largely during the latter part of the eighteenth century, when his myths were regularly published for all masons to read. But this is not always the case.

Sometimes the rituals of Freemasonry make a clear reference to 'traditional history', by which is meant the combination of biblical record and accrued legend which constitutes the story of the masonic ceremony. An example follows the investiture of the new Master Mason, when the text starts: 'We left off at that part of our *traditional history* which mentions. . . .' Likewise, in the Mark degree, there is an explanation of the grip which says 'masonic *tradition* informs us that the shore was so steep. . . .' An explanation given at the installation of the new Master of a lodge starts, 'It is *traditionally* reported that. . . .' Occasionally, therefore, there is an implied view that there is a traditional history which is distinct from real history.

In other places there is an implied claim to antiquity which is in fact not such a claim at all. The first degree Tracing Board lecture starts with:

> The usages and customs among Freemasons have ever borne a near affinity to those of the ancient Egyptians. Their philosophers, unwilling to expose their mysteries to vulgar eyes, couched their systems of learning and polity under signs and hieroglyphical figures, which were communicated to their chief priests or Magi alone, who were bound by solemn oath to conceal them. . . . Masonry, however, is not only the most ancient but the most honourable Society that ever existed, as there is not a character or emblem here depicted but serves to inculcate the principles of piety and virtue among its genuine professors. (Hannah p109)

Whilst this appears to say that Freemasonry is as old as the pyramids, it is in fact saying that all moral behaviour is in a sense a fulfilment of the masonic ideal, and thus present day masons who attempt to conform to this idea can lay claim to be the inheritors of all human societies dedicated to inculcating morality. It is, of course, also true that the oldest known example of dressed stone is in one of the early pyramids.

The 'charge' to the initiate is similar. It says of Masonry:

> Ancient, no doubt it is, having subsisted from time immemorial, and honourable it must be acknowledged to be, as by a natural tendency it conduces to make those so who are obedient to its precepts. . . . And to so high an eminence has its credit been advanced that in every age monarchs themselves have been promoters of the art; have not thought it derogatory to their dignity to exchange the sceptre for the trowel. . . . (ibid p107)

Apart from echoes of the royal patronage portrayed in the Old Charges, this passage also contains a hint that the real history of operative masonry goes back to the time when man first set stone on stone, lost in the days of prehistory. There is strictly nothing wrong with this view, except that any continuity of organisation is lacking. The history of speculative masonry must lie in some sort of organisational continuity with the past, not simply in the history of man's quarrying and working of stone.

Likewise, when dealing with the straight Biblical account of an event, like the use of a password (or more strictly, test word) by Jepthah to distinguish the Ephraimites, there can be no complaint about the story as such. The only complaint may lie in its appropriation by masons as if its use by King Solomon for the masons of his day were a part of real history.

The real problem arises when actual historical personages are taken in tow, not just for masonry in the general sense of building with stone, but as the equivalent of present day officers of a Grand Lodge, simply because they had a connection with a structure in the Bible. This tendency undoubtedly goes back to our Presbyterian divine, James Anderson. As an example, let me quote the Historical (sic) Lecture in the Royal Arch ceremony, as exposed by Walton Hannah:

> Companions, there are three epochs in Freemasonry which particularly merit your attention: they are, the opening of the first or Holy Lodge, the second or Sacred Lodge, and the third or Grand and Royal Lodge.
>
> The first or Holy Lodge was opened Anno Lucis 2515 [this is based on the creation having taken place in 4000 BC, generally following the chronology of Archbishop Ussher], two years after the exodus of the Israelites from their Egyptian bondage by Moses, Aholiab and Bezaleel, on consecrated ground at the foot of Mount Horeb in the Wilderness of Sinai. . . . There were delivered those mysterious forms and prototypes, the tabernacles [sic], the ark of the convenant, and the tables of the Sacred Law engraver by the finger of the Most high, with sublime and comprehensive precepts of religious and moral duty. . . . For these reasons it was denoted the first or Holy Lodge.
>
> Solomon King of Israel, Hiram King of Tyre, and Hiram Abiff presided over the second or Sacred Lodge, which was opened Anno Lucis 2992. . . . (ibid p173)

The traditional dates of events like these in terms of BC and Anno Lucis are carefully given by James Anderson, so the source of this teaching is clear.

The difficulty in expecting modern Freemasons to make any real attempt to tackle clarification of this problem is that the whole complex of traditional history is so ingrained into masonic ceremonial that it cannot be taken out without disfiguring it. It is like the biblical wheat growing with the tares—if you pull out the tares you destroy the wheat. The best that could be done would be to emphasise the traditional and non-historical nature of all such explanations, at least in so far as their connection with Freemasonry is concerned.

INFLUENTIAL FACTORS

Yet a fourth aspect has contributed to the poor standard of masonic history. This is the possibility of influential factors having entered with recruits to the Craft, and having so overpowered the feeble essence of what remained from the operative masons' ceremonial that the history of the influence is seen as the antecedent of modern Freemasonry.

A typical example of this is the claim made for Rosicrucianism. The earliest known speculative initiate in England was the antiquarian and alleged Rosicrucian, Elias Ashmole. The ceremony took place in 1646 in Warrington. We can have no certain knowledge of his motivation for membership, but there have been plenty of masons and outsiders who have speculated that he did so because masonry already contained a Rosicrucian element, or that if not, he intended to provide it with one. The fact remains that our earliest relics of ritual, which date from 1696 onwards, contain no hint of this. The early exposures, such as Samuel Pritchard's *Masonry Dissected* of 1730, are equally bare of any Rosicrucian influence.

Some of the 'higher' degrees, invented during the latter half of the eighteenth century, it is true, have names like 'Rose Croix' and 'Rosy Cross', but their contents as practised in the British Isles have no Rosicrucian element. Even the masonic Societas Rosicruciana in Anglia and its Scottish equivalent—to neither of which I belong—are basically learned societies in which papers are read as a means to progression. The greatest influence is possibly seen in the Scottish Royal Arch, where the rubric for the form of the vault in which the Sacred Law was discovered bears a resemblance to that of Christian Rosenkreuz's tomb, but my own analysis of the ritual reveals that this is entirely superficial. Since it is absent from the Irish and English sources from which Scotland obtained its Royal Arch working, it is probably a case of this resemblance having been added by a Rosicrucian enthusiast at a late date.

Thus, whilst it is possible that Rosicrucianism has some slight influence on the formation of the 'higher' degrees, it is not possible for any reasoned history to suggest that Freemasonry became the secret method by which Rosicrucianism was transmitted. Regrettably, some masons have argued very strongly for Rosicrucianism. Even Frances Yates' *The Rosicrucian Enlightenment* places far too much reliance on John Yarker's unreliable and over-enthusiastic writings. Cosby Jackson, the acknowledged English authority on the Rose Croix degree, has proved in a paper to the Quatuor Coronati Lodge that Rosicrucianism has had no influence on Craft masonry whatsoever. ('Rosicrucianism' passim)

The same principle applies equally to any attempt to elevate any of the possible factors which influenced Freemasonry in the formative years of the ritual to the level of an alternative history. A mason discovers a medieval carving showing a man in a particular posture which, given a certain amount of imagination, is that used by masons as a recognition test today. Immediately an assumed link is forged, and a new history written. I well remember, when on holiday on a large island near Hong Kong, having discovered, at the side of the altar in a temple dedicated to the sea goddess Tin Hau, a statue with the right arm raised in a gesture, remarkably like that used in the Ark Mariner degree. I suggested, tongue in cheek, to a senior mason that here was evidence of the origin of the masonic degree in Chinese fisher folks' religion—and it was only after a few minutes' listening to his enthusiasm that I revealed my cynicism!

CHIVALRIC MASONRY

Perhaps one other major example of the tail wagging the dog should be specifically mentioned: the Crusades. It would seem that the aristocratic and aspiring middle class members of the fraternity in the 1730s were beginning to search for a nobler origin than the poor operative masons could provide. The Chevalier Ramsay, a Scottish exile in Paris, expressed the view in an 'oration' that the true origin of the Order lay in the Crusaders, with their noble concepts of chivalry and honour. Before long, the French Freemasons had invented degrees by the thousand, some of which were based upon imagined continuations of the Knights Templar in what were to them remote places like the Scottish Highlands. This inheritance is still with present day Freemasons in their 'higher' degrees, even if the vast majority of degrees then invented have died a natural death.

The evidence of the simple ceremonial, which was the sole inheritance of the Craft at the beginning of the eighteenth century, gives the lie to any such theory. Official histories deny any connection. Handfield-Jones opens his *Origin and History* by saying:

> This treatise is concerned solely with the modern Masonic Orders of Knights Templar and Knights of Malta, *neither of which have any direct connection* with the Mediaeval Orders founded at the time of the Crusades.
>
> The former was destroyed by Philippe le Bel, King of France in 1314, and in spite of many ingenious attempts to prove that it survived and eked out a secret existence throughout the ages, no authority accepts it today as having any connection with the modern Order. The latter ceased to exist as a military Order when Napoleon Bonaparte annexed Malta in 1798. (p2, emphasis mine)

A similar official booklet dealing with another chivalric Order says:

> I have been invited to set forth what is known about the early story of the Red Cross of Constantine. I must make it clear that the truth is not known, and all I can do is to assemble in as concise and readable a form as possible what is known and what is conjectured about this delightful Order. Also, let it be recognised that *there is no connection whatever* between the mediaeval military Order and our own masonic one; this is unusually important as the former is still in active existence in Europe under the style of 'The Imperial Constantinian Order of St George', the Grand Master of which was His Imperial Highness the Prince Rhodocanakis. (*History and Origin* p485, emphasis mine)

Later, the booklet clearly distinguishes between 'the traditional story of the Red Cross of Constantine' and the possible date of 1780 of 'the masonic Order' being 'first organised'. (pp7 and 11)

Both of these booklets are officially published by the headquarters of the Orders in London, and it is clear that neither sees any hidden connection with the Orders of the past.

THE AUTHENTIC SCHOOL

The attitudes expressed in the two booklets from which I have just quoted are typical of the attitude of all official publications to masonic history today. But a century ago this was not so, and the morass of myth and legend left as an inheritance by James Anderson's historical part of the *Constitutions* and the accretions of those who believed in the importance of what were at most peripheral influences had made masonic 'history' the butt of Ambrose Bierce's caustic pen.

In his centenary history of 'the Premier Lodge of Masonic Research', the Quatuor Coronati Lodge No 2076 of London, Colin Dyer traces the origins of the modern attitude—the tugs by which masonic historians pulled themselves up by their own bootstraps. He sees a start in the opportunity for critical comment in the development of a masonic press in England from the 1830s onwards, followed in the 1850s by the realisation that the Old Charges perhaps indicated an origin in the medieval operative craft other than in Adam's intuition. Various attempts to hold lectures and to form discussion and literary societies were made, and a Masonic Archaeological Institute had a brief life from 1871. But the first successful answer to the growing need was the consecration of the Quatuor Coronati Lodge in 1886.

The memorandum which accompanied the petition for the new lodge read:

> The Founders comprise Brethren who have written on masonic and other subjects; and it is intended besides the ordinary purposes of Freemasonry to gather together brethren connected by similar tastes, and thus devote the energies of the Lodge to a consideration of papers and other communications calculated to throw light upon the History, Antiquities and peculiar customs of the Craft.
>
> It is believed that by carrying out this purpose the general knowledge of these subjects will be extended, and that the members of the proposed new Lodge will take an intelligent interest in the History and Antiquities as well as the Ritual of the Fraternity. (quoted on p11)

Whilst the influence of what was a totally new idea of the function of a lodge was seen in the formation of similar 'research' lodges around the world, perhaps the greatest direct influence was seen in the rapidly expanding Correspondence Circle of those who were not full members but received the transactions, *Ars Quatuor Coronatorum*, now numbering some fourteen thousand masons.

Another direct influence was the publication, ostensibly by R. F. Gould but actually a co-operative effort of several of the lodge members, of the monumental *History of Freemasonry*, which has been read by thousands of masons. The Revd Herbert Poole's revision reached its third edition in 1951, and was being reprinted frequently into the 1960s. In this, Gould demolished one by one the myths and legends that had previously been put forward as 'history', and placed his support firmly behind a theory of evolution from operative masonic lodges, through a transitional period in the seventeenth century when the gentry were admitted on an honorary basis, to the ethical fellowship of the present day. Whilst the details of this smooth evolution have been challenged in recent years, in principle the theory has stood the test of time.

The work of these scholars was not carried on without opposition. The upholders of the traditional view of a descent from the builders of King Solomon's Temple expounded in masonic ritual, with injections of mystery cults here and there, dubbed those who believed that every fact must be proven as 'the authentic school', intending to imply that it was but one school amongst others. This nickname was happily accepted, and is current today. Equally, it must be recognised that many masons, such as 'Vindex', the clergyman author of a sort of answer to Hannah's *Darkness Visible*, still accept the traditional view of masonry as the inheritor of the ancient mysteries. Such masons are likely to express their views in terms of a special understanding: the views of a mason who 'really' understands the 'true' meaning of his membership, thus providing further ammunition for those who see a deep and insidious influence at work in the Order.

OFFICIAL HISTORY

A brief study of the official attitudes of the Grand Lodges of the British Isles makes it clear on which side of the fence they stand. For example, the current *Year Book* of the Grand Lodge of Scotland has a page and a half of 'Notable Masonic Dates' which shows a complete contrast with the story fabricated by the Revd James Anderson. The first ten items are:

Earliest known use of the word 'Freemason'	1376
The Regius Poem	c.1390
The Cooke MS	c.1425
The Edinburgh Seal of Cause	1475
The oldest surviving Minute of a (now extinct) Scottish Lodge	1598
The First Schaw Statute	1598
The oldest surviving Minute of a (still active) Scottish Lodge	1599
The Second Schaw Statute	1599
The First St Clair Charter	1601
H.M. King James VI of Scotland and James I of England, admitted to Lodge Scoon and Perth (p53)	1601

There is absolutely nothing here of the ancient mysteries or the Rosicrucians.

The same *Year Book* contains a list of 'Masonic Reading', which consists of official publications such as the *Constitutions and Laws*, the Proceedings of Grand Lodge, and the like, and seventeen books published elsewhere. One of obvious relevance to the theme of this chapter is Pick and Knight's *The Pocket History of Freemasonry*. With this official commendation, let us see how chapter one begins:

> An immense amount of ingenuity has been expended on the exploration of possible origins of Freemasonry, a good deal of which is now fairly generally admitted to have been wasted.
>
> Many of the doctrines or tenets inculcated in Freemasonry belong to the vast traditions of humanity of all ages and all parts of the world. Nevertheless, not only

> has no convincing evidence yet been brought forward to prove the lineal descent of our Craft from any ancient organization which is known to have, or even suspected of having, taught any similar system of morality, but also, from what we know of the Craft in the few centuries prior to the formation of the first Grand Lodge in 1717, it is excessively unlikely that there was any such parentage. Indeed, it can be very plausibly argued that a great deal of the symbolism which we find in the Craft today is actually a comparatively modern feature and that some was not introduced until after the beginning of the eighteenth century. (p15)

Ireland offers no similar guidance, but Lepper and Crossle's *History of the Grand Lodge*, published by the Lodge of Research which shares premises with the Grand Lodge, comes pretty close to being official. Admittedly it starts with the legendary Gobhan Saor of Celtic mythology, but without suggesting any historical link, moves rapidly through the builders of the round towers to an inscribed square dated 1507, found when a bridge in Limerick was demolished. The book gives numerous examples of square and compasses emblems on graves and furniture from the seventeenth century, all as a precursor to the second chapter on 'The Genesis of the Grand Lodge of Ireland'. There is nothing whatever to imply a link with the ancient mysteries, the builders of King Solomon's Temple, the Crusades, and the like.

THE ENGLISH VIEW

The only official history published by the Grand Lodge of England since the Union is *Grand Lodge 1717-1967*, written by a series of ten senior brethren. Whilst it is basically a history of the two hundred and fifty years since the first Grand Lodge was founded, naturally the first chapter is about 'Freemasonry before Grand Lodge'. In this, a remarkably succinct passage, Harry Carr summarises the dilemma set by the real and traditional histories of Freemasonry:

> That there is indeed a tenuous connection between the Freemasonry of today and the building of King Solomon's Temple, none would deny, since there are so many documents throughout a period of nearly 600 years in which the line of descent is traced with pride. But for the historian of the Craft, who studies its rise and development through the stages that can be examined and proved, the Temple takes its place simply as the traditional background of the Craft. With the passage of centuries, it gradually acquired an allegorical and spiritual significance, so that it ultimately became an integral part of the Speculative Freemasonry of today.
>
> The need for a proper approach to the study of our history must also justify a brief mention here of several ancient societies, religions, and organizations from which modern Freemasonry is supposed to have descended. Among these, the ancient ceremonies relating to the worship of Dionysus, the Eleusinian and the Mithraic mysteries, the spiritual teachings of the Essenes and the Culdees, and the organization and practices of the Roman Collegia, have all been held by writers, zealous for antiquity, to be the original sources from which Masonry took its rise.
>
> It is, indeed, possible to trace among them certain similarities of ideas, of principle, of practices and organization. Resemblances and parallels are incidental and sometimes inevitable: initiatory rites, for example, have tended to follow

> certain well defined patterns throughout the course of history. But studies on these lines have failed—and must fail because nobody was ever able to adduce the evidence that might bridge the gap between those ancient societies and ours. The vital missing links are not lost, for they never existed. The history of Freemasonry begins, not in the Holy Land, nor in Egypt, Greece and Rome, but here in England. (pp1–2)

This view is reinforced in visual terms by the permanent exhibition open to the public in Freemasons' Hall in London. The first of its five sections deals with:

> The development of Freemasonry, directly or indirectly, from the craft of the medieval stone-mason, the initiation of Elias Ashmole of Warrington in 1646 and the development of Lodges in Chester (c. 1670) and Scarborough (1705). The coming together of four London Lodges on 24 June 1717 to form a Grand Lodge, the first in the world, with Anthony Sayer as its first Grand Master. (*An Exhibition*)

The significant point about this list is that there is no reference whatever to any event preceding operative masonry.

The Church of Greece has condemned the Craft because 'in the rituals they saw unmistakable links with the ancient Greek and Egyptian mysteries' (Lawrence p50). The actual history of Freemasonry proves that there is no such link. The condemnation is, to that extent at least, invalid.

The official view of the three Grand Lodges of the British Isles is consistent—no pyramid builders, no ancient mysteries, no Dionysian Artificers, no Roman Collegia, no Crusaders, no Comacine Masters—it is a total official rejection of all that writers like Dr Oliver, A. E. Waite, J. S. M. Ward, Joseph Fort Newton and so many others from James Anderson to the present day have so strenuously offered a credulous audience.

SCHIZOPHRENIA

This, of course, is not the end of the matter. The new initiate is confronted with definite teaching in masonic ritual that conflicts with all that he subsequently reads in modern masonic histories. Only occasionally does he find a clear statement in the ritual that he is being given a 'traditional history'. It is not surprising that the mason who is as deeply impressed as is intended by the ceremonial is reluctant to forgo his first proud impression of membership of an organisation with an immemorial antiquity. He is unwilling to transfer from a literal view of the ritual to a belief that, in masonry, moral teaching is being expressed using 'traditional history' as a vehicle, something of which he can be equally proud.

However, this position is not dissimilar to that of a Christian learning about the Good Samaritan. Jesus tells a story with a deep moral significance. He casts it in a historical mould: 'A man was on his way from Jerusalem to Jericho when he fell in with robbers' (*Lk* 10:30). Yet no one, I suppose, has ever said, 'I will not believe in the story of the Good Samaritan unless you can tell me his name and let me have his home address so that I can check its historical genuineness.' Such a view would be ridiculous, as the truth of the story is seen in its ethical teaching about loving one's neighbour, not in its historicity.

The Christian position becomes more complex with Jonah, where a story that is difficult to believe is also cast into a historical mould: 'He went down to Joppa where he found a ship bound for Tarshish. He paid his fare and went on board. . . .' (*Jonah* 1:3). It is hard to believe that a man could spend three days in the stomach of 'a great fish'. Yet the moral teaching of the story is independent of belief; it is that reluctance to proclaim the truth must be overcome, and that human judgement must not overcloud our view of God's forgiveness. I am not here concerned to express a belief in the historical truth of the story or otherwise, but merely to state that the inspired message that it offers does not depend upon its historicity.

The dichotomy of deep belief in the truth of the Biblical message and its relationship to modern scientific research can be seen in a book which I read with interest; Young's *Christianity and the Age of the Earth*. In this 'a thoroughly orthodox, evangelical Christian' who is also 'a scientist with outstanding academic credentials' in the field of geology, examines the evidence from radioactive decay—including recent fundamentalist objections to its use—and all the other tools available to him for discovering the age of the earth, and concludes that it is indeed 4.5 to 4.7 billion years old. He then departs from his speciality, and adds to this scientific chronology of the inanimate world a direct biblical view of the creation of life.

Convincing or not, Dr Young attempts to reconcile a schizophrenia which, for many evangelical Christians, remains an infinitely larger problem than masons have in reconciling ethical teaching based on the building of King Solomon's Temple with membership of a society dating back only a few hundred years. Christian Freemasons in particular will find no difficulty in living with this problem.

8
Secrecy

VICE OR VIRTUE?

In a Radio 4 phone-in programme which took place in November 1984, the Grand Secretary of the United Grand Lodge of England was careful to distinguish between secrecy and privacy. This was probably because over the years, the word secrecy has become associated with undesirable secretiveness, whilst privacy is seen as a human right.

This has certainly not always been so. Our Lord taught that secrecy was very desirable, equivalent almost to genuineness of feeling, the opposite of outward show. In the Sermon on the Mount, He gives three examples in quick succession:

> When you do some act of charity, do not let your left hand know what your right is doing; your good deed must be secret, and your Father who sees what is done in secret will reward you openly. (*Mat* 6:3–4)

> When you pray, go into a room by yourself, shut the door, and pray to your Father who is there in the secret place; and your Father who sees what is secret will reward you. (*Mat* 6:6)

> When you fast, anoint your head and wash your face, so that men may not see that you are fasting, but only your Father who is in the secret place; and your Father who sees what is secret will give you your reward. (*Mat* 6:17–18)

In contrast to this, it is quite clear that there are no permanent secrets. Jesus taught, 'There is nothing hidden that will not become public, nothing under cover that will be made known and brought into the open.'

These concepts are by no means foreign to Freemasonry. By and large, masonry scores at least some points on the desirable aspects of secrecy—although it has to be confessed that, like many others, Freemasons are not very enthusiastic about fasting! Belief in an omniscient deity is also promulgated in the Craft. The closing prayer in the second degree reads:

> Brethren, let us remember that *wherever we are, and whatever we do, He is with us, and His all-seeing eye observes us,* and whilst we continue to act in conformity with the principles of the Craft, let us not fail to discharge our duty to Him with fervency and zeal (Hannah p93, emphasis mine).

In a modern context, secrecy has acquired the undesirable attributes of espionage, secret police and wrongful covering up of matters that should be public knowledge. Nevertheless, most people readily accept that there should be punishment for revealing national secrets, that industries have a right to develop new products in secret conditions, and that delicate items like a ballot should be conducted in secret. It is a political issue as to whether this applies to Trade Union strike votes, but even the Unions see virtue in conducting their policy meetings in secret. It is equally obvious that a political decision—for example about land resumption by the government—could have very unsettling financial effects, and must be kept secret in the public interest, until the policy is finalised.

Canon R. Lewis emphasised the legitimacy of secrecy in the Church of England Synod debate:

> And the Church, our pure Church, where no secret exists: would a member of Synod please tell me whose names were on the list sent to the Prime Minister for the appointment of the Bishop of . . . ? Which name was the first name? . . . Those who do not know, they will not tell, and why? Because they have been sworn to secrecy. I will say no more. (Synod Proceedings p249)

Privacy has none of the undesirable overtones of secrecy. It goes without saying that conduct between married couples is totally private. Offence is rightly caused when couples have sexual relations in public, or frustrated men expose their private parts. We expect to be able to do most things in life without being stared at or photographed. We are sympathetic to the Royal Family when hounded by the press, even if we still buy the newspapers which wrongfully reveal their private lives.

It is into this delicate balance that Freemasonry must be fitted.

A SECRET SOCIETY?

It is so frequently said that Freemasonry is a secret society, that it is commonly accepted as true without further thought. The Order certainly has a long tradition of privacy, going back at least to the Regius MS of about 1390. In the rules for conduct, set out in this for new masons to follow, is a requirement that what happens in the lodge must be kept secret from all outsiders, and this was sworn by the new member. Of course, it can be argued that the trade secrets or 'mysteries' which ensured the livelihood of the medieval masons are the equivalent of the industrial secrets of today, and have nothing to do with mutual recognition by members of a convivial club. But let us examine how secret—or indeed, how open— modern Freemasonry really is.

A statement called *Aims and Relationships of the Craft* was issued in August 1938 by the three Grand Lodges of the British Isles. At that time, it was published in one or more of the national newspapers. It is still issued to every new English mason in a booklet called *Information for the Guidance of Members of the Craft*, and can be obtained at Freemasons' Hall in London. The same text—but for the name of the issuing body—is printed as the preface to the *Book of Constitutions* of the Grand Lodge of Ireland and as Appendix I to the *Constitutions and Laws* of Scotland. Thus it is abundantly available to any enquirer.

The United Grand Lodge of England more recently published a pamphlet called *What is Freemasonry?* Whilst it may be suggested that its short text cannot do justice to its subject matter, the wisdom of having an easily digestible official statement is plain when it is considered that many a senior mason comes to realise that he still has much to learn. This pamphlet is intended for universal consumption, by masons and non-masons alike.

Every Grand Lodge publishes its own book of *Constitutions,* sometimes under the exotic name of *Ahiman Rezon*. Indeed, England has published this book since 1723, and we are currently at the thirty-fourth edition since the union of the two English Grand Lodges in 1813. This book lays down how the Grand Lodge is constituted, what the duties of its major officers are, how its charitable funds are to be administered, how new lodges may be founded, how elections are to be conducted, what regalia is to be worn on what occasion, who is responsible for lodge property, and the like. It can be bought over the counter at Freemasons' Hall, and so a knowledge of the structure and organisation of Freemasonry is fully available to anyone who takes the effort to find out.

United Grand Lodge holds quarterly 'communications' and an annual investiture of new Grand Officers. These meetings are minuted, and the minutes are printed and circulated to every Grand Officer and lodge. Of course, the minutes contain a list of the members who were present, and this presents a problem, as Grand Lodge believes that the privacy of a mason's membership ought to be respected. There is little doubt that the minutes could be made available to a genuine enquirer, and they are issued without any restriction preventing the masonic recipient showing it to a non-mason.

The same problem presents itself with the *Masonic Year Book* which is now two volumes totalling 886 pages long and contains a complete list of every English lodge and chapter with their places and dates of meeting, as well as a complete list of all living Grand Officers. It also lists donations given to non-masonic causes (which incidentally includes five thousand pounds to every current English Cathedral restoration fund), recognised Grand Lodges overseas, notable dates, and details of English national charities. Because of its lists of names, this is also not purchasable over a counter, but no doubt would be made available to the genuine enquirer. It is not secret in any way, and my father's copy for the year 1936 stood unopened on a shelf in his study for years until he decided that I could make more use of it than he.

Most if not all the English Provincial and District Grand Lodges also print a year book, which is generally similar to that of Grand Lodge, except that more information is given about each local lodge and its officers, and frequently information is also given about 'higher' degree bodies meeting within the same geographical area. Like Grand Lodges, the Provinces and Districts also hold one or more meetings a year, which are also minuted and the minutes circulated. Whilst the circulation is in the main within the lodges concerned, copies are often sent to neighbouring Provinces and to Grand Lodge for reference purposes. This information could be made available for bona fide purposes, in the same way as for the equivalent documents printed by Grand Lodge.

In the nineteenth century, and until relatively recent times, masonic magazines were widely circulated and available at news-stands and in public libraries in Britain. The masonic press had almost died out by the end of the Second World War. When the new quarterly magazine *Masonic Square* was started in 1975, an attempt was made to sell it in the same way, but it failed due to simple lack of interest. Regrettably, this means that one method of finding out about Freemasonry on a casual basis is not readily available to the outsider. But the publishers are perfectly willing for a subscription to be taken out by a non-mason.

Many Grand Lodges publish magazines which every lodge member receives, and are happily made available to outsiders. They vary from tabloids with grinning photos of Grand Masters laying foundation stones to small versions of the *Reader's Digest*. The English *Masonic Quarterley* is a high quality publication. The problem with all such publications is not secrecy, but their lack of continuing interest to a non-mason.

MEETING PLACES

Masonic Halls are not secretly concealed from public knowledge: often they have their purpose displayed in adequately sized lettering over the front door, and may even be signposted from the nearest crossroads to help masonic visitors find them.

The diligent enquirer could well station himself near the front door at half past five on the average weekday, and past him will walk a series of dark overcoated men carrying leather regalia cases shaped like large wallets or small suitcases. They will do so completely openly, with no attempt at disguise. If the enquirer is in a small town—in which case he may have to know the nights of the less frequent meetings—he will recognise a typical collection of townspeople: a local solicitor, a butcher, a banker, a council officer, a taxi driver, and perhaps the local parson. After waiting for a few hours, he will see them leave and return home. Apart from the fact that he had not been inside the Hall to see what went on, no attempt at concealment would have been evident.

Scottish lodges are permitted under Law 179A(2) of the *Constitution and Laws* to advertise their meetings in the local newspaper, with details of the date, time and place of the meeting, as well as certain major items of business. This is quite a common alternative to the usual convening of meetings by posted summons (notice), and the public can thus be aware of part of what is going on in their local lodges.

Non-masons are encouraged to attend an exhibition of masonic history in Freemasons' Hall (60 Great Queen Street, London) and to go on a tour of the Museum and Grand Temple. I am told that about a thousand persons do so each month, including four hundred non-masons. John Lawrence acknowledges the helpful attitude of Freemasons' Hall:

> I was greatly encouraged by the helpfulness and openness of many of the masons I met. I was even able to use the Grand Lodge library for a time until they became aware that my conclusions were not particularly favourable! I was surprised, too,

> at the relative ease of obtaining information. I have never found anyone to be knowingly misleading. (p9)

Compare this review of the actual situation—openly held meetings, in some cases advertised in the press, 'helpful and open' members, and a plethora of published material—with the image of a secret society. Freemasonry is clearly *not* a secret society.

AT LODGE MEETINGS

The fact remains, however, that non-masons cannot attend lodge meetings. Each lodge has an officer, the Tyler, whose duty it is to stand outside the door and persuade non-masons to go away, or to warn the lodge if he cannot do so. The symbol of his office is an unsheathed sword, but it is only a symbol and it is inconceivable that he would use this to keep outsiders at bay. Indeed, the Tyler is generally known to masons as a kindly old man who helped them to prepare for initiation and gave valuable tips as they waited to be readmitted to the lodge.

The Tyler is often a retired person who augments his pension with the fees that he is paid to tyle for a number of lodges. He is almost invariably a past Master, and as such throughout the British Isles would have made a promise prior to being permitted in the chair:

> You agree to pay a proper respect to the Civil Magistrate, to work diligently, live creditably, and act honourably by all Men. ('Summary of the Antient Charges' clause 4)

Respect for the law is therefore particularly incumbent upon him, in addition to the general exhortation to all new masons to pay 'due obedience to the laws of any State which may for a time become the place of your residence or afford you of its protection' (Hannah p108). It is therefore abundantly clear that the Tyler would immediately admit to a lodge a duly warranted officer of the law without demur. The picture painted in one anti-masonic book which suggests that a policeman seeking entry to a lodge would be run through by a rapier can at best be described as wilfully misleading. The Tyler's duty is to ensure that reasonable privacy, which is the right of every human being in a civilised society, is protected. The sword which he bears is a symbol of this duty.

Much that goes on in a lodge meeting could be done in public. The agenda of a typical meeting contains items like reading the minutes, reading correspondence, taking a collection for charity, and it could, for example, include discussion of the organisation of a Ladies' Night or a lodge outing. Other matters which should be regarded as confidential might also be dealt with, such as the result of a ballot for membership, or even more so a discussion and vote on an accusation of non-masonic behaviour (fortunately very few and far between).

However, there is a very good reason why lodge meetings should not be open to the public. A major item on the agenda of most meetings is the ceremonial admission or advancement of a new mason or the installation of a new Master in the chair. These ceremonies have grown up over a long period of time, and have been 'designed' so that the greatest impression and retention of teaching is achieved when the candidate goes through it in ignorance of its contents. Those masons who have acted as guinea pig candidates in lodges of instruction (where the ceremonies are rehearsed) will testify that the second time is not to be compared with the first. Even though sitting on the sidelines to witness what he himself had been through the month previously is very educational for the new candidate, it is not the same thing. So Freemasons are insistent that their privacy should be preserved for the benefit of those who will in the future become fellow members.

There are exceptions to the rule of not admitting non-masons for meetings. In American Grand Lodges and lodges, and in those of countries influenced by American style Freemasonry, the installations of the Grand Master and Master are frequently 'open' ceremonies, and are well attended by wives, families and friends of the members. I have attended the open installation of a Grand Master at which the guest of honour was his boss, a non-mason. I have also read the records of significant speeches made by non-masons at such events, those by members of the Roman Catholic hierarchy being of especial interest.

Another exception—although technically not so—was the invitation extended to a well-known historian, who was not a mason but had specialised in the organisation of medieval operative masonry, to present a paper to the premier lodge of masonic research, the Quatuor Coronati Lodge No 2076. The lodge was opened formally, and then adjourned to admit the speaker, who presented his paper. This was discussed and a vote of thanks was given. He was escorted from the room so that the lodge could be formally closed, and he joined the members for dinner at which no masonic toasts were given. Whilst this may seem complex, how much pleasanter it must have been than to have the paper read on his behalf.

PUBLICATION

Rule 177 of the *Constitutions* of United Grand Lodge gives three cases where privacy from publication is required. The first paragraph is a coverall:

> No Brother shall publish or cause to be published anything which according to the established principles of Masonry ought not to be published.

This clause has an obvious effect on the printing of rituals (normally allowed or tolerated) and full exposures of the ritual (not allowed), and we shall examine this dividing line soon. The third clause is a sensible precaution against the lobbying of a tribunal: it prohibits the publication or circulation of any relevant papers except through the chairman or secretary of the tribunal.

The second paragraph concerns the privacy of ordinary lodge meetings:

> No Brother without the consent of the Grand Master or the Provincial or District Grand Master as the case may be, shall publish or cause to be published the proceedings of any Lodge.

The minutes of a normal lodge meeting are written up by the Secretary between meetings, and read out at the next meeting for confirmation. No attempt is made to circulate them for comment in advance, and thus only one original of each minute exists. Of course, the prohibition is not absolute, as the relevant authority to publish can be obtained. Many lodges have published histories to coincide with a bicentenary, centenary or jubilee, and the minute book is always *the* prime source, often with the minutes of important meetings quoted at some length. Permission will also normally be given to present copies of the lodge history to local public libraries.

There is nothing in this Rule which prevents the Secretary of a lodge delivering the minutes to a court in response to a *subpoena duces tecum*. The Secretary is usually a Past Master, and is subject to the same overriding promises to obey the Civil Magistrate as the Tyler, which I have quoted above. Even if he is not a Past Master, he is subject to the Master for masonic purposes, and would soon be ordered to behave as any normal citizen should in the same circumstances.

Clearly, this is a case of desirable privacy, not secrecy.

MEMBERSHIP LISTS

A dispute about the right of Freemasons to keep their membership private if they so wish was raised with vehemence as a result of Knight's *The Brotherhood*. This has nothing to do with whether a mason is free to reveal his membership: he is, but it is a personal matter, and whilst he should not say that it is not when he is, he still has the liberty to say 'Mind your own business!'.

The issue was put clearly in *Tuesday Call*, the BBC Radio 4 phone in programme, when Stephen Knight and the Grand Secretary, Michael Higham, answered questions put by listeners under the chairmanship of Sue McGregor. Knight, who proved to be much less of a dragon over the air than in writing, said:

> As far as I am concerned masons as much as anybody else have a right to their own privacy and their own private meetings, and I'm not at all concerned about what goes on behind their locked doors. What I am concerned about is who is, it's finding out who, or the opportunity to find out, who is a member and who isn't. . . . Unless you can find out who is a mason, unless there is a published register, and I think that the contents of my book give strong evidence that there must be a public register, if there isn't that then it remains a secret society.

Later in the programme, Higham gave two reasons why he thought that there should be no public register:

> The first one is that Freemasons' lodges are like clubs. Nobody . . . is trying to say that every club should publish a list of its members merely on the basis that because, if they meet in a bar of the club, they're going to transact business and to rig things.
>
> The second [is that] if a Freemason joins the craft on the basis that he's not allowed to advertise himself and he's told not to exhibit his Grand Lodge

> certificate . . ., it could be said that if you publish lists of masons that the publication assists people to advance themselves through their membership of the craft and we're against it for that reason as well.
>
> I don't think it's going to help; I think you've got to trust people in the councils or the judiciary or in the police to do the job they're principally there for, and realise that Freemasons have to think about their priorities. They know that their duty to the law, to their profession, to their council, to their employer prevails over any obligation to masons, and they're reminded of it again and again.

The Grand Secretary did not mention a very practical third reason for not publishing a full list of members of the craft: the logistics of doing so. The *Masonic Year Book* has a 115-page list of living Grand Officers, with their offices, at about fifty a page. If the 350,000 members of every private lodge in England were published with similar details, the list would be ten thousand pages long. Even if it were published in the format and typesize of a telephone directory, it would be a thousand pages long. Even those of Ireland and Scotland would be fat volumes.

Every English lodge sends two returns to Grand Lodge each year, and one of these contains a list of the subscribing members, with further details for those shown for the first time or removed from the list. Thus, on a lodge by lodge basis, Grand Lodge already has all the information needed for a full list. But it is not in a form that enables the question 'Was John Smith a mason?' to be answered; all that can be answered is 'Was John Smith a member of Corinthian Lodge No 1806?' or 'What was John Smith's job, age and home address when he was initiated in Lodge No 1806?' But the records have been slowly computerised, and it is now possible to say exactly how many Freemasons there are in England with no overlaps caused by dual membership–some 350,000. But the information on the forms submitted by lodge secretaries remains substantially the same, and it will never be possible to give the current address and profession of a mason, only those at the time of his application.

The situation regarding annual returns in Ireland is similar to England. In Scotland, it would be even harder to produce a full list, as the annual return for each daughter lodge merely states the number of subscribing members. However, new members are alphabetically indexed, so that 'Has there ever been a Scottish mason called John Smith?' could be answered, but without information as to his current status.

My reference to 'all the John Smiths' brings out another reason for not publishing a list of names: it could easily lead to mistaken identity. The Stalker business of the 1980s is a case in point. A policeman from Manchester was sent to do an investigation in Northern Ireland, and just when he seemed on the verge of getting results, he was withdrawn from the investigation. He was not a Freemason. But a prominent mason in Manchester happened to have the same name as the policeman who had been Stalker's senior, instrumental in making the decision to withdraw him from Ireland. It was strongly implied in the media that a masonic plot had been hatched in collaboration with the masons in Northern Ireland, who did not like the possible results of the investigation. This poor man was literally hounded to death by the media, and his weak heart gave way under the resulting strain. This was the subject of its own investigation, and Freemasonry was specifically exonerated from any blame.

The irresponsibility of the media in England in relation to Freemasonry is indicated by the fact that only one national newspaper— out of the many which had suggested a masonic plot—mentioned that the final report gave the Craft a clean bill of health. It has been suggested by masons that this is a further reason why masonic membership lists should not be publicly available.

However, I am not fully convinced by these arguments against publication of a full list.

It can be argued that the *Masonic Year Book*'s list of Grand Officers is an internal and private matter, just like the lists of members prepared by many lodges for their own use. But it could equally be suggested that, if the full list might be misused for self advancement, why should Grand Officers alone have this privilege? In Scotland, the *Year Book* has a different, more interesting format, but it gives even a brief biography (but with no mention of the business) of each active Grand Office-Bearer.

In the case of the Grand Lodge of Ireland, the *Calendar* also lists all the members of certain 'higher' degrees, and the equivalent bodies in England and Wales have year books with full lists. Why is this acceptable for the 'higher' degrees and not for the Craft?

The Stalker affair merely indicates that if a no-list rule is to be followed, it should be followed scrupulously, so that no lists whatsoever should be circulated. But this would not guarantee any greater privacy, as the media would be even more determined to get the information they sought.

If trust by the public of masons who are councillors, judges and policemen is urged, why should the possibility of the publication of a full list of members being used for personal advancement prevent it? Surely masons can be trusted here too. And the bad mason who seeks personal advancement through his membership will somehow do so anyway.

The main argument against publication would appear to be the logistics of the mammoth task which would be involved. Even more overwhelming may be the legislation regarding improper use of information about individuals collected by computer, possibly making such a publication illegal.

DECLARATION OF MEMBERSHIP

In his address to Grand Lodge on 29 April 1987, the Duke of Kent referred briefly to the inquiry into the affairs of the London Borough of Hackney. The inquiry was originally into the effects of Freemasonry on the Council's operations, but it soon became apparent that Freemasonry was not to blame:

> Although the inquiry found no masonic conspiracy, no 'masonic influence' exercised by Councillors and no improper masonic connections between Council officers and contractors, even among the officers whose conduct was least praiseworthy, the Council may nevertheless adopt recommendations including compulsory declaration of membership in the Craft by Councillors, officers and

> contractors, and disqualification of Freemasons as members of committees or as officers of the Council. This would be on the grounds that there were Freemasons among the Council's officers, that many of the firms bound to the Council by contract had 'masonic connections', and that Freemasonry had not acted as a positive influence to improve standards of performance at Hackney.
>
> In other words, despite no evidence whatsoever of any impropriety of a masonic nature, the Council propose to act on unsubstantiated prejudice. Freemasons would thus be made scapegoats, unprotected by the law which provides redress for other classes of disadvantaged citizens. There is a clear division in the report of this inquiry between fact—the finding that Freemasonry is not to blame—and prejudice, the belief that 'Freemasons are a bad thing'. Too many people's minds it seems were made up before the inquiry began and it will take a long time to persuade people that the prejudice is unfounded.

The topic of declaration was covered in the Radio 4 phone-in programme with Stephen Knight confronting the Grand Secretary of England, in which the latter said:

> If standing orders lawfully require that somebody should declare membership, then any Freemason under the Grand Lodge of England would comply with standing orders. I believe that there is doubt about the legality of such standing orders. There is a law which says that a councillor must declare his financial interest. I don't think there's a law yet which says he must declare his personal ones. There is however a rule of practice which means that a councillor declares his personal interests if they're relevant.

The lady Freemason and Councillor, Joan Fiddie, commented with vehemence:

> I do feel that it's an infringement on civil liberties. If Freemasons have to provide details—and the specific thing is 'and other similar organisations'— should not the register take in the Ancient Order of Foresters, Inner Wheel, trade unions, Rotary, Toc H, *ad lib*? Why just Masonry? . . . Then that would clear the whole council chamber because everybody in some way or other belongs to an organisation. (*Tuesday Call*)

There is a big difference between making a disclosure as a matter of professional trust, and picking on one club—Freemasonry—and making it a unique matter for required disclosure. My own former office had for almost twenty years had a policy of stating on a confidential form, issued solely for the benefit of our clients in tender reports, such things as, 'The proprietor of this firm is the father of the secretary of one of our partners'.

Included in this has been, 'One of the directors of this firm belongs to the same masonic lodge as one of our partners'. I have also felt it desirable to make such a declaration before accepting appointment as an arbitrator. But there is a great deal of difference between saying this as a matter of mutual trust, and being forced to make a declaration by law. I find myself to be in total agreement with my lady 'brother'.

RITUALS

I have already said that the dividing line between the legitimate printing of masonic ritual and improper publishing of exposures is hard to draw.

Several Grand Lodges, including Ireland and California for example, say that no ritual can be printed. They adopt special measures for preserving and promulgating the official working. In Ireland, there is a Grand Lodge of Instruction, in which relatively young masons demonstrate the ceremonial under the watchful eye of very experienced masons, for the benefit of onlookers in various parts of Ireland. In California, one Grand Officer with many assistants all have the task of visiting lodges at work, to correct any imperfections in the working. In both cases, printing of the ritual is improper. Nevertheless, masonic suppliers in California—I do not know about Ireland—do a good trade in exposures of ritual to young masons.

In many American States, such as Massachusetts, an official ritual is printed in 'cypher' and sometimes restricted to the initial letter of every word, and sometimes even with symbols in place of words. There are separate books called 'monitors' in which those lectures which it is felt can be published in full are set out.

In England and Scotland, the situation is totally different. There is no uniform official ritual, though there was one in theory following the union of the two English Grand Lodges. Promulgated in 1816, it was but indifferently enforced. At that time it was felt that no ritual might be printed, but gradually masonic suppliers have printed slim, pocket sized books. Today, only a few old lodges relatively remote from London use individual versions, in some cases still unaffected by what happened in 1816, and which are passed on by 'mouth to ear'. The English and Scottish printed rituals have the vast majority of the text printed in full, with frequent abbreviations of offices, items of equipment and the like, and blanks where a recognition sign is to be demonstrated. The amount of rubric, describing the actions to go with the words, has continued to increase since the Second World War, and the current edition of the *Emulation Ritual* has detailed descriptions of almost every ceremonial movement.

EXPOSURES

Exposures of masonic ritual are considerably older than the mason's own printed rituals. Perhaps the most famous of all time was Samuel Pritchard's *Masonry Dissected* of 1730. This was significant for at least two reasons: it probably caused the Grand Lodge of England to reverse the recognition signs for the first two degrees so as to avoid non-masonic readers claiming masonic charity, and it contained some of the earliest details of the third degree ceremony. Thus, although it was a cause of great concern to the Freemasonry of the time, it has proved to be an invaluable historical document.

The publication of exposures has been a profitable exercise over the centuries. Whilst a part of the motivation has been profit, it has also been a desire to warn outsiders of the evils which the writer saw in masonry, and, particularly, in eighteenth century France, the satisfaction of feminine inquisitiveness. Particularly in the nineteenth century, little attempt was made to be accurate, and the work of Leo Taxil in France, in which he pictured goat-legged demons being conjured up in rites of black magic, remains an extreme example of an 'exposure' which bore no relation to reality at all. Nevertheless, it was believed to be true by credulous Roman Catholics at the time, even within the hierarchy, and his influence is still felt amongst the less educated today. Later in life, Taxil embarrassed his former supporters by announcing publicly that his work had been a complete fabrication.

Perhaps the most significant modern English exposure of masonic ritual was Walton Hannah's *Darkness Visible*. The title sounds ominous, but it is merely a brief quotation from a masonic ceremony which points out the incompleteness of human knowledge without divine inspiration. His book combines a fairly accurate text of a typical English working with his own strong anti-masonic views, written initially as an Anglican priest. When he failed to get the Church of England to vote against Freemasonry, he realigned to Roman Catholicism, but specifically stated that he stood by all that he had written against the Craft as an Anglican.

There are errors in his text, but they are sufficiently insignificant for me to be able to quote it in this book as the basis for my own arguments that Christianity and Freemasonry are fully compatible. Thus the exposures gave me the advantage of being able to talk sensibly about masonic ritual without actually doing more than quote someone else's book. I must stress to the reader that whenever alleged masonic secrets are mentioned, I am quoting an exposure by Hannah or James Dewar, from books which are available to the general public. I am not quoting the actual ritual used in the masonic bodies to which I belonged. This may seem a pedantic point, but I have no wish to break the promises which I made to my brethren. Where occasionally I have quoted from a printed ritual, official or otherwise, I have used passages innocent of any sensitive matter.

THE SECRETS

In considering the dividing line between legitimate printing of books of ritual and improper exposures, it was evident that the difference lay essentially in those parts of the former where there are abbreviations and blanks. Despite all that I have said about the openness of present day Freemasonry and its simple desire for privacy, there remain certain 'secrets' which all masons have promised not to reveal.

Nowadays, club membership can be proved by an instant photograph combining the member's face with his number and date of membership, card validity and the like. When it comes to the 'clubs' that issue credit cards, the photograph is replaced by a hard plastic card with a complex series of numbers impressed in it, although its validity for use depends heavily upon the signature on its rear. Now we have 'chip and pin'. Any organisation—like a trade union—that believes that membership confers privileges upon its members is jealous to limit the claim of those privileges to its members alone. Indeed, I believe that several Trade Unions have obligations and passwords, for exactly the same reasons as Freemasons.

Freemasonry started long before there were instant cameras and hard plastic cards, and indeed even before writing was universal. The purpose of masonic recognition signs is explained to the candidate:

> It is my duty to inform you that Freemasonry is free, and requires a perfect freedom of inclination in every candidate for its mysteries [in the sense of trade secrets; nothing to do with the mystery religions]. It is founded on the purest principles of piety and virtue; it possesses great and valuable privileges; and in order to secure those privileges to worthy men, and we trust to worthy men alone, vows of fidelity are required; but let me assure you that in those vows there is nothing incompatible with your civil, moral or religious duties; are you therefore willing to take a Solemn Obligation, founded on the principles I have stated, to keep inviolate the secrets and mysteries of the Order? (Hannah p98)

The candidate is expected to answer this question freely, without any suggestion or prompt. Later he repeats:

> . . . of my own free will and accord . . . [I] sincerely and solemnly promise and swear that I will always hele [meaning cover], conceal and never reveal any part or parts, point or points, of the secrets and mysteries of or belonging to Free and Accepted Masons. . . . (ibid p99)

He is then told:

> Having taken the Great and Solemn Obligation of a Mason, I am now permitted to inform you that there are several degrees in Freemasonry [this is well known to non-masons too], and peculiar secrets restricted to each; these, however, are not to be communicated indiscriminately, but are conferred on candidates according to merit and abilities. I shall, therefore, proceed to entrust you with the secrets of this degree, or those marks by which we are known to each other and distinguished from the rest of the world. . . . (ibid p101)

The secrets of masonry are therefore the old fashioned equivalent of a membership card.

The fact that exposures exist does not invalidate the mason's personal promise to keep these matters secret. Of course outsiders can find out what the secrets are by reading a book, but the normal mason is determined that they are not going to find out through him. It is a matter of personal honour.

It was the proud boast of Hannah that he had gained entry to a lodge meeting, using a combination of the knowledge gained in writing *Darkness Visible* with the naive faith of the average mason that a man in a dog collar would not tell a lie about his membership. Since that happened, lodges have been more strict, and generally every visitor is now required to produce a Certificate (called 'Diploma' in Scotland) proving his initiation in a lodge of a regular Grand Lodge and an indication that he is not in debt to his own lodge, in addition to the recognition signs. (Certificates were introduced many years ago, but checking had become lax.) Even with the signs exposed by Hannah and his ilk, knowledge of the differences between the workings in the British Isles, Europe and America means that the experienced Tyler or past Master can detect an inappropriate sign.

In fact, most of the 'secret' words of masons are well known to any Bible reader. For example,

ABADDON is in *Rev* 9:11;
MAHER SHALAL HASH BAZ is in *Isaiah* 8:1 and 3; and
SHIBBOLETH is in *Judges* 12:6.

Others are the Hebrew words rendered in English in our Bibles, such as:

BERITH (covenant), in *Genesis* 6:18, etc;
GIBLITE (stone squarer), in 1 *Kings* 5:18; and
SHADDAI (Almighty God), in *Exodus* 6:3, etc.

There is nothing secret about the words themselves, merely about the exact context in which they are used—to establish membership credentials.

The detractors of Freemasonry often paint a picture of a mason standing at the bar of a pub, frantically making signs or standing in odd postures so as to attract other masons like a bee to a flower. A moment's thought will reveal that nothing so unlikely is possible—frequent public use of a recognition signal would quickly render it a matter of universal knowledge. Masonic signs—especially a form of salute and a password— are used simply to establish the bona fides of an unknown visitor before admitting him to a meeting. It is clear that a handshake in a particular manner might be given when non-masons are present, but I recall a mason in Oregon thinking that I was also in the Order before my initiation, because I had apparently given the correct grip by accident! And the long discussion that I had with a Belgian and an American about what the correct handshake would be if no other communication is possible indicates that it is virtually meaningless in an open context when further questions cannot be asked.

It may be asked why it is that masons do not opt for the more efficient mechanism of an instant photograph sealed in a plastic membership card. It is simply a matter of tradition. Masons have been using their own recognition method for so long that it is thoroughly engrained in their ceremonial: it could not be omitted without changing the nature of the Craft.

Masonic secrets—which are simply recognition signs—are trivial in comparison with State secrets, industrial secrets, or even the shared secret hopes of a husband and wife. But to masons they are significant as the guard to their privileges. Small things must not be despised:

> 'Well done, my good and trusty servant!' said the master. 'You have proved trustworthy in a small way; I will now put you in charge of something big. Come and share your master's delight'. (*Mat* 25:21)

9
Obligation

RELATED IDEAS

There are a number of concepts that are closely related, which involve a person in committing himself to do something. I would like to suggest that there is a hierarchy in these concepts:

expressing an intention
giving a promise
giving an undertaking
making an engagement
entering a contract
taking an obligation
making a vow
swearing an oath

In masonic ritual, this view is expressed in part in the words that follow the 'obligation'. The Master says to the candidate:

> What you have repeated may be considered but a serious promise; as a pledge of your fidelity, and to render it a Solemn Obligation, you will seal it with your lips on the Volume of the Sacred Law. (Dewar p137)

A 'pledge of fidelity' and a 'Solemn Obligation' are considered to be superior in significance to a 'serious promise'.

THE SECOND COMMANDMENT

The basic religious law about swearing an oath, affecting Christians as much as Jews, is the second commandment. This occurs in several forms, but the best known is that of *Exodus* 20:7:

> You shall not make wrong use of the name of the LORD your God: the LORD will not leave unpunished the man who misuses his name.

It contains no reference to swearing at all! However, if a person uses the name of God in an oath, it becomes relevant immediately. Perhaps a more relevant version of this prohibition is *Leviticus* 19:12:

> You shall not swear in my name with intent to deceive, and thus profane the name of your God. I am the LORD.

The thirty-ninth and last Article of the Church of England reads:

> As we confess that vain and rash Swearing is forbidden Christian men by our Lord Jesus Christ, and James his Apostle, so we judge, that Christian Religion doth not prohibit, but that a man may swear when the Magistrate requireth, in a cause of faith and charity, so it be done . . . in justice, judgement, and truth.

The form of the oath administered by a magistrate starts, 'I (name) swear by Almighty God that the evidence that I shall give . . .'.

This oath remains a problem for the consciences of many Christians, and the Quakers' well-known refusal to take it represents only the tip of an iceberg of Christians who would really prefer to affirm but do not wish to make a fuss in a court of law. Having lived the greater part of my life in a country where an English form of law is administered but the majority of the population is non-Christian, it seems farcical to me to allow the majority merely to affirm that they will tell the truth, but to insist that Christians 'swear by Almighty God'.

The Book of Common Prayer nevertheless contains some serious promises—even obligations—such as:

> I N. take thee N. to my wedded wife, to have and to hold from this day forward . . . and thereto I give thee my troth. ['Troth' means 'solemn promise', *OED*]

> Will you diligently read the [Canonical Scriptures] unto the people assembled in the church where you shall be appointed to serve? *Answer*. I will.

> Dost thou in the name of this child promise obedience to God's holy will and commandments? *Answer*. I do.

It should be noted that, unlike the oath sworn in a Court, none of these promises is made in the name of God.

THE SERMON ON THE MOUNT

Jesus Christ gave us some quite definite teaching about oaths in the Sermon on the Mount. *Matthew* 5:33–37 reads:

> Again, you have learned that our forefathers were told, 'Do not break your oath', and, 'Oaths sworn to the Lord must be kept'. But what I tell you is this: you are not to swear at all not by heaven, for it is God's throne, nor by earth, for it is his footstool, nor by Jerusalem, for it is the city of the great King, nor by your own head, because you cannot turn one hair of it white or black. Plain 'Yes' or 'No' is all you need to say; anything beyond that comes from the devil.

I think that we must examine this for the source of the objection and the practicalities of saying 'Yes' and 'No'.

The objection is not only to swearing in the name of God, but to swearing by anything that cannot be changed as a result of a broken oath. Taken to its logical extreme, Jesus says that we should not 'swear' at all, that is, *by* anything. Nevertheless, it would seem that when a promise is not *by* something, it is not an oath in the sense objected to by Jesus.

The preference for 'Yes' or 'No' would seem to imply at first sight that the shortest possible form of promise is required. This is of course not so—it is only possible for me to say a brief 'Yes' or 'No' to a clearly defined proposition, and for a complex matter there must be a complex set of conditions. It matters little whether the conditions are in the proposition, or in the promise itself as an extension of the 'Yes'. Anyone who has signed a contract knows that someone has to define clearly what the 'Yes' is being said about, whether the contract was prepared by either party or even an outsider. In the case of a building contract, the architect or surveyor prepares a document several hundred pages long, and two parties say 'Yes' by signing it in front of a witness. It makes no practical difference whether the text is long or short, written or oral, the 'Yes' is simply the culmination of a clearly defined obligation to do something.

Even so, the New Testament contains two passages in which St Paul comes pretty close to a sworn oath:

> *I appeal to God* to witness what I am going to say; I stake my life upon it . . . (2 *Cor* 1:23)

> What I write is plain truth; *before God* I am not lying. (*Gal* 1:20)

The writer of the *Letter to the Hebrews* sees a fully fledged oath as perfectly normal. He writes in 6:16:

> Men swear by a greater than themselves, and the oath provides a confirmation to end all dispute.

He sees a man's oath as a symbol of the greater promises of God. And of course, the Old Testament contains many examples of sworn oaths, for example in 1 *Kings* 8:31–32.

THE MASONIC OBLIGATION

Is a masonic obligation *sworn* in this way? If it is, even if it is in the category of a magistrate's oath, it is very doubtful that a Christian should take it. If not, there is no reason why it should not be made, except of course if the matter being promised were objectionable.

This is how it runs:

> I, John Smith, in the presence of the Great Architect of the Universe, and of this worthy, worshipful and warranted Lodge of Free and Accepted Masons, regularly assembled and properly dedicated, of my own free will and accord, do hereby and hereon sincerely and solemnly promise and swear, that I will always. . . . (Dewar pp134–35)

The first part is purely factual—God is the 'Great Architect of the Universe', and a Christian is in His presence wherever he goes. The candidate is in the presence of the members of the Lodge. He may not know exactly what 'regularly assembled and properly dedicated' means, but since these phrases refer to the lodge and the Master is speaking first, they seem to be matters on which the benefit of the doubt can be given! He has already stated that he is there 'freely and voluntarily'. There is certainly no swearing *by* God, so that it is not the type of oath condemned by the Sermon on the Mount.

The only possible nagging doubt lies in 'hereby and hereon', and this is accompanied by a rubric that the Master touches the candidate's hand at 'hereby' and the Bible at 'hereon'. The rubrics are of course the fruit of lodges of instruction, and certainly were not part of the approved English working of 1816. But if 'hereon' clearly means 'on the Bible', 'hereby' could not with any degree of common sense mean 'by my hand', but it could mean 'by these words', a simple statement of fact. The most logical interpretation is that 'hereby and hereon' should be taken together and seen in the context of the whole obligation, meaning 'I promise by means of these words and with my hand on the Bible.'

The history of masons being obligated touching 'the Book' is an ancient one—at least as old as the Thirty-Nine Articles—and should not be lightly jettisoned. For example, the *Grand Lodge* MS dated 25 December 1583 reads:

> Tunc unus ex senioribus tenent librum, et ille vel illi opponunt manut sub libri, et tune precepta deberent legi & . . . especially ye that are to be chardged take good heede that ye keepe these Chardges right for yt is great perill, a man to forsware himselfe upon a booke. (quoted by Dyer, 'Some Thoughts' p150)

It has proved to be so important for masons to make a promise in this way that non-Christians are also expected to take their obligations on 'the revelation from above which is binding on the conscience of the particular individual who is being initiated' (*Basic Principles* 3). Affirmation is permitted for Quakers by most Grand Lodges, usually with a dispensation from the appropriate officer. However, it would seem that a Quaker might well take the masonic obligation as it is, as it does not contain the feature of a court oath to which Quakers object.

There is nothing inherently unChristian about the form of the masonic obligation. It is at the mid point of an acceptable hierarchy:

promise—obligation—oath

THE CONTENT

The only remaining aspects of the content of the obligations that need concern us are the morality and legality of what is promised. Morality includes a consideration of the accusation made by outsiders that masons promise to help each other in all circumstances. Legality involves a consideration of the suggestion that masons are encouraged to break the law to do so. We will examine these points only in relation to the three Craft degrees, simply for the sake of minimising the space and time involved.

The first degree promise is simply to keep the 'secrete':

> . . . that I will always hele [cover], conceal, and never reveal any part or parts, point or points of the secrets or mysteries of or belonging to Free and Accepted Masons . . . unless it be to a true and lawful Brother. . . . I will not write those secrets, indite, carve, mark, engrave or otherwise them delineate . . . so that our secret arts . . . may improperly become known through my own unworthiness. (Dewar p135)

What is to be kept secret and whether privacy in general is a virtue are covered in a previous chapter.

The second degree simply extends this privacy to members of the first, and adds:

> I further solemnly pledge myself to act as a true and faithful Craftsman [explained in a later 'charge' as to study 'the hidden mysteries of nature and science' from an established moral base], answer signs [by giving the correct sign in return], obey summonses [to attend lodge meetings], and maintain the principles inculcated in the former Degree. (ibid p152)

In the third a number of other clauses are added:

> . . . to adhere to the principles of the Square and Compasses . . . and plead no excuse [for missing meetings] except sickness or the pressing emergencies of my own public or private avocations.
>
> . . . to maintain and uphold the Five Points of Fellowship . . . that my hand given to a Master Mason shall be a sure pledge of brotherhood . . . that the posture of my daily supplications shall remind me of his wants and dispose my heart to succour his weakness and relieve his necessities, so far as may fairly be done without detriment to myself or connections; that my breast shall be the sacred depository of his secrets when entrusted to my care; murder, treason, felony, and all other offences contrary to the laws of God and the ordinances of the realm being at all times most especially excepted.
>
> And finally, that I will maintain a Master Mason's honour and carefully preserve it as my own; I will not injure him myself . . . but . . . will boldly repel the slanderer of his good name, and most strictly respect the chastity of those nearest and dearest to him, in the person of his wife, his sister and his child. (ibid p164)

It is worth noting that there are many inbuilt restrictions to this apparent dedication to the welfare of other masons. The mason in a state of need is only to be relieved to the extent that it does not injure the donor or his connections (family, friends, business associates, and so on). His guarding of another mason's secrets is only to be done when they do not break the law of God or of the land. His obligation to maintain the honour of a fellow mason applies only to the extent that the other mason is slandered, and truthful yet dishonouring comments about a brother need not be resisted.

Nevertheless, the standards of behaviour set for a Master Mason in this obligation are standards which could beneficially govern all human relationships. They may be inadequate in a Christian sense, because they do not go far enough in terms of charity to all men (except perhaps that every male non-mason is a potential mason, and his wife a mason's wife), but this is no reason why a Christian mason cannot take the obligation and from it extend its principles to all men, with fewer if any reservations. As if its inadequacy was felt by some masons, there is an optional 'charge' which is sometimes given after closing a Royal Arch Chapter which says:

> . . . you are expected to extend those noble and generous sentiments still further. Let me impress on your minds, and may it be instilled in your hearts, that every human creature has a just claim to your kind offices. We therefore strictly enjoin you to be good to all. . . . (*Aldersgate* p133)

The masonic obligation—in its generosity within limits—bears a remarkable resemblance to the words of St Paul, "As the opportunity offers, let us work for the good of all, especially members of the household of the faith.' (*Gal* 6:10)

THE PENALTIES

To most Christian non-masons the most distressing aspect of the masonic obligations has been the penalties contained in their tails. I was initiated when no compromise had been effected, and my first degree promise contained the words, as exposed by James Dewar:

> . . . under no less a penalty . . . than that of having my throat cut across, my tongue torn out by the root, and buried in the sand of the sea . . ., or the more effective punishment of being branded as a wilfully perjured individual, void of all moral worth, and totally unfit to be received by this worshipful Lodge . . ., or society of men who prize honour and virtue above the external advantages of rank and fortune. (Dewar p136)

There were similarly gruesome penalties in subsequent obligations, without repeating the 'more effective punishment'. It would seem that these penalties did not exist in a pre-Grand Lodge masonry, and were added during the eighteenth century (Carr 'Obligation' pp130–33). They were probably taken from naval and diplomatic court procedures.

This did not seem particularly offensive at the time of my initiation, and I was more concerned with the interpretation given in the catechism which followed:

> *Senior Warden:* What is that?
> *Candidate:* The sign of an Entered Apprentice Freemason.
> *Senior Warden:* To what does it allude?
> *Candidate:* The penalty of my Obligation, implying that as a man of honour, and a Mason, *I would rather have* my throat cut across than improperly disclose the secrets entrusted to me. (Hannah p103)

Despite what anti-masonic writers have said, I did not promise to cut anyone's throat, even by implication. I expressed an abhorrence of any revelation of masonic secrets by me personally, in terms of preferring to be punished in this way. It was unthinkable that I might ever do so, or be so punished.

The Irish working provides a balance between, 'bearing in mind the *ancient* penalty', and, 'binding myself under the *real* penalty of being deservedly branded as a wretch, base, faithless, and totally unfit to be received amongst men of honour . . .' (unofficial Irish ritual).

Need it be said that no law abiding society could demand that its members inflict the penalties described, and there is no evidence that it has ever occurred. Those who quote the American 'Morgan Affair' should read both sides of that totally unproven story. Even if it were true, one example from history merely proves that men may be misled by their beliefs. The multiplicity of examples of murder and torture committed in the name of Christ means that the Morgan Affair only emphasises the benign nature of masonry.

The punishments inflicted by masons on their members are defined in Rules 179 and 180 of the *Constitutions* as admonition, censure, suspension and exclusion, with the Grand Lodge reserving to itself the right to expel a brother. The *real* penalty remains that of being 'branded' as 'void of all moral worth'.

MODERN CHANGES

Over the past twenty years there has been a permitted alternative, in which any lodge which had so resolved could have its Master say, '. . . ever bearing in mind the *traditional* penalty, that of having the throat cut across. . . .' The purpose of this change was to imply that the penalty never had been inflicted, but that it was traditionally referred to as such. The reference to the penalties could not be erased from the ritual, as it forms the basis for an international recognition system. This change was adopted by less than half the lodges of England, despite the substantial majority by which the resolution was passed in Grand Lodge. As a Christian, I welcomed this change.

It nevertheless remained possible for me to understand those masons, Christians amongst them, who felt that any change was unnecessary, and implied that the old form had in some way been wrong. This view has recently been forcibly expressed by an Episcopal priest, the Revd George A. Burns:

> Masonry, like the Bible, is filled with imagery, symbolism, parables, historical narratives and other literary forms. To interpret any passage literally when it is symbolic would distort the meaning, whether it be in the Bible or in Masonic ritual. Let us take an example from Christ's Sermon on the Mount, from the Gospel according to St Matthew 5:29–30.
>
> 'And if thy right eye offend thee, pluck it out and cast it from thee; for it is profitable for thee that one of thy members should perish, and not that thy whole body should be cast into hell. And if thy right hand offend thee, cut it off and cast it from thee; for it is profitable for thee that one of thy members should perish, and not that thy whole body should be cast into hell.'
>
> As a condition of repentance, our Lord did not intend that we mutilate and destroy ourselves. But if taken literally, a good portion of the population would be blind paraplegics. (Haggard p9)

He then cites the similar example from *John* 6:54–57 about eating Christ as the Bread of Life, and concludes:

> I have used only two examples, of many, where the Bible cannot be interpreted in a strictly literal sense. Masonic ritual also deserves knowledgeable interpretation. The historic and analogous penalty passages of our obligations were never intended to be given literal meaning, nor has such meaning ever been part of Masonic life or practice. Only our enemies could have conjured up such a distortion.

However, change was already in the air. Scottish masonry, well ahead of England, had adopted a far more drastic change in the sixties. For example, *The Cryptic Degrees* contains the instruction:

> That there shall be deleted from the Obligations contained in the Books of Instruction for the Degrees listed in paragraph 4 of the Constitution of Supreme Grand Chapter all reference to the Ancient Penalties and after the respective Obligations have been sealed there shall be added an explanation as follows—'In former times the penalty attaching to the violation of this obligation was that of. . . . We do not now include this penalty in the obligation as we would not wish to, nor indeed could, inflict it. We rely on the moral penalties prescribed in our laws.' (*Cryptic Degrees* p2)

In June 1986, a further change was made by the United Grand Lodge of England, carried by a substantial majority, and required to be implemented in all English lodges by June 1987. This takes the penalty entirely out of the obligation and describes it afterwards as a symbolic penalty associated with the obligation. This is similar to the Scottish change, but escapes the unfortunate implication that a physical penalty ever was inflicted. It still enables a modified form of the catechism which has just been quoted to be used. It made no difference to the nature of Freemasonry and again, as a Christian, I welcomed the change. Even though I sympathise with what Burns says in the quotation above, I feel that a clear distinction between a real promise and a symbolic penalty is advantageous.

Despite the fact that John Lawrence's *Freemasonry—a religion?* was published in 1987, he complains about the original form of the obligation, mentions the twenty-year-old permitted alternative only in passing, and seems to totally ignore the latest changes (pp67–68). His comments were therefore out of date.

10
Strategies Unknown

THE VATICAN VIEW

Central to the exposition of the Vatican attitude to Freemasonry is this passage from *L'Osservatore Romano* for 11 March 1985:

> Above all, it must be remembered that the community of 'Freemasons' and its moral obligations are presented as a progressive series of symbols of an extremely binding nature. The rigid rule of secrecy which prevails there further strengthens the weight of the interaction of signs and ideas. For the members, the climate of secrecy entails above all the risk of becoming an instrument of strategies unknown to them.

The next paragraph is about relativism, and a separate chapter of this book is devoted to the subject.

One of the problems of dealing with quotations from *L'Osservatore Romano* is that of trying to understand what they mean. For example, how can a 'progressive system of symbols' be 'extremely binding'? Such 'symbols' must be something quite different from the square and compasses of masonic symbolism, as there is absolutely nothing 'binding' about them:

> The Square [is] to regulate our actions, and the Compasses [are] to keep us in due bounds with all mankind, especially our Brethren in Freemasonry. (Dewar p137)

They are symbols for moral behaviour, but they are not 'binding'. Likewise, a study of the working tools of the first three and the Mark degrees, and those of the Royal Arch (the Scottish version, not referred to as 'tools' in English ritual) will indicate that they perhaps have a cumulative teaching value, but to say that they are a 'progressive series' cannot be substantiated.

It can only be conceived that the Vatican is referring to the masonic obligations as 'symbols'; they are the only really binding thing about the masonic workings. This is in itself an interesting viewpoint, as when masons have said that the penalties of the obligations are 'symbolic', the critics of the Craft have been very quick to object to them being part of the sworn undertaking.

However, the main point which we will consider in this chapter is the reference to the 'risk of becoming an instrument of strategies unknown'. Is there such a risk in regular masonry, and is it there in certain parts only, or not at all?

WARD

In this field, there have been many enemies within masonry who have seen grandiose visions of its potential, in their view for good. Perhaps the most harmful of these has been J. S. M. Ward, whose writings, together with those of other equally woolly theists, formed the basis for an attack on the Craft by 'An Anglo-Catholic' in the 1930s.

This is the sort of unmasonic rubbish which has issued in the past from the pens of the enemy within:

> The united influence for good and, above all, for peace, which the Masons of the world could exert is enormous. No Chauvinistic government could resist it, and Masonry, tried and tested, is a far stronger and safer implement with which to attain that object than a paper League of Nations. But how to begin. Surely the first step has been made by the alliance . . . between the three Grand Lodges of the British Isles [this might be referring to the Concordat of 1905, concerned purely with internal matters like recognition of each other's Past Masters, new Grand Lodges, etc, or the *Basic Principles for Grand Lodge Recognition* of 1929, neither of which could be regarded as world shattering in its effect]. The next step is to extend that alliance to every Grand Lodge within the British Empire. Next to . . . form a Supreme Grand Lodge of the British Empire. . . . Then, cannot the Supreme Grand Lodge of the British Empire enter into a perpetual alliance with the Supreme Grand Lodge of America, and these two elder brothers with all other Grand Lodges whose principles are sound and who acknowledge the G.A.O.T.U.?
>
> And when this has been achieved then the time is ripe for the formation of the Supreme Grand Lodge of the World, whose Grand Master could be elected for a term of years . . . filling a post compared with which even that of the Pope's will fall into insignificance. Then will this Grand Lodge, by its influence, rather than by mixing in politics, be able to prevent entirely the folly of an appeal to arms, while its constituent members alone will deal with the domestic Masonic affairs of each nation. . . .
>
> Under this banner shall all religions and races meet on the level and, guided by the united wisdom of the best men in Freemasonry and inspired by our age-old principles, we shall be indeed a fit vehicle for the work of the Most High. . . . Freemasonry is, I contend, the mightiest force in the world. All that is best in religion and nationality is united with all that is best in internationalism.
>
> Freemasonry is the survivor of the ancient mysteries nay, we may go further, and call it the guardian of the mysteries. . . . I contend that it comes via the Dionysian artificers, the actual builders of the Temple . . . but the main basis on which the system was built up was the primitive initiatory rites. . . . In short, we find our ritual the foundation of all the religious systems of the world. . . .
>
> In the new age which is passing through the long drawn out travail of its birth, Freemasonry will be there, as of old, to lay the broad foundations on which the new religion will be built. . . . Out of them shall rise a new and better covenant once more, and still will Freemasonry remain to be the Ark of Refuge. . . . (Ward's *Freemasonry and the Ancient Gods*, quoted by 'Anglo-Catholic' pp8–11)

This is only a brief quotation from the turgid prose with which Ward overwhelms his readers. It is all totally irrelevant to true Freemasonry, which categorically denies either the political or religious ambitions which he expresses. It remains a matter of doubt as to whether Ward was giving us the benefit of these views as a Freemason or as a writer—if such a distinction can be made—and if he had done so after 1949, he would have fallen foul of the view expressed in *Aims and Relationships of the Craft*: 'neither in any Lodge nor at any time in his capacity as a Freemason is [a member] permitted to discuss or advance his views on theological or political questions'. Certainly, the evidence which United Grand Lodge presented to the Working Group of the Church Synod contained some very antipathetic comments on Ward.

Our great protection against such nonsense ever becoming dominant lies in the democratic government of the Order.

THE GOVERNMENT OF THE CRAFT

We are concerned with how a Grand Lodge governs itself, and whether there is room for 'strategies unknown' to be evolved and put into practice.

The Premier Grand Lodge of England was founded in 1717 as the first Grand Lodge in the world, and whilst others are sovereign bodies owing no allegiance to England, there is generally a high degree of similarity in the government of the Craft throughout the world of regular masonry. I have witnessed meetings of the Grand Lodges in England, Scotland, Japan the Philippines, and China (Taiwan). I have read substantial parts of the *Proceedings* of the Grand Lodges of Ireland and California, as well as unrecognised Grand Lodges such as Kentucky (Prince Hall Affiliation). I have read the histories of many Grand Lodges such as Queensland, Germany and Pennsylvania. I am conscious of an essential similarity on opposite sides of the globe.

Grand Lodges are fundamentally democratic organisations. Rule 2 of the current *Constitutions* reads:

> The interests of the fraternity are managed by a *general representation of all private Lodges* on the Register, the Grand Stewards for the year and the Grand Officers, present and past, with the Grand Master at their head. (emphasis mine)

Rule 4 moves on to say:

> The Grand Lodge possesses the supreme superintending authority, and *alone* [ie, neither its officers nor the members of any 'higher' degree] has the inherent power of enacting laws and regulations for the government of the Craft, and of altering, repealing, and abrogating them, provided always that the antient Landmarks of the Order be preserved.
>
> The Grand Lodge also has the power of investigating, regulating and deciding all matters relative to the Craft, or to particular Lodges, or to individual Brothers, which power it may exercise by itself or by such delegated authority as in its wisdom and discretion it may appoint.

Rule 5 lists the precedence of members of Grand Lodge, and by doing so amplifies the reference to 'a general representation of all private lodges' in Rule 2 saying:

> 79. The Master, Past Masters qualified [by remaining a subscribing member of a lodge], and Wardens of the Grand Stewards Lodge and of *every other* private Lodge.

Since there are some eight thousand lodges under United Grand Lodge, and each lodge has at least three representatives, Grand Lodge nominally consists of about 25,000 masons, plus say an equal number of Past Masters, representing the half million or so members.

The heads of Grand Lodge and the private lodges of which it consists are democratically elected. Rule 14 provides that:

> The Grand Master shall, according to antient usage, be nominated at the Grand Lodge in December in every year, and at the ensuing Grand Lodge in March the *election* shall take place. The Grand Master, so elected, shall be installed on the day of the Grand Festival. . . .

Rule 105(a) reads:

> Every Lodge shall annually, on the day named in its by-laws for the purpose, proceed to elect a Master *by ballot* from amongst those of its members who have .. . served for one year . . . [in] the office of Master, or of Senior Warden or of Junior Warden, in a regular Lodge warranted under the Grand Lodge. . . . The ballot shall be declared in favour of the member thus qualified who has received the largest number of votes of the members present and voting.

These quotations from the *Constitutions* mean that no policy can be adopted without majority approval, by a potential representation at a level of about one for every ten masons.

In Scotland there is a further refinement, in that overseas lodges can elect a 'proxy Master' to represent them in Grand Lodge. This is actively encouraged by the Grand Secretary, who maintains a list of Scottish resident Past Masters willing to be so elected.

DISSEMINATION

The only doubt about this democratic procedure being effective might seem to lie in the poor proportion of representatives that turn up at Quarterly Communications. In practice, under a thousand masons attend the Quarterly Communications, and twice this number the annual investiture (where admission is by ticket, limited by the size of the 'Grand Temple' in Freemasons' Hall, London).

This is overcome by the detailed printing of agendas with supporting documentation and of minutes of each Communication. These are circulated to each member of Grand Lodge, and this in practice entails two copies being sent to the Secretary of each lodge so that Grand Lodge members—the Master, Past Masters and two Wardens—have access to them.

In addition, for the benefit of every mason from the newly admitted Apprentice upwards, there is the procedure of the 'risings' at the end of every regular lodge meeting. The Master rises three times to formally enquire 'if any brother has aught to propose for the good of Freemasonry in general or of this Lodge in particular', and at the first of these it is customary for Grand Lodge matters to be dealt with. This involves the Secretary announcing any correspondence and minutes received from Grand Lodge, offering to make the latter available to any member for perusal. To assist him in this, the Grand Secretary often includes a slip pointing to items to which attention should particularly be drawn. (The procedure for the 'risings' is given in *Emulation Ritual* pp30–31, but Hannah omits them on p93 of *Darkness Visible*, presumably having failed to appreciate their importance.)

That this is not intended by Grand Lodge as a mere formality can be seen from the paragraph 'Proceedings of Grand Lodge' in *Information for the Guidance of Members of the Craft:*

> On many occasions the Board [of General Purposes] in its report to Grand Lodge has drawn attention to the necessity for members of Lodges to be informed of matters in the proceedings of Grand Lodge of which every member of the Craft should be made aware. . . . An item should appear on the appropriate Lodge agenda after each Quarterly Communication . . .; this should be the regular practice in every case. Masters and Secretaries of Lodges should realize their responsibilities in seeing that their members are properly informed of the business of Grand Lodge. . . . (p17)

My experience of two visits to the Grand Lodge of Japan for its single Annual Communication is that the democracy is more obvious. A smaller Grand Lodge can afford room to have a greater proportion of its masons present, in addition to the three official representatives of each lodge. The two-day-long meetings have much more detailed committee reporting and discussion of resolutions before they are put to the vote.

In contrast, the committee work in the United Grand Lodge of England will have been thoroughly hammered out before the Quarterly Communications, and is usually put as a resolution for acceptance with minimal further discussion. However, examples of resolutions being turned down in London exist, and one example—simply to annoy an overbearing President of the Board of General Purposes—is quoted by Sir James Stubbs (p66). Another is that of the pressure put on Grand Lodge by Provincial masons during the latter part of 1926 which ensured that a ceremony of installation called 'the extended working' was permitted in any lodge under certain conditions (rather than prohibited as the officials of Grand Lodge had wished), so as to ensure a much loved variant practised in the north and west of England to continue (Read: 'The "Extended" Working' pp26–68). A third and very recent example is that of a single Master Mason taking the rest of the fraternity to court over a resolution to sell the Royal Masonic Hospital, which had passed by over two thirds of those apparently qualified to vote, on issues of contitutionality, and winning. There is no 'strategy unknown' here!

Any mason who wishes to know exactly what is happening in the Grand Lodge—to which he has democratically elected his representatives—has an easy mechanism for so doing. Once a mason has become a mason, within the organisation of his Grand Lodge there is no 'climate of secrecy'. There can therefore be no 'strategies unknown'.

GETTING OUT

It is sometimes said, 'Once a mason, always a mason'. In a sense this must be true: the experience of initiation and the knowledge of the masonic passwords and signs cannot be eliminated from a person's mind. Some masons may forget through lack of regular attendance, but in theory the knowledge is always there. On the other hand, nothing can force a person to remain a member of an organisation of which he has become a member of his 'own free will and accord'.

This situation is recognised by the *Constitutions*. Rule 183 provides that:

> A member of a Lodge may at any time resign his membership (either immediately or as from some later date specified by him at the time), by notifying such resignation either by a written notice to the Secretary or orally to the Lodge at a regular meeting.

A member who resigns in this way is entitled to a Lodge Certificate saying that he is not indebted to the lodge, and if he so resigns from every lodge of which he is a member, he retains certain residual rights under Rule 127(ii):

> He shall not be permitted to attend any one Lodge more than once until he again becomes a subscribing member of a Lodge, and upon such one attendance he shall append the word 'unattached' to his signature in the attendance book. . . .

However, nothing in this minor residual right *requires* him to attend any meeting, to rejoin his former lodge or to join another one. The principle of immediate retirement or resignation also exists in Irish and Scottish masonry (Laws 155 and 156A respectively) with somewhat differing residual rights. A resigned member in any jurisdiction is effectively completely 'unattached' from Freemasonry.

A very practical example at the highest level is that of the Marquess of Ripon who resigned as Grand Master and from masonry as a whole on I September 1874, and was received into the Roman Catholic Church six days later. At that time, of course, the two were considered totally incompatible. But it is of interest to note that he resigned specifically not because of any 'strategies unknown'. In 1968, Cardinal Heenan pointed out a portrait of the Marquess to a visitor, the renowned masonic scholar Harry Carr, and quoted him as saying that, 'throughout his career in Freemasonry he never heard a single word uttered against Altar or Throne'. For this reason the Cardinal pledged his support in removing misleading anti-masonic pamphlets from Westminster Cathedral. (Read: 'Let a Man's Religion. . . .' p79)

John Lawrence stressed the moral difficulty of leaving Freemasonry. He writes:

> Many of the factors which give Freemasonry such a wide appeal will militate against a man leaving the craft. I have spoken to a number of masons who when confronted with the challenge of Christ and the need to repent of their committment to the craft, have found it desperately difficult to withdraw.
>
> The most obvious reason for this is the loss of face before friends. In order to join the craft a man must have a formal proposer and seconder. At least one of these will need to be a good friend because he will be putting his reputation on

> the line about the suitability of the candidate. If someone proposes to withdraw, it will appear to be a betrayal of trust, and he will experience a great deal of pressure. I have known of men who have found it necessary to wait for the death of their proposer before they could resign. This presumed 'hold' is not confined to those who introduced the candidate. News spreads.
>
> If a man submits his resignation from the lodge then others around him will very likely wish to question him about his motives. His reputation in the local community may well suffer or indeed he may face a loss in revenue or business because goodwill is withdrawn. . . . (Lawrence pp133–34)

In my experience no such constraints exist. Perhaps the persons who confided in John Lawrence were less committed to the view that Christianity and masonry are incompatible than he. Certainly, the number of actual resignations for a whole gamut of reasons which I heard in my thirty-five years as a mason gives the lie to this passage.

Nothing in his obligation as a mason forces him and his fellow members to participate or continue to participate in something which 'entails the risk of becoming an instrument of strategies unknown to them'. They are at liberty to get out immediately, should they so choose.

THE 'HIGHER' DEGREES

L'Osservatore Romano's reference to a 'progressive system of symbols' leads naturally to a consideration of the so-called 'higher' degrees. But it is necessary to examine where these stand in relation to 'the Craft', meaning the three degrees given in a normal lodge. The 'higher' degrees are those which holders of the third degree are thereby qualified to obtain, sometimes in a chain rather like the three of the Craft. Is it conceivable that these may in some way control the Grand Lodges from which their membership is derived?

The first and obvious practical result of this system is that all masons must be members of a lodge within a Grand Lodge to which—solely within the scope of the *Constitutions*—they have promised obedience. Thus whatever they may do later on, they remain bound by the resolutions of their Grand Lodge. The controlling bodies or members of the 'higher' degrees have no authority whatsoever—simply because of their 'height'— upon the Craft Grand Lodge in any regular jurisdiction.

The second point is numerical. The largest 'higher' degree body in England is the Supreme Grand Chapter which governs the Royal Arch degree, and is run very much in parallel with the Craft from Freemasons' Hall in London. Chapter membership is under forty per cent of that of the lodges under Grand Lodge, and thus on an absolute basis its members could not vote a resolution through Grand Lodge. The same is even more true for other 'higher' degrees. Membership of the Mark degree, the next largest, governed by a separate Grand Lodge at Mark Masons' Hall on St James's Street, is about fifteen per cent of that of United Grand Lodge. The more esoteric the 'progressive system of symbols', the less significant its weighted vote could become in Grand Lodge.

The third objection to the premise that it is possible to control by the 'higher' degrees is the fact that they are themselves as democratic as the Craft, even if with minor variations which are as much a product of size as of principle. As an example, I will take the Order of the Secret Monitor, also governed from Mark Masons' Hall.

The first few Regulations taken from its *Constitutions and Regulations* parallel the Craft, with appropriate changes in the names of the officers, and read:

1. The Government of the Order and the ultimate authority over its members are vested in the Grand Council.
2. The Constitutions and Regulations of the Order may be enacted, altered and repealed by the Grand Council, subject to approval by the Grand Conclave.
4. The Grand Council shall consist of the Grand Supreme Ruler, the Grand Officers, all Past Grand Officers . . . and the Supreme Ruler [equivalent to the Master of a lodge] of each regular Conclave.
6. The Grand Supreme Ruler of the Order and the Grand Treasurer shall be elected annually by the Grand Council at its Annual Convocation.
13. The Grand Conclave of the Order shall consist of all Princes of the Order who are subscribing members of a Conclave. [Members of the Order go through two degrees in succession, becoming a 'member' and then a 'prince'.]
14. No new regulation and no alteration or repeal of any existing regulation enacted by the Grand Council shall take effect until approved by the Grand Conclave. . . .
63. The Supreme Ruler and the Treasurer shall be elected annually by ballot. . . .

The parallels with the government of a Grand Lodge are self evident, but there is also a second tier of greater democracy.

The Grand Council is marginally less representative than Grand Lodge, as it includes only the Supreme Ruler of each subordinate body, not the other two senior officers. But immediately below this is the Grand Conclave, which has to approve all legislation passed by the Council. Because Regulation 13 includes all the 'princes' as members of the Grand Conclave, its membership is virtually that of the whole Order; the smaller total membership of the Order has made it possible to be more democratic, so there is even less chance of a 'strategy unknown' developing.

Resignation is not specifically provided for, but Regulation 120 provides that, 'in all matters not provided for', the Order 'shall be bound by' the *Constitutions* of United Grand Lodge. Thus resignation by any member who feels himself to be subject to 'strategies unknown', despite the extensive democracy of the organisation, can happen with immediate effect.

THE 'SCOTTISH' RITE

It would be improper of me to conclude this consideration of 'strategies unknown' without referring to this rite. It is known in England and Ireland as the Ancient and Accepted Rite, with 'Scottish' added elsewhere in the world, despite its French origin and American development. It is the most common form of masonry outside the Grand Lodges of the Craft, and to an extent overlaps with it.

The 'Scottish' Rite consists of thirty-three degrees, the first three being equivalent to those of the Craft, and the thirty-third and last being the administration of the Rite. Apart from honorary members, holders of the thirty-third degree constitute the Supreme Council, who are self elected and members for life. The only democratic institution lies in the election of the heads of the bodies which confer the degrees up to the eighteenth.

Furthermore, the Supreme Councils meet in nominal adherence to the 'Grand Constitutions' of 1762, allegedly signed by Frederick the Great (who in fact was the Royal Protector of three orders of Freemasonry in Prussia, but was of dubious sanity in 1762), and an amended version dated 1786. In both of these, each degree is regarded as subordinate to its immediate superior, and thus all (including the degrees controlled by Grand Lodges) are in theory subordinate to the Supreme Councils.

In practice, amity is maintained by the Supreme Councils forgoing any rights that they may claim over the Craft Degrees. Thus, the first Supreme Council declared in its *Manifesto of 1802* that:

> The Sublime Masons never initiate any into the blue degrees [ie, Craft masonry] without a legal warrant obtained for that purpose from a Symbolic Grand Lodge. (quoted in Watts p10)

The same applies in the present Rules of the Supreme Council for England and Wales:

> This Council does not interfere with, or militate against, the authority of the Grand Lodges governing the first three Symbolic Degrees, but distinctly recognises such Authority, admitting none to the Ancient and Accepted Rite unless previously raised as a Master Mason in some regularly constituted Lodge. (*Rules, Regulations* p1)

Grand Lodges are very concerned that there should be no derogation of their authority over *all* masons. The fifth of the *Basic Principles for Grand Lodge Recognition* of United Grand Lodge of England (of which Ireland and Scotland have similar versions) says:

> That the Grand Lodge shall have sovereign jurisdiction over all the Lodges under its control; i.e. that it shall be a responsible, independent, self governing organization, with sole and undisputed authority over the Craft or Symbolic Degrees . . . within its Jurisdiction; and that it *shall not in any way be subject to,* or divide such authority with, a *Supreme Council* or other Power claiming any control or supervision over those degrees. (p3, emphasis mine)

Thus the Grand Lodges themselves ensure that their democratic system, in which there cannot be any 'strategy unknown', controls all masons including all members of the 'Scottish' Rite, be he a new candidate or the Sovereign Grand Commander of a Supreme Council.

'THE SCOTTISH RITE CREED'

Even in those halcyon days, between 1974 when the Roman Catholic hierarchy issued a statement clarifying that canon law need not be interpreted to prevent church members becoming masons, and 1985 when the quotation at the head of this chapter was published, statements were issued excluding the Southern Jurisdiction from the benign glow of Roman approval.

It is difficult to examine why this might be, without apparently seeming critical of the organisations to which I do not belong. It claims to be 'The Mother Supreme Council of the World', with jurisdiction in southern and western USA, and with subordinate bodies in Germany, Panama and the Far East. I propose simply to examine a single issue of *The New Age Magazine* from the point of view of a Roman Catholic, and see if this gives any cause for that Church to have specifically picked on the 'SJ USA'. Equally, I shall attempt to determine if it gives grounds for fears of 'strategies unknown'.

The back of the magazine is the same for every issue, starting with the 'Scottish Rite Creed' which is very idealistic and non-specific: 'The cause of human progress is our cause, the enfranchisement of human thought our supreme wish. . . .' It then states what it 'favors' to implement its creed, and commences with patriotism and its symbols, moving through law and order, sovereignty of the people, civil and religious liberty, to free enterprise, all as enshrined in the American Constitution and Bill of Rights. It then treads even more closely upon political issues by expressing support for the government school system, and the principal use of English as a teaching medium. This may be fine in the American situation, but how the non-American members in the overseas bodies of the Rite view it is much more dubious.

However, the crunch comes in the last paragraph on implementation of the creed:

> The complete separation of church and state, and opposition to any direct or indirect diversions of public funds to church-related schools or institutions.

The Roman Catholic Church in America has maintained for years that when a devout member sends his child to a church school, he is being doubly taxed: he pays for his own child's school which runs without government financing, and pays tax to support his neighbour's children in government schools. Not only does the Southern Jurisdiction set its face steadfastly against any support for private schools, but it even objects to the 'indirect diversion' of paying for buses to get children to private schools, and so on. To a Roman Catholic, this attitude is one of opposition to the equitable rights of members of his church.

A subsidiary paragraph at the bottom of the page continues to deal with the relation of Church and State to the Rite:

> The Supreme Council neither makes nor permits to be made in its publications any criticism of any religious faith or church. True freedom demands that each individual have the God-given right to practice without interference whatever religion, his conscience may dictate. The Supreme Council recognizes, however,

its right . . . to safeguard with all legitimate means the fundamental freedoms the Constitution guarantees to the people of the United States.

How does it put this into practice in the issue we are studying?

'THE NEW AGE'

The titles of some of the articles will perhaps give a preliminary idea: The Americanism of Masonry; Our Clinics do more than Just Help Handicapped Children; Why do Jews Celebrate Hanukkah? The Bright Promise of Tomorrow; Free Enterprise—Essential to a Free Society; Every Sect and Opinion; The Gift of Sight; The First Masonic Lodge in Japan; A Portrait of Education; The Martyrdom of Galileo Galilei; Courtesy is Contagious; and Death and Immortality. There you have it—a mixture of patriotism, free enterprise, schooling, doing good in deed and in financial terms, religion, 'inspirational' messages, and just a little bit about Freemasonry. Actually, it is quite like a masonic equivalent of the *Reader's Digest*.

Are we to consider the following extract from the article on Galileo to be against Roman Catholicism?

> Ironically, Galileo's own deep sense of religion led him into the abyss of doctrinal controversy. Optimistically, he wished to convert the theologians from their 'logic-tight' sophistry. After his failure, the Inquisition was alerted. Pope Urban VIII became Galileo's bitter enemy and insisted 'the Earth could not move, because its motion would contradict the Holy Scriptures'.
>
> Urban VIII was ambitious, self seeking, avid of power, and jealous of authority. In short order, Galileo's condemnation read: 'You are vehemently suspected of heresy . . . contrary to holy and divine Scriptures.' Galileo was banished and deprived of his beloved teaching and writing. . .
>
> Galileo was a man of creative personality, a classic humanist trying to advance culture through the use of scientific ideas. Such men have almost always suffered at the hands of church authorities.
>
> It is no small wonder that all great democracies today are alarmed over the danger of mixing Church and State. Such policies overthrow the necessary balance of creeds in a pluralistic society and destroy the rightful equality of all creeds before the law. A reversion to the bloody, embattled days of the past must be avoided. No Galileo Galilei must ever be martyred again! (Lasky p48)

What of the established churches in the 'great democracies' of Sweden, Norway, Denmark, Scotland and England?

However, the Contents page of the magazine does carry a disclaimer, 'The views expressed in *The New Age* do not necessarily reflect those of the Supreme Council or its Officers'. So let us look at the 'Sovereign Grand Commander's Message', which must surely get close to official policy. (The Commander who wrote the message has since retired.) It is titled 'A "Retort Courteous" to Mason-bashing', and deals with some churches' criticisms of Freemasonry. He says:

> The regular and recognized Lodges of Freemasonry could join hand in hand with Christianity to stop crime, cruelty, greed, injustice, and cutthroat competition.

> These streams and tributaries of thought and action could compatibly combine in a confluence to activate the laudable principles of love, compassion, justice, morality, Brotherhood of Man and Fatherhood of God. We can answer our Christian critics, therefore, with Whittier's question in 'Snowbound': 'Where is the Christian pearl of charity?' (Clausen p5)

Later he gives us a résumé of the past history of 'mason-bashing', bringing the Bolsheviks, Horthy in Hungary, Mussolini, Franco, the Nazis, the Japanese allies of Hitler, and the Vichy government of France to our attention. As a sequel he adds:

> Misguided Roman Catholic hierarchies also have blasted forth 'Papal Bulls' from time to time, trickily directed not against individuals but against the whole Masonic movement and prompted primarily because the church leaders could not impose their political, social and religious dictates upon freedom-minded people. They considered the Masons a bar to their desire for domination. No wonder the 'Bulls' frequently have been coldly received or ignored. (ibid pp6–7)

Roman Catholics may perhaps be excused for thinking that there is a policy adopted by the Southern Jurisdiction which is antagonistic to their faith. But is it a 'strategy unknown' evolved in a 'climate of secrecy'? The mere fact that I have been quoting from a published magazine which is easily available surely militates against such a view. It is there for anyone to read.

OPENNESS

It is certainly not hidden from those who seek to enter its portals. The application form for membership of the Long Beach Scottish Rite which I visited a few years ago requires the candidate to sign after reading:

> I approve wholeheartedly of the following fundamental principles: 'The inculcation of patriotism, respect for law and order and undying loyalty to the principles of civil and religious liberty and the *entire separation of Church and State* as set forth in the Constitution of the United States of America.'
>
> I have *never* held or expressed opinions contrary to the foregoing or been affiliated with any organisation which has. (emphasis mine)

Thus the views expressed in *The New Age* are summarised in the application form. There is no attempt to disguise the essentials of the policy of the Rite. I would consider that no Roman Catholic could happily sign his name to such a statement, but then neither could I, nor even George Washington!

Let me quote a passage from the same former Sovereign Grand Commander, which I *do* find myself able to support:

> It is not a secret society. While I personally favor greater visibility, ours is not a secret society. Its design, object, moral and religious tenets and humanitarian doctrines are as open and available as the obvious places where we meet. Its rituals are illustrated with legends and traditions, many from the Middle East. It is not a religion. It is dedicated to bringing about the Fatherhood of God, the

> Brotherhood of Man and the making of better men in a better world, wiser men in a wiser world, happier men in a happier world. (ibid p7)

The Southern Jurisdiction of the Scottish Rite is a vigorous organisation, but it represents a minority of masons. Its members are still subject to the basic rule of their various Grand Lodges. But if that august body is demonstrably not evolving any 'strategies unknown', but instead advocating 'greater visibility', how much less so could the open government of the Craft as a whole.

11 Formalism

PILGRIMAGE

Perhaps I might begin this chapter by leading my readers on a pilgrimage through the personal search for meaning in Christian worship during my teenage years.

My first meaningful attendance at Sunday worship was as a thirteen year old schoolboy, invited by friends to the evening service at Westminster Chapel, then the place of Dr D. Martyn Lloyd Jones' ministry. After this first experience, I attended with zeal for a number of months, and eventually, when the invitation came after one such service to stay for communion, which it was announced could be participated in by 'all who love the Lord in sincerity and truth', I calmly decided that I was qualified. From that day onwards, I regarded myself as a Christian, and started praying and reading the Bible daily. I began to participate in the work of the Christian Union at school, including stuttering my way through a prayer at my first prayer meeting early one cold winter morning in the vestry of the school chapel.

It was the doctor's practice to ascend the large pulpit of the Chapel with nothing but a Bible in his hand, and the long prayer and sermon were, so far as his congregation knew, created on the spot by the inspiration of the Holy Spirit. But even as an admiring schoolboy, I began to realise that the service had a formal structure of alternating hymns and other activities—announcements, prayer, Bible reading and the forty-five minute sermon. I noted more slowly that the long prayer was pretty much for the same things, expressed in much the same way, week by week. In any case, the hymns which were sung with such evident gusto were heavily structured: how could a combination of poetry and music be otherwise? My new enthusiasm for the Christian faith led me to question such formal elements: if everything were truly led by the Spirit, how could formality exist? Surely the sacrifices ordained in the Old Testament had been replaced by the one sacrifice of our Lord, and its formal ritual by true worship from the heart.

This nagging doubt, coupled with the fact that it was an hour's journey by bus and Underground each way from home to Westminster, led me to attend the local hall of the Plymouth Brethren for their Sunday morning Breaking of Bread, where any male member who felt led to do so could read a passage from the Bible, say a prayer, or give a brief message. One of the elders then read the words of institution of the communion from one of the passages in the Bible, whilst a home-baked loaf and goblet of wine stood on a pure white cloth covered table in the centre of the room. This opportunity for active participation by the whole congregation was to me New Testament Christianity in practice, and the elders were kind enough to allow an enthusiastic teenager to participate, even if only christened as an infant in a faithless condition. But again I began to realise that it was the same people who week by week felt led to read from the Bible or say a somewhat similar prayer or message, and I began to feel a distinct need for structured teaching which would help me develop in my new found faith.

I moved to Richmond Baptist Church for a while, and enjoyed the ministry of Alan Redpath, and later of Stephen Olford. But I found the packed Sunday morning service and the evangelistic evening service (which was held in Richmond Theatre because the church building was too small) simply reinforced my concerns at lack of congregational participation in worship and teaching that would lead to Christian maturity. These two factors already seemed more important to me than my original concern about the formalisation of worship, which in any case appeared to develop quickly even in the most unstructured organisation. So, in turn, I attended a nearby Anglican church of evangelical persuasion, as I realised that its liturgical worship was the only way of enabling anything larger than a congregation of twenty or thirty to take part together.

Eventually, this led to my being prepared for confirmation during my first year as a University student. My sponsoring priest (the Principal of St Aidan's College in Birkenhead) had expected me to attend a suitably evangelical parish near my digs, but the morning following my confirmation I overslept the eight o'clock time for that parish, and instead—much to his horror—attended the later sung eucharist in the Anglo Catholic Parish Church of Liverpool. Until the Bishop established a University Chaplaincy, this became my place of regular Sunday worship. I found that the combination of an enthusiastic congregation, an excellent choir, and the beauty of movement and words combined in the liturgy expressed a completeness in worship which all previous forms known to me had lacked.

A total change of environment from England to Hong Kong, and from student life to that of a struggling professional existence, combined with the strains of early married life and parenthood led to some lean years. During these, a determination to worship in church Sunday by Sunday and the demands of lodge activity proved an effective anchor in the storm of life, until I reached what I hope is a degree of maturity in my faith. In this, I happily acknowledge the important part played by the search for religious truth of my wife, whose faith and determination have been a constant challenge to my own lukewarm intellectualism.

Whilst I still hold a high view of the church, I have more recently again come to appreciate the evangelical viewpoint to a greater degree, and am convinced that the ecumenical church, which is Christ's will, will have room for all shades of Christian opinion and worship. My early pilgrimage from church to church should have been unnecessary, as all should have their place within the one catholic Church.

THE CHRISTIAN DILEMMA

I have always been impressed and challenged by what Jesus said to the Samaritan woman by the well:

> The time approaches, indeed it is already here, when those who are real worshippers will worship the Father in the spirit and in truth. Such are the worshippers whom the Father wants. God is spirit, and those who worship him must worship in spirit and in truth. (*John* 4:23–24)

Our Lord's teaching about the dead formalism of the Scribes and Pharisees was relevant to all the types of worship which I had experienced. But whereas, in my earlier years as a Christian, I thought that hypocrisy was the natural corollary of formal worship, and that informality would lead to its reduction, I had failed to see that our Lord worshipped in Spirit and in Truth in the very same synagogues with those whose hypocrisy he condemned. Form in worship does not militate against sincerity.

The early church was already developing liturgical forms as St Paul was writing his letters. To emphasise this, the *Jerusalem Bible* prints the text in verse form in places like *Ephesians* 1:3–14 and *Philippians* 2:6–11, where it is believed that he was quoting such forms. In parallel, the Revelation is full of visions of worship in an ideal heavenly state, offered with incense, vestments, ceremonial gesture and ritual words proclaimed in unison. The early church was evidently very liturgical.

Christians have tended to confuse the advice given to them by our Lord not to worry about what to say in case of persecution, with the inspiration of their message in a normal situation. Jesus taught, 'When you are arrested, do not worry about what you are to say; when the time comes the words will be given to you; for it is not you who will be speaking: it will be the Spirit of your Father speaking in you' (*Mat* 10:19). Outside the context of persecution, St Paul taught, 'We speak of these gifts of God in words found for us not by human wisdom but by the Spirit' (1 *Cor* 2:13). But the latter text says nothing of immediacy, and it seems at least as likely that the Spirit gave St Paul his insight when engaged in prayerful contemplation, prior to addressing his congregation.

The Christian church will always be faced with this dilemma: in order to worship as a community—which the church must be—a structure of some kind is required. Immediately a structure develops, the possibility exists that to some members, worship will cease to be a genuine expression of their convictions. Of course, we should not talk of feelings, as it is not in the least hypocritical to praise the God whom you *know* you should worship when you *feel* spiritually low. Neither is it a denial of the work of the Holy Spirit to use for that purpose prayers which were written by Archbishop Cranmer or other Spirit-filled men some centuries ago. Nevertheless, there will always be Christians who believe that the immediate is sincere, and the quoted prayer is hypocritical, and they must be allowed their place within the church structure.

THE MASONIC POSITION

The position of masonry in regard to formalism must seem quite fixed. It is an essential part of the nature of the Craft that its message is given to new members and its meetings take place in an atmosphere governed by ritualistic procedures, learnt by heart. But there is one essential difference from what I have just been saying: Freemasonry is not concerned with worship. Nevertheless, it is concerned with the inculcation of moral teaching by the use of formally established words. The candidate has previously had no chance to witness the ceremonial, so there is a good chance that, if well presented, it will have freshness and immediacy. It is certainly the aim of each officer to achieve this.

The effect of learning by heart and then repeating the same words may well lead to a diminution of their meaning. But who cannot think of occasions when words learnt by heart have been an invaluable bulwark in a crisis situation. I well remember just such a situation in my life, when a Christian friend and mason quoted the hackneyed text to me, 'We know that all things work together for good to them that love God' (*Rom* 8:28). Hackneyed though it may be, it was just what I needed to carry me through the next few weeks of difficulty. This comfort would not have been available to me if he had not learnt the text by heart.

The masonic view is that it is just such a process of learning and repetition that makes its teaching valuable to the mason: it is available to him at all times, and not just when attending a meeting. Because it is carefully learnt, it becomes a part of his habitual sense of values. One such quotation which has helped me in a management situation is taken from the address to the new Wardens of a lodge: 'It is only by obedience to the laws in our own conduct that we can reasonably expect compliance with them from others.' Without it, I could well have been overbearing in my demands.

The problem with repeating words that have been learnt is that there is a somewhat greater chance that the words will not accord with the actions of the speaker—and this is what we call hypocrisy. But it is easy to overemphasise this. The person who uses his own words to express a high objective may be just as guilty of hypocrisy as is he who repeats a ritual—and may be even more so if he convinces himself that he is being sincere. The person who expresses any standard as an objective which he has not yet achieved is guilty of this sin, yet we cannot say that we should not encourage each other to higher levels of achievement. Every preacher worth his salt sees objectives which he himself has not yet reached, yet his duty is to proclaim his vision.

Moses had a vision, yet he had never been to the promised land when he led the children of Israel out of Egypt, and led them there without entering it himself.

SYMBOLISM

The use of symbols to express its teaching is an essential part of the formal teaching of Freemasonry. Dean Dillistone defines symbol in three parts, which I will shorten somewhat:

> A word or object or thing or action. . . . representing or suggesting or signifying or veiling or illuminating. . . . something greater or transcendent or ultimate: a meaning, a reality, an ideal. . . . (Dillistone p13)

Bevan gives us a classic example of this mind-extension through symbolism. He speaks of 'someone born blind having explained to him what the colour scarlet was by his being told that it was like the sound of a trumpet' (Bevan p10). This is in itself an appropriate symbol, because we are all born blind and need the unseen and spiritual explained to us in this way through the insights of others.

A moment's thought will show how essential this is to religious concepts. Even in a more mundane sphere, all the models of atoms in the form of planets rotating around a sun, or of organic compounds in the form of straws and ping-pong balls, are essential symbols without which we cannot achieve even the most elementary knowledge of the make-up of matter. Electric 'current' is an archaic symbol of electricity as a river, which we still regard as partly useful, even if it is irrelevant to modern electronics.

Each new mason is taught that Freemasonry is 'a peculiar [meaning 'unique'] system of morality, veiled in allegory and illustrated by symbols'. The new mason is introduced to a whole series of symbols, starting with the square and compasses:

> the Square [is] to regulate our actions, and the Compasses [are] to keep us in due bounds with all mankind, particularly our Brethren in Freemasonry. (Hannah p100)

Symbolism is at the heart and soul of Freemasonry.

It is not difficult for a Christian of any persuasion to understand such symbolism; the Bible is full of parallel examples. The Old Testament's use of the story of the dry bones, the man with the plumbline, or the prostitute's husband are vivid examples of the teaching of something spiritual and intangible through the means of something earthly and tangible. The parable of the grain of mustard seed, the sower sowing on differing grounds, or the lost sheep are similarly examples of our Lord teaching profound truths by means of symbols.

TAKING SYMBOLISM TOO FAR

Masons have perhaps tended to take too far the view that sublime truth can be expressed through earthly symbols. An individual mason may gain benefit during and after lodge meetings by extending his own concepts through the symbolism exhibited before him, but senior masonic scholars have given warnings from time to time that this personal edification should not be expressed in rambling lectures and papers for the ostensible benefit of others. As early as 1895, W. H. Rylands said to the Quatuor Coronati Lodge:

> When once fairly launched on the subject it often becomes an avalanche, or torrent, which may carry one away into the open sea, or more than empty space. On very few questions has more rubbish been written than that of symbols and symbolism: it is a happy hunting ground for those, who guided by no sort of system or rule, ruled only by their own sweet will, love to allow their fancies and imaginations to run wild. Interpretations are given which have no other foundation than the disordered brain of the writer, and when proof, or anything approaching a definite statement is required, symbols are confused with metaphors, and we are involved in a further maze of follies and wilder fancies, which bring to mind a certain philological study advanced as unanswerable, that the word curtail is derived from the fact that the tails of curs are always cut short! (quoted in Dyer: *Symbolism* p25)

The book from which this quotation is taken emphasises the need to search for the original meaning of symbols when they were incorporated into masonic ceremonial as the only valid basis for rational discussion of the subject.

However, this tendency to invent personal meanings from symbols is by no means a peculiar fault of practising Freemasons. Their enemies do it too. They develop masonic symbols beyond their stated and original meanings, and not liking what they have themselves developed, condemn the source. I have previously referred to Lawrence's suggestion that the fact that a mason's apron is of lambskin means that it symbolises Christ, the Lamb of God. He introduces the claim made by the investor that it is 'the badge of innocence' as a direct affront to the claim of Christ to alone make a person innocent before God (pp71–72). But in fact the lambskin is the direct descendant of the working mason's apron, and the reason for the claim of innocence is given in a later masonic ceremony. I would summarise it as meaning innocent of betrayal of the masonic obligation. But I would like to thank John Lawrence that his imagination, catalysed by symbols, has given me the new insight that when I donned a masonic apron I was 'putting on Christ'. (*Rom* 13:14)

Lawrence does the same thing with the keystone of the Royal Arch. In the ceremony, this has to be 'removed' to enter a vault. Since the keystone in Lawrence's view is Christ, its removal symbolises the removal of our Lord from masonry. Again, the removal of the stone represents a practical means of gaining access to an underground vault. It has nothing whatever to do with our Lord. In another ceremony, after the keystone has been rejected, it is raised to a place of honour, and one wonders what Lawrence would make of that! I would again like to thank him for this creative use of symbolism, which adds to my edification.

In both these cases, Lawrence is not condemning masonry, but his own imaginative symbolic extension of it. I can see beneficial interpretations even within his own intentionally perverse ones. It is easy to construct adverse symbolic meanings. For example, I could make out a good case against the Church of Scotland for abandoning Christ for the Mosaic law, because it has adopted as its symbol the burning bush instead of the cross. Equally, the publishers of the *New English Bible* could be accused of immanentism or naturalism because the symbol on the cover surrounds the cross with creeping plant tendrils. Symbolism can easily be misapplied.

SACRAMENT AND SYMBOL

It is necessary for a Christian to distinguish between a sacrament and a symbol, because the term 'sacrament' is used too loosely too often, when all that is meant is a symbol of possible religious significance.

The 1662 Catechism defines Sacrament as, 'an outward and visible sign of an inward and spiritual grace given unto us, ordained by Christ himself, as a means whereby we receive the same, and a pledge to assure us thereof'. Modern teaching has tended to widen this meaning. Thus:

> The Church is the *fundamental sacrament* of God's promise and deliverance of the Kingdom of God in Jesus Christ. It is the 'sacrament of universal salvation'. The sacraments, i.e., those seven specific actions which the Church has defined to be sacraments . . . are acts of God to be sure. But they are . . . expressions of the nature and mission of the Church. The sacraments are not simply actions which the Church performs, or means by which the Church makes grace available. They are moments when the Church becomes the Church, manifesting itself as Church to itself and to others. (McBrien pp732–33)

But even this widened meaning clearly distinguishes between a symbol—whether an object or a ceremonial act—which merely points to something higher, following Dillistone's definition, and a sacrament by which God through the church conveys His grace.

Thus it comes as a surprise to read that the German Roman Catholic Bishops listed as a reason for rejecting Freemasonry, that:

> The masonic ritual contained in the three basic craft degrees resembles a sacramental ceremony in both word and symbol. It would appear that a man who has gone through these rites believes he has undergone an objective transformation. (quoted in Lawrence p42)

The only transformation he has undergone is comparable with that of any society membership or graduation ceremony. Before, he was an outsider or an undergraduate, and afterwards he is a member or graduate. This element of initiation exists in baptism or first communion too, but the essential *sacramental* element is missing from Freemasonry, and it neither claims nor wishes to imitate the sacraments of the church.

Lawrence makes the same erroneous identification. Referring to the Rose Croix degree, where the members form a circle and pass round a cup of white wine and a platter of salt and biscuits, specifically 'pledging to each other our fidelity and friendship', he writes:

> The masonic communion is far from scriptural, merely taking the elements and using them in a most indiscriminate way. There is no attempt at consecration. (p108)

Of course there is no attempt at consecration. It is not a communion, but a means of welcoming a new member into fellowship. No divine inward and spiritual grace is sought. There is a Catch-22 situation here: if Freemasonry had a communion, it would be a substitute for the church, and if it uses salt, biscuits and white wine as symbols, because they are a little like those used in Holy Communion, it lacks a proper consecration. In either case it is wrong!

United Grand Lodge's pamphlet on *Freemasonry and Religion* gives a straightforward answer: 'Freemasonry . . . offers no sacraments'.

PRACTICAL PROBLEMS

For the Christian too, there is the problem as to when something is a symbol and when it is not. For example, whilst no one needs to know whether the story of the Good Samaritan is historically true for it to be truth, the same may not apply to the story of Jonah and the whale. Many Christians say that its truth lies outside the historicity of Jonah's being swallowed by a big fish, whilst others insist that its historicity is essential to their faith.

Masons are in danger of emphasising symbolism so much that they fail to realise that some things cannot be symbolic. If the obligation is a symbol, it is not an obligation: and if part of it, even if expressed in the same type of phraseology, is said to be a symbol whilst the rest is not, how should the candidate hearing it for the first time be expected to make the distinction? It is because of this unclear thinking that much of the heated discussion about the place of the penalties in the obligation took place in England.

Not so easy to resolve is the place of the Volume of the Sacred Law ahead of the square and compasses in the quotation which I have just given. The new mason is told 'The Sacred Volume is to govern our faith . . .' in terms which closely parallel those given for the other two 'Great Lights'. But if the Volume is the Bible, the Christian believes that it is really to govern his faith, and it is not a symbol like the square is of square conduct and the compasses of self control. Yet I have heard masons suggest that all Volumes of the Sacred Law are merely symbols of divine inspiration.

My own view is clear: the Bible is not a symbol of Divine inspiration, but its product. The masonic ritual is therefore not all symbolic, but a mixture of symbol and reality. The answer is, of course, that in such a case, the Christian mason can ponder over the issue at his leisure, and it is certainly not the place of masonic ritual to decide the matter in advance for a mature individual.

CONCLUSION

It seems unlikely that it will ever be possible for a Christian who believes that any ritual in worship is not only hypocritical but also evil, to believe other than that masonry is itself equally evil. Such a Christian must first reconcile himself to his fellow believers. If a person believes that formal ceremonial can be beneficial, then he may well find himself able to be both a mason and an active Christian. It is to be hoped that he will continue to clearly distinguish that the purpose of Christian worship is to glorify God, whilst Freemasonry's ceremonial is simply a formal admission or advancement.

Nevertheless, it is interesting that where an established church has imposed a ritualistic form of Christian worship on the population, Freemasonry has not generally become such an important part of community life, whilst the reverse is true in places where the worship of the church has been shorn of ceremonial. Hence the sparse Presbyterianism of Scotland and Northern Ireland has produced a masonic population of something like one tenth of the adult males, whilst the various counties of England have generally been stronger in masonry where the influence of the liturgical Anglican church is less. The ardent Roman Catholicism of the Irish Republic has resulted in the lowest proportion of masons in the British Isles. Whilst church prohibitions may have had some influence on this, the evidence points to the fact that humanity has a ritualistic nature, and if deprived of it in Christian worship, may seek it elsewhere.

This evidence, which was shown by me in a paper on *Masonry Universal*, may lead the reader to believe that masonry has in such a case become a substitute for religion. This is not really the case: all that it may prove is something about the human need for expression through ritual.

12 Morality

PRACTICAL EFFECT

I have already quoted the words that every new mason learns, that Freemasonry is 'a system of morality'. Certainly, its teachings expressed through its ritual would lead one to this conclusion. A speech to the new member likewise says:

> Let me congratulate you on being admitted a member of our ancient and honourable institution. . . . Honourable it must be acknowledged to be, as by a natural tendency it conduces to make those so who are obedient to its precepts. Indeed, no institution can boast a more solid foundation than that upon which Freemasonry rests, the practice of every moral and social virtue. (Hannah p107)

Is this moral aim achieved in practice?

It is said that every barrel of apples contains some rotten ones, and this is true even of the early church as pictured by St Paul. The Corinthians had to be reprimanded for incest, for stealing each other's food, for getting drunk at communion, and for taking each other to court. It seems clear that neither the present day church nor lodge meetings suffer from the laxity condemned by St Paul. But in general terms, I would expect the response of Freemasons to moral teaching, taken as an average, to be somewhat less effective than that of a church. They do not have the same unified faith or the same means of grace and sanctification.

Certainly, Freemasonry has had some rotten apples. This rottenness may well start from the beginning. A member who becomes one for the wrong motivation will no doubt remain one for the same reason (if he does not resign when he finds that his wrong objectives are not being met). It is often said that the church makes sinners into saints, whilst Freemasonry at its best can merely make good men better. My experience is that by and large it succeeds.

PERSONAL ADVANCEMENT

The applicant for lodge membership has to state on the form that he is not joining for personal advancement. He is interviewed by the lodge committee (or Master alone) and quizzed about this aspect. Before being admitted he is required to sign a declaration that he is:

> unbiased by the improper solicitation of friends, and uninfluenced by mercenary or other unworthy motive. (*Constitutions* rule 162)

Immediately he is admitted to the lodge room, he is asked to answer in the affirmative to the same question. Thus this point about unworthy motivation is given at least three times before a person can become a mason. The correct motivation is given in words spoken or signed by the candidate before he is allowed to proceed:

> I do freely and voluntarily offer myself a candidate for the mysteries of Masonry . . .; I am prompted by a favourable opinion preconceived of the institution, and a desire for knowledge.

Nevertheless, it is clear that rotten apples do get into the barrel, as they do in any organisation, be it church, professional association, trade union or golf club.

A PERSONAL VIEW

I used to have an uncle who owned a bakery and restaurant in east Lancashire, who was a keen mason. After a visit one summer holiday, during which he and my father had closeted themselves together for some time, no doubt talking about masonry, I well remember my father saying with a degree of pride that a flour salesman who had called the previous month and had made it clear that he was a mason, and knew that my uncle was too, was unceremoniously asked to leave without an order. That, my father proudly explained as he changed the gears of our Wolseley Hornet on the way home, was because he had tried to use masonry for the wrong purpose.

Some years later, my father was to become Master of his London lodge, and one of the visitors to his installation was his boss. This man, a holder of London Grand Rank, had been his immediate superior for several years previously, and my father knew well that he was a mason. The boss was both delighted and upset to receive the invitation: delighted to discover a keen mason on his staff, and upset that my father had not seen fit to let him know of his membership years previously. My father explained that at work he wished to be judged by his work and not by any irrelevant factor.

Thus my upbringing as the son of a mason emphasised the moral standards imposed by membership. As I have myself entered the portals of the Craft, I have continued in the belief that masons are indeed lifted up to higher moral standards by their membership. Often they are encouraged to give to charity in a way that they would not have done without the Craft. This concern for less fortunate persons may equally express itself in a very considerable amount of work and expense in interviewing petitioners, or simply keeping in touch with widows and orphans. On a less idealistic level, young masons develop the ability to run committees or to express themselves in an environment of brotherly affection, and these in turn will contribute to the fairness and efficiency with which other organisations are run, and their views expressed in public.

I believe that the greatest contribution that masonry makes to a man's moral standards lies in its attitude to work. It seems to me that in this lies its greatest relevance to the average member. He sees it, not as a means of achieving personal advancement by improper means, but as setting standards which are reasonably achievable and relevant to an aspect of life which occupies most of his waking hours, yet which is all but ignored by the churches. Much of this teaching is implied. For example, the repetition of the brief lectures on the working tools drums into even the thickest skulls that, 'as we are not all operative Masons, but rather free and accepted or speculative, we apply these tools to our morals' (Hannah pp106, 124, 148). The teachings on secrecy and fidelity are directly relevant to those aspects of work which require a man to be reliable. As Freemasonry evolved from the medieval stone cutters' meetings, one of its happiest retained attributes has been this relevance to the ethical aspects of work.

But Freemasonry ought to affect the whole of life. This is what a Methodist minister, the Revd R. E. Pierson, wrote about his experience of Christian masons in his early ministry:

> After I accepted my call and entered the ministry I began to preach in a small church in northern Georgia while attending Seminary at Emory University. In that church I met certain men. I really knew nothing at the time about them belonging to the masonic lodge, but there was something about their character, something about their faithfulness to God, something about their commitment, both to the church and to the community of which they were a part that made me begin to look at them and to ask questions. By the life they lived, by the dedication they had, by the fact that they were men who could be trusted and depended upon, there came a time in my life when I asked an elder member of that church if it would be possible for me to become a Mason. (quoted in Haggard p56)

If masons appear to outsiders to 'get on' in life in a way that non-masons generally do not, it would seem that at least some of the credit ought to go to the fact that a sincere mason will be more attentive to the needs of his juniors, more responsive to the reasonable demands of his superiors, and more faithful to the trust which is given him in his daily task. There is nothing in the least secretive or dishonourable in a man applying the teachings of his lodge to his daily life in a way which is recognised as beneficial to the organisation for which he works, the church in which he worships, and the community in which he lives.

CRITICISM

Knight's book on *The Brotherhood* criticised Freemasons for failing to live up to the standards of behaviour which they set for themselves. Most of his examples are pure journalism: no real names are given, the examples are very subjective, and they are presented in such a way that they can be proved neither right nor wrong.

Outsiders forget—or do not know—that Freemasons have their own disciplinary procedures for dealing with members who disgrace their Order, just as much as lawyers or doctors. Indeed, Lee Kwan Yew is reported to have chastised the lawyers of Singapore with the comment, 'Why can't you police yourselves like the Freemasons!' The Grand Secretary's response to quoted cases of misuse of the Craft is very simple: 'Give us the evidence and we will investigate it.' Even this year masons from Dorset and Surrey were expelled by the vote of Grand Lodge, and, traumatic though it may be, more such cases would be of greater benefit both to Freemasonry and the world at large than the unprovable allegations of journalists like Knight.

Knight was much less aggressive when confronted by the Grand Secretary of England during a phone-in debate on BBC Radio 4. He said, for example:

> The influence for good is very great. The potential for good, and the actual influence for good is very great indeed. There's an enormous amount of money which goes to various charities. And I mention all that in my book. I come back to my concern with an organisation which has so many members, many of whom, a minority, are using it for their own purposes, and all I want to happen is for Grand Lodge to say, 'Okay, well this situation is happening to whatever degree, and what we've got to do is to get to the bottom of it and root it out as much as we can'—no one can ever root out all corruption—'root out whatever corruption there [is] to whatever extent in Freemasonry.' (*Tuesday Call*)

This sensible view would be echoed throughout the Craft.

Earlier on he had suggested that a membership list should be published:

> simply to guard against that minority of Freemasons and in speaking of a minority I say that if five per cent of freemasons are corrupt it is still a large number, 25,000 or thereabouts, in this country to guard against any possible future conspiracy between corrupt Freemasons in secret. (ibid)

I cannot argue with the figure of five percent, as it can at best be guesswork. If we differentiate between those who are corrupt and undiscovered, and those who are better known by being found out, the known figure is very, very much smaller, and the unknown figure is pure speculation. Neither Knight, the Grand Secretary, nor I can possibly know.

THE EVIDENCE

Knight admitted that many people saw Freemasonry in an unbalanced way:

> I would like to say that many people feel tremendous paranoia about Freemasonry for their own reasons, and just because somebody has not got promoted or someone else has got promoted whom you don't think should have done, is no reason immediately to jump to the conclusion that Freemasonry is at the back of it. (ibid)

The Brotherhood contains a great deal of unprovable evidence: much of it could well have been invented for the book, and nobody could prove it either way. I do not believe that Knight did this, because of the apparent sincerity of his attitude, both in the book and the radio programme. But I do feel that he may have been so enthusiastic about his self imposed task that he lost sight of the 'laws of evidence' to a considerable degree, and accepted as fact the results of the paranoia which he admits exists. The Church of

England's Working Group admitted that the book is vulnerable to the criticism that it was 'ill researched and included unconfirmed data' (Working Party p41).

The Librarian of United Grand Lodge has ploughed through the book with care, and found twenty-two major statements made by Knight which could be proven wrong. These included a statement that lodge meetings are technically in breach of an ancient Act of Parliament which had in fact been repealed, and a statement that the office responsible for selection of judges was run by masons, which led to a letter to the press by its head stating categorically that his office contained not a single Freemason!

In these and other examples, Knight has been proved to be wrong, but I now propose to consider three examples of the unprovable.

On pages 226–27 of his book, Knight explains the problems that he had with delivering mail to the Common Council of the City of London. First he rang the general enquiry office of the Guildhall, to be told that he could deliver 153 letters to a certain official, rather than post them separately. Then he called on the official and was brusquely told that it was not possible. Knight pointed out that if he posted them they would all have to be delivered, to which the reply was 'presumably'. He asked if there was a Post Room to which he could deliver them, and was told again that it was impossible for the office to accept personal deliveries. Knight then rose from his seat to leave and gave what he says was the handshake of a Master Mason (which as described is not the grip known as such to me), and the official's attitude changed. Knight was therefore advised to go to a different office where he could obtain the addresses he sought. He did this successfully.

Throughout this account, Knight prejudices the reader by a thorough larding of adjectives and adverbs. The official was 'irritated', he spoke 'curtly', he looked 'dismissively'. Knight was 'friendly' and 'hail-fellowwellmet'. After the handshake, the official was 'giving all his attention', 'solicitous' and 'genial'. It is hard to read the account without feeling the change from unjustified antagonism to friendliness.

Yet a second look indicates how hollow is Knight's case. First, the initial answer about delivery was wrong, and the official never agreed to accept letters by hand. Second, we have a situation where Knight was demanding something, apparently wrongly, and when he had given up, was gracious enough to shake the hand of the 'opponent'—naturally his attitude would change! Third, he was directed of all places to the 'enquiry office', where any intelligent person would have gone in the first place. And lastly, Knight never got any better actual service from the man than he would have had, without pretending to be a mason. But such is the quality of Knight's journalistic expertise, that he has us believing that he obtained a special service by so doing.

On pages 180–84 of his book, Knight treats us to a case, which a former Lord Justice of Appeal said was a 'bad judgement' which he said he could 'explain only in terms of this organization'. Central to this story is an odd gesture made by the grandfather of a young girl when giving evidence in support of his daughter's custody of the child. This sign is described in detail:

> He suddenly placed his left arm stiff at his side, his finger tips pointing to the floor, and at the same time craned his head round over his right shoulder, his right hand above his eyes as if shading them. 'It was as if . . . he was watching an aeroplane at the back corner of the court.' (Knight p182)

Knight goes on to say:

> Later, when he aped [the witness's] courtroom antic for my benefit, I was able to tell him that he was making the masonic sign of grief and distress, which is associated with the Five Points of Fellowship, sacred to the Brotherhood. . . . In other words [he] was appealing to the judge to save him from the disastrous cross-examination. (ibid pp182–83)

I am in a number of masonic orders in a number of jurisdictions, and I have never seen or heard of such a sign. A quotation from Hannah should indicate the total variance of Knight's description from what is exposed as reality:

> In the course of the ceremony you have been informed of three signs in this Degree. The whole of them are five, corresponding in number with the Five Points of Fellowship. . . . The sign of grief and distress is given by passing the right hand across the face and dropping it over the left eyebrow in the form of a square. This took its rise at the time our Master . . . made use of this sign as a temporary relief to his sufferings.
>
> On the continent of Europe the sign of Grief and Distress is given in a different manner, by clasping the hands and elevating them with their backs to the forehead, exclaiming 'Come to my assistance, ye children of the widow' on the supposition that all Master Masons are Brothers to Hiram Abiff, who was a widow's son. In Scotland, Ireland and the States of America . . . [it] is given by throwing up the hands with the palms extended towards the heavens, and dropping them, with three distinct movements, to the sides, exclaiming O Lord my God, O Lord my God, O Lord my God, is there no help for the widow's son? (Hannah pp147–48)

In these three descriptions of the international alternative ceremonial gestures given by Hannah, where is 'the left arm stiff at his side' or the 'head round over his right shoulder'? Yet I must have correctly identified the sign which Knight wishes to describe, as all are called 'grief and distress' and are specifically related to 'the five points of fellowship'.

The sign described by Knight bears no relationship to any known masonic gesture. In fact, it is doubtful if it was a signal of any kind. Knight admits that the barrister in question 'did not see or thought nothing of the movement made by [the witness]', and the father seeking custody, 'at the time it happened . . . thought nothing of it other than as evidence of the old man's strangeness'. The very best that a fair assessment of this 'evidence' is that it constitutes a wilful attempt to deceive the readership of the book and prejudice them against Freemasonry.

If the evidence given in these stories is such transparent fabrication, how much is so in the stories where no detection is possible?

In an attempt to prove his bona fides as an impartial investigator, Knight introduced a chapter called 'The Brotherhood Misjudged', in which he gives three cases which he investigated. In these, he slowly builds up the evidence against the Craft, and then notes at the end that another explanation seems far more likely. One is left wondering how much further investigation would have produced the same result in the other examples which Knight uses to prove his case.

JACK THE RIPPER

Knight cannot refrain from quoting his own 'solution' to the mystery of Jack the Ripper, which he gave in full in a separate and earlier book. In this he places great emphasis on the concealment of a message which he suggests was rubbed out by the mason Sir Charles Warren, which read:

> The Jewes are
> The Men That will not
> be blamed for nothing.

He says that Warren had taken no interest in the case until he heard of this message, but when he did so, he rushed to the scene and rubbed it out, because it was 'a *masonic* message'. He says that a masonic ceremony, 'involves the mimed murder of Hiram by three Apprentice masons [who] . . . are named Jubela, Jubelo and Jubelum—known collectively as the *Jewes*' (Knight p54). This identification is central to his theory.

Knight has done some superficial research. What he has failed to note is that the names of the three 'Apprentices' (which is already an error, they were Fellowcrafts) are totally unknown in modern English masonry—by which I mean post eighteenth century. They are referred to in England in 1762, but are now solely a Scottish and American usage. They are mentioned in some modern British masonic reference books, but older books such as Mackey's *Encyclopaedia* skirt cautiously around the 'ruffians' without mentioning their names. I have never ever come across any joint designation of the three, and who on earth would pick on 'Jewes' to designate names whose common feature is 'Jubel . . .'? It is thus extremely unlikely that even an eminent English mason like Sir Charles Warren would know of the names at all, and impossible that he would see 'the Jewes' as a masonic message. That he might be concerned that the average English mason might recognise this unlikely and unknown abbreviation for three names known only in Scotland and America—let alone by any non-mason—is plainly ridiculous.

Yet regrettably this speculation has been promulgated in a film called *Murder by Decree*, starring Christopher Plummer and James Mason, supposedly involving Sherlock Holmes (whose creator, Sir Arthur Conan Doyle, was a lodge member who referred to masonry only once in his genuine writings). This ends in a surrealistic scene in what is supposed to be an empty masonic lodge room, and only after the credits does the viewer get the specific information that the film is fictional.

Warren was not responsible for criminal investigation, but for reform of the Metropolitan Police force, and for stopping the horrifying London riots of those days, some of which were racially motivated. Assuming that the chalked message actually existed, and that it was rubbed out by Warren, is it not logical to assume that it was a semi-literate reference to the Jews, which Warren was afraid would cause further riots against them? (Jackson, 'Sir Charles Warren' passim).

Knight's theory is as speculative as the view that, because the three names end with 'the mystical Brahmin AUM . . ., Freemasonry conceals mysteries from the Far East' (Mackey pp1358–59). No reasonable man would consider it to be evidence against the claim of the Craft to 'make good men better'.

THE POLICE

It is interesting that the Methodist, United Reformed and Anglican Churches, in their recent investigations of Freemasonry, have considered the allegations of Knight unworthy of comment. It could be argued that they are concerned with spiritual values, and that the sort of misconduct which Knight alleges is not of interest to them. Perhaps each church is conscious too that the indiscretions of individuals do not prove the faith of the body as a whole to be false.

The Deputy Commissioner of the Metropolitan Police wrote an article about the *Handbook of Guidance for Professional Behaviour* for the issue of *The Job* for 7 September 1984. In this he suggests that because members of the public are 'sometimes wary when they learn that a police officer is a member of or contributes to any private clubs . . . the conditions of participation in which are not generally known', that police officers who are 'invited' to become Freemasons should consider it 'most carefully before deciding what to do'. He goes on to add that this 'is a matter for judgement, and no supervisor should presume to instruct him—for to do so would be thought an unwarranted interference with private life'.

These are hardly the words of a police officer who believes even a scrap of the allegations of *The Brotherhood*. The Deputy Commissioner is merely concerned about the effect on more credulous people with whom the police must deal.

Needless to say, even this bland comment caused concern in United Grand Lodge, and the Pro Grand Master, Lord Cornwallis, made an offer to the Commissioner, 'to assist with any inquiries they may have about Freemasonry and the police', because, 'Grand Lodge would be as concerned as the police if evidence were produced of Freemasons having misused their membership of the craft'.

In a speech to the Grand Lodge on 12 September 1984, Lord Cornwallis said:

> There is no incompatibility between Freemasonry and police service. The principles of Freemasonry should indeed improve the quality of a Freemason's discharge of his public and private responsibilities, whatever they may be. Freemasons are forbidden to use their membership to promote their or anyone else's business, professional or personal interests, and are subject to masonic discipline if they transgress. Finally, their duty as citizens even more if they are police officers must prevail.

13
Christian Degrees

THE UNSOLVED PROBLEM

When I was installed in the chair of a Preceptory of masonic Knights Templar, I ventured to express my concern at the existence of Christian degrees in the fabric of Freemasonry. I promised that I would give my mind to the subject, and hoped that eventually some sort of solution might be forthcoming.

Other masons do not see this as a problem. Cosby Jackson writes:

> The original members of the Supreme Council for England and Wales would have received their Rose-Croix and Ne Plus Ultra degree through English Knight Templar Encampments, which were entirely Christian. There has never been any suggestion as far as is known that the Ancient and Accepted Rite in England and Wales (or in Ireland and Scotland) should deviate from Christianity; and this has always been an essential qualification for membership. (Jackson, *Rose Croix* p209)

The Grand Secretary of England apparently shares this view. In a radio programme where he was asked about 'Christian lodges' he responded:

> The third degree extends into the Holy Royal Arch, and then after that you're away from the orders of Freemasonry which are administered from Freemasons' Hall into other masonic organisations, still based, as I say on Craft masonry. And one of them is the Rose Croix, and yes there are Christian degrees and there's no trouble about them because they don't practice Christianity in a way which upsets the Christians who belong to it. (*Tuesday Call*)

But to me, the existence of 'Christian degrees' remains a denial of a fundamental tenet of Freemasonry: that all good men and true are acceptable as members, irrespective of their specific religious faith.

How can I say to a Hindu or Muslim brother whom I hold dear and have worked with in lodge for many years, that here at last we come to the crunch, and the 'highest' of the 'higher' degrees are not open to him? Does it help if I explain that it is not really 'higher' in the true sense of the word, since the highest degree is that of a Master Mason, and the highest office that of Grand Master? Does it help if I say that the Christian degrees are not strictly masonic, but Orders of Chivalry to which Christian masons are invited? Should I emphasise that 'pure Antient Masonry consists of three degrees and no more' (preamble to the *Constitutions*), when he is already in the Mark, a Cryptic Council, and the Secret Monitor?

There is no explanation which actually helps; and I find them all to be an embarrassment. Even more embarrassing is the fraternal acquiescence from my non-Christian brethren which invariably accompanies my halting remarks.

HISTORICAL ACCIDENT

The fabric of masonry would be less attractive without these degrees, yet it is difficult to see how any change could be made to admit non-Christians. The series contains ceremonial of extraordinary beauty and impressiveness; I would pick out the Knight of the Holy Sepulchre and St John the Evangelist, the Knight of the Temple, and the Rose Croix degree.

One explanation is that of history. This affected the formation of the Christian degrees in two ways. First, with the so-called 'de-Christianisation' of the Craft following the first *Constitutions* of 1723, when the First Charge opened its portals to good men and true of all denominations or persuasions, it would seem that Christian masons determined to create masonic systems within which the Christian faith was expressed.

The catechetical ritual of the Royal Order of Scotland contains:

> *T:* Where was that Order first established?
> *S.G.G:* On the top of Mount Moriah in the Kingdom of Judea . . . [ie, it has a Christian basis].
> *T:* To what intent was it re-established and amendments made thereon?
> *S.G.G:* To correct the errors and abuses which had crept in among the three degrees of St John's Masonry. (*Official Ritual* pp18–19)

The official history of the Order concludes from a consideration of these few phrases in their historical context that:

> Of the four countries (Scotland, France, Ireland and England) which between 1725 and 1741 were capable of producing the Royal Order, only England had the essentials, and there does not seem to be any shadow of doubt that the Royal Order's birthplace was England.
>
> Because when the Royal Order is first found there were three Degrees in Craft Masonry it is certain that the Order could not have emerged before 1725, and we know from what the Provincial Grand Master of South Britain declared, when signing documents in 1750 for William Mitchell as Provincial Grand Master, that he was executing them in the ninth year of his authority. If, however, the Royal Order only appeared at London in 1741, it would have been too belated a protest against the elimination of the old Christian basis of Craft Masonry. On these grounds it would seem that the date of the institution of the Royal Order at London has still to be traced somewhere between 1725 and 1741. (Lindsay pp37–38)

The Royal Order gives us evidence of the way some Christian masons—perhaps a minority—felt about the way their Craft was progressing at that time. The Order has done all that it can to preserve the actual mid-eighteenth century wording. It gives an explanation of aspects of the Craft in Christian terms, and perhaps the most significant is the identification made elsewhere in this book:

T: What did you hear?
S.G.G: The voice of the Grand Architect.
T: What did it express?
S.G.G: 'Come unto me, all ye that labour and are heavy laden, and I will give you rest.' (*Matt.* xi. 28) (*Official Ritual* pp49–50)

Christian Freemasons have always identified the 'Great Architect of the Universe' with Jesus Christ, and far from shutting Him out of the lodges, have felt His presence in accordance with His promise.

THE CRUSADES

The second strand of historic reaction occurred in France, where the Chevalier Ramsay, a Stuart exile, gave an oration in a lodge in 1736, largely repeated in the Grand Lodge in March 1737, which created an imaginary relationship between Freemasonry and the Crusades:

> At the time of the Crusades in Palestine, many princes, lords and citizens associated themselves and vowed to restore the Temple of the Christians in the Holy Land, to employ themselves in bringing back their architecture to its first institution. They agreed on several ancient signs and symbolic words drawn from the well of religion in order to recognise themselves amongst the heathen and Saracens. . . . Sometime afterwards our Order formed an intimate union with the Knights of St John of Jerusalem. From that time our Lodges took the name of Lodges of St John. The union was made after the example of the Israelites when they erected the second Temple, who, whilst they handled the trowel and mortar with one hand, in the other held the sword and buckler.
>
> After the deplorable mishaps of the Crusades . . . that great Prince Edward, son of Henry VIII, King of England . . ., brought them all back, and this colony of brothers was established in England. . . . Having ascended the throne, he declared himself Grand Master of the Order, gave it various privileges and rights and from that time, the members of our Fraternity took the name of Freemasons after the example set by their ancestors. (Batham pp302–03)

Cyril Batham suggests that this imaginative account was an attempt to make masonry attractive to the French nobility, and to produce some connection between Ramsay's own knighthood in the Order of St Lazarus of Jerusalem and Freemasonry. Certainly it gave Freemasonry a history which went back to the days of the united western church, and would make what might seem to be a new English innovation more respectable in the eyes of French Roman Catholics.

This oration is seen as the start of the period of French inventiveness in creating thousands of degrees based on a mixture of the building of the second Temple, the Crusades, and a continuity with the extinct Orders of Knighthood through the masons of Scotland. These degrees were, of course, largely Christian. And the degrees which were likewise invented in or imported to Britain and Ireland during the eighteenth century and have stood the test of time retain this Christian basis.

This alleged relationship with the Crusades presents problems of its own. Were they good or evil? When I was a young teenager, I attended a boys' group, a sort of cross between the Scouts and Sunday school, called the Crusaders. Its badge was a coat of arms based upon the symbolism of *Ephesians* 6:14–17, about the shield of faith, the breastplate or righteousness and the sword of the Spirit. It apparently accepted the Crusades as a good thing.

When I became a masonic Knight Templar, I was confronted with exactly the same Biblical message, and my enthusiasm for the beauty of the degree led me to search into the background of the original Order. I had not delved far into Runciman before I realised that the Crusades were not by any means all good. It does not surprise me to read in recent evangelical literature that 'there are sinful and demonic elements in all religions . . . [which] is true too in Christianity, seen as a historical phenomenon: we may cite the horrors of the Crusades'. (Evangelical Alliance pp22–23)

It could well be that the masonic 'higher' degrees, stressing the knighthoods of the Christian military Orders, have had a detrimental effect on the position of masonry in Muslim countries. We have failed to emphasise that 'crusade' today means simply campaign: we have crusades against drugs, against crime and even against litter. There is virtually no scrap of evidence of any residual anti-Muslim feeling left in the masonic Knighthoods: the only evidence that I know of is in the second part of the Order of the Holy Sepulchre. A rubric reads that 'the candidate [enters] bearing the crescent', and he is addressed, 'We receive and welcome you on your return from the dangers of warfare' and is asked to deposit 'the spoils and trophies of our victory' (*Ritual No 2* pp39–40). This is quite at variance with the rest of the ritual, which stresses the Seven Corporeal Works of Mercy and the like.

The use of a crescent has no essential relevance to the ceremony, and the offending text could be eliminated at the next meeting of the governing body of the Order. In my view, it should be carefully explained in the introductory text in the ritual booklet of any masonic order based on the Crusades that the masonic chivalric Orders are not in the least anti-Muslim, and any concept of the Crusades is related simply to a spiritual fight against evil, in which they are at one with the devout follower of Islam.

CRAFT EXPLANATIONS

The most recently invented of these Christian degrees (dating from about 1865) contains all the elements that I have described: knighthood and the Crusades, as well as its own explanation of the Craft in Christian terms:

> The symbolic mystery of Hiram's death represents to us that of the Messiah; for instance, the three attacks that were made on the master builder at the three gates of the Temple allude to the three points of condemnation against Christ at the tribunals of Caiaphas the High Priest, Herod the King and Pilate the Roman Governor. . . . (*Ritual No 2* p57)

This reverts to the mid-eighteenth century theme and the Royal Order of Scotland, which explains in catechism and quaint Scots verse the reasons for Craft symbolism in Christian terms, albeit at a different level:

T: How many rule a Lodge?
J.G.G: Three.
T: Why so?
J.G.G: Because there are three equal sides in an equilateral triangle, which is an emblem of the third.
T: And what is the third?
J.G.G: Because there are Three Persons in the Holy Trinity, Father—Son and Holy Ghost, One God.
Omnes: (*All rise.*) To whom be all Glory, Honour and Praise, now, henceforth and for evermore. Amen.

(*Official Ritual* p27)

It is all innocent enough, and the overall effect of participation in the ceremonies perhaps strengthens a brother's faith. Certainly, it cannot be harmful for a Christian to contemplate the life and work of his Saviour in any environment.

SUNDAY SCHOOL

The Secretary General of the Supreme Council for England and Wales, which controls the eighteenth or Rose Croix degree, gave the following evidence to the Working Group of the Church Synod:

> There are three main groups of Christian Degrees in Masonry, known loosely under the titles of the Knights Templar, the Red Cross of Constantine, and the Rose Croix. There is no sort of seniority or progression between these groups; some masons are members of one, some of two, and some of all three [the majority of masons are not members of these orders at all]; but all must first have become members of the Craft or 'probationary' degrees.
>
> As with the other Masonic degrees, the Christian Orders do not aspire to be 'Churches', rather one might consider them as 'Sunday Schools', teaching, very often in dramatic form, the lessons of Scripture and Christian history. Thus the Knights Templar takes up St Paul's metaphor of 'spiritual warfare' against the darkness of this world and demonstrates the meaning of the 'Whole armour of God'. The Red Cross of Constantine's teaching is founded on the conversion of the Emperor Constantine who saw a Cross and was told 'In this sign thou shalt conquer'. Simple lessons, if you like, but surely of value even to the well instructed Christian.
>
> The Rose Croix is one of the thirty-three degrees [of the Ancient and Accepted Rite], though in fact only five of them are ever worked [in England, Wales and Scotland, six in Ireland], the rest being rather wordy and repetitive. Rose Croix is more of a philosophical approach to Christianity, linking it with the age-old Masonic quest for a 'Word'. The Rose Croix ceremony leads the Candidate to an understanding of the opening of St John's Gospel: 'In the beginning was the Word' and goes on to show that he who finds Christ has indeed found The Word. The ceremony rightly describes this as 'the perfection of Masonry'.
>
> In general, then, my Supreme Council would commend the Christian Orders of Masonry as being 'on the side of' the Church, without attempting to replace the Church. If it were possible to make an accurate survey of, say, Churchwardens

> and Sidesmen of the Church of England, one would find a very large proportion of them are Freemasons, and that, of those, the majority will be members of one or more of the Christian Orders. There seems to us to be no reason why the Church and Masonry cannot work together, to their mutual advantage. (quoted in *Freemasonry and Christianity* p49)

I am wholly behind the basis and the conclusion reached by the Secretary General, but it does not answer the nagging question which I posed for myself at the beginning of this chapter.

A POSSIBLE SOLUTION

How then can a Christian resolve the premises of the Craft—as he must have done to remain a Freemason—with membership of a 'higher' degree restricted to Trinitarian Christians? To do so, it seems to me that our definitions of Freemasonry must be substantially changed.

The operative mason of the Middle Ages was a skilled worker, sometimes even a master builder or designer, who constructed the cathedrals, churches and castles of that era to the glory of the ecclesiastics and nobility of their day, and less cynically, through them to the glory of God. The speculative mason of the post-1717 era has no skill in building such monuments, but is seeking to build the spiritual temple which lies within him, equally to the glory of God. This he seeks to do by a search after 'brotherly love, relief and truth', especially the latter.

The search for truth leads first of all to the facts and legends related to the building trade, such as can be seen in the building of King Solomon's Temple, and then its restoration under King Josiah or reconstruction under Prince Zerubbabel. The truth is perceived primarily in the enactment of a simplified drama in which the seeker is a participant. This participation is equally significant at all levels: as a candidate with a totally new experience, as an onlooker witnessing and absorbing the drama, or as an officer who has carefully learned his words so as to deliver them to the greatest effect.

The mason in his search grows to see his forebears no longer as the operative masons of mediaeval cathedrals and Biblical temples, but in fellow seekers of truth. Moses, Aholiab and Bezaleel take pride of place over King Solomon as the first creators of an object which Jehovah deigned to honour. The leader of the team was not the craftsman but the person to whom the Sacred Name had been revealed. Noah, as the first to build a Divinely inspired structure, also takes a major place in the drama. The relationship of David and Jonathan becomes a symbol of true brotherhood. The events in the life of Zerubbabel in Babylon lead to a proclamation of the inevitable victory of truth.

The Christian participates in this ritualised search for truth for the same reason that he reads the Old Testament. The latter is a record of God's revelation to man, and preparation of mankind for the ultimate revelation. By participating in the drama of masonic ceremonial, the mason is taken in a unique way back into these events, and they become more real to him. Of course, he could spend hours poring over the Old Testament books himself, but how many church-goers actually do so, and how many average Sunday worshippers know the Old Testament better than the Christian mason?

Throughout this drama, the mason feels that something is missing. In one degree he is specifically taught that secrets have been lost. If the Old Testament recounts the inspired preparation for the ultimate revelation of truth, to the Christian mason this can only mean that masonry leads to Christ. Thus the ultimate theme of Freemasonry must be the same as that of Christianity; the birth, life, death, resurrection and ascension of Jesus Christ. And these are indeed the themes of the 'higher' degrees which are restricted to Christian membership. Again, these themes are taught by ritual drama, teaching through involvement.

I have recounted this concept at some length because I can personally see no other justification for the existence of the Christian degrees of Freemasonry. But it is essentially unsatisfactory in two respects:

First, should not the incompleteness of the degrees which are based upon the Old Testament lead the mason, having been 'assisted by the secrets of our masonic art', to seek further in his church? Of course, any meaningful confrontation with this person of Christ—whether in church, in a Billy Graham Crusade, in charismatic fellowship, in quiet prayer at home, or as the Great Architect in lodge—is of benefit to Christian growth, but should not the church come first?

And there remains a very important second difficulty. Does not such an explanation leave it open to masons of other faiths to propose their own degrees for the complete search for truth within their own faith? Should not a genuinely masonic organisation, trying to implement the first Charge 'Concerning God and Religion' and yet retain the Christian degrees, actively seek such a balance? Indeed, the Order of Judas Maccabeus, founded in 1972 in New York, may be just such an attempt to form degrees of 'Chivalry' outside their Crusader limitations.

After thirty-five years as a mason, the questions as to how the Christian degrees can be justified—even if they involve only perhaps a tenth of all Freemasons—still remains largely personally unanswered.

14
Priorities

SEPARATION

My father was once the Station Engineer of a public utility in London, which had an employee who was a Plymouth Brother. The latter was expected to do shift work so that the public could be supplied seven days a week. But he did not believe that he should work on the 'sabbath', so he arranged privately for another shift worker to take his place when he was supposed to be on duty on Sundays. Thus the Christian worker could attend his 'hall' on Sunday, and even enjoy his Sunday joint at home, his wife cooking with the utility supplies provided by a fellow worker standing-in in his place.

My father, not surprisingly, expressed indignation at this attitude. But for the Plymouth Brother, there was no doubt about his priorities. As he saw it, he was putting God first. He believed in separation from evil— like work on the 'sabbath'—and therefore likewise refused to join the works' sports club or his trade's Trade Union. It was futile pointing out inconsistencies like, How is it possible for you to do shift work at all when others with whom you work sin by working on Sunday? How can you use any public utility service in your home if it is sinful to work to provide it? Any attempt to use the evidence in the Bible regarding the establishment of the sabbath (the *other* reason in *Deuteronomy* 6:14–15) or our Lord's use of that day for service of others would have been rejected as being the devil's misuse of God's word.

For such people, the question of Christian membership of any organisation like Freemasonry does not arise. It is not organised by sound, conservative evangelical Christians nor restricted to members of that faith, and so cannot be joined. This is what an anti-masonic booklet says:

> 'Christian Brethren, have you any excuse for remaining in the lodge? Brother in Christ, have you any reason for joining the lodge? Does not Christ satisfy you? Is He not All-Sufficient? Must you have fellowship with unbelievers, and *worship in a heathen temple*? For where Christ the Light of the World—is expelled, there is only darkness left; the darkness of sin, unbelief, heathendom, hell.
>
> 'Christian Brother, in the name of Jesus, I ask you to *come out and be separate*. Show to all the world that Jesus is enough, that you can only worship God through the all-prevailing name of Jesus, and with *His* brothers and sisters (*Mark* 3:35) where Jesus, the Saviour of men is not only exalted but is *supreme*.'

> Masonry, like all other Pagan religions and Cults, is based on 'the rudiments (or elementary principles) of the world'. Its salvation is by *works*. True salvation is offered by God as a *free gift* in His Son, Jesus Christ. You must choose Christ or the Lodge! My prayer is that you will choose Christ! (McCormick p70, his emphasis)

Need I say that I find this parody of masonry makes its conclusion unacceptable?

However, other authors express the same viewpoint:

> The attitude of the Christian who recognises the authority of Scripture is not hard to determine. Hear the Word of God: 'Have no fellowship with the unfruitful works of darkness, but rather reprove them'. (*Eph* 5:11)
>
> There are some who say they are strong enough to resist any adverse influence of the lodge. Perhaps they are strong, but to such St Paul gives a relevant admonition: 'Take heed lest by any means this liberty of yours become a stumbling block to them that are weak. . . . Wherefore if meat make my brother to offend, I will eat no flesh while the world standeth, lest I make my brother to offend. (1 *Cor.* 8:9–13)
>
> To the Mason whose conscience is uneasy on account of some feature of the lodge, these words give helpful counsel: 'Now we command you, brethren, in the name of our Lord Jesus Christ, that ye withdraw yourselves from every brother that walketh disorderly and not after the tradition which he received of us'. (2 *Thess*. 3:16)
>
> The final and inescapable word is spoken by St Paul: 'Be ye not unequally yoked together with unbelievers: for what fellowship hath righteousness with unrighteousness? And what concord hath Christ with Belial? And what communion hath light with darkness? Or what part hath he that believeth with an infidel? And what agreement hath the Temple of God with idols? For ye are the temple of the Living God. . . . Wherefore come ye out from among them, and be ye separate saith the Lord, and touch not the unclean thing; and I will receive you. . . .'(2 Cor. 6:14–18)
>
> 'I do not see how any Christian, most of all a Christian minister, can go into these secret lodges with unbelievers. . . . If twenty-five Christians go into a secret lodge with fifty who are not Christians, the fifty can vote anything they please, and the twenty-five will be partakers of their sins. They are unequally yoked with unbelievers.' (Sanders pp151–52)

In this sort of situation, the conservative evangelical relies almost invariably on the advice given by St Paul to the young church in Corinth about the marriage of Christians to non-Christians, and applies it by analogy to lodge membership. As a matter of fact, a lodge is one of the few places where all 'yoking' is equal!

> A Level denotes . . . in its moral sense that in the original state of mankind all were meant to be on a level, and, morally speaking, may be deemed so still; and in its Masonic sense, that you are to maintain the original principles of equality without subverting the distinctions necessary in the concerns of the Craft. (*Irish Book of Constitutions* pp115–16)

The Christian mason in his lodge will find his view respected far more than a Christian architect in meetings of the Royal Institute of British Architects, or the Christian golfer in his largely hedonistic club.

In interpreting the Bible, we must be careful to take each text in the context of the whole. Other Biblical advice on marriage is by no means so apparently harsh, and Christian converts whose spouses do not follow them are advised to *remain* unequally yoked. St Peter taught: 'You women must accept the authority of your husbands, so that if there are any of them who disbelieve the Gospel they may be won over without a word being said, by observing the chaste and reverent behaviour of their wives' (1 *Pet* 3:1–2). If the advice given by the Apostles about marriage has any relevance at all to Freemasonry, then the advice must be applied as a whole, and the lodge seen as a place of silent Christian witness.

PARTICIPATION

I do not know of anyone who really believes that he can be separate from 'the world' in every daily activity—imagine working for a living only with Christians—preferably of the same churchmanship of course—catching buses only with Christians, buying petrol only from Christians, and even shopping only in Christian staffed supermarkets. Despite strident cries of 'Come ye apart', only the Trappist really believes in and practices complete separation from the world, and he does so in the belief that he can do more for the world by involvement with it through 'a good man's prayer'. (*James* 5:16)

The true Christian position is one of participation in the world for the sake of its redemption. The wonderful statement of St Paul in Philippians, perhaps quoted from an ancient liturgy, expresses this:

> Let your bearing towards one another arise out of your life in Christ Jesus. For the divine nature was his from the first; yet he did not think to snatch at equality with God, but made himself nothing, assuming the nature of a slave. Bearing human likeness, revealed in human shape, he humbled himself, and in obedience accepted even death. . . . (*Phil* 2:5-9)

Our Lord was so involved that He was happy to quote others' adverse views of His worldliness: 'The Son of Man came eating and drinking, and they say "Look at him! a glutton and a drinker, a friend of tax-gatherers and sinners!" ' (*Mat* 11:19)

This view of Christian involvement is expressed in contemporary terms in Pope John XXIII's 1963 encyclical *Pacem in Terris:*

> From the fact that human beings are by nature social, there arises the right of assembly and association. They have also the right to give the societies of which they are members the form they consider most suitable for the aim which they have in view, and to act within such societies on their own initiative and on their own responsibility. . . . These societies . . . are to be regarded as an indispensable means in safeguarding the dignity and liberty of the human person, without harm to his sense of responsibility. (quoted in Corriden re: Canon 278)

Prior to this, it seems that, in principle at least, all Roman Catholics would have had to get permission to join any society not formally organised by the Church, be they for the promotion of architecture, golf, or any other 'secular' activity. The new attitude expressed by His Holiness in 1963 might seem to make Freemasonry a logical expression of the aims of the Roman Christian, a view supported at first sight by the omission of any specific prohibition against 'masonic societies' by the new Canon Law.

However, official statements since published by *L'Osservatore Romano* make it clear that such is not the case. Canon 1374 states: 'One who joins an association which plots against the Church is to be punished with a just penalty', and this is still taken to refer to Freemasonry. Such an application has always been impossible in relation to British Freemasonry; the simplest refutation of such an idea comes from the Marquess of Ripon, to whom I have already referred, who could be said really to know both sides of this particular coin. He left Freemasonry only because, wrongly, it was a condition of his admission into the Communion of Rome.

If the Freemasonry practiced by the three jurisdictions of the British Isles is not plotting against the Roman Catholic Church—which it is most assuredly not doing—then Canon 1374 does not apply. As early as 1969, the French lawyer, Alec Mellor, explained to the German masonic magazine *Die weisse Lilie:*

> The text of Article 2335 [now 1374] of the Code of Canon Law is the authority which at present excommunicates these who associate themselves with Freemasonry or other sects, which conspire against the Church or the legitimate civil authorities. Forty years of study of the problem of the relationship between the Church and Freemasonry have brought me to the conclusion that *regular* Freemasonry does not come within this definition. Furthermore this (ie, regular Freemasonry) strictly condemns unorthodox Freemasonry such as the Grand Orient or the Grande Loge de France, just as the Catholic Church does. It is sufficient to say that to me a confusion of regular with condemned Freemasonry appears illogical.
>
> In February 1969, I asked the competent authorities of the French Church whether . . . it would be possible to find out if regular Freemasonry, as represented by the GLNF is affected by these laws. If not, whether it would be permissible for me to submit my candidature to the Grande Loge Nationale Française. The reply of the Church authorities was that the problem was clearly a *de facto* matter. . . . The question would be one for my conscience. . . .
>
> I asked whether it would be certain that in future I would be permitted to receive the Sacrament if I arranged my Initiation. After I received positive affirmation on this point, without which my conscience would not have permitted me to proceed further, I signed my request for admission. (quoted in *CCT* 7 pp178–79)

In my view, his arguments are no less valid today than they were in 1969.

To the Christian who believes that he is put in the world, free to participate in all activity which is not sinful, Freemasonry offers an opportunity of fellowship in a context of mutual respect, which is unequalled in any other secular institution.

TIME SHARING

The assistant Pastor of the congregation which met just up the road from my church had two unusual hobbies. Once in a while he tok a weekend off and went with fellow members of the local Birdwatchers' Club to sit in their hides in the marshes twenty miles to the north, to count the varieties of migrant birds which collected there in the spring and autumn. His other hobby involved him working alone in his workroom restoring old clocks, which he bought in a decrepit state and took great pride in returning to their former glory. Neither had anything to do directly with his faith or his family. Yet no one resented the amount of time that these hobbies took; indeed, many members of the congregation smiled in wry amusement but saw such innocent recreation as a means to a balanced existence.

Many of us have similar recreations. Even missionaries get their furloughs, and during these they are expected to enjoy some holiday between the many meetings at which the missionary cause, even in these cynical days, is placed before interested Christian supporters. The Christian who has spent his working days at a purely secular activity may perhaps devote part of his holiday to a visit to a Keswick Convention or the equivalent, but he still expects to spend some time walking around the lake and in the hills nearby. We all in practice have some personal method of time sharing between the various activities in our lives.

One of the first lessons taught to the new mason concerns this major problem. The working tools of an Apprentice include a ruler or 'gauge':

> But, as we are not all operative Masons, but rather free and accepted or speculative, we apply these tools to our morals. In this sense, the 24 inch Gauge represents the twenty-four hours of the day, part to be spent in prayer to Almighty God; part in labour and refreshment; and part in serving a friend or Brother in time of need, without detriment to ourselves or our connections. (Hannah p106)

This passage points out the four major tensions in the life of the average working believer: his labour occupies him for about forty hours a week; his family ('connections') take up his evenings and weekends; his refreshment in the form of sleep takes up a third of his time; and in the form of recreation it has to be squashed in with the conventionally 'religious' duties of 'prayer to Almighty God' and 'serving a friend or Brother'.

How this balance works out in practice varies from person to person. The workaholic puts too much stress on work—and there are workaholic clergy too! Large international corporations are particularly guilty of fostering the idea that the whole of an employee's time is at their disposal.

THE FAMILY

The family man may submerge himself in home life to the exclusion of a broader outlook for his own life, and hence for his children. Priests of the Church of Rome are expected to have decided that there is not enough time to fulfil their vocation and raise a family, and I have met secular social workers who have slowly come to the same conclusion. It is doubtful if any of the followers of the Christian example set by John Wesley would exist, if he had been more of a family man.

The Christian is generally prepared to devote his Sunday morning to worship, and may spend some time in prayer and Bible study each day, and indeed, this might be regarded as a minimum standard. But the Rector of Liverpool chastised a fellow student of mine for attending Mass daily, saying that he was 'paddling in pools of piety'.

And then we come to that little chink of a man's time into which he must fit his Freemasonry—refreshment. The problem with all aspects of refreshment is that they impinge not so much upon his work as they compete with his family life. Early speculative masonry was only too aware of this:

> You must also consult your Health, by not continuing too late, or too long from home, after Lodge Hours are past; and by avoiding the Gluttony and Drunkenness, that your Families be not neglected or injured, nor you disabled from working. ('Antient Charge' V.5)

Whilst it is not too clear whether the Revd James Anderson was referring to the 'work' of a lodge of speculative masons or the daily labour of the member, the 'Antient Charges' which he produced—or substantially modified—refer to the proper division of time when they say:

> All *Masons* shall work honestly on working Days, that they may live creditably on *holy Days*; and the time appointed by the Law of the Land, or confirm'd by Custom, shall be observ'd. ('Antient Charge' V)

SUNDAYS

The Antient Charges are an encouragement to good behaviour, but for Sundays each of the British Grand Lodges has seen fit to introduce more than mere exhortation. The English *Constitutions* reads:

> In no case may a meeting of the Grand Lodge, or of any Provincial or District Grand Lodge, or of any Private Lodge be held upon Christmas Day, Good Friday, or a Sunday. (Rule 139(a))

Ireland has a simpler provision that 'No Lodge . . . shall meet for labour or refreshment on Sunday' (Law 114). In Scotland, an exception is provided for when lodges formally attend church services: 'for the purposes of Divine or Memorial Services or the Funeral of a brother'. (Law 153)

Masonry thus recognises the principle of time sharing, and gives itself priority only after worship, family and work responsibilities are dealt with. As the third degree obligation has it:

> I further solemnly pledge myself to . . . answer and obey . . . summonses sent to me from a Master Mason's Lodge, . . . and plead no excuse except sickness or the pressing emergencies of my own public or private avocations. (Hannah p135)

THE TIME REQUIRED

Lodges in the British Isles normally meet once a month, with a two or three month summer recess. Many lodges meet less often, such as quarterly. In Scotland, especially in Glasgow, larger lodges meet fortnightly. Extra meetings are sometimes held, but nothing like as routinely as in America. During these meetings, both the administration of the lodge and the ceremonial degree or installation workings are conducted. As the lodge is often preceded by a committee and followed by a dinner, the occasion usually takes about five hours, starting soon after daily work is done, and comprising a complete evening.

Amongst the officers of the lodge are seven who have parts of varying complexity to learn for each of the four ceremonies and for formal opening and closing of the meeting. Most of this learning is done during the month or so before the first occasion that the ceremony is to be performed with a new set of officers, and less intensively to refresh the memory when it is repeated. Freemasonry provides methods to assist the officer become proficient, the most organised of which is the Lodge of Instruction, which often also meets monthly, but without a dinner to follow. Several lodges hold relatively informal rehearsals a few days before the first occasion on which a ceremony is to be worked with a new team. So the mason who accepts one of the seven offices which have ritual to learn will be discovered by his family, secreted in the lounge, pacing the carpet with a ritual book in his hand and muttering to himself, whilst they are watching television in the room next door.

As the mason progresses up the list of offices, he will receive invitations to attend other lodges. In many cases, these will be occasions when his whole lodge visits another local lodge. During the three years in which he is a Warden and then Master, the implied obligation to visit other local lodges for their installations or other occasions will increase, and in some cases, this may become quite an imposition upon his time. He automatically becomes a member of Grand Lodge and the Provincial or District Grand Lodge of which his lodge is a part, and should take part in the deliberations of those bodies. But at least this extra commitment is in the main for his year in the chair of his lodge, and then it reduces to normalcy.

Other officers require more time at home and less visiting of other lodges. The Secretary and Treasurer are cases where the administrative time required cannot be allowed to reduce a mason's work time, and is done therefore at home. Of course, families often help, and many a wife helps her husband draw up debit notes or insert summonses into envelopes. Likewise, the keen Steward of Charities will spend personal time reading up about the masonic charities, and devising means to encourage donations to them. The Almoner may find that he has a very considerable amount of time to devote to a case of distress during his term of office.

A brother who has fulfilled his term as Master then finds that he has extra time commitments. He may accept an office in his Lodge of Instruction and therefore continue to attend that. He may join a Lodge of Research especially for Past Masters, and if enthusiastic spend time preparing papers for presentation. Above all, he may find himself becoming an officer in his Provincial or District Grand Lodge, with routine attendance expected as a matter of course, as well as extra visiting of normal lodges. This degree of commitment will probably settle down to an evening out about once a week.

These commitments do not occur immediately for the new mason, but grow over a period of ten or more years. They are commitments only in the sense that, whenever offered a new office, an extra expectation to attend meetings is there. The office can be, and often is, refused. This may well be for a period of time only, until an expected family or business problem will have been resolved.

PROGRESSION

The degree of masonic participation which I have just explained can be multiplied by a factor of 1.5 by joining another lodge, or by entering each of the various 'higher' degrees. It is a normal expectation that a mason will enter the Royal Arch, and some thirty-five per cent do so in England. Of these, less than half will go into a Mark lodge, and an even yet smaller proportion into the yet further degrees, until out of the 350,000 or so masons in England, some Orders have a mere thousand members. The same proportions apply roughly in Ireland and Scotland (even though the relationships of Royal Arch and Mark are different).

No attempt is made to hide this degree of participation from potential masons. Lodge Committees interviewing potential masons are advised, in my experience, to cover the expected attendance not only at their lodge, but also at a lodge of instruction and Royal Arch chapter during the initial interview.

The most evident feature of what I have been saying is that masonry consists of a graded series of commitments, and at each stage there is a general feeling that, having accepted a membership or an office, it is important not to 'let the side down'. Particularly if a part is to be done which has been learnt, a mason will usually move heaven and earth to attend. The date will have been fixed years ago by the lodge by-laws and shown in the Provincial calendar, and is changeable only in the most extreme situation. Thus a mason is unlikely to be responsive when his wife wishes to attend something else on the night of a lodge meeting, and needless to say, resentment may well develop.

When I was last elected to the Parish Church Council, no dates were fixed. At the first meeting, a Monday was suggested, and I had no objection but asked that it should not be the third Monday, my mother lodge's meeting night. It was explained that no member could be expected to attend every meeting. A few days later, the PCC meeting dates were circulated, and half of them were on the third Monday of the month. When I fail to attend the PCC, I suspect that the vicar believed that I was putting masonry ahead of God in my priorities. Yet I knew very well that in the PCC meeting I would be one of several voices heard on any issue, which would in any case be decided by a majority with no thanks for my dissent. At the lodge meeting,

I had a part to play, and if I did it well I would have contributed to the favourable impression made on a new mason and would earn the thanks of the Master. It was a difficult decision to make.

This is only one typical example of the problems that a busy man has in relating his masonic life to the other commitments which he has, often in absolute terms more important. Senior masons are conscious of this steady growth in masonic commitment, and often advise younger masons against rushing into too many lodges and 'higher' degrees. This forms part of the written advice given to a new Master Mason with his Grand Lodge Certificate in my District, and I suspect that it does throughout British masonry.

MONEY

The principles which I have set down about time sharing largely apply to money too. What a man spends on masonry he cannot spend on his family, save up for retirement, or covenant to his church. On the other hand, far more money than is spent on masonry is spent daily on unnecessarily large lunches and dinners, or yearly on distant holidays in sun drenched luxury. It is again a matter of priorities.

It was apparent from the questions asked of the Grand Secretary in the Radio 4 phone-in programme in November 1984 that many people think that masonry is an expensive hobby. The Grand Secretary denied this, but pointed out that lodges set their own admission fees and annual subscriptions, and they vary—in the latter case from a few tens of pounds to over a hundred a year. The admission fee is perhaps equal to two or three years' annual subscription. In my experience, the interviewing committee for potential masons discussed the cost of masonry with every applicant, irrespective of whether he had discussed it with his proposer and seconder. There is no excuse for a new member who is caught out by unexpected costs.

It is important to note that the duty of the lodge Treasurer includes presenting a set of accounts for approval annually, and that he cannot spend over a certain sum on non-routine items without the approval of the whole lodge. Thus the actual expenditure of a lodge is all on genuine expenses, and is controlled by majority vote.

The cost of meals after meetings, and the drinks that often go with them, is a constant matter of complaint in the current atmosphere of rising prices and expensive catering. But this applies outside the lodge as much as in it. I have attended formal lodge dinners in London costing thirty pounds, and experienced a delightful repast in a village lodge in County Durham where back garden produce was eaten, and the extras brought the cost up to twenty pence each!

The cost of regalia is often overemphasised too. It is expensive for senior officers, but often this is subscribed to by all the members of the lodge of the brother who has received the honour, this being regarded as a credit to the lodge as a whole. New members may have to pay fifty pounds for new regalia when they become Master Masons, and even when the design changes upon becoming Master of the lodge, economical conversions can easily be made. The same amount will be needed again for every extra Order, such as the Royal Arch or the Mark. Much second hand regalia changes hands, and I am happy to possess a couple of Past Master's 'jewels' (medals) which still have the name of a revered predecessor engraved above mine.

At every lodge meeting there is a collection for charity. It is a matter of regret that, despite the lessons taught the Apprentice (the Fellowcraft in Ireland), many brethren give only by such means, a mere pound a month if they attend. Others have bankers' orders paying regularly into central collecting agencies, some covenant to gain tax exemptions, and so on. I know of one brother who, along with his father and grandfather, each give one month's income to masonic charity every year. There is a total flexibility about masonic giving, and the only common feature of all lodges is that it is encouraged. The basic decision which the Christian mason must make is one of priorities—given that every human being ought to exercise his charitable instincts, how much of the total which he can afford should go to Christian institutions, to humanistic do-gooding, and to masonic causes.

The list of four items which I have given completes the picture of masonic expenditure. It is cheaper to go to church than to be a mason. But the Christian mason with his priorities right will respond generously to the financial needs of both. One of the passages of Scripture quoted in masonic ritual is:

> But if a man has enough to live on, and yet when he sees his brother in need shuts up his heart against him, how can it be said that the divine love dwells in him? (1 *Jn* 3:17)

15
A Substitute

THE ISSUE

It is frequently alleged that Freemasonry is a substitute for religion. It is difficult to decide if this is true or not. If a person wishes to prove that it is, he uses a definition of religion that could include Freemasonry, and stresses the fact that every meeting is opened and closed with prayer, said by an officer called the Chaplain, and so on. Those who wish to prove that Freemasonry is not a religion, but merely a club which believes religion to be important, stress the incompleteness of Freemasonry in comparison with a true religion, and the fact that many Freemasons are also devoted members of a church, synagogue or temple.

This is what the rather out-of-date Catholic Truth Society pamphlet says on the subject:

> It has often been said by Masons that 'Freemasonry, although religious, is not a religion'. But that is an impossible subterfuge. For the word 'religious' is an adjective, and it demands an answer to the further question, 'From what religion is its religious character derived?' A man charged with treason does not refute the charge by saying, 'I am loyal!' The vital question is, 'To what country are you loyal?' And so to the Mason we say, 'According to what religion is Freemasonry religious?' And the only honest answer would be, 'According to our own Masonic religion.'
>
> For Masonry has its own dogmas, temples, ritual and moral code. Like all other mystic sects through the ages, it claims to give its members a more profound understanding of the Great Architect of the Universe than is possible to those who have not been initiated into its secret rites and ceremonies.
>
> But Masonry is not only a false religion. It aims at becoming the universal religion, to the exclusion of all others. If it declares that it is non-sectarian, if it denies that it is another 'religious denomination', that is only because it claims to be *above* all sects, upon which it looks tolerantly as merely partially true religions. But it is Masonry which claims to be the true religion, and it aims at becoming universal. (Rumble pp6–7)

Of course, when Dr Rumble answers his own questions, he puts answers into the mouths of masons which are far from the truth. Nevertheless, his conclusion is shared by evangelical Protestants also:

> The World Council of Churches is composed of denominations, some of which deny the basic cardinal doctrines of the Gospel, others avowedly holding the orthodox faith. Romanism has a finger in that pie—an observer from the Vatican

> is appointed to the Council. Since Masonry claims to be 'Religion'— not merely a religion rather, the spirit of ALL religions, it is natural that those established churches infiltrated by Masonry will offer little or no resistance to Church Union, with the Pope of Rome as head of the visible church. . . . Masonry would of course go further and embrace in such a union ALL RELIGIONS, and in this respect closely resembles the Baha'i Faith. There can be little doubt that the present scheme is merely a prelude to One World, One World Ruler, One World Religion, 'The Beast' and 'The False Prophet'. Masonry is important and relevant today because it is playing a part in this false unity.
>
> Masonry encourages a man to be faithful in the religion his heart likes best. Jesus Christ is reduced to the level of the other 'exemplars'—Buddha, Mohammed, Smith and so on—yet all these philosophies and religious leaders are DEAD. . . . Masonic salvation is by works through ritual: God's salvation is by grace through faith in Christ's shed blood. Masonry and other Secret Societies modelled thereon, are relevant today because millions today are trusting in them and are thus diverted from faith in Christ 'THE WAY, THE TRUTH, THE LIFE' *Jn*. 14). (McCormick pp19–21)

Do these views—starting from two extremes and reaching similar conclusions—have any relevance to real masonry, or are they objections to caricatures invented by their authors?

MASONIC VIEWS

I have on my bookshelves a couple of books with similar titles: Whymper's *The Religion of Freemasonry* and Newton's *The Religion of Masonry: an Interpretation*. These titles seem almost to have predetermined the issue: masonry *is* a religion. Whymper's book is quaint Victoriana and need detain us no longer, but since Joseph Fort Newton was a Baptist minister and pastor of the City Temple in London from 1916-19. we shall examine his work briefly. He sees the issue from both directions:

> First of all, there are those who hold that Masonry is a purely social and philanthropic fraternity and has nothing to do with Religion at all, except to acknowledge its existence, accept its fundamental ideas, and respect its ordinances. Having done that in a formal manner, its duty to Religion is done, and it is free to take up its work of 'Brotherly Love, Relief and Truth' the truth being the moral truth and teaching set forth in its symbols and Ritual.

Newton shows that this concept is supported at a high level, and goes on to say:

> It is astonishing how widespread this attitude is, both in spirit and in practice. . . . Indeed, it is much to be feared that the Order . . . is actually in danger of becoming what they hold it to be, merely a social order devoted to fellowship and philanthropy. If such be the future of Masonry, it will assuredly lose what some of us hold to be its distinctive quality and tradition, and become one more society among so many useful and valuable, to be sure but in nowise the Masonry by which our fathers set so much store. (Newton p8)

He goes on to examine what he sees as the opposite view:

> At the other extreme, we find those, both friends and foes, who regard Masonry as a sufficiently organized system of spiritual thought and practice to be entitled to be called a religion. By a religion they mean a definite creed and certain distinctive rites expressing its faith and spirit, and both of these they find in Masonry. Such is the position of the Catholic Church, and of a section of the High Church Party of the Church of England, which is Catholic in all respects except in actual allegiance to the Roman See. They really regard Masonry as a rival religion of a naturalistic kind, to which, by all the obligations of their own faith in Divine revelation, they must be opposed. (ibid pp10–11).

SUPER-RELIGION

Newton's own view of the relationship of the two is as follows:

> As some of us prefer to put it, Masonry is not *a* religion but Religion not a church but a worship [sic], in which men of all religions may unite, unless they insist that all who worship with them must think exactly and in detail as they think about all things in the heaven above and the earth beneath. It is not the rival of any religion, but the friend of all, laying emphasis upon those truths which underlie all religions and are the basis and consecration of each. Masonry is not a religion but it is religious. (*ibid* pp11–12)

Other writers see Freemasonry as a sort of universalistic super-religion. 'Vindex's *Light Invisible*—a poor answer to Hannah's *Darkness Visible* written apparently by an Anglican priest—quotes with approbation:

> In the new age which is passing through the long-drawn travail of its birth, Freemasonry will be there, as of old, to lay the broad foundations on which the new religion will be built. Errors and false dogmas will pass away . . ., but the Real Truth will always remain—for truth is eternal and the bases of truth are within our Order. Out of them shall arise a new and better convenant once more. ('Vindex' p108, quoting J. S. M. Ward's *Freemasonry and the Ancient Gods*)

What is the man in the pew who is a Freemason to make of such rubbish?

THE TRUE POSITION

First, it is my view that we must approach Freemasonry from the standpoint of a believing Christian, not attempt to do the reverse. I believe that this reversal is what both Newton and 'Vindex' have done, despite their ordination as ministers and leaders in the Christian Church.

This means that we must revert to the biblical view of our Lord's position within the drama of history and eternity:

> When in former times God spoke to our forefathers, he spoke in fragmentary and varied fashion through the prophets. But in this final age he has spoken to us in the Son whom he has made heir to the whole universe, and through whom he created all orders of existence: the Son is the effulgence of God's splendour and the stamp of God's very being, and sustains the universe by his word of power. When he had brought about the purgation of sins, he took his seat at the right hand of Majesty on high. (*Heb* 1:1–4)

> I pray that your inward eyes may be illumined, so that you may know what is the hope to which he calls you . . . and how vast the resources of his power open to us who trust in him. They are measured by his strength and the might which he exerted in Christ when he raised him from the dead, when he enthroned him at his right hand in the heavenly realms, far above . . . any title of sovereignty that can be named, not only in this age but in the age to come. He put everything under subjection beneath his feet, and appointed him as supreme head to the church, which, is his His body and as such holds within it the fullness of him who himself receives the entire fullness of God. (*Eph*1:18–23)

These cosmic pictures of Christ—existing before creation and now enthroned in glory—leave no space for a universal super-religion, except that that is exactly what the Christian faith already is! Freemasonry can but be one of the many interfaces which the Christian may use between this Grand Design and the human situation.

Secondly, the Freemason in the pew may take comfort from the official support given to the view that Freemasonry is not a religion. Commenting on the first view of the relationship, which I have quoted above, Newton says, 'It is astonishing how widespread this attitude is, both in spirit and in practice' (ibid p8). This is hardly surprising, as it is close to what the Grand Lodges actually say on the matter.

Every new English mason is issued with a booklet which contains this statement, adopted by United Grand Lodge in 1962:

> It cannot be too strongly asserted that Masonry is neither a religion nor a substitute for a religion. Masonry seeks to inculcate in its members a standard of conduct and behaviour which it believes is acceptable to all creeds, but it refrains from intervening in the field of dogma or theology. Masonry, therefore, is not a competitor with religion, though in the sphere of human conduct it may be hoped that its teaching will be complementary to that of religion. On the other hand its basic requirement that every member of the Order shall believe in a Supreme Being and the stress laid upon his duty towards Him should be sufficient evidence to all but the wilfully prejudiced that Masonry is an upholder of religion since it both requires a man to have some form of religious belief before he can be admitted as a Mason, and expects him when admitted to go on practising his religion. (*Information* p18)

A more recent pamphlet emphasises the incompleteness of the Craft:

> Freemasonry lacks the basic elements of religion:
>
> a. It has no theological doctrine, and by forbidding religious discussion at its meetings will not allow a Masonic theological doctrine to develop.
> b. It offers no sacraments.
> c. It does not claim to lead to salvation by works, by secret knowledge or by any other means. (*Freemasonry and Religion*)

The Christian mason should do all in his power to express this official view to outsiders who suggest to him that Freemasonry is a substitute for Christianity. It is not.

But thirdly, the Christian has to understand that, as Freemasonry is not a dogmatic organisation, its members being merely required to believe in a Supreme Being, there is complete freedom of belief. Hence, Christian ministers like Newton and 'Vindex' are not hunted down by a masonic version of the Inquisition or the church elders of Salem, and expelled from the Order because they do not fully uphold the official view on this subject. They are free to write their books provided they do not come within the narrow prohibited range which I have explained in the chapter on Secrecy. The Christian mason should welcome such freedom, believing that the incompleteness of Freemasonry points to the wholeness of Christ. This does not mean that a Christian must give up his Craft, but that he must recognise its limitations.

MASONS IN CHURCH

One of the places where the relationship of the Craft to the Christian faith becomes most obvious is when masons as a group take part in church worship—perhaps most especially—in funerals. Clergy are particularly sensitive when masons appear to wish to riderough shod over their wishes, often on the basis that the previous Vicar allowed it. The Revd John Gladwyn of the Shaftesbury Project objected to the 'ceremonies and initiation rites of membership of freemasonry . . . breaking out . . . at strongly masonic funerals' (Wade p99). The Revd John Lawrence has more recently objected to a case where a mason asked his vicar to remove the cross from the altar and the name of our Lord from the prayers to be used for a service to be attended by masons.

Now I do recollect myself asking my school's chaplain for permission to remove the cross and candles from the altar of the chapel when, as leader of the Christian Union (and currently attending a Plymouth Brethren assembly on Sundays), I had to organise a meeting of the Surrey Schools Christian Rallies. I regarded them as an unnecessary and distracting bit of symbolism. I am in retrospect glad that he refused, and he rightly implied that, if I wished to arrange for my fellow evangelical fifth and sixth formers to have a rally in his chapel, we took the chapel, cross, candles and all!

Freemasons have even less right to make demands of the minister of the place of worship where they may wish to hold a memorial service or funeral. The United Grand Lodge of England is absolutely clear about this. The following rules were adopted in 1962, thus becoming en 'edict of Grand Lodge' (*Constitutions* Rule 229):

> (i) that Masonic rites, prayers, and ceremonies be confined to the Lodge room. . . .
>
> (ii) that there be no active participation by Masons, as such, in any part of the burial service or cremation of a Brother and that there be no Masonic prayers, readings, or exhortations either then or at the graveside subsequent to the interment, since the final obsequies of any human being, Mason or not, are *complete in themselves* and do not call in the case of a Freemason for any additional ministrations. . . .
> (iii) but that while no obstacle should be placed in the way of Masons wishing to take part in an act of corporate worship, only in rare and exceptional cases should they be granted dispensation to do so wearing regalia; moreover that *the order of*

> *service should in all cases be such as the officiating Minister or his superior consider to be appropriate to the occasion.* (*Information* pp18–19, my emphasis)

Any priest or minister who is confronted by attempts to go beyond the rule set by Grand Lodge should make it the subject of a direct complaint to the Grand Secretary (60 Great Queen Street, London WC2B 5AZ). But this accepted, it is my view that Christian leaders ought to welcome attendance by masonic bodies as a group at church services, since it is a clear demonstration of the incompleteness of Freemasonry.

ATTENDANCE

Masons in church are very much more evident in numbers without the trappings of the Craft, Sunday by Sunday as ordinary worshippers. I have already quoted the opinion of the Secretary General of the Supreme Council for England and Wales on the high proportion of churchwardens and sidesmen who are masons.

Statistics are hard to come by, but a recent article from the United States indicates some affinity between active masonic and ecclesiastical participation. A survey was taken of 422 candidates during the Scottish Rite Spring Reunions in South Carolina. A section of the report dealing with 'Church Affiliation and Attendance' reads:

> As could be predicted, 93 percent preferred the Protestant faith, and approximately 60 percent stated that they were members of the faith of their choice. Ninety-one percent stated that their faith did not object to their membership in Masonry.
>
> As for church attendance, approximately 69 percent attended at least monthly. Those attending church more regularly also went to Lodge more regularly, and vice versa. (Wilkerson p30)

Even making allowance for the differences in church-going habits between South Carolina and the British Isles, the statistics reflect well upon the Craft seen from a Christian viewpoint.

16
Terminology

THE TEMPLE

There remains a problem with terminology. Central to this is the concept of the Temple, and its extension to the meeting halls which masons use: 'Masonry has its own . . . temples' (Rumble p6). Lawrence and the Working Group of the Church Synod make the same objection.

The Temple of King Solomon had a minor place in the Old Charges of operative masonry. During the eighteenth century, as the ritual used in lodges evolved close to its present form, the relationship became closer. The lodge room was seen as being a representation of King Solomon's Temple under construction. Whilst it was appreciated that no profane person could enter the completed temple, masons took pride in the fact that their forebears had been necessarily present daily during the seven years of its construction. This is hinted at during the first degree ceremony, and comes to full force during the next step. One lecture reads:

> At the building of King Solomon's Temple an immense number of Masons were employed; they consisted of Entered Apprentices and Fellow Crafts; the Entered Apprentices received a weekly allowance of corn, wine and oil; the Fellow Crafts were paid their wages in specie, which they went to receive in the middle chamber of the Temple. They got there by the porchway or entrance on the south side. After our ancient Brethren had entered the porch they arrived at the foot of the winding staircase, which led to the middle chamber. Their ascent was opposed by the Junior Warden, who demanded of them the pass grip and pass word. . . . (Hannah p127)

Thus the masonic meeting room and King Solomon's Temple are symbolically identified. In order to assist in this identification, a properly decorated meeting room has two columns at the door in the same way as the medieval masons placed 'Booz and Iachim' at the doorway of Wurzburg Cathedral, and the room—as the church—represents the middle chamber. Thus, despite the application of eighteenth century ideas to a tenth century BC building:

> The ornaments of a Master Mason's Lodge are the Porch, Dormer and Square Pavement. The Porch was the entrance to the Sanctum and Sanctorum, the Dormer the window that gave light to the same, and the Square Pavement for the High Priest to walk on. (ibid p147)

It is not surprising that the room in which lodge meetings are held, which used to be called 'lodge' after the workmen's outhouse to the medieval cathedrals under construction, became the 'Temple'. It is not *a* temple used for pagan worship, but a symbol of the Temple of Solomon under construction, before it was consecrated for worship. Its symbolic name does not make it a place of worship, and I would deny that worship takes place in the room, except in the general sense suggested in my introductory chapter. It is strictly incorrect therefore to call the *building* in which masons meet a temple, although the usage is common. But many masons recognise this differentiation, and my own mother lodge meets in the 'Blue Room' in a 'Masonic Hall'. The headquarters of the three Grand Lodges of the British Isles set the lead by calling their buildings simply 'Freemasons' Hall'.

HOLY GROUND

A lot of consequences flow from this symbolic identification. For example, lodges are supposed to be oriented east west, because the Temple was; and at one point the Master describes himself as 'the humble representative of King of Solomon'. It gets more complicated when we approach the idea of dedication or consecration. These words mean 'set apart for a purpose', and hence it is possible to consecrate a golf club to golf. We are quite happy in everyday speech to say that a man is dedicated to his family. Dedication and consecration have no fundamental difference in meaning, but the latter tends to imply a more religious context. In masonry, there are two consecrations, and they tend to get confused, though not inextricably.

Firstly, there is the consecration of the room and of each lodge which meets in it—in the words of the Consecrating Officer in the Irish ritual—'I dedicate this Lodge of Freemasons to Virtue, Truth and Universal Benevolence' (*Book of Constitutions* p110). This has nothing to do directly with religion.

But the second is much more complex: if the meeting place is identified with the Temple, then it must logically be identified with its location. Reverting to the infrequently used first degree Lecture:

> Our Lodges stand on holy ground, because the first Lodge [ie, the Temple of Solomon] was consecrated on account of three grand offerings thereon made, which met with Divine approbation. First, the ready compliance of Abraham with the will of God in not refusing to offer up his son Isaac as a burnt sacrifice, when it pleased the Almighty to substitute a more agreeable victim in his stead. Secondly, the many pious prayers and ejaculations of King David, which actually appeased the wrath of God and stayed the pestilence which then raged among his people, owing to his inadvertently having them numbered. Thirdly, the many thanksgivings, oblations, burnt sacrifices, and costly offerings which Solomon, King of Israel, made at the completion, dedication, and consecration of the Temple of Jerusalem to God's service. Those three did then, do now, and I trust ever will, render the ground of Freemasonry holy. (ibid pp110–11)

This does not say that a lodge is on holy ground because the land is consecrated to God, as is a church. It merely expands upon the analogy between the Temple and the lodge, and draws the conclusion that there is a tradition of holiness which it is the duty of the mason to uphold. The purpose of the lecture is to give teaching which encourages a better ethical standard.

In the Royal Arch, the symbolism moves to a different period in history, but the 'chapter' still symbolises the Temple. With the exception of chapters in Ireland, the legend concerns its rebuilding after its destruction and desecration during the Babylonian captivity. In English masonry, the senior of the three Principals represents Zerubbabel, the leader of the returning exiles, whilst another important figure is Joshua, the son of Josedech, the High Priest. These officers are called by the names of the persons represented. But in American Royal Arch masonry, due to a slight difference in the way that masonic legend developed across the Atlantic, the senior officer represents Joshua, and he is referred to as the 'High Priest'. Thus we have an *apparently* religious situation—a chapter led by a priest—where *in fact* we have a symbolic representation of three officials leading the 'masons' who rebuilt the Temple. No priestly function whatsoever is exercised. The symbolism is still that of builders in an unconsecrated building.

Whilst it could be said that Royal Arch masonry is more 'religious' than the Craft, there is no attempt to go beyond the limitations which the Craft imposes upon itself: no doctrine, no sacraments, and no claim to provide a means of salvation.

LODGE OFFICERS

There are a number of terms for lodge officers which appear to give masonry a religious context, which I hope can be quickly disposed of.

The Master is referred to as 'worshipful' when being addressed. This means 'entitled to honour or respect' (OED), and is so used of justices of the peace, aldermen and London Livery Companies. A shorter form, 'your worship', is used for magistrates and mayors. Its use by masons has nothing whatever to do with a usurpation by the Master of the honour and respect which are uniquely due to God. Neither is it an appropriation by masons of the proper designation of the orders of Bishop and priest in the traditional ministry of the Church, as if this were so—as is alleged by Lawrence—the masons would have selected 'Reverend' for their titles.

Most lodges have an officer called the Chaplain—it is an optional office. His duty is to say the prayers which open and close each meeting and start off each degree ceremony. Contrary to what Lawrence says in *Freemasonry—a religion*?, he does not have any special duty to instruct the lodge members. The use is analogous to a ship's chaplain, or that of a London Livery Company: the existence of the office does not make the ship or the Company into a religion. There is no rule that a lodge Chaplain must be in holy orders, but if a lodge does have a priest, rabbi or minister in its membership, he often fulfils this role. Nevertheless, many clerics in masonry would prefer to hold a more routine office, on the ground that a lodge meeting should not be a busman's holiday.

Two of the lodge officers are called Deacons, the same as that of the lowest order in the traditional ministry of the Church. The term has a very venerable history in Scottish masonry, appearing to be used as an alternative to Master in operative records from 1424. But their duty bears no resemblance either to the New Testament 'servant' or to the present day stepping stone to the priesthood: their main task is to escort candidates during ceremonial admissions, and to a lesser extent to act as message bearers. A recent paper has suggested that the masonic usage is derived from the Latin *decanus*, meaning a leader of ten men, a sort of corporal (Bruce p151).

The names of lodge offices which appear 'religious' are all analogous to the names of offices in many other secular societies which regard the faith of their membership as relevant and important. They are not an attempt to make Freemasonry into a religion.

CATHEDRALS AND ALTARS

In America, masonic halls, especially those owned by the 'Scottish' Rite, are sometimes called 'Cathedrals'. I recently read in a masonic magazine that one such building in the Philippines was changing its name from Temple to Cathedral because it was more in keeping with the dignity of the Rite. I am appalled at the misuse of a word which should be given exclusively to a church building which contains a 'cathedra', the seat of a Bishop, simply to give dignity to a non-ecclesiastical building. Whilst it would appear to make masonry a competitor with religion, its use is superficial and should be discouraged in practice and disregarded in principle.

Lawrence takes this further, and improperly implies that the main room—the 'Grand Temple'—at Freemasons' Hall in London is a 'Cathedral', even giving its dimensions as apparent proof (it is about a fifth the size of Liverpool Cathedral). He complains that masonic halls frequently are built to look like churches (pp32 and 63). To me as an architect, Freemasons' Hall looks more like a simplified version of the Port of London Authority Building than an ecclesiastical edifice, and the Grand Temple in it has the proportions and character of a concert hall. Indeed, I wish that it were used for some such purpose at weekends so that more of the public could appreciate its architecture.

The headquarters of the Grand Lodge of Scotland on George Street, Edinburgh, looks very like the commercial offices that surround it. Freemasons' Hall on Molesworth Street in Dublin is somewhat more impressive but is not dissimilar to the nearby terraces. Several masonic halls in Britain are converted churches, and they obviously reflect their origins. And it is true that high Victorian masonic halls, like the Grand Temple in Philadelphia, were often built in the best church gothic of the period, but then so were the Old Bailey, St Pancras Station and Glasgow University. No attempt to confuse the public by architectural means can be imputed.

Likewise, Dr Rumble, John Lawrence and the Working Group complain about masonic 'altars'. It is strange that this complaint should have originated in England, because in masonic lodges in England and Wales there is no such thing! Prior to the Union of the rival Grand Lodges in England in 1813, it is likely that in the centre of some lodges stood a cubic wooden table upon which the Bible was placed, and it was called 'altar'. Following the Union, this was eliminated, and instead the Volume of the Sacred Law is placed on the pedestal of the Master—a small table in front of his chair. It has been referred to as the Master's 'pedestal' since the ritual was unified in 1816, and the word 'altar' does not occur in English Craft masonry. The same applies to the Mark degree, the Ark Mariner, and so on.

The Royal Arch situation is marginally more complex. In this, the 'long lost Sacred Law' is found (2 *Chr* 34:13) and according to masonic tradition, this takes place near a pedestal which has the form of 'the altar of incense, a doubled cube'. This is referred to once only as an 'altar' in present day rituals. Since it is a completely unnecessary description absent from early records, Grand Chapter has recently proposed that it be replaced, so that 'a veil covered the altar' becomes 'a veil covered the top [of the pedestal]'. In the installation ceremonies, there will no longer be a requirement for the Principals elect to 'advance to the altar'.

In the Christian degrees, the situation is quite different. For example, the 'preliminary Directions' for the Knight Templar degree commence:

> The apartment represents a Chapel of the Order. In the East is placed an Altar on which are:—a Bible, a Cross, two lighted Candles and an Alms Dish . . . (*The Ceremonies* p7)

The problems associated with these concepts I have already considered in the chapter on the Christian Degrees. I will not discuss them further, except to note, firstly, the importance of the word 'represents', and secondly, the fact that within the Christian denominations the word altar has many significations, from that of the Roman Catholic who believes that no altar is truly such outside his Church, to the evangelical who believes that the Lord's Table is not in any sense an altar.

Although there is no altar in English Craft masonry, the term is used in Ireland and Scotland. Most Scottish lodges have a cubical wooden table in the centre of the room, and in Ireland, the Master's pedestal is moved forward a third of the way down the room. In both cases, the Volume of the Sacred Law is placed on it, and the candidate takes his obligations in front of it.

The 'Religions' section of my *Great Encyclopaedic Dictionary* defines altar as, 'Place of sacrifice, commemoration or devotion, commonly shaped like a table'. It could be suggested with validity that a masonic 'altar' is a misnomer in this context, but if it is not a place of sacrifice or commemoration, in a very real sense it is a place of 'devotion'—at it each new mason promises his allegiance to Freemasonry, to practise its principles, and so on, within the specific limits of religious and civic duty which are imposed. The terminology may not be ideal, but a substitute like 'pedestal' merely describes its shape but not its purpose. Perhaps a new word is needed.

NON-SECTARIAN TERMS

Then there are a number of terms which parallel the reference to God as the 'Great Architect', in the sense that it clearly refers to the Supreme Being without giving it a bias towards any particular religion.

First amongst these is the term 'Anno Lucis'—the year of light—which masons sometimes use, and even mistranslate as 'the year of *masonic* light'. It approximates Archbishop Ussher's calculation from the genealogies of the Old Testament that the creation occurred in 4004 BC, and thus adds four thousand to conventional dates (Scots masons, scrupulously accurate, add the full 4004). Jews today use BCE and CE for their dates, but how much better it seems that our eighteenth-century forebears sought to supply a universal date from the year in which God said 'Let there be Light'. Of course, most Christians today reject Archbishop Ussher's chronology, but the attempt at universality amongst masons remains.

As a second example, I will take the masonic term for Heaven. Without upsetting those who call it Paradise, Nirvana or by any other name, masons simply refer to the place where the 'Great Architect' reigns eternally as the 'Grand Lodge Above'. I have intentionally placed these two concepts side by side, as it is appropriate that the Great Architect should reign in a heavenly Grand Lodge. It is not so called because of any exclusivism, but because of a wish for universalism. It is not for masons to claim knowledge of how to get there, nor the means of grace required. Even less can masons as a whole say that anyone is excluded, but this does not make them universalists. It is open to any mason to believe that certain men will go to heaven, and others to hell. But he cannot, as a mason, tell them so during a meeting or when masonry is involved—and it seems to me to be doubtful whether a Christian should do so in any case. (*Mat* 7:1–2)

LIGHT

In the Masonic Hall which I most frequently attended, at the head of the stair leading to the meeting rooms is the banner of an extinct lodge which prominently displays the text 'Let there be Light' (*Gen* 1:3). My dear wife has commented adversely, on the way up to view the 'Temple' during a Ladies' Night, that masons should not use such texts, because only our Lord is the light of the world. However, the Biblical text refers to the creation of physical light, not to spiritual enlightenment.

Nevertheless, its use by masons is logical, because 'light' is an important part of the first degree. It is closely tied in with the idea of birth. It is important for masons and outsiders to realise that there is a fundamental difference between the teaching of Jesus Christ and that of masonry on these subjects: Jesus taught us of the necessity of being spiritually enlightened by being born again, whilst masonry uses a simple re-enactment of physical birth—at which light is first perceived—to teach equality as the basis of moral judgement. The two are closely related in the first chapter of St John's Gospel, but masonry does not step into the realm of religious enlightenment.

The new mason is introduced to the lodge, with all his money and metallic possessions removed and blindfolded, as 'a poor Candidate in a state of darkness' (Hannah pp94–95). He is literally poor and in the dark, and there is no suggestion that if he is a Christian he is denying that he has already been enlightened by our Lord, or that he possesses spiritual riches. The Master later says to him:

Master: Having been kept for a considerable time in a state of darkness, what in your present situation is the predominant wish of your heart?
Candidate: Light.
Master: Bro. Junior Deacon, let that blessing be restored to the Candidate. (The blindfold is removed.) Having been restored to the blessing of *material* light, let me point out for your attention the three great, though emblematical lights in Freemasonry; they are, the Volume of the Sacred Law, the Square and Compasses. . . . You are now enabled to discover the three lesser lights; they are . . . (pointing to three large candlesticks near the chairs of the Master and two Wardens) meant to represent the Sun, Moon and Master of the Lodge. (ibid p100, my emphasis)

There is a clear distinction between real light and emblematical lights. Later, as a candidate for the third degree, the significance of initiation is further explained:

Your admission among Masons in a state of helpless indigence was an emblematical representation of the entrance of all men on this, their mortal existence. It inculcated the useful lessons of natural equality and mutual dependence. It instructed you in the active principles of universal beneficence and charity, to seek the solace of your own distress by extending relief and consolation to your fellow creatures in the hour of their affliction. . . .

Proceeding onwards, still guiding your progress by the principles of moral truth, you were led in the second degree to contemplate the intellectual faculty. . . . (ibid p135)

The quotation from Genesis shows us that God's first creative act was the creation of physical light. The first perception of light by a new born baby is also an early part of a creative act, and the new child is without possessions. The re-enacted birth of a new mason is accompanied by a restoration to material light, when he is equally possessionless. By this the new mason is taught that all human beings are equal, and that those possessions which he later has are to be shared in a charitable manner.

The symbolism of light used in this sense is the inheritance of all people, and can be used by masons of any faith, for the teaching of new members who are likewise of any faith. This extended symbolism based upon physical light is no derogation upon the true *spiritual* light, who for a Christian is Jesus Christ.

PART THREE

Heresy

17
Modern Views

DEFINITION

Modern writers on the subject of Freemasonry from a Christian standpoint have accused it of many heresies. We must see what the word really means before we can go on to see if such an accusation is really justified.

A heresy is an opinion or doctrine contrary to the orthodox doctrine of the Christian Church, or to the accepted doctrine on any subject (*OED*). It at once becomes apparent that Freemasonry is not itself concerned with heresy. Since the 1723 *Constitutions* were published, its policy has been to admit '*good Men and true*, or Men of Honour and Honesty, by whatever Denominations or Persuasions they may be distinguish'd'. It is thus possible for a lodge to contain within its membership all kinds of heretics, and even perhaps to take a certain amount of pride that, however despised these persons may be for their faith in the outside world, they need fear no partiality within the lodge.

The Christian churches, each of which claims to follow the true, orthodox Christian faith, however much they may differ as to what this is, have no such welcome for the heretic.

Working my way through the Thirty-Nine Articles of my own Church, I find condemnations of the Pelagians in Article IX for their beliefs about original sin; and of those who hold the 'Romish Doctrine' about 'Purgatory, Pardons, Worshipping and Adoration . . . of Images as of Reliques, and also invocation of Saints' in Article XXII. Article XXXVIII condemns the 'boast' of the Anabaptists about communism. Article XXV suggests that the five sacraments which are not 'ordained by Christ' have in part arisen from 'the corrupt following of the Apostles', while Article XIX says categorically that the Churches in Jerusalem, Alexandria, Antioch and Rome have all erred 'not only in their living and manner of ceremonies but also in matters of Faith'. Thus in 1562, whilst the heavy accusation of heresy was thrust towards Rome, my Church was also concerned to condemn Protestant extremism in no uncertain terms.

The 'English Martyrs' are perhaps a symbol of the Christian view of heresy: there are two sets of martyrs. To an Anglican they are the reformed Bishops who were burnt at the stake by the Roman Catholic Queen Mary. To a Roman Catholic they are a very different group of men who died for their Roman faith under Queen Elizabeth. We tend to think of these events as something of the distant past which could never happen today. But are our churches any less ready to condemn those who do not agree in detail with their beliefs?

MODERN NARROWNESS

Modern writers like Sanders, typically of a group of Christians who are classified as Fundamentalist, can write a book on *Heresies and Cults* in which he lists Roman Catholicism, Christian Science, Unitarianism, Jehovah's Witnesses, Christadelphianism, Mormonism, and Seventh-day Adventism along with Freemasonry.

Roman Catholics, at least until very recently, have not been behind their Protestant brothers in condemning those outside their particular fold:

> The Protestant Church is not the true Church: It is notoriously not one in faith or worship; every shade of opinion is represented among its members, some of whom, among them Protestant Bishops, reject miracles and deny the Divinity of Christ. From a doctrinal standpoint, Protestantism can be described as a chaos rather than a religion. . . . Not one of these sects claims infallibility.
> The Schismatic Greek Church is not the true Church: It is not one in government . . . ; it is not really a church but an assemblage of churches. It is not Catholic or Universal; it is chiefly confined to portions of the Greek and Slavonic races. . . . It does not claim infallibility. (Archbishop Sheehan p143)

Jesus knew that unity was a fragile thing: indeed, if he could see the details of the future centuries during His earthly life He must have been inexpressibly sad. One of his last prayers was:

> Holy Father, protect by the power of thy name those whom thou hast given me, that they may be one as we are one. (*John* 17:11)

Christians, not least by their very readiness to condemn the firmly held beliefs of those who can equally claim to be led by the Holy Spirit, have converted the pagans' admiration of the early martyrs into a cynical comment: 'See how these Christians love one another!'

SELF EXAMINATION

There is a growing view amongst present day Christians of all persuasions that when a church condemns a group of its members or other believers for heresy, it is in fact condemning itself for having failed to present the whole Christian faith in a balanced way.

This is how a modern evangelical writer commences his sympathetic, if firm, study of *The Four Major Cults:*

> You may have heard the expression, 'The cults are the unpaid bills of the church'. Though this statement does not tell the whole story, there is a good deal of truth in it. Cults have sometimes arisen because the established churches have failed to emphasise certain important aspects of religious life, or have neglected certain techniques. . . . People often find in the cults emphases and practices which they

> miss in established churches. ... Every heresy which has obtained wide acceptance has been so accepted because of the grain of truth which was found in it. (Hoekema p1)

A similar view is being expressed by modern Roman Catholic theologians, even if not backed up by the hierarchy. When Hans Kung was prohibited from practising as a 'Catholic Theologian' in 1979 because of the views he expressed in *The Church—Maintained in Truth*, he wrote a postscript called 'Why I Remain a Catholic', which says:

> The Catholic theologian will always start out from the fact that the gospel has not left itself without witness to any nation, any class or race, and he will try to learn from the other churches. ... Precisely in his specific loyalty, the Catholic theologian is interested in the *universality* of the Christian faith embracing all groups. ... And there is no doubt that a number of those who describe themselves as Protestant or evangelical can be and are in fact catholic in this sense ... There ought to be joy at this, even on the part of the institutional church. (Kung p82, his emphasis)

It is evident that Christians are gaining a new view of ecumenicity which excludes calling any fellow Christian a heretic. The Holy Spirit is not bound by human divisions created contrary to the expressed will of Jesus Christ.

MASONIC HERESY

This trend has not affected Christians in their readiness to condemn Freemasonry for heresy. There has been no reappraisal of the churches of their own shortcomings which may be the complement of the alleged heresy. But we are of course in a different field—Freemasonry does not claim to be a religion or a church, and indeed it states that the philosophy of its secular society is *per se* incomplete. Nevertheless, I believe that a case along this line can be made out, and we shall examine it in Part 4 of this book.

Those critics who have accused Freemasonry of heresy have done so on a very narrow front—a sort of proof-text approach. They appear to have got hold of a printed ritual book or an exposure, searched through it strenuously without absorbing any overall meaning, aiming only to find a phrase or sentence here or there which appears to support a particular heresy. Or they look through books published by enthusiastic masons, not necessarily Christians, and certainly not necessarily of the same denomination as the critic, to see if they can find evidence of heresy there. They then jumble all their findings together, shuffle the pack of heresies, and write a book to support their accusations.

The non-mason Christians who read their work see all these awful names—Gnosticism, Satanism, Pelagianism, and the like—and react with that horror of heresy which is inherent in their Christian upbringing. They are shocked that an organisation can exist with so much unchecked heresy in its midst. The Freemasons, who probably constitute the majority of the purchasers anyway, read the book sadly, shake their heads at the travesty of their organisation which is portrayed, and put the book on their bookshelves after a couple of chapters. Perhaps these natural reactions are wrong in both cases, as, rather than passive apathy, an active search for the truth is what is needed.

In the following chapters, the various heresies of which Freemasons stand accused are analysed, to see what the names of heresies actually mean, and whether the accusation really is justified. This will be seen in the light of the whole context of the official pronouncements of the Grand Lodges and the ritual used in the meetings of their private lodges. An attempt will likewise be made to analyse the degree of support which may be given to the view of individual authors, who are at perfect liberty within the Craft to be as heretical as they like—seen from a Christian viewpoint—without incurring any censure.

18
Deism

MASONIC ACQUIESCENCE

Many masons have acquiesced in the view that the Order is Deistic. This is particularly true in Germany, where there are two basic types of initiation: one derived from Scandinavia and called 'Christian' because Trinitarian belief is a necessary qualification for membership, and the other derived more directly from England and called 'Deistic'. I received a letter from a particularly knowledgeable German mason, making this very distinction. They serve as convenient labels for two of the parts of the United Grand Lodges of Germany.

But the German masons are not alone in this. Some years ago two papers were read in the Quatuor Coronati Lodge No 2076 in London on the subject of Deism, which attracted a substantial amount of comment at the meetings and in subsequent correspondence. Since this is almost exclusively about the meaning of the 'First Charge' in the *Constitutions* of 1723, it would seem necessary to reproduce the relevant parts of its wording first:

> A Mason ... will never be a stupid Atheist, nor an irreligious Libertine. But though in ancient Times Masons were charg'd in every Country to be of the Religion of that Country or Nation, whatever it was, yet 'tis now thought more expedient only to oblige them to that Religion in which all Men agree, leaving their particular Opinions to themselves ... by whatever Denominations or Persuasions they may be distinguish'd. . . . (p50)

It is worth again noting that the final form of the *Constitutions* was the work of a Presbyterian minister, the Revd Dr James Anderson, and the book is generally known as '*Anderson's* First Book of Constitutions'.

J. R. Clarke, the author of the first of the two papers read to the Quatuor Coronati Lodge said, 'The wording of the Charge makes it clear that henceforth Freemasonry was deistic in principle' (Clarke p50). He talks of '1723 having been set for the official permission to extend Freemasonry to deists' (ibid p54), and says, 'The transition from Christianity to Deism as the primary requirement of the Craft has been a gradual process' (ibid p55). Needless to say, these comments were attacked—in some cases vehemently—in the subsequent discussion and correspondence, and the outcome was a second paper by Lt-Col Eric Ward, putting the author's firm view in its title, 'Anderson's Freemasonry not Deistic'.

The idea that Freemasonry enshrines Deism is certainly held outside members of the Order. An article in the *Lafayette Sunday Visitor* which I have quoted more fully in the chapter on Naturalism contains the sentence, 'The religion of Freemasonry can best be described as Deism.' The Archbishop of York said in 1989 that it is the Deism of Freemasonry that does not attract him.

It would seem therefore that those who regard Deism as a heresy which is inherent in the Craft have a potentially good case, but that the views of those masons who disagree (myself included) should be examined carefully before a final condemnation is made.

SOME DEFINITIONS

It soon became clear in the debate in the Quatuor Coronati Lodge that different masons meant quite different things by Deism. In particular it was constantly confused with Theism, and it was suggested that this was because in the early part of the eighteenth century the two terms were not differentiated. They apparently have the same meaning, as *Deus* and *Theos* both mean God. But they have long been totally different in their application.

Theism is simply one of many general descriptions about belief in God. Thus monotheism means belief in one God, polytheism means belief in many gods, atheism implies belief in no god. Trinitarian Christians are accused by Unitarians of being tritheists, a term which Christians reject, saying that belief in the Trinity is not a denial of their monotheism. Theism as a term—simply meaning belief in God—can therefore be applied without any sense of being derogatory to Jews, Muslims and Christians.

It is a term which regular Freemasons happily accept, as is implied by present day official statements:

> The first condition of admission into, and membership of, the Order is a belief in the Supreme Being. This is essential and admits of no compromise. (*Aims and Relationships of the Craft*)

This is simple Theism. In distinct contrast, Deism is an established and specific system of belief. It signifies:

> The theory that God's contact with the world ceases with his having made it, in contrast with theism, which regards God as continuously involved in the world, although not identical with it.
>
> In the history of theology, deism has also denoted a movement, chiefly English and 18th century, of which the main concern was to subordinate historical revealed religions, such as Christianity, to the permanent canons of the natural religion whose principles were inherent in human reason. . . . Underlying the various forms of religious practice, it was felt there must be some basic unity of religious principle. (*New Caxton Encyclopedia* p1845)

It is important to appreciate that Deism involves specific beliefs, and it is just as dogmatic as Christianity.

The Jews saw Yahweh Sabaoth (the LORD of Hosts) as a king leading His army into battle. Jesus Christ gave us, above all else, the image of God as a

Father loving and caring for his children. The Deists created the image of the divine clockmaker, who, having made the universe and wound it up, left it to run down inexorably, with no further contact with the maker until the end of time. The only possible revelation of the maker is that inherent in the clock, and any attempt by the ticking universe to contact its maker through prayer is a delusion.

Here is an example of what the Deist John Toland wrote in 1698 about the Bible:

> To believe the Divinity of *Scripture*, or the Sense of any Passage thereof, without rational Proofs, and an evident Consistency, is a blamable Credulity, and a temararious Opinion, ordinarily grounded upon an ignorant and wilful Disposition; but more generally maintain'd out of a gainful Prospect. For we frequently embrace certain Doctrines not from any convincing Evidence in them, but because they serve our Designs better than the Truth. (quoted in Gay p59)

This is hardly the sort of person who would be able to accept the consistent masonic use of the Volume of the Sacred Law.

WERE MASONS EVER DEISTS?

If the Revd Dr James Anderson, author of the first *Constitutions* and minister of the Swallow Street Chapel in London was a Deist, then perhaps we would be justified in seeing the First Charge as an insidious attempt to draw all his fellow masons into that system of belief. It is just possible that in the Presbyterian Church of that time, ministers existed who had been convinced of the truth of Deism, yet still held to their ministry in the church.

Anderson's beliefs however were quite definite. There exist a book and printed versions of four of his sermons. The title of the book, published ten years after the *Constitutions*, is enough to convince: *Unity in Trinity and Trinity in Unity* with the subtitle, *Dissertation against Idolators, modern Jews and Anti-Trinitarians*.

In the first book of *Constitutions*, the 'historical' section contains the phrase, 'God's Messiah, the great Architect of the Church' (p24), clearly not the opinion of a Deist in any sense.

In the second edition of 1738, Anderson saw fit to elaborate on the First Charge, and included references to 'the 3 great Articles of Noah', implying a belief in a common revelation that had been made to all mankind. A literal belief in the truth of the account of Noah's flood, during which all mankind except he, his sons and their wives perished in the deluge, means that everything known to Noah is necessarily the inheritance of all mankind. The commandments known to Noah therefore constitute a universal revelation of God's will, from which no human is excused.

This type of amplification in the Antient Charges was a common practice, and to an extent the changes made in England and elsewhere reveal the trend of official thought in masonry in general. Anderson's reference to our Lord in the historical part was also expanded:

> In the 26th Year of [Augustus'] Empire, after the Conquest of *Egypt*, The WORD was made *FLESH*, or the LORD JESUS CHRIST IMMANUEL was born, the Great Architect or *Grand Master* of the Christian Church. . . .
> King HEROD died a few Months after the *Birth* of CHRIST, and, notwithstanding his vast Expence in *Masonry*, He died rich. . . .
> In his 20th Year after *Augustus*, or the *Vulgar A.D.* 34. The LORD JESUS CHRIST, aged 36 Years, and about 8 Months, was Crucified, without the Walls of *Jerusalem*, by *Pontius Pilate* the *Roman* Governor of *Judea*, and rose again from the Dead on the 3d Day, for the Justification of all that believe in him. (original emphasis)

Perhaps John Lawrence's wilful attempts to mislead his readers can be judged, after reading the quotations above, by his statement that 'The twelve chapters in [Anderson's] *Book of Constitutions*, trace the craft through many religious figures yet expressly exclude Christ' (p26). How could such a fundamental error not be intentional in someone who claims in his Introduction to have made a prolonged and detailed study of Freemasonry?

A convincing case could be made out that, far from having changed to a Deistic base, Anderson and many of his fellow masons considered that the Craft was still wholly Christian, even if tolerated by and tolerating liberal Jews. It is hardly a matter of surprise that the early versions of the First Charge translated into French were given as, 'On a juge plus a propos de n'exiger d'eux que la religion dont tout chretien convient' ('. . . that religion in which all Christians agree'). (Naudon p71)

It is also apparent that Deism was not being inculcated by the Freemasons of the period. The articles in *Ars Quatuor Coronatorum* to which I have referred give many instances of Christian terminology being retained throughout the eighteenth century. However, one official and specific refutation of Deism during the century was not noted, and is worth quoting at length:

> SECT. I. *Concerning* GOD *and* RELIGION.
>
> Whoever, from love of knowledge, interest, or curiosity, desires to be a *Mason*, is to know that, as his foundation and great cornerstone, he is to believe firmly in the ETERNAL GOD, and to pay that worship which is due to him, as the great *Architect* and *Governor* of the universe. A Mason is also obliged by his tenure, to observe the moral law, as a true *Noachida* (Sons of Noah; the first name for Freemasons); and if he rightly understands the royal art, he cannot tread the irreligious paths of the unhappy *libertine*, the *deist*, or stupid *atheist*; nor in any case, act against the great inward light of his own conscience.
> He will likewise shun the gross errors of bigotry and superstition; making a due use of his own reason, according to that liberty wherewith a *Mason is made free*. For although, in ancient times, the *Christian Masons* were CHARGED to comply with the *Christian* usages of the countries where they sojourned or worked (being found in all nations, and of divers religions or persuasions) yet it is now thought most expedient that the brethren in general should only be CHARGED to adhere to the *essentials* of religion in which all men agree; leaving each brother to his own private judgement, as to particular modes and forms. Whence it follows, that all Masons are to be *good men and true*—men of honour and honesty, by whatever religious names or persuasions distinguished; always following that golden precept of 'doing unto all men as (upon a change of conditions) they would that all men should do unto them.'

> Thus, since Masons, by their tenure, must agree in the three great articles of NOAH, Masonry becomes the center of union among the brethren, and the happy means of conciliation, and cementing into one body, those who might otherwise have remained at a perpetual distance; thereby strengthening and not weakening the divine obligations of RELIGION and LOVE! (*Ahiman Rezon* as approved by the Grand Lodge of Pennsylvania in 1781, quoted in Carpenter p6, original emphasis)

It is evident that, in so far as the masons of Pennsylvania reflected the opinions of their parent Grand Lodge across the Atlantic, the spirit of masonry in the late eighteenth century specifically *excluded* Deism as an acceptable philosophy for its candidates.

In my comments on a still later paper by the Revd N. Barker Cryer to the Quatuor Coronati Lodge, I stated:

> Perhaps wisely, the author has not embarked upon another excursion into the realms of Natural Religion, Deism and Theism and their various meanings in the eighteenth century and today. However . . . we have hopefully eliminated the accusation that, because of the First Charge, Freemasonry is inherently Deistic. What Anderson was doing was creating an environment in which he, a Presbyterian, could meet on an equal basis with a Deist, without either feeling inferior to a member of the established Church and, even more important, without denying the absolute importance of religion in a member's personal life. In so doing he gave birth to an Order in which each of us can meet not only with Jews and Deists, but also with Muslims, Hindus, Buddhists and so on, on a basis of perfect brotherhood. (Barker Cryer p67)

After further study, I withdraw one idea expressed in those remarks. I no longer think that a committed Deist would have been acceptable as a member of the Craft, then or now. His inability to accept any revelation or his belief in the superiority of natural religion would have made the use of any Volume of the Sacred Law repugnant to him, and his belief in the pointlessness of intercession would have made masonic prayer equally objectionable.

THE GREAT ARCHITECT

In order to ascertain whether present day regular masonry is Deistic, it is necessary to prove that in its official statements and in its ritual, it permits and encourages its members to believe in intercessory prayer, and in a revelation other than what can be discovered from a study of the clockwork mechanism of the universe.

Let me premise this consideration by stating that the expression 'Great Architect of the Universe' is not Deistic. It may be seen as containing the idea that God designed the universe as if it were a building, and then like an architect, left it to its inhabitants. However, the expression is nowhere developed in masonic ceremonial to suggest this. When a Christian says that God created the universe and then says no more, no one suggests that he is a Deist. There is no need for him to make a complete credal statement every time he opens his mouth.

This masonic name for God is nevertheless non-sectarian. United Grand Lodge stated:

> The names used for the Supreme Being enable men of different faiths to join in prayer (to God as each sees Him) without the terms of the prayer causing dissension among them. (*Religion and Freemasonry*)

To the Christian Freemason, the concept of the Great Architect is just as reminiscent of the eternal creative process in the church as it is of the universe:

> You are built upon the foundation laid by the apostles and prophets, and Christ Jesus himself is the foundation-stone. In him the whole building is bonded together and grows into a holy temple in the Lord. In him you too are being built with all the rest into a spiritual dwelling for God. (*Eph* 2:20–22)

As explained by Dr James Anderson, the 'Great Architect of the Church'—as well as of the Universe—is Jesus Christ. 'Through him all things came to be'. (*John* 1:3)

Radio Bible Class's *Our Daily Bread* for 7 December 1987 had the usual aphorism at the bottom of the page: it was 'The humble Carpenter of Nazareth was also the mighty Architect of the universe'. As a Christian mason, I take this thought with me into every lodge meeting.

INTERCESSION

Even the Deists admitted that a man might utter praise to his Creator, but he must not ask Him to interfere with the perfect clockwork mechanism which must necessarily run its course. Thus intercession and petition are excluded from Deistic prayer. How then do masons pray when they meet?

Every English lodge meeting begins with the prayer:

> The Lodge being duely [sic] formed, before I declare it open, let us invoke the assistance of the Great Architect of the Universe on all our undertakings. May our labours, thus begun in order, be continued in peace and closed in harmony. (Hannah p86)

The new member has the following said for him at his passing:

> We supplicate the continuance of Thine aid, O merciful Lord, on behalf of ourselves, and him who kneels before Thee; may the work, begun in Thy Name, be continued to Thy glory, and evermore be established in us by obedience to Thy precepts. (ibid p177)

Other prayers used in the various ceremonies are covered in other chapters, for example, that on Gnosticism. The two examples above should clearly indicate that the candidate for Freemasonry is immediately involved in a non-Deistic environment of intercessory prayer.

REVELATION

The *Basic Principles for Grand Lodge Recognition*, approved by the Grand Lodge of England in 1929, states:

> That a belief in the G.A.O.T.U. [Great Architect of the Universe] and His *revealed* will shall be an essential qualification for membership.
> That all initiates shall take their Obligation on or in full view of the open Volume of the Sacred Law, by which is meant the *revelation* from above which is binding on the conscience of the particular individual who is being initiated. (*Information for Guidance* p3, emphasis mine)

Not only does this state categorically that there is a revelation from above other than that of the creation, but it requires a book signifying this to be displayed to the initiate. *Aims and Relationships of the Craft*, approved in 1938, goes further and requires that, 'The Bible, referred to by Freemasons as the Volume of the Sacred Law, is always open in the Lodges' (ibid p1).

The candidate is introduced to the Volume during his initiation with these words of the Master of the lodge:

> Let me point out to your attention what we consider the three great though emblematical lights in Freemasonry; they are, the Volume of the Sacred Law, the Square and Compasses; the Sacred Writings are to govern our faith, the Square to regulate our actions, and the Compasses to keep us in due bounds with all mankind, particularly our brethren in Freemasonry. (Hannah p100)

Later, he is charged, 'As a Freemason, let me recommend to your most serious contemplation the Volume of the Sacred Law'. (ibid p107)

There can be no doubt that a belief in a supernatural revelation is as central to the Craft as it is incompatible with Deism. There can be no Deism in present day regular Freemasonry.

19
Relativism

THE CRITICISM

The issue of *L'Osservatore Romano* for 11 March 1985, in the midst of a long but unspecific exposition of the evil of Freemasonry, gave the reasons why the Congregation for the Doctrine of the Faith has condemned it:

> Freemasonry . . . does not impose any 'principles' in the sense of a philosophical or religious position which is binding upon all its members, but rather . . . it gathers together, beyond the limits of the various religions or world views men of good will on the basis of humanistic values comprehensible and acceptable to everyone. . . . Even if it is stated that relativism is not assumed as a dogma, nevertheless there is really proposed a relativistic symbolic concept and therefore the relativising value of such moral-ritual community, far from being eliminated, proves on the contrary to be decisive.

What is this Relativism? My dictionary defines it as, 'the doctrine that knowledge is of relations only' (*OED*). In the context of the Vatican pronouncement, it would seem to mean a belief that one religion can only be considered in relationship to another religion, and that none has any absolute value. To anyone who believes, as almost all Christians do, that one religion is superior to all others and is absolute, relativism is an unacceptable doctrine.

The Church of England Synod's Working Group complains that Freemasonry leads to Indifferentism. I take this to be very similar in meaning to Relativism, but perhaps taken to its extreme. In Indifferentism, it matters not what your religion is, as all are an approximation to the truth and equally valid. In Relativism, one religion may be considered superior to another, but this can only be decided by comparing the two, as there is no absolute standard.

As a Christian, I believe that only the faith taught and practice exemplified by the Son of God can be a complete revelation of the truth—at least in so far as man can understand it—and even the faith of the Old Testament is incomplete and partial. As the Letter to the Hebrews starts:

> When in former times God spoke to our forefathers, he spoke in fragmentary and varied fashion through the prophets. But in this the final age he has spoken to us in the Son whom he has made heir to the whole universe, and through whom he created all orders of existence. . . .

As a Christian, I can accept neither Relativism nor Indifferentism.

OTHER FAITHS

Throughout the ages, Christians have adopted one of three basic positions when confronted with other religions. They have sometimes rejected them absolutely as being of the devil; they have accepted them to varying degrees as being incomplete revelations of partial truth; or they have accepted them as being sufficiently comparable (if marginally inferior) for study and even for mutual growth in truth.

The position adopted has depended largely upon the degree to which the believer has considered the image of God, in which all mankind was created, to have been distorted by the Fall. Thus the believer who emphasises, 'the LORD saw that man had done much evil on earth and that his thoughts and inclinations were always evil' (*Gen* 6:5) will tend to see other religions as evil, whilst those who consider St James' teaching about 'our fellow-men who are made in God's likeness' (*James* 3:9) will hold a high view of other faiths.

When St Paul made his famous speech before the Court of the Areopagus in Athens he was prepared to start from their existing religion to lead them to Christ. He said:

> Men of Athens, I see that in everything that concerns religion you are uncommonly scrupulous. For as I was going round looking at the objects of worship, I noticed among other things an altar bearing the inscription 'To an Unknown God'. What you worship but do not know—this is what I now proclaim.
> The God who created the world and everything in it, and who is Lord of heaven and earth, does not live in shrines made by men. It is not because he lacks anything that he accepts service at men's hands, for he is the universal giver of life and breath and all else. He created every race of men. . . . They were to seek God, and, it might be, touch and find him; though indeed he is not far from each one of us, for in him we live and move, in him we exist; as some of your own poets have said, 'We are also his offspring. . . .' But now he commands mankind, all men everywhere, to repent. . . . (*Acts* 17:22–30)

St Paul was prepared to study pagan religious practice. He acknowledged that in man lies a natural instinct to seek God, and that God is willing to be found. He was prepared to quote a pagan writer with approbation. But the ultimate revelation lies in our Lord, approached with penitence.

MODERN EVANGELICAL VIEWS

A conservative evangelical view, albeit not specifically about other religions but about what he calls heresies and cults, is put by Sanders. He condemns them all as equally evil:

> The spate of subtle propaganda which comes over the air on the various radio networks, has strengthened the conviction that it is incumbent on Evangelicals,

> not only to indoctrinate their own members, but to raise a warning against the insidious encroachments of these Satanic counterfeits of true religion. Too long we have allowed the cults to win by default. . . .
>
> May the Lord Whose honour this book seeks to defend, bless it to the enlightenment of some and the emancipation of others of its readers. (Sanders pp5–6)

Other evangelicals have a different attitude. Demos Shakarian, founder of the Full Gospel Business Men's Fellowship International, believed that a devout Jew was directly inspired by God, in parallel with Shakarian himself, to help at a crucial time in his life (Sherill pp111–16). The Evangelical Alliance sees real virtue in other faiths. After emphasising the supremacy of Jesus Christ and the evils of syncretism, it is still prepared to say:

> *Other faiths are not devoid of truth.* Our acknowledgement of Christ as Lord of all does not oblige us to think of other faiths as entirely in error. Lesslie Newbigin well says, 'The Christian confession of Jesus as Lord does not involve any attempt to deny the reality of the work of God in the lives and thoughts and prayers of men and women outside the Christian church. On the contrary, it ought to involve an eager expectation of, a looking for, and a rejoicing in the evidence of that work. . . . If we love the light and walk in the light, we shall also rejoice in the light wherever we find it.' There is much in other faiths which is in harmony with the Christian faith, e.g. the sense of the tremendous majesty of God, so clearly proclaimed by Islam and also by the Bible, . . . and the love and adoration of a personal God, found in Sikhism and the *bhakti* movements in Hinduism. We can see here the Divine Word enlightening all men, the Word which is Jesus himself; for all truth is his truth. . . . But our glad acknowledgement of this fact must be qualified by our conviction of the supremacy of Christ. (Evangelical Alliance p22)

INCLUSIVISM

An article by Alan Race, the Director of Studies at Southwark Ordination Centre, and therefore presumably representing at least one acceptable Anglican belief, reviews the 'Catholic Theologian' Hans Kung's attitude as expressed in 1964:

> The traditional model of preparation-fulfilment, already familiar to Christians in their designation of Jesus as the Christ-completion of Jewish hopes, was also applied to the other world religions. These religious cultures were 'pre-Christian, directed towards Christ'. The theory was essentially an extension of an old view. So Justin Martyr, speaking of the universal activity of the *logos* in creation, could write that 'those who do the good which is enjoined on us have a share in God'. All that remained for Rahner, and Kung, to add was the modern awareness of humanity's rootedness in history and the realisation that a person's access to the divine must necessarily take a particular socially-conditioned form, and anonymous Christianity [the author terms this 'inclusiveness from above'] could take shape. . . . But inclusiveness did not mean that all religions were equally valid. The qualification 'from above' relates to the axiom that Christ is the author of salvation for both Christians and others. Thus the incarnation, as the *sine qua non* of the saving presence of God in all religious traditions, functions to link,

> inclusively, Christianity with other traditions. What is experienced openly in Christianity is known hiddenly in the non-Christian traditions. Christianity, as Kung said, was the extraordinary way of salvation, and the other religions represent the ordinary ways of salvation. (Race p179)

However, Race goes on to say:

> Anonymous Christianity has been criticized on many grounds, chief among them being the sense of Christian patronizing it suggests. By the time Kung wrote *On Being a Christian* eleven years later, he expressed his objection to it forcefully: 'This is a pseudo-solution which offers slight consolation. Is it possible to cure a society suffering from a decline in membership by declaring that even non-members are 'hidden members'? . . . So Kung turned to develop what I have termed inclusivism from below. Could other religious truth, he asked, 'be brought into its full realisation in Christianity: without a false, antithetic exclusiveness, but with a creative rethinking, resulting in a new, inclusive and simultaneous critical synthesis'? (ibid pp179–80)

He concludes:

> To hold Jesus as non-normative yet universally relevant is to hold together both the reality of God as glimpsed in Jesus . . . and the necessity to witness to this in dialogue, without assuming Jesus to be the final (decisive) truth about God before the dialogue begins. . . . The purpose of the dialogue will be to develop criteria whereby a world ecumenism, which respects differences and yet encourages the 'sharing of truth that leads to enrichment', can be pursued . . . This is the new direction Christianity is being called to in the age of inter-faith dialogue. (ibid p185)

I have to confess that I was left behind with 'early Kung', and am unable to progress with him to 'inclusivism from below'. However, Kung can hardly be said to represent the general view of his church; in 1979, but a few years after he published his most up-to-date ideas, he was deprived of his status of 'Catholic Theologian'. Although this was primarily for his views on infallibility published in that year, no doubt his earlier work also fell under a shadow. (Kung p75)

MODERN ROMAN CATHOLICISM

In terms of relativism, I find myself totally in sympathy with Father McBrien's summary of the present Roman Catholic position:

> Why are there many religions rather than one alone? Because God is available to all peoples, widely differentiated as they are by time, by geography, by culture. . . . Revelation is received according to the mode of the receiver, and the response to revelation (religion) is necessarily shaped by that mode of reception. If all religions have the same source, why are they not all equally valid? Because perceptions of revelation are subject to distortion, and so, too, are the modes of response. Common sense, though not a highly refined philosophy of human values, should tell us that a religion which worships through a communal meal is superior to one which practices human sacrifice.
> What is to be said, finally, of the 'validity' of the non-Christian religions?

> (1) They are 'valid' religions insofar as they implicitly share and practice the values inherent in the one true religion of Christianity (the theory of 'anonymous Christianity');
> (2) they are 'valid' religions but are also lesser, relative, and extraordinary means of salvation;
> (3) they are 'valid' in varying degrees, to be sure, but Christianity has much to learn from them and they from Christianity.
>
> Dialogue, therefore, must characterise our relationships with each other. The call to dialogue, however, does not require us to withhold criticism of other religions. The question of truth is always pertinent. . . .
>
> Present official teaching acknowledges the salvific value of nonChristian religions (without prejudice to the unique and central place of Christianity in the economy of salvation) and calls for religious liberty for all and dialogue among all. (McBrien pp279–81)

However, this benign view is difficult for even some of the most ecumenical of Protestants to accept. Bishop Stephen Neill wrote:

> For an understanding of the change that has taken place in the Christian attitude towards these non-Christian religions, nothing can be more strongly recommended than the study of the document of Vatican II called *Lumen Gentium* in the light of the Gentiles. The Fathers assembled in council go very far in their appreciation of these other forms of faith. . . .
>
> Some feel that the Council went too far, and did not adequately safeguard the uniqueness of the Christian revelation. The use of the word 'salvific', conveying salvation, in a number of Roman Catholic writings on these non-Christian faiths, seems to imply a view of salvation that would not be everywhere acceptable. But the generosity of the approach of Vatican II has called forth wide response both in the Christian and in the non-Christian worlds. . . . Wherever human beings in any way at all are seeking the unseen Father of our spirits, it is good that they should be approached with reverence and the desire to understand. (Neill pp10–11)

This long introduction has been necessary to establish what is current Christian thought about Relativism within the ranks of the church, before we can consider the accusation levelled at Freemasonry. We have the totally exclusive position of Sanders representing a significant fold of our Lord's scattered flock, the totally relativistic position adopted by Race within the teaching ministry of another fold, whilst between them the official teaching of a third encourages dialogue whilst still emphasising the primacy of Christianity.

INTOLERANCE REGARDING THE CRAFT

In view of this overwhelming evidence that intelligent Christians today believe in the 'salvific value' of other faiths, or at least that they are 'not devoid of truth', it is strange that in considering Freemasonry the Church of England's Working Group should say that masonic prayers are:

> an offence to the Christian belief that none come to God save through Jesus Christ our Lord; and for some it would appear to be a denial of the divinity of Christ. (p25)

Why is the toleration afforded to other faiths in our multi-faith society denied when masons practise toleration?

The Working Group was even intolerantly critical of its own leader and other Christians:

> These questions need to be considered in the context of contemporary interest in and experiment with inter-faith services. Only last year, the Bishop of Rome himself was in Assisi praying for peace alongside Buddhists, Sikhs, Jews, and medicine men of North American Indian tribes. When he listened attentively to their prayers was he joining in them or unobtrusively dissociating himself from what was going on? Was the whole affair, in which the Archbishop of Canterbury was himself prominent, just an exhibition of spiritual sleight-of-hand or ecclesiastical hypocrisy? (pp37–38)

No wonder a former Archbishop of York was prompted to criticise this aspect of the Working Party's Report when it was debated in the Synod. Whilst his speech was spiced with humour, he was deadly serious in intent when he said:

> There are of course questions to be asked about religious syncretism. I have already made the point in another context that there is much work to be done by Christians in discerning where the true meeting points between faiths lie. But I do deplore the suggestion in paragraph 112 of the report that one can make simplistic judgements about what is going on in an inter-faith service. [He then quoted the paragraph which I have given above.]
>
> I think that is unworthy of a Church document. We badly need good contexts in which people with different religious convictions can work together, without abandoning those convictions or without ignoring them.
>
> Freemasonry, as I understand it, has tried to provide such a context. We may not like its style. I would certainly myself have some difficulty worshipping an Architect, with or without Church Commissioners' approval (Laughter). And, despite what some people say, I am not greatly attracted by Deism. But I think the Craft needs to be commended for at least trying to solve an exceedingly difficult problem. (Quoted in a circular from United Grand Lodge dated 21 July 1987.)

Of course, and with the greatest of respect, the Archbishop was wrong in two matters: masons do not worship an Architect, but pray to God described as the Great Architect of the Universe; and masons are not Deists. But the contrast between the position taken by the Archbishop in company with most present day Christians, in relation to the outdated intolerance of the Working Group, is very evident.

THE MASONIC POSITION

Freemasonry was changing from a trade association to a private club throughout the seventeenth century, but its members were all, nominally at least, Christian. At the beginning of the next century, a new central organisation, called the Grand Lodge, was formed in London, initially to govern the lodges in the cities of London and Westminster, soon to spread throughout England, and to be copied elsewhere. An important religious change was introduced when the Minister of the Scottish Church in London, the Revd Dr James Anderson, undertook the task of revising the 'Old Charges' 'according to a new and better method'. To quote him once again:

> . . . he will never be a stupid Atheist, nor an irreligious Libertine. But though in ancient Times Masons were charg'd in every Country to be of the Religion of that Country or Nation, whatever it was, yet 'tis now thought more expedient only to oblige them to that Religion in which all Men agree, leaving their particular Opinions to themselves; that is, to be good Men and true, or Men of Honour and Honesty, by whatever Denominations or Persuasions they may be distinguish'd . . . (1723 *Constitutions* p50)

The meaning of this passage has been gone over again and again, but we must perforce repeat the exercise. Anderson does not say that all religions are of equal value, that masons have a duty to compare various religions to find the truth, or that they must give up any specific religion to become a member. He is merely stating the membership rules of a club. They are:

'stupid Atheists and irreligious Libertines are prohibited membership, ie, the members must have faith in God.
'good Men and true', etc, means that members should have adopted and practiced moral standards.
'leaving their particular Opinions to themselves' means that they must not use masonry to propagate their personal faith.
'by whatever Denominations or Persuasions they may be distinguish'd' implies that there is no restriction whatever on the content of their personal faith imposed by membership.

There is no Relativism or Indifferentism imposed or implied by this rule of membership. It is less relativistic, for example, than membership of the Royal Institution of Chartered Surveyors or a suburban golf club, where religion is totally irrelevant to membership, and anyone who mentioned it to any excessive degree would be considered odd and unlikely to progress within the committee. Indeed, it would be correct to conclude from Anderson's text that Freemasonry is specifically *opposed* to Relativism—it demands a religious faith of its members which is at a minimal level, and expects them to practise it at that level at the very least. It simply asks that, whilst in meetings, they do not discuss it.

Is this still the view today? This is what the Grand Lodge of England says on the subject:

> Freemasonry is far from indifferent to religion. Without interfering in religious practice, it expects each member to follow his own faith, and to place above all other duties his duty to God by whatever name He is known. Its moral teachings are acceptable to all religions. Freemasonry is thus a supporter of religion. (*Freemasonry and Religion*)

It is essential to add to this the important point that Freemasonry is incomplete in a religious sense:

> Freemasonry is not a religion, nor is it a substitute for religion. . . . Freemasonry lacks the basic elements of religion: it has no theological doctrine, and by

> forbidding religious discussion at its meetings will not allow a Masonic theological doctrine to develop. . . . (ibid)

Because of this it follows that a Christian Freemason does not belong to a 'moral-ritual community', as suggested by *L'Osservatore Romano*, apparently under the impression that such a thing can exist in a vacuum. He belongs to a total community which includes his family, his place of work, his recreations, and his church, all more important in practical terms than his masonic lodge.

RELATIVIST MASONS?

Further, a believer in absolute relativism as such might well not be admissible to regular Freemasonry:

> All Initiates shall take their Obligation on or in full view of the open Volume of the Sacred Law, by which is meant the revelation from above which is binding on the conscience of the particular being initiated. (*Basic Principles for Grand Lodge Recognition*).

If the relativist or indifferentist had no preferred Volume of the Sacred Law, he could not be initiated. If he believed all to be equal, how could he pick one as binding upon his conscience?

The critics of the Craft seem determined not to distinguish between the attitude of Freemasonry as an *organisation* to the several religions of which its membership is composed, and that of *individual* Freemasons to their own faith. For some reason they do not make the same mistake when considering the Royal Institute of British Architects or the local golf club. In such organisations it is quite acceptable for a staunch Baptist or Roman Catholic to participate fully, without the openness of the organisation to all religions (or to believers in none) compromising his faith.

It seems natural to the mason that his lodge membership is but an extension of the same concept—he enters as a staunch Baptist or Roman Catholic, and so he remains. Lodge membership does not involve relativism or indifferentism, real or implied.

A SCAPEGOAT

Does the quotation from *L'Osservatore Romano* with which this chapter begins and the view of the Working Group represent a search for a scapegoat for the infiltration of their churches by Relativism and indifferentism? Certainly it could be said that the 'inclusivism from below' of the Roman Catholic Hans Kung, supported by an Anglican theological teacher, might represent a typical true source for the problem.

I will conclude this chapter with a quotation from the end of a book written by another Anglican priest charged with the task of educating the parish priests and theologians of the future:

> When a fully Christian position has been reached, the difference between the Christian and the non-Christian is no longer a disagreement about beliefs but has simply become a difference in spirituality. In recent centuries the factual or descriptive elements of belief have been steadily whittled away, until nothing serious is left of them. When the purge is complete, we see that spirituality is everything. . . . Disagreements between different religions and philosophies of life are not disagreements about what is the case, but disagreements about ways of constitution human existence, disagreements about forms of consciousness and moral policies. (Cupitt p263)

> God simply *is* the ideal unity of all value, its claim upon us, and its creative power. . . . Just as you should not think of justice and truth as independent beings, so you should not think of God as an objectively existing superperson. That is a mythological and confusing way of thinking. The truth, we now see, is that the idea of God is imperative, not indicative. To speak of God is to speak about the moral and spiritual goals we ought to be aiming at, and about what we ought to become . . . The true God is not God as picturesque supernatural fact, but God as our religious ideal. (ibid p270)

It appears that the probable sources of present day relativism and indifferentism are to be found within the Church itself. Is Freemasonry being wrongly used as a scapegoat?

20
Naturalism

THE OBJECTION

On 5 December 1983, the official newspaper of the Vatican carried a brief boxed article titled 'Declaration on Masonic Associations'. This gave no reasons for its statement that 'membership . . . remains forbidden' but I have been sent an article from the *Lafayette Sunday Visitor* which speculates upon them. It suggests:

> The major reasons have always been the *religious naturalism* of the lodge and the nature of the Masonic oaths. The lodge offers a plan of salvation and a particular religious teaching which most Christians find deficient. The Great Architect of the Universe is not the Triune God of Christianity . . . The religion of Freemasonry can best be described as Deism. Because of the *religious naturalism* and the oaths, many Christian churches forbid or discourage Masonic membership. . . . (emphasis mine)

In this chapter, I propose to consider the issue of Naturalism, having expressed my views on the related concept of Deism and the completely different issue of masonic oaths in earlier chapters.

My dictionary defines Naturalism (omitting the irrelevancies of botany and nudity) as 'Moral or religious system on purely natural basis; philosophy excluding the supernatural or spiritual', and a 'naturalist' as 'one who believes in or studies naturalism' (*OED*). The meaning of the Vatican condemnation nevertheless presents some difficulties, as there is inherent in all Christian belief the idea that God is in some way revealed in nature.

The Protestant reformers tended to see in 'nature' something so defaced and deformed by the Fall that it must be rejected as valueless to establishing truth and reality. On the other hand, Roman Catholics have continued in the tradition of St Thomas Aquinas, and see nature and grace together as means of establishing truth and achieving salvation.

NATURE AND GRACE

The Roman position is defined in some detail by Father McBrien:

> The Catholic Tradition has always been insistent that the grace of God is given us, not to make up for something lacking to us as human persons, but as a free gift that elevates us to a new end and unmerited level of existence. Hypothetically, we

> could have a natural end. . . . The real, historical order, however, is already permeated with grace, so that a state of 'pure nature' does not exist. In other words, if grace supposes nature, nature in its own way supposes grace, insofar as the grace of Christ sustains us in our actual existence and orients us toward a supernatural end, the Kingdom of God. . . .
>
> Much of Protestantism, meantime, has so emphasised the depravity of the natural human condition apart from the grace of God that the natural order can only be viewed in thoroughly negative terms.
>
> 'Nature,' to be sure, is not a Biblical concept but arises from subsequent theological reflection on the New Testament's proclamation of 'the grace of God through Christ.' We infer who we are as creatures of God by reflecting on who we have become through Christ. . . .
>
> 'Nature' . . . is not purely positive because it is a concept one derives from reflecting on something higher, namely, grace. It is not a purely negative concept because it implies the rationality of the human person and the person's fundamental relationship to God, to other persons, to the world, and to its history apart from grace. (McBrien pp151–52)

Later, Father McBrien goes on to consider the relationship of creation to revelation:

> The doctrine of God, and the doctrine of revelation as well, presupposes a doctrine of creation. How could we know that there is a God unless God were somehow available to us? And how can God be available to us except through the created order? And how can we begin to express our understanding of God except in terms of our perceived relationship with God? That relationship is a creaturely relationship. God is the source and sustainer of our very being.
>
> Matter is not evil, as some of the earliest heresies insisted. It comes from the creative hand of God, in one and the same creative act by which God brought forth spiritual realities: 'God looked at everything he had made, and found it very good'. (*Genesis* 1:31) (ibid p225)

There are of course many Protestants who would object to the view of the early Reformers as much as does Father McBrien. The development of biology as a science owes much to the 'naturalists' of the seventeenth and eighteenth centuries, who by and large were Protestants or Anglicans, convinced that they were revealing the glory of God in their work. But, put in crude terms, the Roman Catholic position is half way between the rejection of nature of the Protestant reformers, and the viewpoint of the theological naturalists, that nature is the only vehicle of revelation.

Naturalism thus overlaps with Deism to a very great extent, and this chapter will only consider what Freemasonry has to say about nature, especially in comparison with the biblical record.

NATURE AS REGULARITY

The most important reference to nature apparent to every member of a lodge is the example set by the solar system for regular behaviour. In a masonic sense, 'regular' does not mean particularly 'at equal intervals of time', that being only one example of regularity. It means 'in accordance with the law'—Latin *regula*—and thus, as every lodge opens:

W.M.	Bro. Junior Warden, [what is] your place in the Lodge?
J.W.	In the South.
W.M.	Why are you placed there?
J.W.	To mark the sun at its meridian, to call the Brethren from labour to refreshment, and from refreshment to labour, that profit and pleasure may be the result.
W.M.	Bro. Senior Warden, your place in the Lodge?
S.W.	In the West.
W.M.	Why are you placed there?
S.W.	To mark the setting sun, to close the Lodge by command of the Worshipful Master, after having seen that every Brother has had his due.
W.M.	(*To Senior Warden or Immediate Past Master*) The Master's place?
S.W. or I.P.M.	In the East.
W.M.	Why is he placed there?
S.W. or I.P.M.	As the sun rises in the East to open and enliven the day, so the Worshipful Master is placed in the East to open the Lodge and employ and instruct Brethren in Freemasonry. (Hannah p86)

There is a similar simplified exchange between the Master and the Senior Warden only, when the lodge is closed.

After the initiation ceremony there is an optional lecture about the 'First Degree Tracing Board'—an oil painting with a symbolic depiction of a lodge on it—which contains similar teaching about the solar system:

> Our Lodges are situated due East and West, because all places of Divine Worship as well as regular, well formed, constituted Lodges [note that lodges are not places of Divine Worship] are or ought to be so situated: for which we assign three Masonic reasons: first, the Sun the Glory of the Lord, rises in the East and sets in the West. . . . (ibid p111)

At his installation, the Master is charged by one of his predecessors:

> As a pattern for imitation, consider that glorious luminary of Nature, which, rising in the E., regularly diffuses light and lustre to all within its circle; in like manner it is your peculiar province to communicate light and instruction to the Brethren of your Lodge. (*Emulation Ritual* pp201–02)

The concept expressed in these passages is in harmony with the purpose of the solar system expressed in the account of the creation:

> God said, 'Let there be lights in the vault of heaven to separate day from night, and let them serve as signs both for festivals and for seasons and years. Let them also shine in the vault of heaven to give light on earth.' So it was; God made the two great lights, the greater to govern the day and the lesser to govern the night; and with them he made the stars. God put these lights in the vault of heaven to give light on earth, to govern day and night, and to separate light from darkness; and God saw that it was good. (*Gen* 1:14–18)

Jeremiah is prepared to use the regularity of the solar system as an analogy for more personal matters:

> These are the words of the LORD: If the law that I made for the day and night could be annulled so that they fell out of their proper order, then my covenant with

> my servant David could be annulled . . ., so also could my covenant with the levitical priests who minister to me. (*Jer* 33:20–21)

The masonic picture of the solar system as an example for good order in personal relationships has not departed from the biblical format. It is teaching which any Christian can accept and use outside the lodge in his work, at home, and in his work for his church.

CREATION AS BEAUTY

Needless to say, it follows that masons see beauty in nature. In the First Degree Tracing Board lecture from which I have just quoted, the candidate is told:

> The Universe is the Temple of the Deity whom we serve; Wisdom, Strength and Beauty are about His Throne as pillars of his works, for His Wisdom is infinite, His Strength omnipotent, and Beauty shines forth in the whole of creation in symmetry and order. The Heavens He has stretched forth as a canopy; the earth He has planted as a footstool; He crowns His Temple with Stars as with a Diadem, and with His hand He extends the Power and Glory. The Sun and Moon are messengers of His will, and all His Law is concord. (Hannah p112)

Compare this to *Psalm* 19:

> The heavens tell out the glory of God,
> the vault of heaven reveals his handiwork.
> One day speaks to another,
> night with night shares its knowledge . . .
> In them a tent is fixed for the sun,
> who comes out like a bridegroom from his wedding canopy rejoicing like a strong man to run his race.
> His rising is at one end of the heavens,
> his circuit touches their farthest ends;
> and nothing is hidden from his heat.
>
> The law of the Lord is perfect and revives the soul.
> The Lord's instruction never fails,
> and makes the simple wise . . . (vv 1–2, 4–7)

The Psalmist goes straight from a consideration of the beauty of the solar system to a consideration of law and order. Again it can fairly be said that there is nothing in the masonic teaching about the beauty of nature which is incompatible with the biblical revelation.

THE MYSTERIES OF NATURE

It is not surprising that, in a ceremonial developed over a long period of time with anonymous contributions made by many masons, there are some inconsistencies. One of these lies in the teaching on the study of nature. Almost the last few words of an initiation ceremony encourage the new mason:

> to dedicate yourself to such pursuits as may at once enable you to be respectable in life, useful to mankind, and an ornament to the society of which you have this day become a member. To study more especially such of the liberal arts and sciences as may lie within the compass of your attainments, and without neglecting the duties of your ordinary station, to endeavour to make a daily advancement in Masonic knowledge. (Hannah p109)

Part of a new mason's duty is to study nature, in so far as the traditional designation of 'liberal arts and sciences' includes natural science.

In the next degree, there is a similar concept.

> You now stand to all external appearance a just and upright Fellow-Craft Freemason, and I give it to you in strong terms recommendation ever to continue and act as such; and, as I trust, the import of the former charge neither is, nor ever will be, effaced from your memory, I shall content myself with observing that, as in the previous Degree you made yourself acquainted with the principles of moral Truth and Virtue, you are now permitted to extend your researches into the hidden mysteries of Nature and Science. (Hannah p124)

Thus the masonic teaching is that true scientific knowledge should be based upon a strong moral foundation. There is nothing in the two quotations above about natural religion, and the 'mysteries of nature' are exactly the same thing as the 'laws of nature'—laws which have always existed in nature but which remain unknown until 'discovered' by scientists. If a study of the hidden mysteries of nature is heretical, then so is all scientific research. No Christian nowadays objects to this, except perhaps to the lack of any corresponding moral basis and commitment— something which the sequence of masonic teaching implies is essential.

PROOF OF IMMORTALITY

The charge towards the end of the third degree ceremony contains a third type of reference to nature which is perhaps harder for us to understand today. It says:

> . . . you may perceive that you stand on the very brink of the grave. . . . Let the emblems of mortality which lie before you lead you to contemplate on your inevitable destiny, and guide your reflection into that most interesting of all human studies, the knowledge of yourself . . .; continue to listen to the voice of Nature, which bears witness, that even in this perishable frame resides a vital and immortal principle, which inspires a holy confidence that the Lord of Life will enable us to trample the King of Terror beneath our feet, and lift our eyes to that bright Morning Star, whose rising brings peace and salvation to the faithful and obedient of the human race. (Hannah p140)

To the Christian mason, this passage refers to our ultimate participation in the victory of our Lord. The 'bright Morning Star' is He referred to in *Rev* 22:16, 'I, Jesus . . ., am the scion and offspring of David, the bright star of dawn'. But what does this have to do with the 'voice of Nature'?

It seems to me that the compiler of this passage was seeing nature in the sense that St Augustine saw it when he said, 'Thou hast created us for thyself, and our heart cannot be quieted till it may find repose in thee.' (*Confessions* 1:1). If man has 'knowledge of himself' he will find in his own heart a natural revelation of immortality and an urge to seek salvation.

St Augustine was not without a Biblical warrant for his opinion. St Paul wrote:

> The created universe waits with eager expectation for God's sons to be revealed. It was made the victim of frustration . . . yet always there was hope, because the universe itself is to be freed from the shackles of mortality and enter upon the liberty and splendour of the children of God. Up to the present, we know, the whole created universe groans in all its parts as if in the pangs of childbirth. (*Rom* 8:19–22)

The whole universe—and more especially the whole of mankind—has an inbuilt sense of incompleteness without God's ultimate victory over evil. If God created us in this way, it is *natural* to seek fulfilment in that victory. The whole saga of man's religious quest is testimony to the truth of St Paul's words.

I can envisage another possibility: the evidence that Jesus Christ rose from the dead is unmistakably there in the Bible. Some people who have studied the resurrection account to scoff at the minor contradictions between the four Gospels have been convicted and converted (such as Frank Morison, the author of *Who Moved the Stone*?). The evidence of a life after death is there, and it is 'natural' to believe in life beyond the grave.

Both of these interpretations are consistent with Christian conviction. The view of natural revelation put forward in the masonic ritual in the context of life after death is not contradictory to the Christian faith.

THE BIBLICAL POSITION

In the early part of this chapter, I dwelt at some length on the Roman Catholic position—that nature and grace are interrelated. As a final consideration of natural religion, let us look at the New Testament's view of man's natural inheritance.

St John the Evangelist saw that every man has Christ within him. He wrote:

> The Word then was with God at the beginning, and through him all things came to be. . . . All that came to be was *alive with his life*, and that life was the light of men. The light shines on in the dark, and the darkness has never mastered it. There appeared a man named John, sent from God . . .; he came to bear witness to the light. *The real light which enlightens every man* was even then coming into the world. (*John* 1:2–6, 8–9, emphasis mine)

The idea of a natural revelation—despite Father McBrien's view to the contrary—is present in the Bible. St Paul writes:

> It is not by hearing the law, but by doing it that men will be justified before God. When Gentiles who do not possess the law *carry out its precepts by the light of nature*, then, although they have no law, they are their own law, for they display the effect of the law inscribed on their hearts. Their conscience is called as

> witness, and their own thoughts argue the case on either side, against them *or even for them*, on the day when God judges the secrets of human hearts through Jesus Christ. So my gospel declares. (*Rom* 2:13–16, emphasis mine)

St Paul actually envisages that a person can achieve salvation through conformity to the law of nature. Of course, this text must be taken in the context of the whole Christian revelation, and a battery of arguments can be produced that it does not compromise the unique grace given through our Lord.

Freemasonry has quite a lot to say about faith, but this will be covered in the chapter on Pelagianism. Suffice it to say that the statements in masonic teaching about nature are wholly compatible with the revelation of Jesus Christ and the balance of Holy Writ. A Christian who enters a lodge is in no way required to substitute natural religion for his faith in our Lord.

21
Pelagianism

THE ENGLISH HERESY

Pelagius was an English monk who shook the church during his residence in Rome around AD 400, by maintaining that original sin was personal to Adam, and that until a child sinned he needed no salvation. Even so, a person could achieve his own salvation by his own effort, by living according to Divine law—in other words, he believed in justification by works. Some cynics have maintained that this has for ever remained an English heresy in the 'good-chap-ism' of the middle class. A decent bloke who behaves and is helpful to others will surely get to heaven!

This view is, however, not confined to the English. The American Bible study notes called *Our Daily Bread*, which we used in my family for our daily prayers (I must give my wife all the credit for this), contained a comment following the reading for 31 July 1986, as follows:

> *How do you get into Heaven?*
> This question will bring a variety of answers. A confusion of views is evident from this sampling of opinions gathered from the Radio Bible Class program *Sounds of the Times:*
> . . . 'Keep the Ten Commandments.' (San Francisco)
> 'How I live my life . . . being kind to people.' (Boston)
> 'Be a good person.' (Gainesville)
>
> [eight irrelevant answers omitted]

Pelagius was condemned by the whole church. But justification by faith alone is not a *Christian* doctrine, but merely a *Protestant* one. It was made by Martin Luther into the keystone of the Reformation. Freemasonry as an organisation cannot be expected to take sides in this matter, and it is to be hoped that masonic teaching ought to be compatible with the beliefs of all divisions of the Christian Church, as well as those of other religions. But since modern Roman Catholics see 'the differences between Trent and the Reformers as more verbal than substantive' (McBrien p42), I hope that this chapter will be considered relevant to all Christians.

THE CRITICISM

Some critics of Freemasonry have suggested that the Craft has inherited the Pelagian tradition. The Revd David Littlefair, Vicar of Charles with St Matthias of Plymouth, was prompted to write:

> There is no doubt in my mind from the hundreds of conversations I have had with Freemasons and their wives (and widows), that many believe salvation comes by good works done and upright lives well lived. The Christian faith however declares categorically that salvation is by faith alone, faith in Jesus Christ whose work in dying on a cross 'carried the can' for our sinfulness. His death and our response to His sacrifice on our behalf, procure our salvation. No amount of good works will put us right with God.
>
> Good works should come out of our response in love to a loving and gracious God who wants us to care for our fellow beings. . . . I do know what I'm talking about because I too was a Freemason.

Without being quite so explicit, James Dewar sees the same dilemma in Christians becoming masons:

> Freemasonry is . . . vulnerable to the criticism that it rests upon the false teaching that man can perfect himself by his own efforts. The lodge Master in his charge to the initiated candidate tells him: 'No institution can boast a more solid foundation than that on which Freemasonry rests, the practice of every moral and social virtue.' If Freemasonry is considered a religion, then Christians have a particularly appropriate Scriptural authority for its rejection:
>
> > The stone (Christ) which was set at nought of you builders is become the head of the corner. Neither is there salvation in any other . . .
>
> Article XI of the Church of England declares:
>
> > We are accounted righteous before God, only for the merit of our Lord and Saviour Jesus Christ by Faith, and not for our own works or deservings. Wherefore, that we are justified by faith only is a most wholesome Doctrine, and very full of comfort.
>
> The argument is enlarged, however, by Article XIII, which . . . states:
>
> Works done before the grace of Christ, and the Inspiration of the Holy Spirit, are not pleasant to God, forasmuch as they spring not of faith in Jesus Christ . . .; yea rather . . ., we doubt not but that they have the nature of sin.' The problem here is particularly relevant to those raised by Freemasonry. The phrase 'forasmuch as they spring not of faith in Jesus Christ', however, indicts the efforts of all good and conscientious non-Christians. It permits of no compromise and so has prompted many Christian doubts and reservations. The late Dr. William Temple described the Article as 'unfortunately, even calamitously expressed'. (Dewar pp182–84)

I have to confess that I am delighted to be in the good company of one of the greatest of Archbishops of Canterbury. I find sufficient justification for this in *Romans* 2:14, which is quoted in the chapter on Naturalism. However, this is not the place to discuss Christian doctrine, but to see whether a Christian must deny this doctrine if he becomes a mason.

The Working Group of Synod reached the same view as Littlefair and Dewar:

> The newly raised Master Mason is told:
>
> > Thus the working tools of a Master Mason teach us to bear in mind and act

> according to the laws of our Divine Creator, that, when we shall be summoned from this subluminary abode, we may ascend to the grand Lodge above, where the world's Great Architect lives and reigns for ever.

The question arises: Is the Master Mason being assured that if he lives a good and moral life he will inevitably 'ascend' to live with his Creator? Is this really what is meant? Comforting though this may be for some, it appears to have the marks of a familiar English heresy—Pelagianism—since the grace and forgiveness of God in Christ and the power of the Holy Spirit are being ignored. (p34)

THE BIBLICAL BALANCE

It is my belief that the balance between faith and works exhibited in masonic ritual is close to that of the New Testament. The New Testament has a multiplicity of passages which suggest the importance of one or the other, and masonic ritual also does this. If the balance is similar, then a Christian can interpret such references with the same presuppositions as he interprets the Bible.

The classic balance is between Saints Paul and James, who both refer to Abraham to give an apparently opposite answer. This is what St Paul says:

> If Abraham was justified by anything he had done, then he has a ground for pride. But he has no such ground before God; for what does Scripture say? 'Abraham put his faith in God, and that faith was counted to him as righteousness . . .' For it was not through the law that Abraham, or his posterity, was given the promise that the world should be his inheritance, but through the righteousness that came from faith. . . . The promise was made on the ground of faith, in order that it might be a matter of sheer grace, and that it might be valid for all Abraham's posterity, not only for those who hold by the law, but also for those that have the faith of Abraham. . . . . Those words were written, not for Abraham's sake alone, but for our sake too: it is to be 'counted' in the same way to us who have faith in the God who raised Jesus our Lord from the dead; for he was given up to death for our misdeeds, and raised to life to justify us. Therefore, now that we have been *justified through faith*, let us continue at peace with God . . . (*Rom* 4:13, 13, 16, 23–5:1, emphasis mine)

Now contrast this with St James:

> My brothers, what use is it for a man to say he has faith when he does nothing to show it? Can that faith save him? . . . if it does not lead to action, it is in itself a lifeless thing. But someone may object: 'Here is one who claims to have faith and another who points to his deeds.' To which I reply: 'Prove to me that this faith you speak of is real though not accompanied by deeds, and by my deeds I will prove to you my faith.' You have faith enough to believe that there is one God. Excellent! The devils have faith like that, and it makes them tremble. But can you not see, you quibbler, that faith divorced from deeds is barren? Was it not by his action, in offering his son Isaac upon the altar that our father Abraham was justified? Surely you can see that faith was at work in his actions, and that by these actions the integrity of his faith was fully proved. Here was fulfilment of the words of Scripture: 'Abraham put his faith in God and it was counted to him as righteousness'; and elsewhere he is called 'God's friend'. You see then that a man is *justified by deeds* and not by faith in itself (*Jam* 2:14, 17–24)

No wonder Martin Luther called the *Letter of James* 'an epistle of straw'! But by the time St Paul has dealt with the immorality of the young church in Corinth, one is left in no doubt that he and James are really looking at two sides of the same coin.

Particularly in the teaching of Jesus, there are many passages which would appear to support a belief that works are of the utmost importance. In *Luke* 18:18 onwards, we read of a 'man of the ruling class' who asked Jesus, 'Good Master, what must I do to win eternal life?' Jesus recited those of the ten commandments which are concerned with human relationships to him, and the man replied, 'I have kept all these since I was a boy'. Jesus replied that still one thing was lacking, but it was not faith. It was, 'sell everything that you have and distribute to the poor, and you will have riches in heaven; and come, follow me'.

Even more striking is the passage in *Matthew* 25:31–46:

> 'When the Son of Man comes in his glory and all his angels with him, he will sit in state on his throne, with all the nations gathered before him. He will separate men into two groups. . . .
> Then he will say to those on his left hand . . . 'when I was hungry you gave me nothing to eat, when thirsty nothing to drink; when I was a stranger you gave me no home. . . .' And they too will reply, 'Lord, when was it that we saw you hungry or thirsty or a stranger . . . and did nothing for you?' And he will answer, 'I tell you this: anything that you did not do for one of these, however humble, you did not do for met' And they will go away to eternal punishment, but the righteous will enter eternal life.

(I have cut this passage down tremendously, and it should be read in full length to be appreciated.)

I hope that in these brief quotations, I have given a due balance to the New Testament passages which talk in terms of justification by faith alone, by faith shown through works, or even—'tell it not in Gath'—by works alone. If, taken as a whole in both cases, the balance of Scripture is followed in masonic ritual, I suggest that the latter cannot be considered heretical.

MASONIC RITUAL

Masonic ritual is not concerned with salvation, but with membership and progressive education in Freemasonry. It is therefore not surprising that there are few references to either faith or works as a means of getting to Heaven. It contains prayers which marginally touch upon eternal existence, it refers to faith as a virtue, and the explanations of the 'working tools' appear to imply justification by works. Is this unbalanced in relation to the New Testament revelation?

It would seem that this issue ought to be settled once and for all by the question and answer which the candidate is required to give on his entry:

W.M.	In all cases of difficulty and danger, in whom do you put your trust?
Can.	In God.

W.M. Right glad am I to find your faith so well founded: relying on such sure support you may safely rise and follow your leader with a firm but humble confidence, for where the name of God is invoked we trust no danger can ensue. (Hannah p96)

Not only is there no suggestion that good works are a basis for any trust, let alone for salvation, but also the position of this statement at the very beginning of a mason's life means that all subsequent activity must be seen in its light. An abstract balance of probabilities that God exists is not enough: the object of belief is a Person in whom trust can securely be placed.

However, we are looking for an overall balance, and should search for any other relevant references. When the newly initiated mason is shown the Volume of the Sacred Law (the Bible for Christians) he is told, 'the Sacred Writings are to govern our *faith*' (Hannah p100). Whilst it could be argued that this is pure Protestantism, it cannot be said to be unChristian.

Then there is the lecture about the 'First Degree Tracing Board', which is optional but printed in all English 'Rituals' to be read privately or recited in lodge as time or inclination permit. This contains the statement as to the object of faith:

> The covering of a Freemason's Lodge is a celestial canopy of divers colours, even the Heavens. The way by which we, as Masons, hope to arrive there is by the assistance of a ladder, in Scripture called Jacob's ladder. It is composed of many staves or rounds, which point as many moral virtues, but three principal ones, which are Faith, Hope, and Charity: Faith in the Great Architect of the Universe, Hope in Salvation, and to be in Charity with all men. It reaches to the Heavens and rests on the Volume of the Sacred Law, because, by the doctrines contained in that Holy Book, we are taught to believe in the dispensations of Divine Providence, which belief strengthens our Faith, and enables us to ascend the first step; this Faith naturally creates in us a Hope of becoming partakers of the blessed promises therein recorded, which Hope enables us to ascend the second step; but the third and last, being Charity, comprehends the whole, and the mason who is possessed of this virtue in its most ample sense may justly be deemed to have reached the summit of his profession. (ibid p112)

The object of this faith is 'the Great Architect of the Universe'. Dewar would say, along with many critics, that this 'is not the Triune God of the Christian religion, but one left deliberately ill defined enough to be embraced by men of differing creeds' (p181). This is a contradiction in itself—if He is 'embraced' by a Christian, the Great Architect of the Universe is the Holy Trinity.

This teaching as to the relative value of faith, hope and charity is taken from the famous passage of St Paul (1 *Cor* 13). Charity has, however, been downgraded in common usage to mean giving away money to the needy, and masons have proved to be no exception to this. It might justly be suggested that 'charity' means good works to the average mason. During the ceremony, the initiate has been introduced to this subject twice. First, the 'Charity Charge':

> I shall immediately proceed to put your principles, in some measure, to the test, by calling upon you to exercise that virtue which may justly be denominated the

> distinguishing characteristic of a Freemason's heart—I mean charity. I need not here dilate on its excellences; no doubt it has often been felt and practised by you. Suffice it to say, it has the approbation of Heaven and earth, and like its sister mercy, blesses him who gives as well as him who receives. ... Whatever therefore you feel disposed to give, you will deposit with the Junior Deacon; it will be thankfully received and faithfully applied. . . .
> Should you at any future period meet a Brother in distressed circumstances, who might solicit your assistance, you will . . . cheerfully embrace the opportunity of practising that virtue you have professed to admire. (Hannah p106)

Immediately afterwards, in the 'working tools', the idea of works is extended beyond mere giving of money into service:

> The twenty-four inch gauge represents the twenty four hours of the day, part to be spent . . . in serving a friend or Brother in time of need, without detriment to ourselves or our connections.

Whilst these passages emphasise the importance of good works, they certainly do not imply that they are a means of justification. However, in the second degree there is no mention of faith, but the presentation of the working tools contains:

> The Square teaches morality, the Level equality, and the Plumb-Rule justness and uprightness of life and actions. Thus by square conduct, level steps, and upright intentions we hope to ascend to those immortal mansions whence all goodness emanates. (*ibid* p124)

The Christian mason, confronted with this, should remember that the second degree is built upon the first with its teaching, however elementary, about faith. He has just been told that 'the import of the former charge neither is, nor ever will be, effaced from your memory'. All must be understood together.

The reference to 'mansions' is no doubt based upon Jesus' description of His Father's house in the Authorised Version of *John* 14:1.

THIRD DEGREE

The third degree ceremony commences with a prayer for the candidate, which includes the words:

> Almighty and Eternal God, Architect and Ruler of the Universe . . . endue [the candidate] with such fortitude that in the hour of trial he fail not, but passing safely under Thy protection through the valley of the shadow of death, he may finally rise from the tomb of transgression to shine as the stars for ever and ever. (*ibid* p132)

Lawrence says that 'this prayer clearly sets out the aim of the degree' which is 'to withstand some hitherto undisclosed time of trial and rise through this into eternity' (p86). Let us see if this is true.

In the ceremony which follows there is a point at which the candidate is physically 'raised'. It is suggested to him that he represents the hero of the degree, Hiram Abif, being disinterred after his murder, so as to be buried in a suitable place for the master craftsman of King Solomon's Temple. At no time is it suggested that he represents anything different from this, and certainly there is no 'resurrection'. He is reminded that, as he has symbolised a physical death in the ceremony, he will himself eventually suffer actual death, and must prepare himself for it. This he will no doubt do within the context of his own religious faith.

The prayer is that the candidate will find salvation. But the concept of salvation being achieved merely by passing through a masonic ceremony is totally and absolutely lacking. The prayer is biblically based, this time on *Psalm 23*. There is also a hint of the seven promises 'to he that overcometh' in the Book of *Revelation*. There is a clear implication in the prayer that faith is present, otherwise how could the candidate receive the protection prayed for. Death as 'the hour of trial' is hardly an 'undisclosed' matter; to most people it is too lightly considered, and the ceremony confronts each Master Mason with it as the ultimate issue that must be faced by all men.

Lawrence, as is so frequently the case with anti-masonic writers, has created his own symbolism and meaning for a masonic ceremony, and because he does not like the result, condemns Freemasonry. If his interpretation were true, I would also condemn it.

Later in the ceremony the candidate's attention is drawn to a 'retrospect' of the two earlier ceremonies. For the first degree it relates works to faith in a definite but non-doctrinal way:

> It instructed you in the active principles of universal beneficence and charity, to seek the solace of your own distress by extending relief and consolation to your fellow-creatures in the hour of their affliction. Above all, it taught you to bend with humility and resignation to the will of the Great Architect of the Universe; to dedicate your heart, thus purified from every baneful and malignant passion, fitted only for the reception of truth and wisdom, to His glory and to the welfare of your fellow-mortals. (ibid p137)

Note, however, that neither relief and consolation nor a dedicated heart are seen as a means to justification.

Towards the end, there remains what is perhaps a relic of the days when all masons were Christians:

> . . . a holy confidence that the Lord of Life will enable us to trample the King of Terror beneath our feet, and lift our eyes to that bright Morning Star, whose rising brings peace and salvation to the faithful and obedient of the human race. (ibid p140)

Note that 'peace and salvation' comes to the 'faithful and obedient', again a balance of faith and works. The 'bright Morning Star' to a Christian is of course Jesus Christ—'I Jesus . . . am . . . the bright and morning star' (*Rev* 22:16 AV). However, there is no reason why a brother who holds another faith should not interpret these words in another way.

Neither this last passage nor the opening prayer in the third degree offers a means of justification. And it is not wrong for a Christian to pray for the eternal life of any person of any religion, nor to express the hope that he may attain it.

THE ROYAL ARCH

It would seem logical to extend this search for Pelagianism into the Royal Arch degree, as 'it is the Master Mason's completed' (ibid p172). Hence if the third degree offers hints of good works as a means to enter a future life, the Royal Arch should confirm it.

At an early part of the 'exaltation' ceremony, a short catechism reminiscent of that of the initiate takes place:

Z.	Bro. A.B., in all cases of difficulty and danger, in whom do you put your trust?
Can.	In the True and Living God Most High.
Z.	Glad are we to find your *faith* continued on so firm a basis. You rise [sic] and follow your conductor. (ibid p160).

The basis from which all subsequent teaching in the Royal Arch must be judged is thus, like the Craft, a statement of *faith*. However, the ceremony itself contains no reference that might suggest a way of salvation.

The second of the three lectures given at the end of the ceremony contains a very sombre equivalent of the 'working tools' of the lodge:

> The stroke of the Pick reminds of the sound of the last trumpet, when the ground shall be shaken, loosened, and the graves deliver up their dead; the Crow being an emblem of uprightness, points to the erect manner in which the body shall arise on that awful day to meet its tremendous though merciful Judge; while the manner in which the body is laid in the grave is fully depicted by the work of the Shovel, and we with humble but holy confidence hope that when these earthly remains have been properly disposed of, the spirit will arise to immortal life and everlasting bliss. (ibid p177)

There is nothing Pelagian here. The Christian may suggest that the bodily resurrection indicated by the first two tools is incompatible with the immortality of the human spirit implied in the third. The immortal soul is pagan Greek belief; the Apostles' Creed says that Christians believe in 'the resurrection of the body'. Even so, Biblical evidence supports use of the word 'spirit' in the context of death. Jesus said, 'Father, into thy hands I commit my spirit' (*Luke* 23:46). St Stephen cried, 'Lord Jesus, receive my spirit' (*Acts* 7:59). The masonic wording merely expresses a hope for immortality, without any doctrinal view as to how it is to be achieved. (See also James Barr's chapter on 'Athens or Jerusalem?' in *Old and New in Interpretation*, especially p52.)

The third lecture contains a series of recognition signs and provides them with a totally speculative origin in events in the Old Testament. Whilst they may depict the presumed attitudes of mind of Adam and Moses, they clearly have no basis as such in the biblical record. This is surely so obvious that it cannot be claimed that they are there to mislead the new 'exaltee', but to express Royal Arch teaching through those attitudes:

> The Royal Arch signs mark in a peculiar manner the relation we bear to the Most High as creatures offending against His mighty will and power, yet still the adopted children of His mercy. (ibid p178)

> [by one sign] we confess that we can do no manner of good or acceptable service except through Him from whom all good counsels and just works do proceed, and without whose Divine and special favour we must ever have remained unprofitable servants in His sight.
> [by another] we throw ourselves on the mercy of our Divine Creator and Judge looking forward with humble but holy confidence to His blessed promises, by which means alone we hope to pass through the ark of redemption into the mansions of eternal bliss and glory. . . . (ibid p179)

Again, there is no hint of Pelagianism in this teaching; quite the reverse. There is perhaps a means suggested by which a person may receive eternal life; not a masonic scheme of salvation, but a trust in God's promises. This presents no problem to the Christian mason, as the promises in which he trusts are those given by our Lord.

This chapter may fitly be summarised by the official statement on *Freemasonry and Religion* issued by the United Grand Lodge of England in 1985:

> Freemasonry lacks the basic elements of religion. . . . It does not claim to lead to salvation by works, by secret knowledge or by any other means.

It would appear that the Working Group's specific rejection of this clear statement (p34) was based on a wilful extraction from masonic ritual of those passages which emphasise the value of morality and charity, ignoring any that refer to faith. I could easily do the same thing with the Bible. The balance of teaching in the ritual in fact corresponds very well with that of the Christian Scriptures.

22
Gnosticism

HANNAH'S ACCUSATION

In his book, *Darkness Visible*, the Revd Walton Hannah accuses Freemasonry of Gnosticism, mentioning it three times. His first reference is confused, as it mixes up Gnosticism with justification by works, something which would surely be impossible to anyone who had read the *First Letter of John*. Hannah writes:

> Although Masonry also echoes Gnosticism in claiming to impart an esoteric light that is *sui generis,* it disdains (or at least ignores) any conception of God reaching down from Heaven to save and heal mankind. At best, 'Freemasonry is regarded as a human groping after that very thing which God himself has established in the Christian Church' . . . It is a religion of complete uprightness and respectability, of justification by works, but not of holiness or humility. (pp40–41)

The possibility of the Craft representing justification by works alone is covered in the previous chapter. His second reference is to a question as to what would happen if the Church of England denounced masonry, would the English Craft become as anti-clerical as the Grand Orient of France? He merely uses Gnosticism as a comparison, apparently comparing himself with Irenaeus! We shall see.

His third reference is to a prayer that he claims *used* to be included in the Rose Croix degree:

> The prayer in the Black Room until recently contained the phrase 'grant that we being solely occupied with the work of our redemption . . .' And the Resurrection in the Closing ceremonies is defined significantly as the 'hour of a Perfect Mason'. Our Lord's redemptive act is treated as a type and allegory of the experiences which a Mason must undergo in his quest for light, not as a unique and objective act of redemption wrought for him by God. This is, of course, a purely Gnostic conception. (p206)

It seems odd that present day masonry must stand accused because of a prayer that *used* to be used. Is it not to be permitted to amend itself intelligently in inessentials when confronted with criticism? And whilst I do not wish to go into the Rose Croix degree here, it seems to me that the ceremonial is capable of taking a completely different interpretation.

Every Christian must go through the experience of entering into a relationship with Jesus Christ, without depriving the crucifixion and resurrection of its uniqueness. Every Communion Service is a representation and symbolic re-enactment of the 'one oblation of Himself once offered'. St Paul identifies his own experiences with a participation in the suffering of our Lord, yet he does not stand accused of Gnosticism! (But see Bultmann p190 for his use of Gnostic language.)

DEFINITION

Gnosticism is the name given principally to a group of sects and writers of the late Roman-Hellenistic era, especially in Alexandria. The general doctrine of *gnosis*, Greek for 'knowledge', was a mixture of religious, ethical and cosmological notions derived from various Near Eastern sources. According to this view, God reveals the truth to certain groups of the elect and initiated, who by dint of preparation are able to receive it, and this, rather than works or faith, ensures their salvation.

Much was made of the dualism between God, who is perfect, and the material world which is said to have been created by a fallen divinity. A saviour who, though remaining detached and unincarnate, was identified with Christ, enlightens men who are blind prisoners in this world and so liberates them from ignorance, but only the elect. Thus the gnostic was above the moral laws ordained by an inferior demiurge. Hence alongside ascetic practices, there was amongst gnostics a freedom of conduct that attracted severe censure from orthodox Christians. ('Gnosticism' p2747)

Gnosticism was already making an initial appearance in the New Testament period. It seems highly probable that the *First Letter of John* was written against the sect (Brown p55ff). The first letter to Timothy concludes with:

> Timothy, keep safe that which has been entrusted to you. Turn a deaf ear to empty and worldly chatter, and the contraditions of so-called 'knowledge' [*gnosis*], for many who lay claim to it have shot far wide of the faith. Grace be with you all! (1 *Tim* 6:20–21)

Bearing in mind what I have said above, it is not difficult to understand why many people, both within and outside Freemasonry, have seen certain similarities. However, there is no identity of purpose, and thus to equate gnosis with masonry requires the critic to add to masonry a salvific object which it does not claim to possess.

VICOMTE DE PONCINS

A whole chapter of de Poncins' book on *Freemasonry and the Vatican* is devoted to 'Occult Theology and Gnosticism'. Presumably he regards the latter as a specific case of the former, and he starts off by asking if 'there can be such a thing as occult theology secretly animating Freemasonry'. He then goes on to quote certain modern rabbis who relate the Craft to the Kabbala, although it is not clear if they are masons or not. He continues with quotations from Freemasons of the 'mystical' type such as Stewart and

Wilmshurst who are only too anxious to state that only those Freemasons who are as mystical as they are truly understand what they are doing in their lodges.

There are quotes from Italian articles, whose authors claim the Revd J. T. Desaguliers, LLD, FRS, Grand Master of England for 1719, as a Rosicrucian:

> The Rose-Croix naturalist, John Theophilus Desaguliers, and James Anderson, a Protestant minister, and others, held a meeting on 24 June, 1717, in London, which was attended by the members of the four lodges which were active at that time.
> The aim of the reunion was to unite the Fraternity of the Free and Accepted Masons with the Alchemist Society of the Rose-Croix, so that the Rose-Croix could shelter their alchemistic research and their gnostic and rationalistic ideas behind the respectable facade of the Fraternity. . . .
> The Assembly unanimously accepted this union. Thus, on 24th June, 1717, out of this compromise, was born Freemasonry . . . the workshop of pure Gnosticism [which] took up a stand against the Christian Church, the workshop of falsified and corrupted Gnosticism. (de Poncins p126, quoting *La Massoneria* of 1945)

Anyone who has studied the evidence which exists about the foundation of the first Grand Lodge will know that this is pure rubbish—the motive was purely social. There is no evidence whatsoever that Desaguliers or Anderson were present; indeed it can be said with little short of certainty that they were not. It is unbelievable that a pair of clergy, whose Christian beliefs were well known then and now, could have hatched a plot to use Freemasonry 'against the Christian Church'.

It is evident that there are masons—at least the author of the article quoted—who believe such rubbish in defiance of the historical record, but to condemn the Craft for Gnosticism as a result would be equally mistaken. Unfortunately, this is exactly what Vicomte de Poncins does.

He digs through the works of irregular masons and those with a mystical bent, and whenever he discovers the word 'gnostic', he quotes their views as proof that Freemasonry is Gnostic:

> The alert Thinker can discern a supreme teaching which runs through all our symbolism. If we are able to grasp its most profound significance, our judgement will be illuminated with a radiant clarity of understanding. It is then that, possessing the Gnosis, we are able to claim that we know the meaning of the letter G. (ibid p128, quoting Wirth)

Compare this with the bald masonic ritual. In explanation of the building of King Solomon's Temple, the second degree mason is told:

> When our ancient Brethren were in the middle chamber of the Temple their attention was peculiarly drawn to certain Hebrew characters [the Tetragrammaton] which are here depicted by the letter G, denoting God, the Grand Geometrician of the Universe, to whom we must all submit, and whom we ought humbly to adore. (Hannah, op cit, p129)

I have come across no other teaching in the rituals of the English Orders of Freemasonry to which I belonged which modifies this simple explanation that G = God in any way. One Irish ceremony refers it to a Hebrew word in a marginal note in the Authorised Version of the Old Testament, long before *gnosis* had been thought of. Oswald Wirth's explanation is personal speculation.

But, whilst there is no possibility that early speculative masons were planning to attack the Christian Church, Freemasons do not see themselves as a substitute for the Inquisition or the witch hunters of Salem. Whether gnosis is a good thing or not is a subject about which no Grand Lodge can express an opinion. The admission qualifications for new masons would probably admit Gnostics almost as easily as Christians, Muslims and Jews, and if Gnosticism still has its adherents, we would expect a few of them to be found amongst Freemasons.

The evidence produced by Vicomte Leon de Poncins that some masons—especially irregular ones—have expressed belief in Gnosticism, is irrelevant to the question as to whether Freemasonry and Christianity are compatible.

RITUAL

There are two passages in masonic ritual which warrant examination, because they possibly imply Gnostic belief.

The prayer said following the entry of a candidate for initiation is as follows:

> Vouchsafe Thine aid, Almighty Father and Supreme Governor of the Universe, to our present convention, and grant that this Candidate for Freemasonry may so dedicate and devote his life to Thy service as to become a true and faithful Brother among us. Endue him with a competency of Thy Divine Wisdom, that, *assisted by the secrets of our Masonic art, he may the better be enabled to unfold the beauties of true Godliness*, to the honour and glory of Thy Holy Name. (Hannah p96, emphasis mine)

The words which I have emphasised give the impression that 'the secrets of our Masonic art' are adding something to a man's religion without which he could not achieve 'true Godliness'. That *would* almost be Gnosticism lacking only the element which requires knowledge of a secret to achieve salvation. But it does not actually say this. It prays that 'Masonic art' may be used by God to 'assist' the candidate to 'true Godliness'. It is not a way of salvation; it is not exclusive to masonry; but most important, its objective is worthy.

As an example, it would be possible for a Christian social worker to do his job for many years with enthusiasm in the context of a Church mission, and claim that caring for his fellow men over the years had brought him closer to 'true Godliness'. A similar Christian social worker doing the same thing in the context of the Welfare State would be justified in making a similar claim, even though what he did was wholly outside the official context of the Church. He would be genuinely able to say that his work had the better enabled him 'to unfold the beauties of true Godliness'. Examples could be multiplied at length of a Christian finding that something done in a non-Christian context had enabled him to progress in his faith.

I could go further in this and say that for a Christian, anything that does not produce the product of godliness is prohibited. George Herbert's hymn is relevant:

Teach me, my God and King,
  In all things Thee to see;
And what I do in anything,
  To do it as for Thee. (quoted in Mudditt p492)

If a Christian, in addition to his livelihood, cannot see his visit to the golf club or the pub, his holiday in Majorca and all the other multiple activities of his life in this context, he should not be doing them.

The prayer said for the new mason is a devout prayer to God that masonry may be such a context for him: that the ritual, the use of the Bible, the exhortation to higher moral standards, charitable giving, and all the other factors which go to make up the fabric of the Craft, may result in greater godliness.

The second extract from the ritual presents greater problems. It is in the 'Mystical Lecture' of the Royal Arch, which deals with the 'signs' of that Order. This is how Hannah exposes it:

> . . . we are taught by the Reverential or Hailing Sign to bend with humility and contrition beneath the chastening hand of the Almighty, and at the same time to engraft His laws on our hearts. . . . This sign was . . . adopted by Moses, who, when the Lord appeared to him in the burning bush, at the foot of Mount Horeb in the wilderness of Sinai, thus shaded his eyes from the brightness of the Divine presence, and placed his hand on his heart in token of obedience, and this sign was afterwards *accounted to him for righteousness*. (Hannah pp178–79, emphasis mine)

A comparison with *Exodus* 3:6 indicates that Moses did indeed cover his face, but whilst he was subsequently obedient, there is no indication of any gesture to signify it. However, the problem with the potential Gnosticism of this text is that it may be taken to imply that knowledge of the sign is a means of salvation.

In my chapter on Pelagianism, I stressed the differences between Sts Paul and James as to whether Abraham was justified by faith or by the demonstration of that faith in the form of works. The writer of the *Letter to the Hebrews* deals at somewhat greater length with Moses:

> By faith, when Moses was born, his parents hid him for three months, because they saw what a fine child he was; they were not afraid of the king's edict. By faith Moses, when he grew up, refused to be called the son of Pharaoh's daughter, preferring to suffer hardship with the people of God rather than enjoy the transient pleasures of sin. . . . By faith he left Egypt, and not because he feared the king's anger; for he was resolute, as one who saw the invisible God. By faith he celebrated the Passover. . . . By faith they crossed the Red Sea. . . . (*Heb* 11:23–29)

The lesson that we are to learn from the life of Moses is that he achieved practical results because he had faith in God. It was quite clearly the practical expression of faith and not the sign used by Royal Arch masons that 'was accounted to him for righteousness'.

Is it possible for a Christian mason to find an interpretation of this sign in a way that is consonant with New Testament teaching, and is not an exclusive piece of Gnostic knowledge?

The sign with its two parts is a symbol of the two most important aspects of Moses' faith. He had a revelation of God's nature expressed as the Tetragrammaton 'Yahweh' or 'Jehovah'. Man's proper reaction to God's awful righteousness is expressed in shading the eyes from the Divine presence. He was commissioned to go forth and act. Man's need to respond in obedience to God's commission is expressed in placing the other hand on the heart. Thus the whole sign, given by a Christian Freemason, reminds him of this double duty; he is to believe in a righteous God, and he is to show his belief in action. There is nothing specifically masonic in this, and every well lived Christian life is a demonstration of the Royal Arch sign.

This sign is thus to be interpreted in the spirit of intercession for the exaltee. Without any claim to exclusivity, by the practical application of its significance, its user may be better enabled 'to unfold the beauties of true Godliness'.

THE OFFICIAL POSITION

The official position is given in *Freemasonry and Religion*. In a section called 'Freemasonry compared with Religion', it gives three reasons why it is not a religion. The second clearly is intended to refer to the accusation that masonry is a modern form of Gnosticism:

> It does not claim to lead to salvation by works, by secret knowledge or by any other means. The secrets of Freemasonry are concerned with modes of recognition and not with salvation.

Any interpretation of masonic ritual or practice that departs from this principle is thus personal opinion, and cannot be regarded as inherent in the nature of the Craft.

ALTERNATIVE RITUAL

As an appendix to this chapter, I would like to mention that the ritual which is 'exposed' by Hannah is not that used throughout the Craft in Britain. As an example of a prayer in a Scottish working which has quite different wording, I quote:

> Vouchsafe Thy blessing, Almighty Father and Supreme Master of the Universe, upon our present labours. Grant that this Candidate now in our midst may be so enlightened by Thy Wisdom, so supported by Thy Strength, and so adorned with the Beauty of Thy Grace, that he may prove a true and faithful brother of our Craft, to the honour and glory of Thy Holy Name. (MacBride p24)

Irish ritual is uniform, as demonstrated by the Grand Lodge of Instruction in Dublin. There are, however, alternative prayers for the candidate, and one of them does not contain the allegedly gnostic phrase. Likewise, neither the official Scottish ritual for the Royal Arch nor the Irish contain the specific reference to Moses. Whilst it can be argued that a fully Christian explanation of the English passages is possible, the point must also be emphasised that they are not an *essential* part of Freemasonry.

23
Syncretism

THE ACCUSATION

An exchange took place on BBC Radio 4's phone-in programme *Tuesday Call* on 13 November 1984. Questions were being asked of the Grand Secretary of England, Commander Michael Higham, and the author of *The Brotherhood*, under the chairmanship of Miss Sue MacGregor:

Sue MacGregor.	Let me . . . move on to Mr Leslie Hopkins who's in Devizes in Wiltshire? Hello Mr Hopkins!
Leslie Hopkins:	Good morning, Miss MacGregor and gentlemen. How can Freemasonry and Christianity be compatible as Freemasonry is essentially syncretistic and Christianity is not?
SM:	Can you explain, Mr Hopkins, what you mean by syncretistic?
LH.	Well a mixture, well, syncretism is explicitly condemned throughout the Old Testament and implicitly in the New Testament, whereas the Freemasons' Great Architect of the Universe is a compound word derived from the Chaldean, Hebrew, Assyrian and Jewish sources.
SM:	Yes. I think Commander Higham that a lot of Christians are bothered by the fact that the Masons take an oath to the Great Architect of the Universe who appears to be above the Christian God and Jesus Christ for instance. What do you say to that?
Michael Higham:	First of all, there is no Masonic god. The oaths of Freemasonry are not taken to a god, the name of God is involved. Freemasons must believe in a Supreme Being, but that doesn't mean that Freemasonry is a substitute for religion. It is a way of pulling together men of any faith which requires the belief in a Supreme Being under one society.

The argument then got lost in the necessity for belief, the omission of the name of Christ from masonic ceremonial, and so on. The question of syncretism was never really tackled.

THE OLD TESTAMENT

The questioner suggested that 'syncretism is explicitly condemned throughout the Old Testament'. It must be admitted that at times this condemnation was almost neurotic. For example, on the return from the Babylonian Captivity, we read:

> Some of the leaders approached [Ezra] and said, 'The people of Israel . . . have not kept themselves apart from the foreign population and from the abominable practices of the Canaanites, the Hittites . . . and the Amorites. They have taken women of these nations as wives for themselves and their sons, so that the holy race has become mixed with the foreign population. . . .'
> While Ezra was praying and making confession, a very great crowd of Israelites assembled round him . . ., and they all wept bitterly. Then Shecaniah . . . said to Ezra . . . 'let us pledge ourselves to our God to dismiss all these women and their brood, according to your advice, my lord, and the advice of those who go in fear of the command of our God. . . .' (*Ezra* 9:1–2, 10:1–3)

On the other hand, it must also be acknowledged that during the Captivity, Ezekiel had a vision of a peaceful land that saw all those within the boundaries of Israel as living in harmony:

> These are the words of the Lord GOD: these are the boundary lines within which the twelve tribes of Israel shall enter into possession of the land. . . . The land which I swore with hand uplifted to give to your fathers you shall divide with each other. . . .
> You shall distribute this land among the tribes of Israel and assign it by lot as a patrimony for yourselves and for *any aliens living in your midst* who leave sons among you. They shall be treated as native born in Israel and with you shall receive a patrimony by lot among the tribes of Israel. . . . This is the very word of the Lord GOD. (*Eze* 47:13–14, 21–23, emphasis mine)

Far from there being a continual and absolute demand for purity, syncretism—symbolised by marriage—was always present in Israel as a tension. The whole book of Hosea is based upon this analogy.

Practical examples of syncretism can be seen in the worship of the Jews, as expressed in its setting. When Moses revealed the divine plan for the Tabernacle (*Ex* 25:10–27:21), and Bezaleel and Aholiab were chosen for its execution (*Ex* 31:1–11), the structure which they built showed a remarkable resemblance to the temple of the sun-god in Egypt from whence they had just escaped. After all, 'Moses was trained in all the wisdom of the Egyptians'. (*Acts* 7:22)

Equally so was the design for King Solomon's Temple. Here again the divine plan was revealed to King David (1 *Chr* 28:19) but the execution was put into the hands of a craftsman from Tyre, the servant of King Hiram, who had himself erected a magnificent but totally pagan temple in his capital city. The plan and detailed decoration of King Solomon's Temple, whilst still owing something to the antecedent Tabernacle, owed much to the design of the pagan shrine in Tyre.

Again, by the time of our Lord, Herod's Temple had been completed, owing much to its Jewish antecedents but influenced by Hellenistic and Roman architecture. Thus the setting in which Jesus worshipped was a syncretistic mixture of Egyptian, Tyrian, Greek and Roman architecture.

Of course, it can be argued that syncretism in architecture and theology are different things, but is not the culture of any age a single whole? The Tabernacle may have owed much to Egyptian architecture, but what of the scapegoat? I was brought up to believe in this as a beautiful symbol of our Lord, the sins of the people laid on his head, to be sent out to die in the wilderness. Now what does the evangelical *New Bible Dictionary* say about it?

> SCAPEGOAT. The word Azazel occurs only in the description of the Day of Atonement. There are four possible interpretations. . . . 4. It is the name of a demon haunting that region, derived from *'azaz* 'to be strong' and *'el* 'God'. Most scholars prefer the last possibility, as in v. 8 the name appears in parallelism with the name of the Lord. As a fallen angel, Azazel is often mentioned in *Enoch* (6:8 onwards), but probably the author got his conception from *Lv.* 16. The meaning of the ritual must be that sin in a symbolical way was removed from human society and brought to the region of death. (Douglas p1077)

Must this not be regarded as syncretism enshrined in Holy Writ?

I have referred to the Babylonian Captivity above. Biblical passages which reached their final form after the captivity have a more developed concept of the conflict of Good and Evil than those of earlier origin: the Jews had developed their theology by the experience of living with other faiths. (An example lies in the contrast between 2 *Sam* 24:1 and 1 *Chr* 21:1.) I would go so far as to suggest that, without some degree of syncretism, religion stultifies and dies.

NEW TESTAMENT

The New Testament deals with a much more limited period of time, and the evidence of syncretism is less. Leslie Hopkins admitted that it is only *implicitly* condemned, but I wonder if this is really true at all. Of course, passages exist like that with which St John the Elder concludes his First Letter: 'My children, be on the watch against false gods' (1 *John* 5:21), but this might be interpreted in the same way as 'You cannot serve God and Money' (*Matthew* 6:24), implying a need for Christians to get their priorities right.

Any reading of the New Testament reveals that the writers expressed themselves differently to different audiences. The *Letter to the Hebrews* is different from St Paul's *Letter to the Philippians*. *St Matthew's Gospel* is different from *St John's*. Father Raymond Brown distinguishes seven different church characteristics on the basis of the later New Testament writings (*The Churches* pp19–30). The most obvious contrast lies between those writings expressing themselves in Jewish thought concepts for Jews, and those using Greek terms so that gentiles could understand. As St Paul said:

> I am a free man and own no master; but I have made myself every man's servant, to win over as many as possible. To Jews I became like a Jew, to win Jews; as they are subject to the Law of Moses, I put myself under that law to win them, although I am not myself subject to it. To win Gentiles who are outside the Law, I made myself like one of them, although I am not in truth outside God's law, being under the law of Christ. To the weak I became weak to win the weak. Indeed, I have become everything in turn to men of every sort, so that in one way or another I

> may save some. All this I do for the sake of the Gospel, to bear my part in proclaiming it. (*1 Cor* 9:19–23)

The writer of *Acts* gives us a clue as to how far St Paul the Jew was prepared to go in presenting the gospel in Greek thought concepts in his speech at the Court of the Areopagus at Athens, in *Acts* 17:22–34.

It can be argued that St John the Evangelist was strongly influenced by the thought of the mystery religions which were prevalent in Ephesus, where he probably wrote his Gospel. Whilst not admitting their correctness, he used expressions that he had evolved from their beliefs. In due time, *St John's Gospel* became the book of the Gnostics, a heresy which all but overcame the orthodox Christian faith (Brown, *Epistles* pp49–86).

Rudolf Bultmann's book on *Primitive Christianity* has a substantial section on 'Primitive Christianity as a Syncretistic Phenomenon', and in his introduction, he writes:

> The cradle of primitive Christianity as an historical phenomenon was furnished by late Judaism, which in turn was a development from Hebrew religion as evidenced in the Old Testament and its writings. . . . At a very early stage in its development it came into contact with Hellenistic paganism, a contact which was to exercise a profound influence on Christianity itself. The paganism itself was equally complex. Not only did it preserve the heritage of Greek culture; it was also enlivened and enriched by the influx of religions from the Near East. From [its environment] it assimilated many traditions, while to other traditions it adopted a critical attitude. It also took up the same questions as were being asked in these other religions, and by attempting to answer them, it found itself *ipso facto* in competition with other missionary religions and philosophies of its time. Only by paying attention to what Christianity has in common with these other movements shall we be able to discern its difference from them. (Bultmann p11)

Syncretism is inevitable if a faith is to reach out to the situation of an outsider. It may be disguised by alternative jargon such as contextualisation, indigenisation or inculturation—even of theology (Meeking and Stott pp76–77)—but the real problem is not whether syncretism is permissible, but how far it is permissible for a Christian to go.

THE CHRISTIAN CENTURIES

The years since have seen many Christian solutions to this problem.

The conflict with Islam produced the Iconoclasts, and the compromise which was reached is evident in every Orthodox church to this day: there are no three dimensional images. The influence of this decorative idiom was felt as far west as the Adriatic coast. Yet no Venetian Roman Catholic would refuse to worship in St Mark's Cathedral because it is wholly Byzantine in its decoration and is therefore a product of syncretism with Islam.

Pagan Greek philosophy has had a profound effect on Christian theology:

> Plotonius (AD 205–270) was the founder of neo-platonism, a modified version of Plato's thought. He attempted to join ideas from Greek philosophy to the mysticism of Eastern monism. Neo-platonism deeply influenced both the medieval Christian mystics and the idealist philosophers of the eighteenth century

> European Enlightenment, which shaped much modern Western thinking. (Nicholls p32)

> Augustine . . . adapted from the neoplatonists their model of the mind's ascent to knowledge. He claimed that understanding of God, who can only be known through the incarnate Son, comes solely as God illumines the willing minds of those who have already taken Christian truth on trust. 'Believe in order to understand' was Augustine's principle here. (Packer p145)

> Thomas Aquinas was [scholasticism's] greatest, most creative and most influential figure. (A pope declared his theology to be eternally valid as recently as 1897!) . . . He took as his basis the orthodox theological heritage, particularly as spelt out by Augustine. But he sought to recast it in a different philosophical mould—that provided by the recently rediscovered writings of Aristotle. Aristotle's philosophy prompted Thomas to conceive God not as a static essence . . . but as a being whose essence is precisely his constant activity: the dynamism of the one who is the first cause of everything that is not himself.

> Aristotle's method was to examine everything in terms of causes. This prompted Thomas to develop 'natural theology', supposedly real and sure knowledge of God gained by reason alone. . . . He claimed that the findings of natural theology are the proper basis on which the truths of supernatural revelation (knowledge of the God of grace) should be received.
> Thomas differed from Augustine on the question of knowledge. . . . In this Augustine followed a modified form of Plato's thought, Thomas a modified form of Aristotle's. (ibid p146)

> When the Reformers revived (as they did) Augustine's Bible-based teaching on God's sovereignty in providence and grace, and the decisiveness of his predestination, the sense of God's aliveness and closeness gave their doctrine traumatic impact. (ibid p147)

The whole gamut of Christian teachers from the first century to the present day have seen pagan Greek philosophy as beneficial to the exposition of the gospel.

When, after the conversion of Constantine, the fourth century Christians were for the first time able to build places of worship, they chose the pagan courts of justice as their model. Gradually, over many centuries, gothic architecture evolved; not a 'style', but a response to a given set of building materials and a conviction as to how God should be worshipped. The Renaissance shattered this, but where did the new church architects turn for their inspiration? Two central shrines of Christendom—St Peter's Basilica in Rome and St Paul's Cathedral in London—are witness to a return to the inspiration of pagan Roman buildings, be it the Baths of Caracalla or the Pantheon. But Christians do not refuse to worship in these churches because they are syncretistic.

It would seem that there is a dividing line between two degrees of syncretism. The first degree is that in which the Christian church or the individual believer has found a broadening of faith through assimilation of part of the practice, technique or even philosophy which has evolved in another religion. This may well be disguised as 'inculturation' or 'indigenisation'. The second degree is where an attempt is made to combine different religions on an equal basis. There is clearly a parallel with relativism and indifferentism, to which a chapter has already been devoted, and in a sense, the two degrees of syncretism are the practical expression in religious form of theological relativism and indifferentism.

The classic example of syncretism in Christianity is the celebration of Christmas. The pagan mid-winter festival drew its inspiration from the cycle of seasons and the death and rebirth of the land. The birth of Jesus Christ occurred at roughly the same time, so the two celebrations fused and the distinction became blurred. Nearly everyone has a roast bird for Christmas dinner. Many eat Christmas pudding, drink until replete, decorate a Christmas tree, hang up holly and mistletoe, and burn a yule log in the fireplace, without realising that these are all pre-Christian rites (Cadogan). We may grumble about the loss of meaning of Christmas, but is the vicar to be treated as a heretic if he places a tree next to the communion table in his church and celebrates Jesus' birth in this way?

FREEMASONRY

In this context, is the Craft relatively more guilty of syncretism than the Christian Church?

In the quotation which heads this chapter, Leslie Hopkins attacked Freemasonry for this heresy because he claimed that the Royal Arch word is in four languages. The word itself is the subject of a separate chapter, so let us look at the question of languages. Does the fact that a word consists of three syllables in four languages make it syncretistic? Of course not! Many a theological text book contains words in Hebrew, Greek, Latin and even German, perhaps even within the same paragraph, and this does not make them synchretistic.

Is it possible for a person who believes in syncretism to be a Freemason? Yes, it must be, as the masons examine only if he believes in a Supreme Being and regards a particular book as his Volume of the Sacred Law. Provided that he has not taken his syncretism so far that he is unable to identify a Volume which he holds sacred, he fits the membership criteria. Thus a person who apparently believes in syncretism and sees it in his own interpretation of masonry is not expelled from the Order. Mr Hopkins later quotes an Anglican priest and mason as having written that Freemasonry is 'the heir and legitimate successor of the ancient mysteries' and that 'the masonic Hiram is Osiris, Persephone, Bacchus, Orpheus, Camus or Mithra . . . but quite legitimately he is also Christ'. The fact that one odd-ball clergyman believes such things in defiance of historical fact is no reason to assume that all masons do so—certainly I do not. But he was probably a much loved lodge member whose participation was most welcome.

The essential point that must be made is that he would not have any opportunity to develop such a theory in discussion with other members and then promulgate it within his lodge. Item 7 of the *Basic Principles for Grand Lodge recognition* says, 'The discussion of religion and politics within the Lodge shall be strictly prohibited'. On the other hand, neither Freemasonry as an organisation nor its members as such can condemn syncretism:

> If Freemasonry once deviated from its course by expressing an opinion on . . . theological questions, it would be called upon not only publicly to approve or denounce any movement which might arise in the future, but would also sow the seeds of discontent among its own members.' (*Aims and Relationships*)

The recently issued pamphlet on *Freemasonry and Religion* represents the continued official policy of the United Grand Lodge of England:

> Freemasonry . . . demands of its members a belief in a Supreme Being but provides no system of faith of its own [ie, it can neither support nor condemn syncretism]. Freemasonry is open to men of all religious faiths. The discussion of religion at its meetings is forbidden. [ie, syncretists might be admitted, but cannot discuss their views with other masons in lodge].
>
> There is no separate Masonic God; a Freemason's God remains the God of the religion he professes. Freemasons meet in common respect for the Supreme Being as He remains Supreme in their individual religions, and it is *no part of Freemasonry to attempt to join religions together* [ie, syncretism is specifically denied as an aim of the Grand Lodge]. *There is therefore no composite Masonic God* [ie, the product of syncretism does not exist].

Some Christian pastors see benefit in this relationship of faiths in a neutral environment. A Baptist minister, the Revd Roger L. Frederickson, writes:

> In the first place, I feel that Freemasonry tends to underline and highlight certain of the values and principles to which we are committed in the church. I do not look upon Masonry as a competitive matter whatsoever to our church work, but I view it as a supplementary movement. Both the church and Freemasonry are strengthened by each other.
>
> Secondly, I believe that the sense of universal brotherhood in Freemasonry is a very wholesome, meaningful fellowship for this day and age. Where there is so much divisiveness and suspicion in our world, we need the intermingling of men of many creeds and faiths and Freemasonry provides this. (quoted in Haggard p14)

The religious person who becomes a mason can therefore expect to meet with persons of several faiths within its confines, but can expect to be subject to no pressure whatsoever either to change his faith or to combine it with that of other members. He will indeed be encouraged—if he understands what is happening with any depth—to go out and improve the practice of his existing faith. A Christian is therefore better protected from the insidious influence of syncretism at a lodge meeting than he is in church.

24
Satanism

A YOUNG GIRL

A few years ago, my private secretary was a charming, convent-educated, Portuguese girl from Macau. She had worked for me for well over a year, and during that time, since I was running my own practice and was lodge Secretary, I had asked her to type more than a few letters on masonic matters as well as the minutes of my lodge meetings. So much for the 'secrecy' of the Craft! But I knew that, as a thoroughly competent secretary, whatever information she gleaned would go no further.

Eventually she plucked up courage to start a conversation which ran like this:

Mr Haffner, is it true that you worship the devil at your lodge meetings?
No, it's not true, Nina, we pray to God. Where did you get such an idea?
Well, the nuns told me that the Freemasons worship the devil. Do you pray to Jesus Christ?
It's true that we don't use the name of Jesus in our prayers, because we are not all necessarily Christians. We call . . .
Well, all I can say is that if you don't pray to our Lord but you do pray, you can only be praying to the devil.
Nina, let me assure you that we certainly do not pray to the devil.

Whether she was really satisfied with that exchange or not, I do not know, as she left the room, never mentioning the matter again, and she continued typing lodge minutes without further demur.

Freemasons should not be unduly upset by an accusation of Satanism. Christians have accused one another of being Satan's embodiment throughout the centuries. The classic example is the explanation of the number 666, the mark of the beast from *Revelation* 13:18:

> The number has . . . been used against the Catholic Church: *Italika Ekklesia* (Italian Church) of which Eliot remarks that 'the name of no other national church would give the same result!'; *He Letana Basileia* (the Latin Kingdom) of which Clark observes, he has tried out more than four hundred other kingdoms without again finding the results of 666 which fits Rome; *Papeiskos* which is taken to mean pope. Roman Catholics have tried the same game suggesting; *Loutherana*, that is Luther; *Saxoneios* which means Saxon, again representing Luther. (Ford pp216–17)

But if Freemasons do stand accused of this, far more than heresy is involved. It is a fundamental inversion of what we masons claim for ourselves that we 'unite with the *virtuous* of every persuasion in the firm and pleasing bond of fraternal *love*'. (Antient Charge I, present day version, my emphasis)

LEON DE PONCINS

An attempt at a more serious accusation of Satanism against masons than my secretary's occurs in Vicomte Leon de Poncins' *Freemasonry and the Vatican*. In common with other religious persons who emphasise the existence of the devil, his credibility suffers because of the difficulty modern sceptics have in taking such accusations seriously. But I have no wish to discuss the existence of a personal devil, an impersonal force of evil, or an anti-progressive instinct within mankind. I am merely concerned with the evidence the Vicomte has produced and its relevance to the regular masonry to which I belong.

It must be understood that the first chapter of his book is devoted to proving that regular and irregular masonry are indistinguishable. His evidence for this is largely that a well-known regular French mason, Alec Mellor, acknowledges his thanks to his personal sources in *La Franc-Maçonnerie a l'Heure du Choix* in a list which does not differentiate between members of the regular and irregular Craft. This is evidence of Mellor's courtesy, and has nothing to do with regularity. I do not expect to find separate acknowledgements of Roman Catholics, Anglicans, Protestants and non-Christians in books about the Christian faith, and neither would a reasonable person expect the equivalent of a masonic author.

Since the fundamental split between the two masonic factions occurred specifically over the elimination of references to God in the *Constitutions* and ritual of the latter, it is particularly on religious matters that this differentiation *must* be made. Evidence of a particular belief in masons of one type proves nothing about the other.

The fifth chapter of de Poncins' book is devoted to 'Satanism, Naturalism and Freemasonry'. The two are unrelated and I have devoted a separate chapter to Naturalism.

He again uses Mellor as a beginning for his argument, but in fact the passages which he quotes deal with the history of Satanism, and eventually with the accusation levelled against Freemasonry. It includes quotes of—literally—old wives' tales:

> According to a very reliable witness, the furniture of a lodge was being sold one day, and an old peasant woman came up, very curious, to the Master's chair, asking to see the slot where the Devil put his tail whenever he took his seat! (quoted in de Poncins p81)

This is of course no evidence at all!

De Poncins then moves on the encyclical *Humanus Genus* of 1884, where His Holiness Pope Leo XIII contrasts 'the Kingdom of God on earth, namely the true Church of Jesus Christ' with 'the kingdom of Satan, under whose sway and in whose power are all those who, following the baneful example of their leader and of our first parents, refuse to obey the divine and eternal law' (ibid p81) I can accept His Holiness' teaching as applying to a personal battle between good and evil in the personality of every man. As it stands, however, it sets off the Roman Catholic church as the sole expression of the Kingdom of God, whilst every other organisation of whatever kind from a suburban tennis club to the House of Commons is in the sway of the devil.

To quote this encyclical merely shows how out of date de Poncins is. I have quoted Father McBrien's summary of the present view of the Roman Church in my chapter on Relativism, but let me simply quote one sentence: 'Present official teaching acknowledges the salvific value of non-Christian religions (without prejudice to the unique and central place of Christianity in the economy of salvation) and calls for religious liberty for all and dialogue among them' (McBrien pp280–81). Since the time of Pope Leo XIII, his simplistic black and white has been replaced by multiple shades of grey.

De Poncins continues quoting Pope Leo XIII, as on a number of occasions he specifically related the concepts of Belial and war against God to Freemasonry. The most up-to-date quotation is from 1902, except for a secondary requotation dated 1959. As Roman Catholics no longer believe that everything outside the confines of their church is under the absolute control of Satan, these quotations have no relevance.

THE SERPENT IN IRREGULAR MASONRY

He then moves on to an extremely convoluted quotation dated 1877 from a mason of the Grand Orient of Belgium, Senator Goblet d'Alviella, who is himself quoting a French Deputy who may or may not have been a mason. The Deputy was speaking in favour of peoples' libraries, and was in turn quoting Genesis, apparently in favour of the serpent in the story of Adam and Eve. We are not given a reference for the quotation as a whole, nor are we able to know if the original mason favoured or disapproved of what he quoted, or whether it was meant seriously. One clear statement by the original mason would be strenuously denied by regular masonry: 'Masonic progress . . . takes a man obedient to God . . . and makes him a morally emancipated freethinker'. It was at this period that regular masonry—not surprisingly—broke off relations with the Grand Orient of Belgium, but there is still a great deal of difference between advocating freedom of thought and worshipping the devil.

It is very important to note that Grand Lodges do not keep indexes of proscribed books which masons are prohibited from reading. Neither do they conduct witch-hunts whenever a book about masonry is published and decide if the author ought to be allowed to remain a mason or not. It is true that there is a restriction on discussion of religion during meetings—and this extends to subsequent dinners and social events—as well as a restriction on publishing minutes and those parts of the ceremonial which are supposedly secret. But there is nothing to prevent a mason writing a book giving his own personal views about religion, politics and his ideas about masonry. Many of the masons who have written such books have a personal axe to grind. Such intensely personal views in no way represent the official view of the Craft, and cannot be used as a basis for deciding the nature of Freemasonry. These and all Vicomte de Poncins' subsequent quotations are of this nature: unofficial, personal opinion.

There are three pages of picked quotations from another irregular mason, Oswald Wirth of the Grand Lodge of France, who is clearly of the mystical school of masonic thinkers who have plagued both regular and irregular masonry with their nonsense about the ancient mysteries of Egypt and Greece over the years. In all three pages, the closest he gets to Satan is in one quote which refers to the 'Serpent' as held sacred by 'the initiated'—but he is referring to the ancient mysteries and not to Freemasonry! De Poncins gives a single quotation from Gustav Bord which talks of Freemasons as representing, 'human pride, the spirit of evil in revolt against God', and adds, 'Many similar texts can be found in French and European Masonry'.

I can add to the Vicomte's collection. Maria Desraimes was initiated in an all-male lodge, Les libres penseurs du Pecq—which was promptly expelled from the Grande Loge de France—and became the founder of the irregular 'Droit Humain' masonry. In 1881 at a Congress of Free Thought, she extended the admiration for the serpent expressed by a few irregular masons to the person of Eve:

> I repudiate Mary as a sign of renunciation, submission and nullity. My preferences go to Eve because she symbolises the desire to elevate, to instruct and to understand. . . . Families should cease to impose religious practices and instruction on children, so as to impair their liberty of conscience and endanger their intelligence, health and morality. (Brault p132)

This has nothing to do with regular masonry.

IRRELEVANT EVIDENCE

There follows a naive suggestion that all books written in English must be by regular masons, with a page and a half of quotations from T. M. Stewart's book *Symbolic Teaching: or Masonry and its Message*. These amount to a view that official Christianity, especially Roman Catholicism, has obscured the true teaching of Jesus Christ; the non-dogmatic nature of masonry is to be preferred. Nowhere is Satan mentioned. A few quotations from J. D. Buck's *The Genius of Freemasonry* show a similar viewpoint. De Poncins accuses W. L. Wilmshurst of Gnosticism, probably true, but without producing any quotations to prove his point.

It would be tedious to continue, and I will try to be brief in my summary. De Poncins quotes at length from a Frenchman who had repudiated Freemasonry, but the closest he gets to the devil is to suggest that the idea of 'man's being sufficient to himself' is 'truly diabolical egoism'. Then he quotes a German Freiherr and mason who believed in socialism (which I suspect de Poncins regards as closely allied to Satanism). Then there are six-and-a-half pages of quotations from Jewish authors who refer neither to Freemasonry nor to the devil, with the justification that, 'As we can see, these ideas closely resemble those advanced in the authoritative [sic] studies on the Nature of Freemasonry from which we have quoted above'. (ibid p96)

The Vicomte's final words in this chapter refer to Stalin, Ribbentrop, Adolf Hitler and Trotsky. There is no conclusion about Freemasonry or Satanism. The total irrelevance of his whole case is surely proved by the fact that the persons to whom he refers—more conceivably possessed by Satan than anyone else in recent world history—were the diehard enemies of the Craft.

ALBERT PIKE

A pamphlet giving seven reasons why a Christian cannot be a Freemason draws attention to a reference to 'Luciferan doctrine' in what it claims was an instruction to the Supreme Councils of the world emanating from Albert Pike. I have not been able to identify the text.

Albert Pike is regarded as a regular mason, and any accusation that he *officially* taught Luciferism is potentially damaging. He was the head of the Southern Jurisdiction of the United States of the Scottish Rite from 1859 to 1891. During that period, he revised its ceremonial and gave it much of its present character. Like many of the subsequent holders of that office, his position as Grand Commander of 'the Mother Supreme Council of the World' led to a degree of megalomania—fortunately not a characteristic of the present incumbent—but even 'the great' Albert Pike would not have presumed to instruct equal and sovereign bodies what to do. The text allegedly from his pen is therefore suspect.

I am not alone in being unable to identify the quotation. United Grand Lodge has concluded that it was invented by A. C. de la Rive for an anti-masonic tract *La femme et l'enfant dans la franc-maçonnerie universelle* of 1894, allegedly quoting a circular of 14 July 1889. The present day successor to Pike has confirmed that the Supreme Council has no record of such a circular (*Freemasonry and Christianity* pp47 and 49).

Albert Pike was a many sided character. An issue of the *New Age* magazine was devoted to his significant part in the development of the Southern Jurisdiction. I recently visited the headquarters of that body, and looked with great interest at the display devoted to him. In contrast, the brethren of the Prince Hall fraternity despise him for his racist statements in connection with his own devotion to Freemasonry.

When I visited the local headquarters of the Rite in Portland, Oregon, I was presented with a copy of his book, *Morals and Dogma*, first published in 1871. The 'greatness' of the book, which until about 1980 was issued to every new member, lies in its turgidity and woolliness. The latter militates against its containing any matter related to its title, which implies specific rules for action and belief. But if there were to be any reference by Pike to Satan which revealed his actual personal belief, it would certainly be found in *Morals and Dogma*.

There are indeed eleven indexed references to Satan, two to Lucifer, and four to the Devil in the 861 pages of the book, though they overlap. Most of these occur in a passage a few pages long, in which Pike follows a meandering path through the rubbish dump of extinct religions. He mentions Satan in connection with the Ophites (p563) and the Manicheans (pp 565–67). In a passage about light, he refers to Satan as 'the negation of God . . . the personification of Atheism or Idolatry'. He describes him as 'a force, created for good, but which may serve evil' (p102), presumably a reference to *Isaiah* 14:12–15. In a passage about Hermes, he relates Tuphon, 'the source of all that is evil in moral and physical order', to 'the Satan of Gnosticism' (p255). Very similarly, he suggests that the Babylonian god Ahriman, whose image was a dragon, was 'confounded by the Jews with Satan and the Serpent-Tempter'. (p258)

A more directly positive passage is:

> It is WISDOM that, in the Kabalistic Books of the Proverbs and Ecclesiasticus, is the Creative Agent of God. Elsewhere in the Hebrew writings it is 'Debar lahavah', the Word of God. It is by His uttered Word that God reveals Himself to us; not alone in the visible and invisible, but intellectual creation, but also in our convictions, consciousness, and instincts. Hence it is that certain beliefs are universal. The conviction of all men that *God is good* led to a belief in the Devil, the fallen Lucifer or Light-bearer, Shaitan the Adversary, Ahriman and Tuphon, as an attempt to explain the existence of Evil, and make it consistent with the Infinite Power, Wisdom and *Benevolence of God*. (p324, emphasis mine)

There are two more references. Pike refers to the return from the 'Persian' captivity and the development of a belief in 'the Devil, a bad and malicious spirit, ever opposing God', explaining that Satan means simply 'Adversary' (p661). Finally, he refers to the Devil in a factual manner in a brief overview of Dante's *Divine Comedy*. (p822)

I have reviewed all these passages to give the reader an idea of the real content of Albert Pike's thought. His extensive knowledge of comparative religion, if undisciplined, may have led him to seek a common ground in all religions, but Pike clearly did not advocate the worship or 'doctrine' of Satan.

ENCYCLOPAEDIAS

A more subtle view that Freemasonry has something to do with the occult and witchcraft is regrettably being promulgated by the publishers of modern specialist encyclopaedias. One such example is the series published weekly a few years ago, called *Man, Myth and Magic*. The series contained excellent articles on all the major religions, and one—equally excellent—on Freemasonry. But I cannot imagine the Anglican, Roman, Methodist or any other Church being thrilled at being classified along with myth and magic, even if the articles do not actually say that they have anything in common. Equally so, the implication that Freemasonry has something to do with anything other than 'man' (with perhaps a little 'myth' in its 'traditional histories') is obnoxious.

Another worse example is Crow's *A History of Magic, Witchcraft and Occultism*. This is not simply a matter of having a good article about the Craft mixed up with others in an encyclopaedia. The title of the book implies that everything mentioned between its covers is concerned with at least one of the three parts of the title. It is thus amazing to a regular mason to find that chapter 29 is called 'Some Magical Fraternities', and the summary of the chapter reads:

> Freemasonry Templar Revivals—Ancient and Accepted (Scottish) Rite—Order of the Palladium—The Illuminati–A Mysterious Character—Cagliostro's Egyptian Masonry—Ancient and Primitive Rite of Memphis and Mizraim—The Golden Dawn—Order of the Temple of the Orient—A Theurgic Rite—Martinism. (p8)

Imagine therefore the surprise with which the opening words of the chapter were read by me:

> *Freemasonry.* We do not intend to include the Masons in the magical fraternities. No one would consider Craft Masonry in England as working black magic! Nevertheless, masonry is throughout symbolic. It is well known that Masons wear symbolic jewels and aprons . . .

Field Marshals, Cardinals, Kings and Judges also wear clothing symbolic of their office! Why mention masonry in this chapter at all, if it is irrelevant to the subject of the book?

The chapter also deals with other deviant forms, such as the long defunct 'Strict Observance' and rites foisted on credulous members of the Craft by the charlatan Cagliostro. These accounts are each rather brief and superficial, and cannot be said to really deal with the question as to whether their rites have anything to do with either masonry or the occult.

It should be noted that this book was published by the Aquarian Press. This publisher has also started publishing serious books about Freemasonry. But it also publishes books on magic, occult, vegetarianism, ley lines, theosophy, and a whole gamut of subjects that can only be described as 'odd'. Its first serious masonic book was Alex Home's *King Solomon's Temple in the Masonic Tradition*, a very down to earth account of the masonic tradition as exemplified in masonic workings, of Biblical evidence, of archaeology, and so on. But an Anglican priest in my own former lodge, whilst impressed with the book, felt constrained to object in conversation to the advertising of books about the occult on its cover. When picking up a catalogue of the Aquarian Press, the impression given is that Freemasonry has a connection of some sort with all the other subjects. This is simply not the case.

Here again, it is important to distinguish between scholarly study of the lives and writings of masons who have dabbled in the occult, and a belief that this is what masonry is all about. Other serious books from the same publisher include Ellic Howe's *Magicians of the Golden Dawn,* John Hamill's introduction to *The Rosicrucian Seer,* R. A. Gilbert's to *The*

Magical Mason, and the like. Its most recent masonic book is John Hamill's *The Craft*, actually published by Crucible, 'an imprint of Aquarian Press'. The change of name for its new range of books is most welcome.

When looking for masonic books in Foyles, the visitor has to find them in a corner of a room labelled 'Occult'. Why does the management not catalogue them like most librarians, under 'Social Studies'?

This regrettable tendency is not confined to this side of the Atlantic. The best known American masonic suppliers, Macoys, has in its catalogue of books Manley P. Hall's *An Encyclopaedia of Masonic Hermetic, Quabbalistic and Rosicrucian Symbolical Philosophy: the Secret Teachings of all Ages*. This is advertised as containing 'information' on:

> Atlantis and the Gods of Antiquity; Life and Writings of Thom Hermes Trismegistus; Initiation of the Pyramid; the Virgin of the World; Sun, a Universal Deity; Zodiac and its Signs. . . .

None of this can have any possible connection with the masonry that I have experienced. When will the masonic suppliers stop trying to sell such junk to their brethren?

PSYCHIC CASES

The Working Group of the Church of England Synod received many letters in support of the Craft, but chose to publish only two letters. These were both from ex-masons who had found their membership to be psychically disturbing. The first of the two contained a clear implication of devil possession, or Satanism if you like:

> For a long time, even after my conversion, I defended masonry, and maintained that I was able to reconcile its philosophy and precepts—supposedly based on teaching morality and charity—with Christianity.
>
> But in His time, and in His own gentle way, the Holy Spirit began to show me how blind I had been, and how effectively the enemy [the Devil] can use his weapons of subtlety and rationality in the blinding process. It was to the point of having my eyes fully open, and my heart sufficiently convicted of the evils attaching to masonry and the powerful bondage it imposes. It was one of the hardest things I have ever had to do getting rid of my regalia, masonic literature and all the outward trappings of this evil craft. But this was not enough; the Holy Spirit showed that another step had to be taken in order to completely release me from the bondage I was in, and that was to approach a brother in Christ who would pray for my release. This he did, with the laying on of hands.
>
> What a beautiful sense of lightness and freedom I experienced when that oppression was lifted! (p55)

The second letter emphasises the normality of the patient except with respect to Freemasonry, which gave him 'obscene sexual images'.

These cases should not be taken lightly. But they are so far removed from the reality of ordinary experience that they have an anecdotal quality—no condemnation could rationally be based upon them. If the Craft was proving to be a form of bondage to these men, it was failing to provide in their cases what it was intended to provide, and every mason should wish them well in their 'liberation'.

Such psychic disturbance with 'obscene sexual images' has been the lot of the devout over the centuries. One need but read the life of St Anthony of Egypt to realise that there can be no logical identification of Freemasonry as its cause.

RONALD

John Lawrence gives a similar example of his friend Ronald, to whom he devotes a whole chapter. This does not say that Freemasonry is satanic, but the belief is implicit. I will summarise it.

Ronald was a PCC member, and was proposed for initiation by another member. He was a mason for sixteen years, and reached the office of Junior Warden. A couple of years before that, at a meeting to which he was invited by his vicar, Pat laid her hands on him and prayed in tongues, and he felt a tremor from head to foot. He spent the next six months reading the Bible in every spare moment. Over a year later he knelt in personal dedication after hearing the ministry of the Revd Peter Scothern. Despite the fact that his vicar had introduced him to this charismatic experience, he felt that the vicar was inadequate, and felt a need to change to another parish.

He found that he could not say that part of the Junior Warden's work in lodge which runs, 'No institution can boast a more solid foundation than that on which Freemasonry rests—the practice of every moral and social virtue'. The Holy Spirit said to him, 'You cannot say that. You have Jesus as your foundation'. Later, the Spirit said, 'Come out', so he resigned. As a symbolic act of exorcism, he burned his regalia, whilst Pat said, 'Praise the Lord—we have been praying for you about this—even though we did not know that you were a mason!' Later he gave several testimonies at Birmingham Cathedral about why he had resigned from the Craft.

He was guided back to his former church, yet nevertheless still found it dead. He went on a pilgrimage to the Holy Land, where Calvary became very real to him. He became the first President of the local chapter of the Full Gospel Business Men's Fellowship International, which became the mainstay of his Christian life. By now the cathedral seemed dead too. The Bishop did not respond as he would have liked to being sent a copy of *Christ, the Christian and Freemasonry*, and he presumed from this that many of the clergy were masons.

The Lord's guidance then led him to a church on a housing estate with 'a born-again Spirit-filled vicar'. But the congregation was Anglo-Catholic, and resisted the vicar's ministrations, fearing that 'they were losing their catholicity' (I cannot resist adding, God bless them!). The vicar left, and Ronald was led to *Isaiah* 52:11–12, and for this reason he and his wife are leaving the Church of England.

In this autobiography, Ronald was kind enough *not* to quote the words of those verses which he applies to the Anglican Church. But they should be referred to, as they say:

Away from Babylon; come out, come out,
  touch nothing unclean.
Come out from Babylon, keep yourselves pure,
  you who carry the vessels of the LORD.

But you shall not come out in urgent haste
  nor leave like fugitives;
for the LORD will march at your head,
  your rearguard will be Israel's God.

Ronald's case emphasises the problems that more than a few charismatics have. They are forever dissatisfied with the organisation of the visible church, forever seeking the excitement that they felt when they first prayed in tongues, forever believing that every emotion and urge that they have is the prompting of the Holy Spirit. Do not misunderstand me—I used to attend a chapter of the Full Gospel Business Men's Fellowship myself, and know and love many members. In most, the Holy Spirit teaches deep humility. In my younger years as a Christian I too found a need to search for fullness in worship. But I find Ronald unattractive in his feeling of superiority to the majority of Christians, and I wonder what John Lawrence is trying to tell us.

Ronald felt guided by the Holy Spirit to leave his parish church and go to the cathedral. He felt guided to leave Freemasonry. He felt guided back to his old parish church, and then to an Anglican church on a housing estate. Now he feels guided to leave the Church of England. Surely no absolute lesson can be learned from this—if the Holy Spirit can guide a person to three different Anglican churches, and then guide him out of them all, then it can at best be a personal guidance unrelated to the validity of the Church of England as a part of the Church Universal. The Holy Spirit does not make *Isaiah* 52 His guidance to the many charismatic Anglican priests like Colin Urquhart, or their congregations. So if this guidance to Ronald was purely personal, what about His guidance with respect to Freemasonry?

Of course, Ronald should have left it in the circumstances, but this proves nothing about the good or evil of the Craft.

MASONIC REALITY

My own knowledge of masonic ritual is of course incomplete, even within the jurisdictions of the British Isles. But it is as comprehensive as that of most masons, expanding into many 'higher' degrees and chivalric orders. I am unable to put forward any suggestion of any part of any working that could conceivably be interpreted as involving Satanism or devil worship of any sort.

The most recent accusation of this type occurs in Knight's *The Brotherhood*. In chapter 25, 'The Devil in Disguise', he suggests that the Royal Arch word contains a syllable which means Baal, the old Canaanite fertility god, and that Baal has been identified by some writers on demonology with the Satan. This particular accusation is examined in my chapter on Ba'al.

The only part of a masonic ceremonial which appears to see cosmic forces in conflict is in the third degree, and this is also referred to elsewhere in this book. According to one of the exposures, the candidate is told by the Master:

> . . . in this perishable frame resides a vital and immortal principle, which inspires a holy confidence that the Lord of Life will enable us to trample the King of Terror beneath our feet, and lift our eyes to that bright Morning Star, whose rising brings peace and salvation to the faithful and obedient of the human race. (Dewar p170)

It seems to me that the 'King of Terror' who we as masons hope to trample under our feet can only be the devil, at least to those who believe in a personal evil being. To those that do not, it must be a personification of the force of evil, or evolutionary hangovers in the human personality.

Although he was speaking personally, in a radio programme on 13 November 1984, the Grand Secretary, Commander Michael Higham, said very firmly in answer to a question as to whether an atheist or agnostic could belong to the Craft:

> Not if you don't believe in a Supreme Being. It doesn't match. The whole business requires a belief in a Supreme Being, and a Supreme Being [who] is a *benign* Supreme Being. There's *no question of devil worship* in Freemasonry. (*Tuesday Call*, my emphasis)

He reiterated this somewhat later in a talk at St Margaret Pattens' Church in London:

> To be admitted and to remain a Freemason, a man must believe in the Supreme Being (and . . . the God must be a *good* one). (Higham p31)

The reality is that there is no hint of Satanism in regular Freemasonry.

25
Ba‘al

THE EFFECT OF RITUAL CHANGES ON THIS BOOK

This chapter is about a word (or three-part compound word) that was conveyed to candidates in the English Royal Arch ritual until February 1989, which had proved to be particularly offensive to critics of masonry. It was exposed by Hannah et al as ‘Jah-bul-on’, and it has been alleged that the middle syllable refers to the pagan god Ba‘al. The word was taken out of the ceremony by the democratic vote of Supreme Grand Chapter not long after the first edition of this book was published. This is the only chapter of this book which by now, preparing for a second edition, is thoroughly out of date.

The issue naturally arises as to whether the chapter should be wholly rewritten or not. The answer is a compromise. Much of the previous text dealing with the meaning of Ba‘al and its overt and disguised use in the Bible has been retained but shortened. Most of the text dealing with how objections arose has also been kept intact. However, the reasoning behind making the changes that Grand Chapter adopted are set out so far as they are known to me – the recommendation was the product of the Royal Arch Ritual Working Party set up in 1986, of which I was not a member. The change was a product of questioning by masonic scholars whose capability in Hebrew was notable, coupled with a sensitivity to the views of the Methodist Church and the Church of England. These questions had arisen before in places like the Quatuor Coronati Lodge, but had been brushed aside by conservatism until the churches brought pressure to bear. What is wholly regrettable is that those churches that used the alleged reference to Ba‘al as a cudgel have not reconsidered the issue of masonic membership by believers since the object of the cudgel blows has been removed.

There is another reason for leaving this chapter substantially alone. The Supreme Grand Chapter of England has jurisdiction over ‘English Constitution’ private chapters in England and Wales and overseas. But because of the unique relationship of chapter to lodge in England, the product of negotiations at the Masonic Union of 1813, Supreme Grand Chapter has no international connections. A foreign Royal Arch mason is tested by membership of a recognised Grand Lodge and knowledge of the ceremony, and not by membership of a chapter under a recognised Grand Chapter. Thus there is no list of recognised Grand Chapters who might be informed of the English changes. And so far as is known, every other Grand Chapter which ever had the word exposed as 'Jah-bul-on' or something similar in its ritual has retained it. Hence some residual justification of the word has been kept by me.

THE NAME OF GOD

The Old Testament tells us that God revealed His Name to Moses. This is recorded in *Exodus* 3:13–15. A common variant of this Name is used in the masonic ceremony of the Royal Arch. There is evidence that this word formed part of the Master Mason's degree in the second quarter of the eighteenth century, but it was soon an essential part of the Royal Arch degree, and as such was combined with a second word. The fact that the second word is referred to as a 'name' of God in some of the (very varied) Royal Arch rituals has been taken by the critics of Freemasonry to mean that masons have a separate God of their own, necessarily therefore incompatible with Christianity.

This is what the 'Introduction to the Old Testament' in the *New English Bible* has to say about the Name of God:

> This personal proper name, written with the consonants YHWH was considered too sacred to be uttered; so the vowels for the words 'my Lord' or 'God' were added to the consonants YHWH, and the reader was warned by these vowels that he must substitute other consonants. This change having to be made so frequently, the Rabbis did not consider it necessary to put the consonants of the new reading in the margin. In the course of time the true pronunciation of the divine name, probably *Yahweh*, passed into oblivion, and YHWH was read with the intruded vowels, the vowels of an entirely different word, namely 'my Lord' or 'God'. In late medieval times this mispronunciation became current as *Jehova*, and was taken over as *Jehovah* by the Reformers in Protestant Bibles. (p xx)

In common with most of its predecessors, the *New English Bible* uses 'LORD' in small capitals to represent *Yahweh*. The American Standard Version has 'Jehovah' and the *Jerusalem Bible* and *New Jerusalem Bible* have 'Yahweh'.

THE BIBLICAL TRADITION

There is a well established Biblical tradition of coupling the divine Name with an attribute to make a new name of special significance. There are eleven such (Stone, passim), seven being expanded Divine Names, and four applied to holy objects and places:

Jehovah Elohim, translated in most Bibles as 'the LORD God', starting in *Genesis* 2:5 and then repeated so frequently that we forget that it is a compound Name, or even that *Elohim* is plural. It should also be noted that *Elohim* is the commonest word in the Bible for 'gods', being so used some two hundred times. 'You shall have no other gods [*elohim*] to set against me.' (*Ex*. 20:3). Yet no one has suggested that the Biblical use of *Jehovah Elohim* is a compound word disguising polytheism!

Jehovah Sabaoth, meaning 'LORD of Hosts', is used about two hundred times. 'Who then is the king of glory? The king of glory is the LORD of Hosts.' (*Ps*. 24:10)

Jehovah Rophe, meaning 'the LORD your healer', *Ex*. 15:26.

Jehovah M'Kaddesh, 'the LORD who hallows you', *Le*. 20:8.

Jehovah Tsidkenu, 'The LORD is our Righteousness', *Je*. 23:6.

Jehovah Rohi, 'The LORD is my shepherd', *Ps*. 23:1.

Jehovah Elohe Israel, 'the LORD the God of Israel', *Ju*. 5:3.

Jehovah Jireh, meaning 'the LORD will provide', the place where Abraham offered a ram in place of his son, *Ge*. 22:14.

Jehovah Nissi, 'the LORD my banner', the name of an altar built by Moses, *Ex*. 17:15.

Jehovah Shalom, meaning 'the LORD of peace', the name of an altar built by Gideon, *Ju*. 6:24.

Jehovah Shammah, 'the LORD is there', the name to be given to Jerusalem after the exile as seen in a vision by Ezekiel, *Ez*. 48:35.

The Name and word formerly used in the Royal Arch ceremony are thus within a well established Biblical tradition of compounding the Divine Name revealed to Moses with an attribute to produce a new name for God or a special place, without in any way inventing a new or separate religion, or creating a separate God. Because the word has been eliminated from the English Royal Arch ceremony, this relationship of the ineffable name to a series of attributes has been lost to English masonry.

BA'AL AN EVERYDAY WORD

Despite the fact that no known Royal Arch ritual uses the word *Ba'al*, the suspicion remains that whenever a word that sounds something like it is translated as 'Lord', we have *Ba'al* in another Semitic dialect, be it Chaldee, Syriac or something similar. Was this really 'the devil in disguise'?

Throughout the Old Testament, the word *ba'al* is an ordinary everyday word, with ordinary everyday meanings. It is true that it is used sixty-nine times to represent a Canaanite god or gods, although often not as a proper name but as a description. It is used as a proper name of other things or persons many times. For example, *Baal* is the name of a city in *1 Chronicles* 4:33. In 1 *Chronicles* 5:5, 8:30 and 9:36, it is the name of a Jewish person.

It is used even more frequently in combination:

Baal Gad, Baal Hazor, Baal Hermon, Baal Meon, Baal Perazim, Baal Shalisha, Baal Tamar, Baal Zephon, Baalah, Baalath (feminine of *Baal*), *Baalath Beor* and *Baale* are names of towns or places.

Baal Hanan and *Baalis* are the names of kings.

Baal Berith, Baal Peor and *Baal Zebub* are the names of gods.

The latter (Lord of the Flies) is used by Jesus Christ to represent the devil. With that exception, there is nothing satanic about the list. No more so, for example than the names Diana or Chloe are satanic because they are personal names derived from pagan gods.

However, what is much more significant is the use of *baal* translated into other words. It is translated as ‘master’ four times (according to Young's *Concordance*), an example being:

> The ox knows its owner, and the ass its master's [ba‘al's] stall, but Israel, my own people has no knowledge. (*Is*. 1:3)

This is very important, as by analogy, Yahweh is the Ba‘al of Israel. Another translation is as ‘owner’ (twelve times):

> But if the thief is not found, the owner [ba‘al] of the house shall appear before God, to make a declaration that he has not touched his neighbour's property. (*Ex*. 22:8)

A third translation is as husband (eleven times):

> A capable wife is her husband's [ba‘al's] crown. (*Pr*. 12:4)

Because in all these uses, *Ba‘al* is disguised by being translated, its ordinary everyday meaning and use have been obscured. Perhaps the accusation of creating a ‘devil in disguise’ should be made primarily against the scholars who translate the Bible!

This view is supported in authoritative studies of the Bible:

> Yahweh was ‘master’ and ‘husband’ to Israel, and therefore they called him ‘Baal’, in all innocence; but naturally this practice led to confusion of the worship of Yahweh with the Baal rituals, and presently it became essential to call him by some different title; *Hosea* (2:16) proposed is [more commonly *Ish*], a different word meaning ‘husband’. (Douglas p109)

Hosea's reform was not implemented, and outside the book of *Hosea* God is never referred to as *Ish*. Nevertheless the use of *ba‘al* as a description of Yahweh had fallen into abeyance by the time of our Lord's ministry.

As far as Freemasonry is concerned, the remote possibility of its use to designate a divine attribute in a ritual representing a period when it was in everyday use as a description of ‘the True and Living God’ would be fully legitimate.

If the masonic use of ‘Bul’ was condemned as ‘blasphemous, disturbing and even evil’ by the Church of England's Working Party, what is to be said of the Bible's use of Ba‘al alone and in combination on a more frequent basis?

BA‘AL IN AN INTERFAITH CONTEXT

In the story of Elijah, *1 Kings* 18:17-40, there is a well-known account of his confrontation with the prophets of Ba‘al, who were supported by the evil queen Jezebel. He arranged a contest on Mount Carmel in which many pagan prophets were to call upon their god to set a burnt offering on fire, which after many hours they failed to achieve. Elijah then set up a cultic altar of twelve stones with trenches dug around the stones, and set the wood and bull carcase carefully on top, and finally poured water over everything three times until the trench was full. Then he alone prayed to Yahweh and immediately fire fell from heaven and consumed everything, even licking up the water in the trench. Thus Elijah, acting alone, proved the superiority of Yahwism, and all the prophets of Ba'al were killed by the people.

The story is one of a contest between two religions. We would ourselves see other reasons why Yahwism was superior, for example, child sacrifice was an evil practice that had been rejected since the time of Abraham (*Genesis* 22:1-19), even if there was a lapse with Jephthah (*Judges* 11:29-40).

We consider that today we are entitled to look at other faiths and consider them in comparison with our own and to give a value judgement. Christianity is superior to the cargo cult of New Guinea because the latter is based on a misconception of the meaning of planes that landed bringing supplies during the Pacific War, not conceivably on contact with a true god. But in a multi-faith society, where the contest is much more equal, we refrain from condemning other faiths out of hand. We adopt a position of dialogue with other faiths, not to convert their adherents, but in order to understand. If the object is conversion, then no true dialogue exists.

When a Muslim prays to Allah, we accept that this has at least a level of equality with Jewish prayer to Yahweh, to Parsee prayer to Ahura Mazda, and with Christian prayer to the Trinity. We might even be shy of writing of Allah as 'god' with a small 'g', especially as in Bible translations into Arabic the Jewish/Christian God is also called 'Allah'. This is much the same as Isaiah calling Yahweh 'Ba'al' when describing him as the 'Master' of Israel (*Isaiah* 1:2-3).

THE SOURCE OF OBJECTIONS

In a chapter in his book *The Brotherhood* called 'The Devil in Disguise', Stephen Knight, tries to prove that the second Royal Arch word is a name for a specifically masonic god. His book has been stated by United Grand Lodge to be shallowly researched and as quoting the unproven opinions of third parties as facts, and so on. This finding was agreed in by the Church Synod's Working Group (p41).

A typical example of Knight's shallowness is what he says as a start to his condemnation of the second Royal Arch word:

> In the ritual of exaltation, the name of the Great Architect of the Universe is revealed as JAH-BUL-ON—not a general umbrella term open to any interpretation as an individual Freemason might choose, but a precise designation that describes a specific supernatural being a compound deity composed of three separate personalities fused in one. Each syllable of the 'ineffable name' represents one personality of this Trinity:
>
> JAH = Jahweh, the God of the Hebrews.

> BUL = Baal, the ancient Canaanite fertility god associated with 'licentious rites of imitative magic'.
> ON = Osiris, the Ancient Egyptian god of the underworld.
> Baal, of course, was the 'false god' with whom Jahweh competed for the allegiance of the Israelites in the Old Testament. But more recently, within a hundred years of the creation of the Freemasons' God, the sixteenth century demonologist John Weir identified Baal as a devil. . . . (Knight, p236)

With disregard for logical thought, Knight makes assumptions about the meaning of the second Royal Arch word which appear nowhere in any known masonic ritual, and then treats them as if they were true. He proceeds to suggest that the words of an obscure sixteenth century demonologist are relevant to twentieth century masons. Knight is attacking only what his imagination has led him to believe is the meaning of the second word, with no reference to the only relevant meanings—those which used to be explained to every new Royal Arch mason.

Knight probably got his perverse explanation of the three syllables from Hannah's *Darkness Visible,* in which he says:

> This word, JAH-BUL-ON, is explained in the Mystical Lecture as consisting of certain titles or attributes of divinity to which in English no-one could take exception. Yet this word is made up (as is also explained) of the Hebrew Jahweh coupled with the Assyrian Baal, so utterly repugnant to the prophets even as a symbol, and the Egyptian On or Osiris. (p35)

That is it—no explanation is offered of the jump from 'attributes of divinity to which . . . no-one could take exception' to Baal and Osiris. The suggestion that the lecture actually said that Jahweh is coupled with Baal and that On is Osiris is wilfully misleading—it said nothing of the sort.

Elsewhere, Hannah's exposure says that to masons, *On* means 'Father of all', yet Knight, copying Hannah, says that it refers to Osiris. Likewise the exposure of the ritual says that *Bul* means 'Lord' or 'on high', without any identification with the god Baal. Yet Knight, again copying Hannah, says 'BUL = Ba'al'. No explanation of this massive and illogical accusation is given. But regrettably, this specious logic was swallowed hook, line and sinker by the Church of England Synod's Working Group.

Lawrence goes even further, and makes the astoundingly misleading statement that:

> In the ritual the 'u' of Bul drops out and two 'a's are inserted. It is very clearly a reference to Baal, although several combinations involving these letters produce everything but his name. (p101)

Lawrence appears to be relying on the fact that vowels did not exist in the original Hebrew text of the Old Testament, and any vowel might in theory be inserted. There was however no such substitution in the ritual, and Lawrence was again misleading his readers. But at least he admitted that the word Ba'al appears nowhere in any masonic ritual.

WHERE DID THE WORD ON THE TRIANGLE ORIGINATE?

Research done after the decision of Grand Chapter was made has indicated that the original word was not the one that has now been discarded. The Royal Arch is a mid-eighteenth century development, and early references are of that time. A book published in Dublin in 1744 states that 'some years before a brother was made a Royal Arch mason in London,' with no further details. The first record of an actual ceremony comes from the American colonies, Fredericksburg, in 1753.

It has always been known that masonic ceremonies based on a strange mix of Zerubbabel's story and the crusades developed in France in the early eighteenth century and were known perversely as *ecossais* degrees. It is therefore not surprising to learn that details of a ceremony have been discovered known as the *Rite de Bouillon* (undoubtedly named after the crusader Godfrey of Bouillon), which was practised in a lodge meeting at the Ben Johnson's Head Inn in Pelham Street, Spitalfields, London, in the 1730s. It was not very like the present day Royal Arch ceremony, more an embroidering of the Master Masons' degree, but it had some clear connection with later developments. The ceremony included reference to four letters on a jewel (medal) which the candidate was told comprised 'the true name of God,' obviously the Tetragrammaton. And the word used to test those present was 'Zabulon' which the candidate was told meant 'Where God resides.' This seems quite feasible, there being three relevant Hebrew words, viz, *zabal* = 'to exalt,' *zebul* = 'height, lofty abode,' and *zebulon* = normally the proper name Zebulun but also meaning 'dwelling.' Thus the words in the *Rite de Bouillon* would have been combined as 'Zabulon-JHWH,' and might with reasonable propriety be translated as 'dwelling of the LORD' or more loosely 'where God resides.' There was no connection whatever with Ba'al.

It is evident that anglicisation of this word, pronounced originally by a Frenchman, would quickly lead to its becoming 'Jabulon.' Having discovered a beginning, the downward evolutionary path is fairly easy to recreate:

'Zabulon' was anglicised to 'Jabulon' in the late 1730s.

The two words were taken together, as 'Zabulon-JHWH', meaning 'Where God resides.'

By the 1770s, 'Jabulon' was split into syllables as 'Jah-bul-on' (A similar word exists in American rituals, separated from England by the War of Independence, so the change must have been made before that time).

The imperfect Lutheran rendering of 'JHWH' as 'Jehovah' was introduced.

Each syllable of 'Jah-bul-on' was explained separately in the way that the ritual current until 1989 continued to explain it. However, the idea of 'Where God resides' was continued in the explanation of 'Bul' as 'in heaven or on high.'

The characters at the angles of the triangle, *aleph*, *beth* and *lamedh*, were probably added in England in the new ritual of the 1830s (since I understand that no other jurisdiction uses them) with an explanation by masons whose knowledge of Hebrew was minimal.

Thus the Royal Arch word, starting from a perfectly innocent meaning, developed in a way that led, in the perception of critics, to blasphemously equating Yahweh with Ba'al.

Regrettably, going back to the original explanation was out of the question in 1989, as the origin of the word explained above was unknown: the *Rite de Bouillon* was only discovered afterwards.

INTERIM PROPOSALS

That parts of the Royal Arch ritual were unsatisfactory had been made clear over several years. The Revd Canon Richard Tydeman was a voice that proclaimed this in masonic circles as early as 1979, and others took up the theme well before the churches jumped on the bandwagon, following in the footsteps of anti-masonic writers like Hannah (1974) and Knight (1984). When in sensitive response to the complaints of the Methodists and Anglicans, Supreme Grand Chapter's senior officers decided to look into the matter, there was adequate material available to solve the problem, difficult though it might seem to be. In the first edition of this book, I wrote in support of the *status quo* to the best of my ability as a layperson with no deep knowledge of biblical Hebrew. I was able to show that it was not possible to make Ba'al out of the words as used, but unable to see that the Hebrew letters used in the ceremony did not make sense as described. I was thus able to prove to my own satisfaction that there was no actual reference to Ba'al, and that no blasphemy was intended by Royal Arch masons as they communicated their 'secrets'. Nevertheless, I noted the probability that within months of the publication of the first edition, the offending words would be omitted from the ritual rather than simply modified (p219 in the previous edition).

I have had made available to me the text of a submission titled 'The Mystical Lecture' – which is the place where the explanation of the Royal Arch words is given – by Raymond Thornhill. It is probably from 1988. Although I do not have the minutes of the meetings that formulated the proposal that the chapter representatives in Grand Chapter eventually democratically accepted, if indeed any were kept, it is possible to piece together at least some of the process from this.

A proposal had been put forward by two senior masons, Colin Dyer and Harry Mendoza. My recollections of both as fellow members of the Quatuor Coronati Lodge are vivid. Dyer was a revered scholar who brooked no opposition to his theories, but was usually right. He was a nominal Christian with little understanding of theology. He was a staunch supporter of the semi-official *Emulation* and *Aldersgate* workings. In contrast, Mendoza I recollect as a charming and scholarly Jew, but who was also perhaps over-committed to the rituals that he had grown to love over the years. Regrettably Dyer died in the early days of the working party and he was replaced by Roy Wells, likewise a venerable member of Quatuor Coronati. So the proposal that was put forward by the working party was more of a tinkering with the existing ritual than a cleansing sword. And it was against this compromise that Thornhill wrote what, within a masonic context, is as close to a tirade as it would be possible to get.

He commenced by setting out his CV: first class honours in Classics at Durham in 1938, followed two years later by a first in Theology, and a fellowship in Semitics for two years. After war service he lectured in Semitics at Manchester and then in Hebrew at Durham, which last post he held for 34 years.

He objected semantically to the word on the triangle: the ritual confused 'word', 'compound word', 'words' and 'syllables' in describing it, when it was clearly three words. He objected to its being described as in four languages, because there was no such thing as 'Chaldee', the languages of Chaldea being Aramaic and Accadian. Further, the words are not in Syriac or Egyptian, and only three Hebrew words were used, and to each he raised strong objection. He pointed out that the explanations may have been acceptable to early nineteenth century English divines, but not to a genuine Hebrew scholar following the great developments in understanding ancient languages since the 1850s. For example, '*b*' is indeed a preposition meaning 'on' but there is no Hebrew word *ul* meaning 'heaven' or 'high'.

He then moves on to 'the characters at the angles of the triangle' and mounts an equally devastating attack. The brunt of this is against the wholly mistaken statement in the ritual then current that the Hebrew letter *aleph* corresponds with the Latin alphabet's vowel 'a'. In Hebrew it is a soundless consonant, but one to which vowels can be attached, usually forming part of the typical Hebrew construction of a three-consonant 'root' to which various vowels might be inserted to form nouns and verbs in various tenses. More confusing is the existence of another soundless consonant *ayin*, which happens to be the one used in ba'al.

My own study of Hebrew conducted since the first edition of this book was published leads me to comment thus. Potentially 'the aleph, the beth and the lamedh of the Hebrew' could form several words with various added vowels. It would be necessary to add two vowels—*qames* vowel points—to the three consonants to get *ba'al*, where the *aleph* is represented by an inverted comma facing left. But, according to 'Brown-Driver-Briggs-Gesenius', there is no word in Hebrew consisting of two vowels within *beth aleph lamedh*: the notorious ba'al being *beth ayin lamedh*, romanised with the inverted comma facing right.

Thornhill then criticised more phrasing, like a proposed change from, 'engaged yourself never to pronounce,' to, 'promised never to repeat', and from 'it is in four languages,' to, 'it is said to contain at least four ancient languages,' and so on. He was very definitely in favour of simple and clear statements rather than weakened or vaguer language that in effect was unchanged in meaning. He then moved on to criticise a suggestion that words on the triangle should remain as a separate password unconnected to 'Jehovah', its three syllables/parts/words being said to mean 'Omnipotent, omniscient, omnipresent,' which are words taken from elsewhere in the ritual but which would have been almost wholly misapplied in the proposed context.

THORNHILL'S COUNTER-PROPOSALS

Thornhill approved of one of Canon Tydeman's earlier general recommendations to Grand Chapter:

> The second solution is to preserve the heart of what is being taught, and look around hopefully for other symbols which could be used to illustrate those lessons . . . though I fancy it might prove almost impossible to find better illustrations than the ones our predecessors produced, however inaccurate they were. (*Proceedings*, SGC, November 1979)

But if Tydeman could think of none, Thornhill made proposals which were of considerable merit. The words on the triangle should be replaced by *'Elohim*, giving—with the word on the circle—Jehovah Elohim (*Yahweh 'Elohim*) which is the name used for example in the JE passages of Genesis 2-3, and given in most English language Bibles as 'the LORD God'.

The characters at the angles might remain the same, but properly used as consonants and combined with vowels in different ways. For example, *'Ab* still means 'Father', but correctly spelt in Hebrew with an added vowel 'a'; likewise *'El* with an added 'e' is a normal abbreviation for *'Elohim*, meaning 'God' or 'gods'. The combinations of four words made up in this way would be, 'God is Lord, God is Father and God is One,' and this would have remained in full accord with the teaching of Deutero-Isaiah. It would have been less sectarian than the residual Trinitarianism of the old explanation.

Thornhill amplified this by adding that the story connected with the Royal Arch might still be the return of the exiles, but bringing with them the strict monotheism taught by Deutero-Isaiah, suggesting that verses from *Isaiah* 43-45 might be incorporated in the ritual. The lost secret would then be the monotheism which was lost when Solomon and his successors started worshipping false gods. This thematic suggestion was expanded at very considerable length making up an admirable new version of the previous 'Mystical Lecture' based on an entirely accurate account of the history of the Jewish people from Solomon to Ezra. He stated that the previous version contained 'blemishes which are a standing disgrace to R.A. masons'.

In actuality, the words on the triangle and the characters at the angles of the triangle, as well as the use of Alexander Pope's *Universal Prayer*, and at the final recommendation of the working party, were voted out of existence in February 1989 as far as English Royal Arch masonry was concerned. This was probably the best solution in the circumstances. Both the Dyer/Mendoza/Wells compromise and even the Thornhill replacement would have remained the subject of attacks of financially motivated exposé-writers as well as thoroughly well-meaning Christians. The first preserved the words intact and merely moved them apart and rephrased the explanations, whilst even the second retained the probability of *beth-aleph-lamedh* being interpreted wrongly and disadvantageously as *Ba‘al*.

But it strikes me that the great disadvantage of Thornhill's suggested Mystical Lecture would have been that it replaced a non-sectarian story of building repairs containing an obvious connection with the work of operative masons with an explanation—which verged on doctrine if not theology—of the rediscovery of ethical monotheism during the Babylonian exile. It made a marvellous story but it was more suited to B'Nai B'Rith than to an organisation whose members are Christian, Jewish, Muslim, or of other faiths.

THE PROPOSAL TO GRAND CHAPTER

So, on 8 February 1989, a proposal was put to Supreme Grand Chapter by the President of its Committee of General Purposes. Here are some of the comments that he made:

> The essence of the Royal Arch is a reverence for God dramatised by the discovery of His Sacred Name in the vault, along with his Holy Will and Word manifest in the scroll bearing the first words of the VSL [Volume of the Sacred Law, the Bible]. The earliest evidence of the Royal Arch Working available to us indicates that the Sacred Name was found beneath the Arch in the form of the Tetragrammaton. (*Proceedings*, SGC, February 1989, p175)

He was of course referring to the Royal Arch legend, not making a claim that this is what actually happened to three workers on their return from Babylon. And the 'VSL' that is used in all English chapters is the Authorised Version. He continued:

> Now the word on the triangle [the notorious Jah-bul-on] . . . has been described as the name of God in three or more eastern languages. Differing interpretations have been made about the meaning of the second and third syllables. There is little doubt that it is a fabricated word . . . This is reinforced by numerous 18th century rituals to the word on the circle as the Word with a capital 'W' and the other as a substitute . . .
>
> Be that as it may, following the 1834 revisions leading rituals elevated that word unequivocally to the realms of divinity and the Exaltee [candidate] is told he is about to have revealed to him for the first time the [sacred and mysterious Name of . . . God].
>
> For many candidates this comes as something of a shock, for mysterious it may be, but it is certainly not the name of . . . God . . . To continue along this path is to convey the impression that we have found a new and secret name for God which is known only to RA Masons . . . By removing the word on the triangle there is no longer any confusion and the Exaltee is free to concentrate on the easily recognisable and uplifting ceremony. We submit that we do not need the substitute for the Word. We have the Word itself . . . (ibid pp175-76)

He summarised the resolution set out in the paper of business:

> They refer to the removal of the word on the Triangle and the Characters at the angles of the Triangle and the taking of the obligation by the Principles on the VSL, either in the West or at the Pedestal or Altar.
>
> If these Motions are carried certain changes will become mandatory . . . (ibid, p176)

The 'VSL' in this case would of course be that volume which is binding on the conscience of the person involved, produced for the purpose of the obligation. The Bible would not be removed from its place for this to happen.

In seconding this proposal, Douglas Burford, a Grand Officer that year and a member of the Working Party, said:

> Although we are barred from topics of religious discussion within our assemblies, the fact remains that Masonry is, as it has always been, supportive of religion and not merely of the Established Church of this country.
>
> Although as the President has said, the initiative for change came from within our own ranks, we nevertheless cannot forget, nor can we continue to be insensitive to the feelings of those Companions who derive their living from the teaching and ministration of religion nor indeed those who, with their families, take great comfort from their particular faith.
>
> We are not a religious sect and we really have no need for yet another word for God. Certainly not, what is in reality a non-word, which by default became a Name. (ibid p177)

In personal correspondence, Burford has indicated to me that he had especially in mind here the case of the former Methodist minister of Epsom, who had been the Provincial Grand Chaplain of Surrey and who had been called to a new posting in north Oxford. He was told on arrival that he must give up Freemasonry or lose his job. With a wife and four children to educate he had no option but to resign his masonic memberships.

In Grand Chapter, Burford went on to describe the attitudes of Royal Arch masons whom he had met and with whom he had discussed these things on recent journeys throughout southern England and Wales, and mentioned the hundreds of letters that the Working Party had received and carefully read. There was a general feeling that change was needed. He noted that no private chapter followed with exactitude the ritual laid down in 1834, and indeed there was considerable variety, and concluded that, for this variety to have developed, 'change is not uncommon in our Order'.

So the proposal was passed and 'the word on the triangle' no longer exists in the English Royal Arch.

CONCLUSION

There is no real evidence that the second Royal Arch word contained the names of pagan gods or the devil, actual or disguised. There is no evidence that the use of this word is an attempt to combine differing religions into one, or to found a new religion just for masons. Its use as a compound description of Jehovah is within well established Biblical traditions.

The word was simply an expansion of a description of God to display His eternity, omnipotence and fatherhood, and our own inability to fully comprehend His nature. May these concepts not be legitimately regarded as 'the most exalted ideas of God', which if truly understood will 'lead to the exercise of the purest and most devout piety'? (Hannah, op cit, p183). This is not specifically masonic knowledge, and any Christian can experience these Divine attributes in worship and in daily life. Royal Arch masonry may have assisted the Christian mason in his understanding and appreciation of the Divine nature, especially when seen against an Old Testament background, but it could do no more than that.

Perhaps the most frustrating aspect of the argument outlined in this chapter is its pointlessness. There are twelve Hebrew words rendered as 'Lord' in most translations of the Bible, such as the King James, *Revised Standard* or *New American Standard* versions. Two are actually substitutions, used in place of Yahweh and Jah, and the first in particular is used about six thousand times. If the word 'Lord' which is used as the substitute were *translated* back into Hebrew, 'Ba'al' would be as good a translation as any.

PART FOUR

Conclusions

26
Learning

A MODEST PART

The processes of learning and teaching are complementary halves of the same endeavour. But one implies a superior position and the other an inferior. In this chapter I am proposing to look at what the churches—as the superior position—might learn from the existence of Freemasonry, and its modest success in the British Isles. The Craft is at least holding its own and in some areas expanding, when there is a massive slide away from most of the churches.

In this, Freemasonry cannot presume to teach the churches as if it were a well trained teacher, but I would suggest that the churches might find a few factors from which they might learn.

WORK

When I became a Master Mason, my lodge presented me with the Bible upon which I had taken my obligation. It is a straightforward Authorized or King James version, with spaces for inscribing the presentation and family details. There is also a thirty-two page introduction by H. L. Hayward called 'Freemasonry and the Bible', inserted ahead of 'To the Most High and Mighty Prince, James'. Hayward was a prominent American masonic author, but the Bible is published in Scotland, and it is presumed that the publishers either selected the text as appropriate to Scotland, or specially commissioned it.

Hayward is obviously expressing his personal views. Nevertheless, his text was a part of my early masonic education, and it dealt with the 'philosophy of work' in a masonic environment. He wrote:

> This projection and perpetuation of the practices and thought of a body of Medieval working men could not have occurred had it not possessed something uniquely its own of great worth and interest to men. Freemasonry is not the consequence of a miracle; it has perpetuated itself like mathematics . . . in such states as Britain, or France or Rome only because like them it had in its possession something men were in want of, and would go to lengths of labour and sacrifice to obtain. It is this possession which is the true (or 'royal') secret of Freemasonry.
>
> What is that 'secret'? The answer is plain, because it is written large over the whole history of the Fraternity. It is a true, and sound, and genuine *philosophy of work*, and the Medieval Freemasons were the first men ever to find out such a

> philosophy; they found it out not from theory, or tradition, or books, but from what their own daily work of building cathedrals and other fabrics of architecture forced upon their minds. (p14)
>
> In the beginning the philosophy of work which the Freemasons had found out, and which they themselves could grasp only one step at a time, they kept to themselves as a private possession, and even as a secret. After a time they came to see that what was true of their own work was true of work in the other crafts and gilds. Next they came to see that it was true of the many forms of work that artists, scholars, thinkers, teachers used as much as workers with tools. Finally they came to see that it was true for workers not in England only but for the whole world. (p18)
>
> The story that work was a curse upon Adam and Eve was an old Oriental pessimistic tale so soon forgotten that in the next chapters after it [in the Bible] the writers of the books glorified the men who worked great things for their people, built cities and found out the arts; and the Man in whom the Bible reaches its climax, who is set forth as the very type and model, who in himself has embodied what God wished men everywhere to be, not a king, or a pope, or a noble, or a privileged person, but a carpenter, and was one for eighteen years . . .
>
> In the Bible one man does not own another man, nor does he prey upon him; its virtues are those of men who are working together in harmony, peaceableness, kindliness, charity, pity, and good fellowship. It was these same truths, and others consonant with them, which the first Freemasons saw at a time when other men saw them not at all. (p19)

The Scots have perhaps always had a higher view of work than the English, and in some Scottish lodges the candidate for initiation is required to be 'able and willing to work for my living if need be'. Nevertheless, there is a clear value placed upon work in every Craft working. The *working* tools of an apprentice teach that part of every twenty-four hours is to be spent in labour, just as some is to be spent in 'prayer to Almighty God'. The placing of Hiram Abif the craftsman on a level with two kings in the creation of King Solomon's Temple is another typical example of this theme.

Freemasonry teaches that equal responsibility is to be taken by and equal honour given to labour and management, in a legend about the builders of the Temple:

> They then passed to the middle chamber of the Temple where they went to receive their wages, which they did without scruple or diffidence: without scruple, well knowing that they were justly entitled to them, and without diffidence, from the great reliance they placed on the integrity of their employers in those days. (Hannah p129)

It may be that the labour and management relations in Britain are beginning to move closer to this relationship encouraged by the Craft for two centuries. However, within masonry this is not a political platform, but a guide to personal ethics.

This view of the value of a man's working life is relevant to everyday experience. We need not digress into artificial distinctions between labour and management. The fact remains that every man expects—and even if temporarily unemployed, this expectation is still there—to spend the greater part of the waking hours of every weekday at labour, and to be respected and paid his due value for it.

CHURCH VIEWS

The churches generally will give lip service to this concept too. But I well remember my disappointment when the two Archbishops of the Church of England produced 'A Short Guide to the Duties of Church Membership' at the request of the Church Assembly in 1956. Here was a list of nine fundamental duties, and the closest that this got to me as a student, shortly I hoped to be a working man, was the first clause:

> To follow the example of Christ in home and daily life, and to bear witness to Him.

Then followed a list of very important things: daily prayer, Bible reading, Church attendance, receiving Communion, service to Church, neighbours and community, giving money, upholding marriage, and providing a Christian upbringing for children. But there was nothing about endeavouring to glorify God in a person's work, and I resented its lack of application to my case.

The old prayer 'for the whole state of Christ's Church militant here on earth' is a summary within the Communion Service of what the church thinks it should be praying about. About the man at work, where he spends eight hours a day, there is no petition. Of course, excuses can always be made for the old *Book of Common Prayer:* one would not expect them to have been correct in their attitude to work in 1662! But the 1928 prayer 'for the whole state of Christ's Church' is no better. Bishops, priests and deacons, men in authority in government, missionaries, teachers, the congregation present in general, the sick and the dead are all well and truly prayed for, but not the average, ordinary person at work. In the new *Alternative Service Book,* the equivalent prayer in 'Rite A' is simply a precis of the 1928 prayer. The 'Subject Index of Prayers' has nothing about Labour, Work and the like.

It seems clear that in practical terms the Anglican Church is not concerned about the person at work, be they factory worker, government clerk, banker or architect. It apparently believes that the Christian life of any worker ceases whenever they enter their place of work, and recommences when they leave it. If ever considered in between, it consists solely of witness to their fellow workers. Other limbs of the Body of Christ seem to be no less at fault than the Anglicans.

Can the churches learn something from Freemasonry in this context?

COMMON HUMANITY

Freemasonry is not concerned with providing a means of salvation, but regards this as something which each person will find within their own religion. Freemasonry is thus not concerned to prove itself to be better than any other fraternity, or indeed to prove itself to be the only genuine fraternity out of many. It is therefore free to look at what all people have in common, rather than at what distinguishes one from another.

The first obvious common ground of humanity lies in the concept of a common Creator. Since we all have the same Father in creation, we must all be brothers to each other, irrespective of any religious belief, and certainly irrespective of masonic lodge membership. In this sense, becoming a mason is simply a recognition of something which already exists: the brotherhood of humanity.

The three degrees of Craft masonry take the candidate through a recollection of other things that all people have in common: birth, development and death. As the exposure of Hannah puts it:

> Your admission among Masons in a state of helpless indigence was an emblematical representation of the entrance of all men on this, their mortal existence. It inculcated the useful lessons of natural equality and mutual dependence. . . . Proceeding onwards, still guiding your progress by the principles of moral truth, you were led in the second degree to contemplate the intellectual faculty, and to trace it from its development, through the paths of heavenly science, even to the Throne of God Himself . . . To your mind, thus modelled by virtue and science, Nature, however, presents one great and useful lesson more. She prepares you, by contemplation, for the closing hour of existence; and when by means of that contemplation she has conducted you through the intricate windings of this mortal life, she finally instructs you how to die. Such, my Brother, are the peculiar objects of the Third Degree in Freemasonry. (Hannah p137)

The same type of common humanity theme exists in the whole of the masonic structure. Perhaps the Royal Arch could be said to emphasise the common sinfulness of humankind when confronted with a vision of a righteous God. The Ark degree indicates that we have common stock, not just in creation, but also in descent from those who were saved from the deluge by the Ark. The Secret Monitor teaches the common value of human friendship. The 'Red Cross of Babylon' proclaims that, no matter how adverse the conditions, Truth will prevail.

In contrast to this, the churches have emphasised what divides one man from another: Christian from non-Christian, Baptist from Catholic, Creationist from Evolutionist, Dispensationalist from true Evangelical, Liberal from Fundamentalist, and born-again from nominal Christian. Forgetting for the moment that the previous chapters about heresy are largely about accusations of *revived* heresy levelled at masonry, for the most part they are about what fellow Christians have believed deeply to be true, and have been prepared to suffer and to die for. This in itself indicates that the leaders of our churches over two millennia have emphasised what separates person from person. We have failed to learn from what St Paul taught the Philippian church: 'You must humbly reckon others better than yourselves.'

Looking through my bookcase, I find that I have more books about factionalism than I have about the search for unity, and I do not believe that I am untypical. I have James Pike's *Modern Canterbury Pilgrims And Why They Chose The Episcopal Church*, Alexander Stewart's *Roman Dogma and Scripture Truth,* Gabriel Hebert's *Fundamentalism and the Church of God,* Peter Moore's *Bishops But What Kind?,* Anthony Hoekema's *Four Major Cults* and James Barr's *Escaping from Fundamentalism*, just to pick a few at random.

The Gospel of John speaks of the Word of God as 'the real light which enlightens *every* man' (1:9) before it says, 'to those who have yielded him their allegiance, he gave the right to become children of God' (1:12). As succinctly put, 'in a theological evaluation of the non-Christian world religions . . . the starting point for a solution lies not in the theology of election but in the theology of creation' (Golka p280). Freemasonry has nailed up a signpost pointing the right way for almost three hundred years, but it cannot travel the path itself—except that of existential experience—because of its prohibition of theological discussion.

Is it possible that the churches might learn something from the emphasis on common humanity given by Freemasonry?

THE LAITY

British Freemasonry has never been anti-clerical. Indeed, men of the cloth have generally been a prized asset, and not too long ago it was possible for lodges to have a reduced initiation fee and subscription for such members, if not to waive them altogether, as an encouragement to membership. Nevertheless, masonry can exist with or without clerical members, whereas most of the Christian church believes that it cannot do so. I belong to a fold of the flock which requires its priests to be ordained by a Bishop who has himself been made in succession to the Apostles (subject to certain irregularities in the early church which make those alleged to have occurred with the Reformation insignificant!). Thus there is a great gulf fixed between the clergy and laity which can be crossed only with great effort.

Freemasonry describes itself as 'a progressive science', and although this phrase refers to the progression of a candidate through the Craft degrees, it could be taken to apply equally to office in a lodge. The officers are listed in a specific order, and, all going well, each year a new Master will appoint a member to the next office up the list. Certain offices are assumed to be outside this progression, basically those with an administrative function such as Secretary, Director of Ceremonies or Almoner, and it is considered desirable for a Past Master to fulfil these functions. But the principle still exists, that there is a progression in office, and that each office has a function to fulfil that requires attendance at virtually every meeting.

Now compare this with the laypersons's part in a Parish Church Council. Unless they are honorary secretary or treasurer, they are just voting members, expressing cautious views in the face of strong opinion deeply felt by the Vicar. They feel that a single vote makes little difference to what the Vicar will do or organise anyway. (I hasten to state that this is not a criticism of my present Vicar!) There is little or no formal organisation of function, nor any concept of progression.

Now a council of twelve could readily have twelve committees, with one member heading each. Topics like Administration led by the honorary secretary, Finance by the treasurer, and then Worship, Visitation, Evangelism, Public Relations, Fellowship, Prayer and Bible Study, Youth and Sunday School, Music, Fabric and Furnishings, and Community

Service, would make up a list of twelve very important aspects of church life. Each member of the council could form their own sub-committee to deal with the aspect for which they had been chosen, to get the task in hand moving, and report back at every meeting.

The offices could be, say, grouped into fours, each deemed to be of equal importance, and a person who had served in one office in all the groups could have some recognition conferred by the Bishop when he visits the parish. It is meaningless to say that such things should not be coveted by the laity, if recognition is coveted within the clergy. Modest badges of office for the laity who undertake responsibility, a shadow of the opulence of some masonic regalia, should not be despised by clergy who wear their birettas and chasubles—or even their Geneva collars—with panache. Further, without derogation to the priesthood, a progressive means of advancement by the laity to that office could be devised.

Within masonry, the progressive system does not attract all people. Some will always be content to sit on the sidelines, and this is not altogether bad. What is apparent in masonry—particularly in America— is that there seems to be an ideal size for a lodge, beyond which attendance drops off. The wish for a participatory role may be frustrated by a limited number of offices compared with the total membership in a large organisation. How much more is this true of the church!

The progressive system of Freemasonry may have faults, but it does encourage continued interest, a sense of loyalty, and a feeling that absenteeism is letting the members down. Could it be that the churches might also learn something from this?

OTHER FIELDS

There may well be other fields into which this chapter could be expanded. There is the possibility of multiple congregations using a single building, analogous to trusteeships in masonic halls, thus reducing the ridiculous overheads of separate congregations meeting once a week in different buildings. Careful designation of priorities to a small number of institutions for charitable giving would lead to a greater interest in Christian charities. Demonstrations of differing liturgies to other congregations would lead to a greater understanding of one another than the exchange of pulpits for a unity week service. A clearer designation of membership of churches on a common basis would help statistical analysis, and assist in planning. Other aspects inherent in the Craft might be equally relevant.

The purpose of this chapter has not been to criticise any Christian church or denomination, or to imply it. It has been to briefly examine a few of the differences between the organisation of the Craft and the various churches, particularly my own. The present day relative success of the Craft in maintaining the interest of its current membership, and even attracting increased membership without recruitment drives, may well be worthy of study.

27
Teaching

CRITICISM

Criticism is in itself a good thing. Provided that it is truthful and fair, it prevents us becoming complacent and encourages us to improve our standards. The recent criticism of Freemasonry by various Christian churches has been useful in forcing the officials of our Grand Lodges to confront the Craft as a whole with the problem of the content of the obligations, the real nature of privacy, the difference between a name and a word, between initiation and worship, and so on. Christian criticism has been *teaching* masonry, and the process has been beneficial.

Criticism by means of unprovable assertions by writers like Stephen Knight, and harangues against their own caricatures of masonry by fundamentalist preachers and loony left politicians have been less helpful. There is nothing that masonry can do in response to untruths and half truths, except be more open about what it really is, and hope that those who have taken note of the accusations will be fair enough to study the reality as well.

My long series of chapters about heresies is a response to a series of accusations made over many years by worried Christians. Generally their worries have been unfounded, and only the official 'No Comment' answer from United Grand Lodge has served to give them continued credence. Almost all of them have been the result of taking a sentence or two out of context, or the unofficial writings of an individual mason—who could well be a heretic personally seen from a Christian viewpoint, as masons in lodge are not permitted to be heretic hunters—and failing to apply the balance which is already inherent in masonic teaching.

The result of the furore in Britain has been an overall benefit, so far as can be seen at present. Recruitment is up somewhat, no doubt as a result of greater awareness of the Order. Masonry is less complacent, and therefore in better shape. It is to be hoped that church leaders will continue to provide criticism of Freemasonry, so long as it is well researched and constructive in intent, and free from ridiculous accusations of immorality, Satanism and the like. Only then is there a chance that the masonic fraternity will treat the comments of the churches with respect. As it stands, the masons in England have paid more than enough respect to an unbalanced Working Party report made within the Church of England and to the *Guidance* of the Methodists, which was better in content but illogical in its conclusions. The consequential changes made by the masons have not result in any redrafting of church reports and this in itself militates against any further changes being made.

INCOMPLETENESS

The greater lesson that Freemasonry has learnt from recent criticism is a reaffirmation that, in relation to religious faith, it is incomplete. It has never claimed to be a complete philosophy except in the mouths of over-enthusiastic members. The enforced study of the relationship of Freemasonry and religion has reinforced this sane view.

As a private club, taking new members in search of enlightenment and setting them on a path which points them to a religious faith to be found elsewhere, Freemasonry can be a modest handmaid of religion. I am well aware that this phrase has upset Christian leaders, who say they do not want a handmaid. But if the Craft assists a single Christian in his/her faith and its practical application, that is what it is.

Many clergy have seen it in this light. The Revd Dr David A. Williams, a Presbyterian pastor, writes:

> Because of the high moral and humanitarian ideals of Freemasonry a many faceted relationship with the church is an informal and unofficial actuality. It is this similarity of the high principles of religion and the sublime humanitarian objectives of Freemasonry which sometimes creates the impression that Masonry is also a religion. Freemasonry is not a religion, although it may be religious in the sense of its support of high and worthy projects, such as homes for the aged and hospitals, youth activities and aid to the needy, the crippled, and the handicapped. (quoted in Haggard p12)

A Salvationist, Major H.H. Lawson, writes:

> Masonry has provided the most profound lessons to be found anywhere—and you find them, carefully followed, complementing your own private faith. (quoted in Haggard p136)

These comments by church leaders who are masons should not lead us into complacency. Freemasonry does not offer any teaching to the Christian that cannot be found—or at least should be able to be found—within his church organisation. It must be acknowledged that for many Christians the Craft is a totally superfluous extra, like the golf club down the road or a ladies' coffee morning. For these people, the incompleteness of Freemasonry in comparison with Christian fellowship is sufficient reason to reject it. But the five million or so masons around the world who remain within the Craft regard it as a positive help in life's stormy sea.

Freemasonry seeks no recruits by formal campaigns. It demands that its candidates are motivated by 'a favourable opinion preconceived of the order', and sees such an opinion as being generated by the multiple good examples of devotion and concern exhibited by its members. Freemasons will be the first to acknowledge that this is often not as evident as they would like, but to persons who have no favourable opinion, no obligation to seek membership exists.

PRIORITIES

Closely related to the incompleteness of Freemasonry in comparison with any religion is the allocation of priorities. If masonry is not a religion or a competitor with religion, it must be shown to be so in terms of time.

If we might consider first of all where any person's priorities should lie, ignoring the Craft, and then try to fit into the overall scheme. This is my list of a dozen items:

Maintaining a relationship with God on a daily basis.
Worshipping with the Christian community every Sunday.
Putting faith into practice in daily living.
Fulfilling obligations to the country in matters of law.
Fulfilling obligations to the immediate family.
Work.
Developing fuller relationships with the immediate family.
Maintaining relationships with the wider family and close friends.
Participating in church activities other than worship.
Participating in unessential events related to work.
Participating in voluntary community activities.
Leisure activities.

It is hard to draw up such a list without finding very quickly that there are exceptions to the best of rules. This is particularly so when a position of responsibility is accepted which requires the normal priority to be upgraded, because a group of people would otherwise be inconvenienced. Thus the chairman of a golf club may well give its activities a much higher priority than would a normal member, and rightly so.

Into this list of priorities, where does Freemasonry fit? I would insert it at two places. After 'fuller relationships with the immediate family' I would insert attendance at all regular masonic meetings. I appreciate that some family members can be so demanding in terms of 'fuller relationships' that some masons might never get to their lodges, but we must assume that reason prevails! And then I would fit voluntary masonic activity, such as attending lodge social activities or visiting other lodges, ahead of 'leisure activities'—pretty well at the bottom of the list. This of course would not apply during that Master's year in the chair, or to the Junior Warden organising a social function, and for a period of time the priority of such functions would need to be upgraded.

But criticism by the churches of masonic priorities should teach masons to reappraise them intelligently.

OPENNESS

Another period of soul-searching which has resulted from the recent criticism of the Craft has been a deeper consideration of the difference between secrecy and privacy. Masons do still have things which they wish to keep secret because they have promised to do so, no matter how much these may have been exposed by authors possessing every shade of motivation, from financial gain to religious fervour. But masons have now realised that the relevant parts of the rituals are minute in relation to the parts which *can* be spoken of, to wife and family, and even to the press. And those who respect the men who are masons should respect this wish, and not push for answers in public about things which have been pledged secret.

Masonry too wishes to retain its legitimate privacy, as does every human organisation, be it a conclave of Cardinals electing a Pope, or a professional body preparing a list of exam results. Every lodge meeting is a committee of the whole, and alone has executive power: a perfectly normal situation for privacy to be expected as of right. The nature of masonic ceremonial will remain such that it is best appreciated by a new member existentially, because he has not seen or read in advance what will happen. So no criticism of the Craft is likely to result in lodge meetings being opened to the public. Neither is it likely to result in published membership lists being made available—a mason may freely tell his friends that he is one, but should not without permission reveal the names of other masons.

But having said that, a significant change has been wrought by the critics, in that masonry is prepared to come out into the open, once the basic need for privacy has been met. The permanent public exhibition of masonic history at Freemasons' Hall in London is a welcome change, and about forty per cent of the visitors are not masons. Equally so has been the appearance on the radio and television of the Grand Master, the Grand Secretary and the Curator of United Grand Lodge's Museum. Another significant change has been the suggestion that not only in London but also in every Provincial and District Grand Lodge, there should be appointed two senior masons charged with the task of replying to misinformed letters and articles, in the hope that some of the media may have conscience enough to publish the sane reply as well as the scurrilous criticism!

OFFICIAL SUPPORT

The Craft has certainly been bedevilled with its own authors. Many cases have been quoted in this book, no doubt originally intended for consumption by masons alone, and for their mutual encouragement, which go way outside the boundaries of sanity in their claims for what the Craft could do for the world, how religiously significant is its ceremonial, how ancient its history, and how perfect its morality.

I think that we were all a little suspicious of the *Nihil Obstat* and *Imprimatur* notices that used to appear in books written by and for Roman Catholics. It conjured up pictures of the Inquisition and the burning of books now often thought innocent enough, but it did have the virtue of letting readers know in advance whether they were going to read something which the Roman hierarchy supported. Does masonry need an equivalent system, without the unpleasant nuances of *Nihil Obstat?*

The list of books recommended by the Grand Librarian of Scotland published in the *Year Book* which is presented to every new mason of that jurisdiction, is an excellent start, but England and Ireland have not followed suit. It is no doubt better to encourage reading of beneficial literature than to condemn books holding views which contradict the very essence of Freemasonry. Some means of enlightening the average new mason and the non-masonic public as to what literature represents a sound view of the Craft should be sought. A seal of approval issued by the Grand Lodge Board of General Purpose to publications which it hopes will be extensively read, with a clear statement that this does not mean that the book represents the official view of Grand Lodge, would be a possibility.

MAINTAINING A BALANCE

Intelligent criticism of Freemasonry has cleared the mind of masons as to what they are. Various pamphlets have been published by United Grand Lodge for public consumption, the first official statements of this kind ever issued in the British Isles. For both mason and outsider, these clarify the nature of Freemasonry to the public, its relationship to religion, and the primary duty of public servants who are masons. Clarification of this sort can only be beneficial, and it is a welcome lesson that has been taught by the churches.

This book has been an extended attempt to clarify in my own mind why critics of the Craft have said what they have said, when it rings largely so untrue in relation to my own deep involvement in masonry, whilst retaining an undiminished involvement in the work of my parish and Diocese.

I hope that my fellow masons will join me in this ambition, as it would be a tragedy for them and for the Christian church if the *Contribution to Discussion* of the Church Synod's Working Group were taken to be more than that. Disgruntled as the church-going mason may feel, the words of the writer to the *Hebrews* are very relevant:

> We ought to see how each of us may best arouse others to love and active goodness, not staying away from our meetings [church, not lodge!], as some do, but rather encouraging one another. (*Hebrews* 10:23–24)

The place of the Christian mason on a Sunday morning is not polishing his car, trimming his lawn, or even learning his ritual; he should be in church.

A FINAL WORD

My personal commitment to the work of our Lord through my parish and Diocese will inevitably have resulted in a degree of imbalance in the emphasis of this book. In fact, the time occupied by my daily activities until my retirement was largely that of an architect and husband. Despite what my wife said about it, I certainly did not spend my days piously alternating from masonic hall to church and back again. The reader may well feel as a result of the emphasis that I have given that Freemasonry is a very 'religious' organisation. It is not.

It is a fellowship which starts and ends its meetings with prayer, and believes that all human activity takes place under the watchful and caring eye of God. It welcomes men (and women's lodges welcome women) of all faiths into membership, believing in an already existing human brotherhood of which the masonic title is but a recognition. It believes that—no matter how important a person's specific religious sect and political party may be—within the bounds of masonic activity sectarian religion and party politics may not be discussed. It encourages its members to put into practice the precepts of their own religion, and the moral teachings of the fraternity.

Its fellowship includes participation in ceremonies in which the quality of the role played is a matter of friendly competition. It includes good meals and a sensible consumption of modest wines. It includes witty speeches which eschew vulgarity, and efficient administration of its internal business. It involves collecting money from members—and occasionally friends of members—for charities which to an ever increasing extent express concern for the whole community and its problems. But it reserves the right to attend to the needs of the widows and orphans of former members and those of masons who have fallen on hard times as a first priority. In such activity, its members find fulfilment and enjoyment.

The Freemason members of the Church of England Synod's Working Group specifically dissociated themselves from any conclusion that Christianity and Freemasonry are incompatible. They saw 'difficulties' which I hope I have lessened for concerned masons by the commentary which I have given in this book. Methodist *Guidance*, written by non-masons, has accepted that many church members who are in the Craft see no incompatibility between the two.

Freemasons ask that only those who have preconceived a favourable impression of the institution should apply for membership. Their regulations provide an easy method of resignation for the few who may come to believe the Order to be incompatible with their religious beliefs, whether as a matter of doctrine, of time sharing, or for any other reason. There should be no masons with an uneasy conscience about their involvement. Those Christians who prize their membership of the Craft are mature adults who can confidently be expected to grow in their faith, with lodge activity playing its part. They seek to participate in privacy and with freedom.

PART FIVE

Recent Developments

28
Positive Views

INTRODUCTORY

In this latter part of the second edition, completely new text has been added to cover some ecclesiatical reports on Freemasonry which were not known to me when I wrote what is now the first edition. First I will consider those reports which leave masonic membership up to the freedom of choice of the individual. Then I will consider some more negative reports and the detrimental effect on individuals that church prejudice has had. And finally I will look at a new academic approach to Freemasonry which may well enable antagonism based on ignorance to be overcome.

The assistance of John Hamill of Freemasons' Hall, Great Queen Street, in locating relatively recent anti-masonic assessments by various churches is acknowledged. United Grand Lodge probably has the best collection of anti-masonic material available in this country.

I have not in fact used all that he produced for this exercise, but have selected those which appeared most relevant. The situation in the Diocese of Sydney in New South Wales can be disregarded because the church in that diocese is myopic, and clergy who show any independence and do not conform to the fundamentalist doctrines preferred by its archbishop are allegedly discriminated against. The leadership gives support to dissenting Anglicans in other dioceses who seek to leave them to form a 'pure' church. In a nutshell, the leaders of the diocese give the appearance of being against everyone with whom there is any disagreement, and masons can regard themselves as honoured to be included in this universal venom. (This comment is based on a fuller article published in the *Church Times* in 2004, and in fairness it should be pointed out that there was a letter supporting the Archbishop of Sydney in the correspondence column the following week.)

The two reports with which this chapter starts, although now nearly twenty years old, were not known to me when the first edition was written. They exhibit a breath of fresh air from northern Europe when compared with the confrontational approach of the British churches.

THE CHURCH OF SWEDEN GOES POSITIVE

The Church of Sweden is perhaps the closest of all non-Anglican churches to the Church of England. It is the established church of the country, governed by bishops who claim to have received the apostolic succession continuously despite the Reformation, and it retains liturgical worship. Indeed, in many ways it is more Catholic than typical Anglicanism, in that its clergy never ceased to wear vestments to preside at 'mass' throughout its history. One women's religious order has had a continuous existence, so that the religious life did not need reviving as happened in England in the nineteenth century. The major difference is that it is part of the Lutheran tradition, whereas Anglicanism was influenced to an extent by Calvinism in the sixteenth and seventeenth centuries. Not surprisingly, it has been in communion with Anglican Churches for many years, strengthened recently by the Porvoo Agreement which brought other Scandinavian and Baltic churches together with the Anglicans. Adherents of the Church of Sweden represent two thirds of the population and the only significant minority are those who claim to be non-religious or atheists.

Freemasonry in the Scandinavian countries differs from that in other countries in that it consists of a single rite of twelve degrees which requires a Christian qualification for entry. It is thus more closely analogous to the British masonic Knights Templar and similar chivalric orders, except that the qualification extends to the very beginning of masonic life, and even the Entered Apprentice must be prepared to confess to his Christian faith. Despite differences in all the ceremonies, mutual recognition exists with the closest equivalents of the various degrees in regular Freemasonry worldwide.

The Swedish Synod of Bishops conducted a trial and pronounced its judgement on 21 March 1985. The complaint was against an archbishop and four diocesan bishops, and it had been brought at the end of the previous year by Rolf Sjoland. It was that the five defendants were members of the Masonic Order, which it was alleged was a religious sect distinct from the Church of Sweden. Vow-taking existed in its ceremonies which involved acceptance of the religion and doctrine of the Order. Membership by bishops of the Swedish Church, it was alleged, was incompatible with their *episcope*. The petition was supported by a description of masonry from *Dagen,* a newspaper that had been published only three days before the complaint was made.

The Synod consisted of a lady member of the Supreme Court as chair, a retired archbishop, a laywoman, a former Justice and a university professor.

The accused were each given an opportunity to defend themselves. Three did so briefly. Archbishop Weskstrom simply denied the assertion of incompatibility. Bishop Palmqvist of Harnosand gave a little autobiography and mentioned that in his diocesan seat it was a long-established tradition that the bishop and dean were masons. He would not have joined but for the tradition, but his experience was that he could view masonry positively; it had broadened and deepened his contacts and he was able to give masonic symbols a Christian interpretation. Bishop Brannstrom of Lulea argued that the Order is neither a religion nor a sect, but an association with an ancient ritual which requires its members to be Christians. You do not cease to be a Christian when vows are taken which concern only the Order's survival. The charge should be dismissed as an interference with Swedish law concerning freedom of association.

Bishop Lonnebo of Linkoping offered a longer defence. He quoted the first words of the 'Objects' clause of the Grand Lodge: 'The Swedish Freemason's Order is a society resting on a Christian foundation . . .' and noted that Mr Sjoland had not proved that this was not true. Freemasonry was 'a game for grown-up men with serious objects' including personal commitment and charity. It was for people who cherish living cultural history, symbolic language and beauty. Everyone had the right not to join, and for him membership was not of absolute importance. But he strongly asserted his right to membership, and to make that decision for himself. He was perfectly capable of deciding if membership conflicted with his calling as a bishop. With even greater energy he would assert his right to privacy, and to hold a secret as an individual. No one had the right to accuse others of abusing this public trust without evidence. He was astonished that modern journalists were increasingly indignant at people who could keep secrets and hold to vows.

Bishop Lindegard of Vaxjo likewise quoted from official documents. He noted that there is a development in masonic ritual from the Old Testament through John the Baptist and Andrew to Christ himself. Freemasonry is not an alien religion. The order is not secret, but its ritual is conducted in secret, and this is for educational reasons, because of the greater impact of something heard for the first time. The ranking system also inculcates the need for gradual inculcation of the values for which the Order stands. Any suggestion that the masonic ritual copies baptism and the eucharist is a mistake, and for many members the ritual has been the means by which church membership has been discovered and strengthened. The Order's anniversary celebration in March is conducted during a 'high mass' in one of Stockholm's churches, and it is the usual form of service, unamended for masonic participation. He cited the memoires of Archbishop Henrik Reuterdahl, who had died in 1870, as proof that there was nothing inconsistent between his church and Swedish Freemasonry. Modern bishops and priests would make the same testimony, and could point to their presence in Swedish lodges as 'showing a Christian profile'.

Mr Sjoland was given a proper opportunity to counter the defences. He responded to the Archbishop and two other bishops by quoting the Masonic Order's *General Laws* to the effect that the Order is 'an independent society', showing that it is distinct from the church. In the Order's religious test, the possibility of a 'separate religion' is mentioned, again making this distinction. Bishop Lonnebo's contention that the Masonic Order is Christian proved nothing, because many religious movements make the same claim. Mr Sjoland drew a parallel with a so-called 'Christian society' which had been declared to be non-Christian by the Bishop's Council in 1978.

Mr Sjoland continued: because he has to take a religious test, the initiate of the Order must be treated thereafter as a practiser of the religion of the

Order. Bishop Brannstrom had also claimed freedom of association, but whether this extends to bishops is a matter for the Church of Sweden to settle. The Church was not entitled to place freedom of association above the rules governing a bishop's duties.

The Synod delivered its judgement. The Swedish Constitution guarantees freedom of association for general or individual purposes. This does not mean that there is absolute freedom, and some actions conducted in such associations may be illegal or undesirable and require punishment or discipline. The Synod therefore had a duty to examine the claim that members of the Masonic Order—including the accused bishops—had taken a vow of faith which was distinct from the doctrines of the Church.

The complainant had given some information on the ritual but the Synod had not had the opportunity to verify if it was what was actually used. Nevertheless, what it had read gave no evidence that the person becoming a mason adopts a set of doctrines inconsistent with those of the Church. Quoting the *Swedish Masonic Order's Fundamental Charter, Book 2* which had been submitted by Mr Sjoland, the candidate is asked if he would confess the Masonic Order's religion and abandon his own. If the applicant twice answers 'Yes' to this question he is considered to have 'failed the test', whilst if he twice answers 'No' he is considered to have passed. Hence the complainant's own documentation does not support his allegation. There was no reason to assume that any of the persons complained of had surrendered the Church's doctrine or broken their Bishop's vows.

The Synod is empowered only to examine questions of abandonment of duty or surrender of doctrine, and it is not empowered 'to make general recommendations on fitness'. The Synod therefore considered that the complaint did not warrant any action on its part. It rejected any possibility of appeal against its decision.

Freemasonry in Scandinavia clearly differs from that practised elsewhere (although there is a similar system in parts of Germany), but the complaint was similar to that experienced in other countries. The question asked of the candidate for initiation which demands a freely given answer parallels that process in other forms of masonry. The judgement of the Synod was a robust rebuff of unfounded complaints which is generally applicable.

THE CHURCH OF FINLAND SAYS YES

The Research Institute of the Lutheran Church in Finland published a 24-page pamphlet in English by Harri Heino called *Freemasonry and the Christian Faith*, which was itself a summary of an 87-page book in Finnish published in 1986.

The Finnish Lutheran Church is very similar indeed to the Church of Sweden, which has been described above. It is joined with Anglican churches through the Porvoo Agreement, which aims at things like exchange of its clergy and full intercommunion based on a common experience of episcopacy, a common sacramental theology, and the like. Some ninety per cent of the population belong to this Church, with minorities of Orthodox, Pentecostalists and Salvation Army at about one per cent each.

The Freemasonry of Finland is very different from that of Sweden. There is a small group of lodges with some 1,400 members which practice the Swedish Rite in Swedish, and this means that it is limited to the Swedish-speaking population. But the majority of Finnish freemasons, numbering some 5,000, are members of the Grand Lodge of Finland which was formed from lodges chartered by Finnish returnees from America, which worked initially under the Grand Lodge of New York. The first initiate of the first lodge established in 1922 was the internationally renowned composer Sibelius, who afterwards wrote pieces for performance during lodge ceremonies, and this calibre of candidate has to an extent continued. The American ceremonies for the first three degrees, albeit more dramatic than the English, are clearly from the same source of English, Irish and Scottish lodges formed in America before the War of Independence. Attached to this are some 'higher degrees' which without exception are derived from England. Finnish language Freemasonry may thus be said to be directly comparable with England.

The study starts by noting that from the earliest days people have expressed doubts about Freemasonry, notably the Roman Catholic and Orthodox churches, but also Protestants. This it ascribes to its secrecy, its international nature, and the high social status of the membership. This questioning reached a peak in 1984, when the Finnish papers contained over 400 articles on masonry, and the official view of the Lutheran Church was frequently requested. (p5)

During 1985 and 1986, meetings took place between seven persons nominated by the Parish Institute of the Church and eight by the Grand Lodge. The former are all presumed to have been pastors/priests and certainly all held doctorates in theology, and included the author Harri Heino. The masonic delegates included two pastors, a consul, the President of the Court of Appeal, and three university professors. (p6)

The discussions held in the 1970s and early 1980s between the German Lutheran Church and the United Grand Lodge of German Freemasons were used as a basis for deciding topics of discussion. Great attention was given to finding and agreeing reliable sources, noting that official Masonic sources are actually few and that the ritual varies considerably. The masonic delegates were prepared to make available the actual ritual texts used in Finnish lodges, probably the first time in Finland that these had been seen by outsiders. (pp7–9)

A historical study notes the vicissitudes caused to the Craft by Russian occupation and prohibitions from 1808-1917 and during the Second World War (p11). There follows a study of the structure of the various degrees, noting the overall dependence for membership in the 'higher degrees' on continuing membership of the three degrees conferred in a 'blue' lodge. (pp12–13)

A study of ethics notes that Freemasonry seems to be the product of the Enlightenment and thus places trust in ethical progress. The rituals stress obedience to the authorities and a virtuous way of life with commitment to mutual care. There was no evidence that Freemasonry was used for immoral purposes (p15). Commitment to the rules within masonry was limited by the condition that 'they do not contradict moral or national duties or rights'. There was no proof of any misconduct by the judiciary in Finland when masonry was involved; the general ties of open friendship create as much tension. (p16)

Freemasonry is not a 'secret society' because it is registered under the laws of Finland. The reason for keeping the ceremonies secret are pedagogic, and this is explained to the candidate before he makes his vows. In theory everything else is public, though it was noted that there was difficulty in getting information. The penalty attached to the obligation was accepted as being symbolic, and 'is a heritage from the time of operative lodges'. To take it literally is 'the most common misunderstanding by outsiders'. (p18)

Teaching given to candidates for the second degree is quoted:

> 'The conception of Freemasonry is based on the confession of one God. To acknowledge God means receiving strength through prayer and living in the hope of eternal life. Masonry . . . is not a competitor with any religion because there are no doctrines in its teachings. However, Masonic work, as well as the principles of Freemasonry, is [sic] religious in their nature. Masonry requires a man to have some form of religious belief before he can be admitted as a Mason'. (p19)

Other passages to similar effect are quoted. It is also noted that the rituals are 'practically filled with Biblical quotations'. In the Craft degrees these are from the Old Testament, and therefore some critics from the nineteenth century found that masonry was 'a form of Judaism and forms a conspiracy with it'; a view which reached its peak under Naziism. The reality however is that the rituals of the first three degrees with New Testament elements were stripped of those so that Jews (and later those of other faiths) might become members at the end of the eighteenth century, and the additional degrees with a specifically Christian element developed, notably in France, as a reaction. (p20)

The study notes that the candidate for the eighteenth degree called 'Rose Croix' must first profess 'the Triune Christian faith' and that during the ceremony 'the whole *pericope* of the Suffering Servant of the Lord from the book of Isaiah is read as well as the Hymn of Love from the First Epistle to the Corinthians' (p21). The symbol of the pelican in her piety is examined and found to be Christian, as is the rose and of course the cross. Likewise a Preceptory of Knights Templar is opened 'in the name of Christ our Prophet, Christ our Priest, Christ our King'. The candidate represents a pilgrim and he is accepted as 'a defender of the cross'.

The discrepancy between the actual history of Freemasonry, starting in the latter half of the seventeenth century, and references to the Greek and Egyptian mysteries, hermeticism, alchemy, the Essenes, Rosicrucianism and the like is noted. The majority of masons accept that there is no historical connection with such occult elements and it was only 'after Freemasonry had spread to the followers of other religions' that such elements entered masonic teaching as a comparison. (pp22-23)

The study concludes that 'the nature of basic masonry is that of a generally religious kind'. Some masonic 'systems' seem to believe that the teachings of masonry contain supplementary knowledge passed to members from earlier esoteric circles; the higher degrees of the Swedish rite connected with the Knights Templar legend are accused especially. (p23)

The study concluded that, based on the ritual texts and other masonic sources:

> Finnish Freemasonry is probably best characterized as a monotheistic religious activity or religious philosophy based on the Old Testament. Within the 'higher' additional degree systems, Finnish Freemasonry assumes that the candidate has a Christian belief and supports his Christian conviction and religious identity. (p23)

The study found support for this conclusion in the work of G. Schenkel, who saw it not as directed against the Bible or faith, but positively as the ennoblement of mankind and the growth of one's personality. It confronts its members with life and death and offers broadly human ethical ideals to follow. It differs from the ancient mysteries 'because its rituals do not aim at deity or at the creation of union with God' (p24). It noted that masonry as defined in these ways would not find support in the dialectical theology of Karl Barth (an influential Swiss theologian, 1886-1968) and his followers.

However, the study concludes that the self-conception of Finnish Freemasonry is compatible with more up-to-date Christian theology because:

> General religiosity is part of the general revelation given to all mankind, as a search and longing for unity with God and as a presentiment of God's existence and, especially within ethics, even a far-reaching knowledge about the will of God. (p24)

This writer would note that the Finnish church's conclusion is simply another way of expressing Paul's Areopagus address: 'From one ancestor he made all the nations . . . so that they would search for God and perhaps grope for him and find him—though indeed he is not far from each one of us'. (Acts 17:26–27)

THE URC FINDS METHODIST 'GUIDANCE' INADEQUATE

The United Reformed Church was formed in 1972 by the union of the English Congregational Union and the Presbyterian Church. Thus two groups formed in 1662 by the 'great ejection' of some 800 clergy from the Church of England following the restoration of the monarchy, both owing allegiance to the teachings of Calvin as expressed through the *Westminster Confession* of 1646, became a single church. The URC has about 300,000 members, smaller than the Methodists.

The General Assembly of 1986 considered Freemasonry in one of eight resolutions, and the Appendix which set out the report of the Mission and Other Faiths Committee was received and commended for 'study and reflection by masons and other alike'. In other words, it was not a document which condemned masonry. Indeed, in a preamble it noted that the

Methodist report was issued shortly after the 1985 Assembly and that responses showed that 'there is a need for a document which is more informative about certain aspects of Freemasonry'. The two-page, small type 'Appendix' passed by the 1986 Assembly provided this.

The initial paragraphs outline the history of Freemasonry. The Appendix contrasts 'operative' medieval masonry with its 'old charges' which gave an idealised history dating back to Solomon's Temple, Euclid, and so on, with the gradual development of 'speculative masonry' which is 'a peculiar system of morality, veiled in allegory and illustrated by symbols'. It contrasts the undogmatic and tolerant attitude to religion which in Britain supported the orthodoxy of the age, with the radical freedom of thought seen in Continental masonry which caused the disfavour of the Roman Catholic Church. It notes that masons are proud of the fact that members of different faiths may join. It provides a third contrast between the masonic belief that it is not a 'secret society' but a private society with some secrets, with the fact that anyone can obtain the supposed secrets from one of many exposés. It accepts that reticence about disclosure of membership is based on a belief that it must not be used to advance personal interests.

The Appendix moves on to ritual. It also accepts that the gruesome penalties were never enforced, because the true penalty was 'being branded as a wilfully perjured individual'. It notes that though the candidate enters the lodge blindfolded, he is not offered spiritual enlightenment but is 'restored to the blessing of material light'. The raising of a Master Mason is not a false resurrection but part of a warning that masons must be resolute. The secrets that the masons undertake never to reveal are 'substituted secrets' and do not contradict the Christian belief that new life is to be found only in Christ. It notes that the 'other degrees' are relatively modern, even if some claim a basis in the medieval orders of chivalry. It briefly discusses the Royal Arch word, which at the time of writing of the Appendix still included the word Jah-bul-on which has since been removed from English masonry, and quotes the masonic explanation without speculating as to whether Bul is Ba'al, and so on.

This acceptance of the masons' own explanation of matters which have produced extended criticism is in marked contrast with the fanciful explanations put forward by anti-masonic propagandists and accepted hook, line and sinker by some churches in earlier reports. The URC places on non-masons a need to understand why people become Freemasons and what value they derive from it, and on masons the need to allay suspicions about their activities.

The writers of the Appendix can see that many URC members are unlikely to be attracted to membership, for reasons such as the desirability of open discussion on any topic, the building up of a community of men and women together, the use of more obvious ways to discover moral values, and the need for time to be spent on fundraising outside masonic charities. But they stress that 'it would be unfair to question the motives of those who do become masons'. The Appendix sees the motives of family connections, interest in ritual and antiquities, and admiration of known masons as all innocent enough. It regards it as unfair to question masonic testimony to the value of membership and sees masonic charitable giving as putting their fellow church members to shame.

But it balances this positive view with the fact that masons bring suspicion on themselves by excessive secrecy. It notes that masonic influence on certain areas of public life is almost impossible to prove or disprove. Finally, it calls upon Christian masons, by remaining in the Order, to ensure that such things do not happen.

Thus the Appendix turns Methodist *Guidance* upside down, and leaves it entirely up to the individual to decide freely whether or not he or she should apply for initiation.

A POSITIVE REPORT IS ACCEPTED

The Southern Baptist Convention, with eighteen million members, is the largest single ecclesial body in the United States with the exception of the Roman Catholic Church. They do not describe themselves as a 'church', believing that New Testament usage limits that term to the local congregation and the single universality of true believers in heaven and on earth. Any organisation co-ordinating activities is called a 'Convention' in the US, and a 'Union' in Britain. Bearing in mind that its membership depends not on infant baptism but consists solely of those who have made public testimony to their faith in Jesus Christ and been baptized as an adult, the proportion of active to nominal membership is high. The Convention covers the territory known as the 'Bible-belt' of the USA, renowned for its fundamentalist approach to the Scriptures and doctrine.

In 1993 the Home Mission Board of the SBC published *A Study of Freemasonry* as the result of a resolution passed in June of the previous year, the operative wording of which was, 'To appoint an ad hoc committee for the study of the compatibility with Christianity and Southern Baptist doctrine of the organization known variously as Masonic Lodge, Masonry, Freemasonry and/or Ancient and Accepted Rite of Freemasonry' (*A Study* p1). The booklet produced was a substantial 75-page document which is probably the most comprehensive of any study of Freemasonry produced by any church or ecclesial body. Interestingly enough, the 'background' chapter noted that no mention of Freemasonry had appeared in the Convention annuals since it was formed in 1845.

The second section (chapter) paints a very brief picture of Freemasonry and related bodies as it exists around the world. Concentrating thereafter on the US, it first notes the division between Caucasian and Black (or Prince Hall) masonry as a historical fact, but recognises that this is being bridged by mutual recognitions of the two Grand Lodges in many States. There is good coverage of masonic charitable activities, looking at obvious examples like the $306 million budgeted for 1992 alone for the 22 Shriners' Hospitals where all treatment is free (pp7–8), and going so far as to note that Job's Daughters, an organisation for young unmarried women related to masons, provided babysitting for wives of men involved in Operation Desert Storm so that they could attend support group meetings. (p9)

The third section gives a brief list of 14 justifications offered by critics for being opposed, varying from, 'It is anti-Christian or Satanic', to, 'It provides cover for people attempting to overthrow governments'. (p10)

The *Study* moves on to note the difficulty in reaching objective conclusions. For example, the spurious quotation of a speech by Albert Pike, head of the Scottish Rite, Southern Jurisdiction, USA, during the nineteenth century, in which he supposedly said that 'Lucifer is God' is frequently quoted against the Craft, but has been found to be the invention of a French anti-mason and anti-Catholic, who was trying to embarrass both groups. Its creator, de la Rive, whose pen-name was Leo Taxil, admitted in 1897 that what he had written was a hoax, but it is still cited by anti-masons (p12). The search for legitimate and authoritative literature on masonry is discussed at some length, and it was noted that full facilities were made available immediately on request to the committee by three masonic libraries (p19). It is notable that *A Study* contains no anecdotal correspondence about devil possession and the like which disfigured the *contribution to discussion* of the Church of England. The neurotic and tortuous windings of a deranged mind can hardly be used as genuine evidence.

Passing by a chapter on origins, the next question considered is whether Freemasonry is a religion or a fraternity. It notes that most masons are adamant that it is not a religion (p23), and even quotes legal decisions to that effect in the US State courts (p25). On the other hand, most of the opponents of Christian masonic membership find some reasons why it is a religion, or that it teaches that one religion is as good as another (p27). There is a particular objection to the term 'Worshipful Master' (p28), no doubt so in the US because there is no common reference to mayors, judges, heads of liveries, and other public officials using similar words.

The 'ritual'—that is the formal wording of the ceremonies conducted in lodge meetings—is then considered. Its very formality prevents Christian witness during meetings. Its alleged bloodthirsty oaths are found to be obnoxious and the changes being made in several Grand Lodges, such as that of Pennsylvania, to eliminate their impact are welcomed. Although many rituals explain that these 'obligations' are symbolic, this is not recognised by the critics quoted in *A Study* (p31). Indeed, the committee quotes a reversal of actuality, suggesting that every mason is made to swear to *kill* other masons, whereas the actual wording is that a mason would be prepared to suffer punishment rather than betray his trust. But the committee welcomes changes being made by several Grand Lodges—as indeed had been done by the English, Irish and Scottish Grand Lodges well before *A Study* was written. Another objection is to the term 'altar' (not used in English Craft Freemasonry, see pp 149–50 ante), and for some unstated reason the use of biblical words as passwords is offensive too. Many of the symbols used in the lodge are commented upon in a negative way, but in fairness *A Study* accepts that symbols like bride's veils, Christmas trees and Easter eggs are equally questionable yet happily used in most churches. Most of the matters raised in this chapter have been covered in the detailed chapters of *Workman Unashamed*. This book was cited by the committee but not mentioned in this particular connection.

The next chapter is probably the most serious in the booklet, on 'God'. Most of it is devoted to the Royal Arch word usually quoted as being Jah-bul-on, which critics see as denoting an unacceptable and syncretistic mixture of Jewish and pagan names (p39). It notes that this name was dropped from English masonry in February 1989, and suggests that American masons should follow this lead (p41). It then goes on to consider the phrase 'Great Architect of the Universe', accepting that the framer of the first masonic *Constitutions* of 1723, a Presbyterian minister, obtained the concept from the Protestant Reformer John Calvin, whose usage is quoted from three places in his writings: 'supreme Architect', 'Architect of the world,' and 'great . . . Architect' (p42). *A Study* finds that 'Freemasonry requires no specific belief about God'. (p45)

The booklet then considers the masonic attitude to Jesus Christ. After noting that in lodge a mason cannot refer to Christ, it points to an exception in the *Masonic Code* of the Grand Lodge of Alabama which permits a mason to insert the name of his own God in formal masonic prayer (p46). It then quotes several passages from rituals which refer to Christ, but it is clear that they are from what are known as 'Christian Degrees'. In conclusion, it was noted that masons may speak to one another about Jesus Christ as much as they like outside the lodge, and that Christian masons, as they receive the blessing of light, would be reminded of 'the light of the World'. (p49)

It is typical of conservative Christian critiques of Freemasonry that they fail to address the question of non-Christian prayer and belief. Most churches nowadays have some recognition of the reality of prayer by non-Christians, particularly as such believers testify as readily as Christians to the fact that God answers prayer. They accept that when another faith expresses beliefs in God that match their own, for example that he is holy, loving, and merciful, that these beliefs are true no matter who utters them. *A Study* failed to recognise that this possibility exists.

Regarding masonic use of the Bible, it was considered an affront to place it on a level, both physically and in the ritual wording, with mere symbols such as the square and compass. Moving on to 'Salvation and Future Life', the argument hinges upon whether Freemasonry is a religion. It quotes Ankerberg and Weldon's antagonistic view that 'Freemasonry . . . presents its own plan of salvation,' and ignores official statements to the contrary. It quotes from burial and memorial services produced by Grand Lodges which include wording such as, from the Texas *Monitor of the Lodge*: 'We place [the deceased mason] in the arms of our Heavenly Father who grants love and protection to those who put their trust in him.' It concludes that 'Freemasonry does not save anyone,' probably the first statement in this section with which the English masonic authorities would agree.

It is good that the next chapter is devoted to the influence of Albert Pike, mentioned already above. The current head of the Scottish Rite, Southern Jurisdiction, USA, says that Pike's well-known *Morals and Dogma* 'does not represent dogmatic teachings for Freemasonry' and Pike himself is quoted as saying that 'everyone is entirely free to reject and dissent from' his book. It then mentions another book by Manley P. Hall whose book's title may be shortened to *An Encyclopaedic Outline of . . . the Secret*

Teachings of All Ages. It contains a great deal of mystical material that has nothing to do with Freemasonry, even when it claims to be writing about it. The committee considers that masons will 'find themselves hard-pressed' if such books continue to be recommended reading for the education of masons, something with which this writer would heartily concur.

A section on anti-masonic movements mentions the Morgan Affair, a matter of concern only to Americans. It notes that Russian Communism, Italian Fascism, German National Socialism and the Spanish dictator Franco all condemned Freemasonry, but in this section it draws no conclusion. The next chapter is in effect a continuation, since it reviews the anti-masonic positions adopted by a number of churches, often also condemning other organisations considered to be similar such as the Odd-Fellows and Elks. The Wisconsin Evangelical Lutheran Synod even condemned Trades Unions, Rotary and the Boy Scouts in the same breath.

The greater part of *A Study* is a tedious reiteration of the issues raised in this book, but with a more scholarly and balanced response to them than in almost every other church-produced report on Freemasonry. However, section 15 is a fascinating account of the involvement of senior members of the Southern Baptist Convention. It notes as a preliminary that in 1798 two Baptist Associations, those of Charleston, South Carolina, and Shaftesbury, Vermont, reached similar conclusions that the only objection was to the vow of secrecy and that membership 'be left with the judgement of the individual.' It also notes that in 1991 a survey of 1,433 Baptists holding some sort of office in their local churches showed that a majority in each category (varying from fifty-six per cent to seventy-four per cent) felt that a statement from the church on Freemasonry was 'not very important at all,' or had no opinion. Of the respondents, five per cent of pastors and eighteen per cent of deacon chairmen (with other categories ranged between) had a masonic involvement of some kind. It estimates that up to 500,000 Southern Baptist men are masons. (pp64-65)

To take just one example of an individual, the committee writes:

> George W Truett (1867-1944), pastor of First Baptist Church, Dallas (1897-1944) president of the SBC (1927-1929), president of the World Baptist Alliance (1934-1939), and trustee of Baylor University and Southwestern Baptist Theological Seminary, was a Scottish Rite Mason. He was raised a Master Mason in 1920 in Dallas Lodge No 760; he received the 32nd degree in 1921. Of his Masonic membership Truett said:
>
> 'From my earliest recollection, sitting about my father's knees, who was a Mason, and hearing him and fellow Masons talk, I imbibed the impression in early childhood that the Masonic fraternity is one of the most helpful mediating and conserving organizations among men, and I have never wavered from that childhood impression, but has stood steadfastly with me through the busy and vast hurrying years.' (quoting Denslow: *10,000 Famous Freemasons*, vol 4, Missouri Lodge of Research, 1961).
>
> Truett, in perhaps his most famous sermon, preaching on the steps of the US Capitol in Washington DC, on May 16 1920, addressed the 15,000 people gathered:
>
> 'The right to private judgement is the crown jewel of humanity, and for any person or institution to dare to come between the soul and God is a

> blasphemous impertinence and defamation of the crown-rights of the Son of God . . . Everyone must give an account of himself to God. Each one must repent for himself, and be baptized for himself, and answer to God for himself, both in time and in eternity.' (quoting Powhattan W. James: *George W. Truett: A Biography*, Macmillan 1945).

There are fifteen other brief biographies of senior Southern Baptist pastors who were known to have been enthusiastic masons. (pp65–68)

The committee notes that Ankerberg and Weldon's anti-masonic book quotes some who hold an opposing view, summed up by, 'Either follow God or follow Masonry'. But a non-mason Southern Baptist pastor is then quoted as saying that the masons known to him were good Christians and indeed possibly 'more active than most church members and are instrumental in the spiritual growth of their peers'. The committee concludes that there is no agreement on masonic membership but that, 'Many fine conservative, Bible-believing, soul-winning men can be found on both sides'. (p68)

The final and very brief section notes the slow decline in membership of the Grand Lodges in the same geographical area as the Southern Baptists and suggests that if they considered the concerns raised by Christians this decline might be halted. (p69)

The section on conclusions advises that membership in Freemasonry, as resolved in 1798, 'be left to the private judgement of the individual' (p71). A seven-page precis of favourable and unfavourable points made in the *Study* was issued by the Home Mission Board in March 1993, and an extended recommendation was printed in bold type. This included:

> We recommend that consistent with our denomination's deep convictions regarding the priesthood of the believer and the autonomy of the local church, membership in a Masonic Order be a matter of personal conscience. Therefore we exhort Southern Baptists to prayerfully and carefully evaluate Freemasonry . . . (p6)

In an anti-masonic work, Harold Berry commented:

> It was a surprise to many evangelicals in June 1993 when delegates at the Southern Baptist Convention, after reading a seven-page report from its Home Mission Board, passed a resolution that "membership in a Masonic order [should] be a matter of personal conscience." (Berry p39)

He gives an article in *Christianity Today* from July that year as his authority for this welcome news. I have been told that Dr Garry Leazer, the Baptist who was head of the committee which wrote *A Study* (Robinson p93) soon afterwards applied for initiation.

ADVICE TO PRESBYTERIAN MINISTERS

Although the Church of Scotland is the established church of that land, it is Presbyterian, part of the Calvinist tradition, and very different from the Church of England with its mixture of Catholic and Protestant practice. It claims some 2 million members. The Grand Lodge of Scotland is also coterminous with that country's borders, and although proud of its own traditions and antiquity (eg, the earliest minute book of an existing lodge goes back to 1599), in all essentials it is similar to English masonry, including largely parallel structures for the 'higher degrees'. If anything, a higher proportion of the adult male population are members than in England, and most of these will be members of the Kirk.

The church issued a generally negative report in the form of a Pastoral Letter advising masons to act in accordance with their consciences, but pushing very hard indeed for an opinion against masonry. But in its appendices there is a section of 'Advice to Ministers' which is so positive in its effect that it has been placed in this section.

It is here for the first time that an attitude is expressed that does full justice to the Freemason members of the church. It rightly points to unease felt by non-mason ministers in dealing with lodge-sponsored church services, funeral services for masons, and so on. It points out that their first loyalty is to Christ and to the unity of his Church, 'even where there is profound disagreement about the nature of Freemasonry' (p15), by implication saying that the minister's duty is to the whole Church, masons included.

This advice given is summarised as:

> Where a lodge expresses a wish to attend a church service as a whole, this should not be refused—the church is open to everyone.
> If the lodge wishes to have an ordained minister who is its chaplain conduct the service, this is entirely up to the local minister who has sole control.
> If the lodge wishes to attend wearing regalia, this is no different from scouts in uniform, mayors in chain-of-office, etc, since it expresses no formal approval of the organisation in question, and it should be left to the individual mason to decide what he will wear.
> A funeral with masonic connections should be conducted in accordance with the approved forms of the Church, but once the blessing has been said the funeral is finished, and the family may arrange whatever masonic ceremony it wishes after the service. ('Masonic' funerals are not permitted by the English Grand Lodge because the funeral services of the church are seen as complete in themselves.)

And most significant of all:

> Great care must be taken that pastoral care of Freemasons and their families is in no way affected by the doubts of the minister about masonry.

The appendix notes that masonic bodies are at pains to point out that they see no conflict between Church and lodge and that their members, being Christian, are encouraged to support the Church. The Church should see this as a challenge, and must ask what human needs are being met in masonry that the Church is failing to provide. The three important points picked out in the appendix are the need for companionship, the need to express the value of all lay ministry, and the importance of ritual and symbolism. There is something amiss if people find that these needs are not met in Church.

The latter point is interesting, as in a paper titled 'Masonry Universal—a

Geographical Study', which I presented in 1978, based on the statistics then available to me, a comparison of the counties of Britain showed that generally the densest masonic provinces reflected the densest Free Church counties in England:

> The overall picture of Scotland as the masonically dense part of the British Isles is quite true . . . It is instructive to compare its [the map's] shadings with the strengths of various denominations of the Christian faith . . . Relative masonic weakness in eastern England perhaps reflects the strength of ritualistic Anglicanism in this area. (p19)

29
The Negative

SCOTTISH BAPTISTS SEE ONLY INCOMPATIBILITY

The Baptist Union of Scotland has an affiliated membership of some 50,000, making it a relatively small ecclesial body. Few of its members are thought to be masons in any case. In contrast to the report to the Southern Baptists of the USA, the Scottish Baptists produced an entirely negative report. Although it was produced just before *Workman Unashamed*, there is no reason to believe that they have changed their outlook in the meantime.

An undated 11-page pamphlet was produced by the Baptist Union of Scotland titled *Viewpoint: Baptists and Freemasonry.* The group that wrote the pamphlet was appointed following a Council meeting in January 1987 as a result of those church members who insisted that the Union should give clear guidance. It consisted of four members of the Doctrine and Inter-Church Relations core group and four others. It was initially hoped that of the four 'outsiders', two might be sympathetic to masonry and two not, but it proved impossible to find two Scottish Baptists who were prepared to represent masonry. They relied on input from an English Baptist who was prepared to help but could not be a group member, and from a Scottish Baptist who had recently renounced masonry.

It is particularly sad to note that the group asked for help—in a letter—from the nearest Scottish lodge and in response received a telephone call asserting that there was no incompatibility but refusing any help whatsoever. This is the only instance known to me where masonic authorities have not been fully frank and open with enquiries from the churches. The lodge should have made an immediate reference to the Grand Secretary, and that is what eventually happened, and a cordial meeting was held. They reported that the group found an openness which had been unexpected and a real appreciation of the issues raised, although they also 'detected a definite holding back'. (p10)

Other masonic sources were provided by the written remarks of the English Grand Secretary on the Report to the Synod of the Church of England (p10). The booklet records that it considered four other church reports, noting that most of them strike a note of pastoral concern rather than indulging in 'wild dramatic claims' (p8). It preens itself that the answers of the other church reports it mentions are similar to that of the group and sees this as an indication that it is correct. In quoting the most negative single passage in the Church of England Report—'blasphemous, disturbing and even evil'—it failed to point out that the masons on the working party did not agree the majority report. (p9)

The *Viewpoint* first examines the development of Freemasonry from the operative guilds. It states that an 'elaborate mythology and complex rites' are drawn from many sources including (surprisingly to me) other religions (p2). It is concerned that the ordinary mason does not know what happens in the higher degrees and that in these 'lies the greatest cause for concern', but fails to explain further. It notes charitable giving amounting to £12 million in the UK in 1986, and that much of this goes to institutions which are not limited to masonic participation. It also notes that membership is male, but that women may join the related Eastern Star (true of Scotland only, there are two Grand Lodges in England for women, and another for both sexes).

It accepts that masons themselves deny that their order is a religion, but goes on forthwith to say that it is, because even if religious discussion is prohibited, 'the whole movement is shot through with religious and mystical elements' (p3). It then states that it is an inadequate religion because it derives from the deism of the eighteenth century. It accepts without question the derivation of the latter syllables of the former Royal Arch word Jah-bul-on as being derived from Ba'al and Osiris, which the ritual does not support and comes entirely from mischievous anti-masons. Presumably the 'holding back' noted above was about this word, which the Grand Lodge of Scotland representatives would probably not be willing to discuss as being outside their purview.

Somehow the group obtained the completely false idea that, whereas the name of Jesus Christ is not mentioned, He is 'put side by side with Confucius, Mahamet [sic] or Zaroaster [sic] who seem to be regarded as subordinate deities' (p4). There was an anecdotal comment that in one instance the name of Christ was requested to be omitted from a masonic church service, with the further comment that this was known to be unusual and that a minister who was also a lodge chaplain had said that he would not omit Jesus' name in any church service. The same sort of criticism, but on a sounder basis, arose from the masonic use of several Volumes of the Sacred Law depending on the faith of the candidate. The removal of a blindfold to bring the candidate to material light was criticised because the teaching fails to offer Jesus Christ as spiritual light. (What would have been said if it did offer Jesus, and outside the church at that?) It suggests, even while noting masonic denials, that eternal life is offered the candidate by his being raised following the example of Hiram Abif. It seems to this writer that the rituals were being mischievously interpreted in an adverse way that few if any masons have ever accepted.

On the question of secrecy, the group questions whether commitment can be made to an unknown obligation, which for no clear reason it suggests involves 'a strong element of deception' (p5). Furthermore the oaths involved 'smack of vain swearing' and imply a degree of commitment that ought only to be given to Jesus Christ as Lord. It moves on to state that 'in the whole complex of words and ideas' masonry involves occultism, with some ex-masons testifying to the need for spiritual deliverance (p6). Finally, it considers masonry in society and notes the difficulty of proving that wrongful influence has been used. It nevertheless suggests that the guidelines issued to the Metropolitan Police show that masonry and police service are incompatible, and commends the journalistic and proofless assertions of Stephen Knight's *Brotherhood.*

The conclusion is that the Christian Freemason 'may find himself compromising his beliefs'. The 'clear conclusion . . . is that there is an inherent incompatibility' and that 'commitment to the movement is inconsistent with a Christian's commitment to Jesus Christ as Lord.' The *Viewpoint* then concludes by quoting *1 John* 1:5-7 about walking in the light. (p6)

It recommends further reading, and the books concerned had all been consulted by the group. Without exception, they are written by anti-masons and are wholly negative (pp9–10). There is no hope that the average Scottish Baptist might gain a balanced viewpoint by following this advice. Most of the books had been noted by this writer and many if not all their points answered in the pages of the first edition of *Workman Unashamed.*

The whole argument eventually hinges on the question of commitment. One is led to question how this view of the massive nature of the masonic candidate's commitment is supported. The promises actually made involve keeping secret things like passwords, attending meetings, following the *Constitutions* when administering the lodge, maintaining moral principles, and the like. But there is no reported examination of the masonic obligations in *Viewpoint* to see what exactly is being promised, and if it were, it would have been found to be a rather over-glorified promise to be a good member of the club. It is certainly less than the commitment of marriage, but the existence of monastic orders shows that some have found even that to be incompatible with Christianity!

THE CHURCH OF SCOTLAND WRITES A PASTORAL LETTER

The General Assembly approved the 'Report of the Panel of Doctrine on Freemasonry and the Church' in 1989. In an introduction, the convenor of the Panel admits that the Report is incomplete because it is limited to the Craft (ie, not the 'higher degrees') and Christianity, and is addressed only to members of the Kirk who are Freemasons rather than to the Kirk or to Freemasons in general. It immediately states that the matter ought to be left to the conscience of the individual. It refuses to deal in compatibility and incompatibility and considers that the prior claims of the gospel are self-evident. It therefore aims to point to practices which it considers unworthy of allegiance to Christ. The panel consisted of six august ministers and one lady. The pastoral letter with lead-in material was published as *The Church and Freemasonry* in 1990 and it was hoped that it would be widely disseminated.

The terms of reference were rather detailed and extended:

> To examine the theological issues involved in Church members being also Freemasons; to consider the compatibility or otherwise of Freemasonry with Christianity; and in particular to determine whether its rituals and the teachings of Freemasonry are consistent with the Church of Scotland's belief in the gospel of the sovereign grace and love of God, wherein through Jesus Christ, his only Son, our Lord, Incarnate, Crucified and Risen, he freely offers all men, upon repentance and faith, the forgiveness of sins, renewal by the Holy Spirit and eternal life. (p1)

The panel was also instructed to consult the Grand Lodge of Scotland. But it did so only towards the end of its deliberations, and it is admitted that much of the study over two years was done before consultation. Nevertheless, cordial reception by the Grand Secretary and other office-bearers of the Grand Lodge was gratefully noted. The panel produced a list of questions, and 'the frank answering of these questions was much appreciated', especially comments concerning the role of parish ministers. A meeting was held with the Grand Master Mason, a past Grand Master Mason, two Grand Chaplains and nine other named representatives and some others (p2). At this meeting they received advice on how to contact the bodies governing the Royal Arch and the Scottish Rite, and there too found a willingness to enter into useful discussion. (p3)

In the pastoral letter, the good points of masonry are noted, that fine people including many church members are masons, and that masonic charity extends well outside the fraternity. But then it went on to theological problems, and dissected the prayers used in lodge meetings. The terms used for God it saw as a 'theology', defined—I suggest very inadequately, see 'Academia' below—as 'a knowledge of God', and sees them not as 'vacuous words' but as meaningful even before a Christian or Muslim hears them and attach their own meanings. The name of Jesus is not only suppressed, it is not required: 'Brothers in Christ, this is unworthy of you'. (p4)

Nevertheless, the letter admits paternalistically that 'there are many fine Christian men who are also Freemasons' (p5). But it wishes to point to the truths of the gospel and then to ask masons to assess their Freemasonry in that light. It also points to the primacy of the Bible in a Reformed (ie, Calvinist) Church, and this leads to concern about a morality that claims validity apart from the gospel, which it suggests must be deficient. None of the good things of masonry, including its important place in Scottish history, justifies deviation from the doctrine of the Church of Scotland or the world Church (p7). The letter then expounds at some length with a number of biblical quotations the idea that prayer is acceptable only through Jesus Christ.

Privacy is accepted as merely a symbol, since the 'secrets' are well known, but it is 'a wholly inappropriate symbol' because if Christ cannot be proclaimed then masons must be labelled as Gnostics, and a paragraph is spent explaining this (p8). A comparison is then made between masonry and inter-faith worship and dialogue. In the later, differences are to be discussed and considered, and this is not possible in masonry, because theological discussion is proscribed. To the argument of masons that this is to produce brotherhood and harmony, the answer is given that brotherhood can exist only in Jesus Christ. 'Not to confess Christ' is again unworthy of Christians; so, 'we invite you to reconsider your involvement in Freemasonry' (p9).

Having stated at the outset that membership of the lodge is a matter left to the individual conscience, the Report goes all out to push the conscience in a single direction. There is no suggestion that the opinions of the many Grand Lodge office-bearers who so willingly assisted the panel might be given weight. The Report must therefore be classed as negative.

There are then three appendices, strictly not part of the pastoral letter. The first (p10f) concerns what it calls 'Christian' Orders, with inverted commas. The panel met with the Supreme Council for Scotland of the Ancient and Accepted Scottish Rite and were shown the main rituals, those of the eighteenth and thirtieth degrees, including in each case an 'exegesis' which is apparently issued to candidates. It concluded that the central facts of the life of Christ are 'removed from historical reality' by becoming part of 'a mysterious journey towards moral perfection'. The many references to Christ did not alleviate their concern that the candidate is somehow making an atonement for himself. It seems that the panel would not have been happy unless Calvinist doctrine had been specifically spelt out.

The second appendix (p13f) is about the use of the Bible. The individual writer of this notes that the stories in masonic ritual are not entirely based on the Bible, but have some relationship to it. For example, Hiram Abif is mentioned in 1 *Kings* and 2 *Chronicles*, but the legend of his death is not in the Bible. This is somehow unsatisfactory, and it is even more so since it does not mention Christ, 'the centre of the entire biblical revelation'. Further, the Hebrew used in the Royal Arch, like 'Jah-bul-on', is very poor Hebrew indeed (p14). Hebrew scholars in the Quatuor Coronati Lodge have long questioned the poor Hebrew of the words and thus on that subject at least are in agreement with the appendix; this opinion formed part of the case for their deletion from English Royal Arch masonry some sixteen years ago.

The appendix further maintains that if it is a secret word, that is also unbiblical because 'God did not speak in secret'. Perhaps the writer had not read *Daniel* 12:4, *Revelation* 10:4, or studied the 'Messianic secret' of Mark's gospel. Perhaps he had not studied the Sermon on the Mount where Jesus commends secrecy (see p69 ante).

The third appendix is advice to ministers. This is in reality so positive that it has already been considered under that category.

Comments of the Grand Master Mason on the Report are printed in the *Proceedings* for 3 August 1989. He stated that all must be saddened by it; it was weakened and in part inaccurate because the panel chose not to discuss it in draft form with Grand Lodge office-bearers as had been offered. He noted the good relations that had existed in Scotland for 400 years, shattered only by questioning after the Second World War. He noted the rise of bigoted fundamentalism in all religions. Since Freemasonry had not changed, the church must have done so.

However, he stated that the most important thing must be that brethren must not resign from their churches, a slippery path towards denial of God.

Freemasonry should adopt a higher public profile, otherwise how will people preconceive 'a favourable opinion of the order' and thus become proper candidates? Thirdly, masons should look into the way their meeting halls and clubs (a Scottish concept) are run, so as never to be a cause of community complaint. He was convinced that the controversy over masonry was a storm in a teacup, a minor ripple in the long stream of masonic history. He concluded with the wording with which the Scottish ritual has the Master close his lodge: 'May Brotherly Love prevail and every moral and social virtue cement us.'

IRISH PRESBYTERIANS IGNORE ADVICE

The Presbyterian Church in Ireland has some 400,000 members, largely in the north. It is nevertheless easily the largest Protestant church, although the Anglican Church of Ireland, widely regarded as Protestant, has an only slightly smaller membership. Irish Freemasonry is united despite the partition, though its largest concentration is in the north. The headquarters is nevertheless in Dublin, and all the masonic bodies including the 'higher degrees' are administered from Molesworth Street. Because the Roman Catholic prohibition on masonic membership is largely effective, the proportion of masons in non-Roman churches must be correspondingly very high.

In 1991 the Irish Grand Secretary received a letter from Professor T.S. Reid, head of the Department of Practical Theology and Pastoral Studies of the Union Theological College of the Presbyterian Church in Ireland saying that their Doctrine Committee had been instructed to conduct an investigation into 'the Beliefs and Practices of Freemasonry'.

The Grand Secretary replied, as would any other masonic official, that a mason's beliefs were his own, except that a qualification for admission was belief in God. Membership ought to reinforce a person's beliefs and the practices inculcated are 'irreproachable'. Clergy and laypersons are represented in its membership. He suggested that, rather then randomly consulting 'masonic sources' he should confine himself to Presbyterian ministers who were masons. He enclosed a list of past and present Grand Chaplains and, since he had no record of their denominations, suggested that those be selected who were Presbyterians. He suggested that meetings might take place in Freemasons' Hall in Dublin where all facilities could be made available, and where they could view a patchwork tapestry which listed the masons who, as Presbyterian ministers, had participated in resuscitation of the Presbyterian Orphan Society in 1908, the outgoing and incoming Moderators being prominent amongst them. A few basic documents were sent with the letter.

Six months later a meeting took place, the Deputy Grand Master heading a delegation of four masons including an Anglican archdeacon and a Presbyterian minister, both past Grand Chaplains, whilst the Church was represented by Professor Reid, two other professors and another clergyman. A report by the Church delegates made a few days later is quoted at length in the Grand Lodge *Annual Report* for 1991. The masons had expressed a sense of mystification at the examination taking place, and they felt that they had nothing to hide and much to gain by it. The masons at the meeting answered all questions asked of them openly. These included questions asked about the 'higher degrees' without any of the reticence felt in Scotland, probably because all the degrees of Irish Freemasonry are governed from bodies meeting in the same building. The answers given were in full accord with the view expressed in this book. The Presbyterian delegation was given a tour of the Molesworth Street building, and its museum, both of which it was noted are open to the public. The *Annual Report* also includes the main text of a letter sent subsequently by the Grand Secretary giving different references to God in different degrees, and indicating that although prayers begin and end each meeting, no religious instruction is given. Further basic documentation was enclosed, which included the *Newsletter* of Leinster Lodge No 115 in Colombo, Sri Lanka, as a living example of a lodge where men of several different religions meet in 'peace, love and harmony'.

The next Grand Lodge *Annual Report*, that for 2002, included the full text of the four-page report on the Investigation submitted to the General Assembly of the Presbyterian Church in June of that year. Hence the Irish masons would no doubt be better informed of the opinion of the Church than most of the church membership.

After introductory paragraphs the committee stated that it had noted the generally negative opinion of other reports such as those to the Church of England and the British Methodists, but failed to mention the positive or 'matter of conscience' reports. It noted that Irish masonry is somewhat different from that in both England and Scotland—one difference being that the Irish ritual is oral and unpublished. It recognised the openness of the Grand Lodge and also 'much that is positive and praiseworthy in Irish Freemasonry'. It also recognised that the limitation of masonic charity to relatives of masons is paralleled by restrictions on Presbyterian charities to Presbyterians as part of the law on charities in Ireland, but noted that in Belfast the masons had recently raised over £300,000 for medical research. It accepted that, contrary to the popular misconception, masons do not promote one another's professional or business interests.

There were nevertheless 'matters which give us concern as Christians', the first being that belief in God is not identical with belief in 'the God and Father of our Lord Jesus Christ'. Prayer to him is not the same as prayer understood in Islam, Judaism and other religions, and the uniqueness of Jesus as 'high priest' is stressed, cf, *Hebrews* 4:14,16. Although it is acknowledged that masons do not have a 'composite deity', setting religions side by side is inconsistent with the uniqueness of the claims of Jesus Christ. Masonic use of the Bible is objected to, both because of the lectionary restricted to King Solomon's temple and John's Gospel, and the fact that other sacred books may be set alongside the Bible. It regarded itself as unable to comment on the Christian degrees such as Knight Templar since the ritual was not available in print in Ireland to be studied for doctrinal soundness. It regarded ideals such as 'the brotherhood of man under the

Fatherhood of God' as too vague, and stated that human brotherhood can only truly exist by God's adoption though faith in Jesus Christ. Paul's quotation of a Greek philosopher in *Acts* 17:28 was presumably ignored.

Thus everyone, mason or not, should assess everything that they do 'in the light of the grace and love of God'. They refused to judge masons, especially those with whom they had met who found no tension to exist in membership of the Order and the Church. But they also recognised that many Christians have found them to be incompatible. They referred to *Romans* 14–15 where Paul considers the individual conscience, expounding this as the duty of every Christian to respect every other, and yet to consider the effect of one's own actions on others. They conclude:

> Christ has the first and final claim upon our obedience. As Christians we cannot serve Him and someone or something else. Participation or non-participation in Freemasonry must be decided in the light of that imperative.

Of course, the Irish Christian Freemason would see this in a positive light; he would regard himself to be mature enough to have considered the relationship of his faith with masonry and were it to be seen as a problem, he would no longer have remained a mason. He would see his membership as a private matter that is not advertised and need not have any effect on others unless they were prying busybodies.

The Investigation report has an Appendix which apparently resulted from a meeting with three ministers who were past and present Grand Chaplains, and sight of a copy of a paper by another minister on 'The Masonic Order and Religion'. This paper was not reproduced in the Investigations, but is printed in full in the 1992 *Annual Report* of Grand Lodge. These ministers stated that when acting as masonic chaplains they were addressing the same God that they addressed from the pulpit of a Presbyterian church. They also stated that every mason worships the God in whom he believes. The committee reported that no mason minister that they had met was conscious of any tension between membership of the Order and his church. They concluded:

> We had a firm impression of sincere men who valued the fellowship they experienced in Masonry and were mystified that other Christians should think it could be unchristian for them to be members of the Order.

The Grand Lodge submitted a response to the Investigation report. Most of this was obvious but restrained riposte, but notable was a comment on the remark that, 'there was a time when the relationship between our Church and the Masonic Order was closer and more extensive than it is today', to the effect that it was the church that was inconsistent, not masonry.

When the Investigation report was put before the General Assembly on 3 June 1992, unusually the adoption of the report did not form an agenda item. A resolution was proposed which effectively threw away the careful advice of the committee:

> That the General Assembly in the light of the Doctrine Committee's report on the beliefs and practices of Irish Freemasonry, disapprove of communicant members of the Church being involved in Freemasonry.

An amendment was proposed which was in effect the adoption of the report, which called upon 'all masons who are members of our Church to consider seriously the danger of divided loyalties'. This amendment was lost and the original motion was carried. Nine members of the General Assembly asked that their names be recorded as dissenting, and this did not include the proposer and seconder of the amendment, so it can be assumed that there was a much larger number of unrecorded names.

An amusing ending to this negative view of compatibility may be seen in a letter to the *Church Times* published on 17 December 2004, referring to a prognostication of the disintegration of Anglicanism:

> Many Masons are now asking themselves whether the origins of this sad development, the Church's trend towards heterodoxy and its increasing appetite for secular and sexual politics, are compatible with the high moral and religious ideals of Freemasonry.

There is certainly an element of 'Physician, heal thyself' there.

30
Faults of Negative Reports

NON-ACCEPTANCE OF REASONABLE EXPLANATIONS

The negative reports of the various churches and ecclesial bodies to their governing bodies or to their membership are incestuous, each one studying the work of the other and repeating their findings in different words. This is not in itself bad, in that ecumenism is desirable, but it is bad when wrong interpretations of masonry get repeated with ever increasing authority when they were never proved in the first place. Where less ecclesial incest exists, such as in Scandinavia, an openness to a positive view has prevailed.

It is not possible to understand Christianity in any depth without having made a commitment to Jesus Christ. It is likewise not possible to fully understand Buddhism without having sought to follow the Noble Eightfold Path. It is possible to talk to practising Buddhists and to write about their expressed teaching, but what the non-Buddhist will produce will be but a shadow of what the disciple feels. It is therefore a well-known principle of inter-faith study that what is written about a particular faith should be written by or at least approved by a participant in the religion that is being explained. If Freemasonry is to be considered as a religion, which its adversaries maintain, then the same principle must be applied. Yet in practice they study the ritual to find adverse things, and yet when an explanation is given, they ignore it and substitute their own.

This is particularly true of the interpretation of the word (or words) Jah-bul-on, which is repeatedly explained in anti-masonic reports as representing Yahweh, Ba'al and Osiris. The actual explanation given in the ritual does not say this, yet the imaginative explanation of Walton Hannah is preferred. As the Southern Baptist *Study* states:

> Hannah offers no explanation or documentation for this charge. Haffner and other masons insist the ritual for the Royal Arch degree, from which this identity allegedly comes, 'says nothing of the sort'. Still, this charge has taken on a life of its own and is commonly repeated. (p39)

Despite masonic explanation, such were the objections raised by the Church of England that the English governing body of the Royal Arch degree voted to remove the word and its explanation from the ritual in February 1989. It was so determined to enforce the change that it threatened disciplinary action against a venerable chapter which failed to comply. Since this was sixteen years ago, it is fair to assume that the majority of Royal Arch masons in England and Wales have never heard the word. However, the chapter in this book titled 'Ba'al' was written before the change was made, but it has been thought best not to modify it completely, because the same change has not been made in other jurisdictions. Though I am more than happy that the omission was made, not least because of the poor Hebrew of 'the word on the triangle', the justification for its continuing use elsewhere still stands.

AVOIDING PLURALISM

The greatest criticism of the anti-masonic reports and guidance offered to church members is that none of them face up to the fundamental question of what happens in non-Christian prayer. There is ample evidence that such prayer is as fully answered as the prayer of the most devout Christian believer, and it would be a denial of reality to suggest that it is wish-fulfilment for pagans but true divine response for Christians. All the anti-masonic reports retreat into a sixteenth or seventeenth century ostrich-head-in-sand situation, where all that matters is correct Christian doctrine and everything else is ignored. The only report which has attempted to go beyond this was the last paragraph of the positive *Study* of the Church of Finland. The vast majority ignore the fact that we live in a pluralist society.

This is especially noticeable in the churches that adopt a close to fundamentalist theological stance. *Viewpoint: Baptists and Freemasonry*, for example, sets out 'the nature of our Christian commitment' based on the *Baptist Union Declaration of Principle*, which is undated in the pamphlet but probably dates back to the formation of the Union in 1750 (Barrett p706). From this it draws out five 'affirmations':

> 'There is one God, Father, Son and Holy Spirit, who has revealed himself *uniquely* in the Son . . .';
> 'Jesus Christ as Lord is the *sole* and absolute authority . . .';
> 'The Bible is *uniquely* the book of God's revealed truth . . .';
> 'Salvation is *solely* through repentance and faith . . .';
> 'In believer's baptism we affirm our prior commitment to Jesus Christ . . .' (p7)

It contrasts these with statements taken from *The Universal Book of Craft Masonry*, which is not listed amongst its recommended books, nor is its claim to be a masonic authority indicated. Be that as it may, what it says is not far from the truth, and one of the quotations is, 'Freemasonry recognises no distinctions of religion, but none should attempt to enter who have no religious belief . . . and prayers to Him [Deity] form a frequent part of the ritual' (p8). The contrast between 'uniquely' and 'solely', repeated several times in the affirmations, and the lack of religious distinction in Freemasonry could not be more complete. But where is there any statement from the Scottish Baptist Union about prayer offered by Jews, Muslims, Hindus, Parsees, and so on? It is surely a question which no church living with relevance in a pluralist society can avoid.

THE BIBLICAL WITNESS TO PLURALISM

Such ecclesial bodies, claiming to be Bible-based, are selective in their usage and ignore biblical material with which their doctrinal presuppositions do not concur. For example, there is a series of passages running throughout the Bible which indicate a much broader view of human relationships with the divine than the one that is limited by the covenant in the Old Testament or the *sola fides* of the New. Here are a few examples:

Before the covenant:

Accepting that Genesis is myth enshrining spiritual truth, what was it that caused Cain and Abel to feel the need to offer sacrifices, when no example had been set by their parents nor had they received any instruction from God (*Genesis* 4:34)?

Why was it that human beings felt a need to call upon the name of the Lord, and how did they discover the divine name (*Genesis* 4:26)?

How is it that Enoch had the capacity to walk with God (Genesis 5:24) and how was he able to please God (*Hebrews* 11:5)?

How did Noah achieve this same capacity (*Genesis* 6:9) and how did he know that he should offer sacrifices and what to offer (*Genesis* 8:20)?

After the Abrahamic covenant:

How did Melchizedek, outside the covenant with Abraham, achieve the status of 'priest of God Most High' (*Genesis* 14:18)?

How is it that Pharaoh could use the same name for God that Joseph used without converting to Joseph's religion (*Genesis* 41:16, cf 38)?

How could Jethro be a priest outside the covenant (*Exodus* 2:16) and yet offer acceptable worship to God in Moses' and Aaron's presence (*Exodus* 18:12)?

How could Moses require the high priest to perform an annual ceremony in which one goat is sacrificed to Yahweh and another let loose for the pagan god Azazel (often disguised in translations as the 'scapegoat') (Leviticus 16:8)?

How could Jephthah suggest that the land given by the two Gods Yahweh and Chemosh should be the basis of a territorial division (*Judges* 11:24)?

How could Solomon import a pagan chief artisan from Tyre to be the builder of a temple (2 *Chronicles* 2:13–14) which archaeology indicates was similar in design to Tyrian temples, and yet it could be blessed with divine presence (2 *Chronicles* 7:1–4)?

How could Naaman be encouraged in syncretistic worship of both Rimmon and Yahweh (2 *Kings* 5:18–19)?

How could Isaiah by implication make Ba'al the God of Israel when Ba'al is the name of a pagan god (*Isaiah* 1:3, 'master' in Heb is *baal*)?

How could Isaiah see Cyrus as the Lord's anointed (actually using the word 'Messiah', *Isaiah* 45:1) when he never converted to Yahwism and indeed was probably an enthusiastic Zoroastrian throughout his life?

How could God decide to spare the people of Nineveh at the five-word proclamation of Jonah, without any mention of covenant, even though they had merely repented and not converted to Yahwism (*Jonah* 3:4,10)?

How could Malachi have the Lord say that he was better worshipped by the pagan nations all around than by his covenant people (*Malachi* 1:11)? (Some translations mistranslate the Hebrew into the future tense to bury the problem as a prophecy of Christian worship).

In the New Testament:

How could John describe 'the Word' as 'the true light which enlightens everyone' (*John* 1:9) or his life as 'the light of all people' in a creational context (*John* 1:4) if he did not believe that everyone is to an extent enlightened?

How could Jesus commend the good deeds of a person whose faith was misguided if not pagan (*Luke* 10:33–37)?

How could Paul speak of all people having a capacity to 'search for God and perhaps grope for him and find him' because 'he is not far from each one of us' (*Acts* 17:27)?

How could Paul write of Gentiles (outside the covenant) instinctively fulfilling the law because it is written on their hearts and their consciences (*Romans* 2:14–15)?

How could Paul write that 'all Israel will be saved', even though the Jews of his day were not converting as readily as he hoped, if he believed that salvation was available only through Jesus Christ (*Romans* 11:26)?

The answer to all of these questions is that an openness to other faiths is a minimum biblical requirement because in their own way they have salvific value. There is a built-in response to the divinity in every human soul. Yet not one of the anti-masonic church reports recognises this strand of biblical material, and the only one that does so, albeit in a very short statement, is the positive report from Finland.

PRACTICAL PLURALISM

In his fine book on *Christian Theology—An Introduction* by Alister McGrath, used respectfully as the text book of a course taken by me before I became a Reader, three different views of other faiths which are generally adopted by Christians are set out. He calls these Particularism, Inclusivism and Pluralism, and the terms explain themselves. There is an earlier chapter in this book on Relativism (pp176-184) which still stands and need not be repeated. In that I set my heart on Inclusivism on p179, and I noted that this is a position adopted by some Evangelicals (p178) and Catholics. (p179) McGrath is customarily content to state alternative doctrinal viewpoints without going firm as to which is in his opinion the correct one; but here he opines that the Pluralist has abandoned Christ. (p538)

The problem is that we live in a pluralist society, and society demands a theology that faces up to and explains it.

A useful account of the Chaplaincy at Heathrow Airport appeared in a recent issue of the *Tablet*:

> It is here, in this chapel, that Christianity, Judaism, Sikhism and Islam shake hands every day over tea and biscuits. Yet the scene that greets me is a

> quintessentially English mix: two Salvation Army officers, a husband and wife pair neatly buttoned in their trademark uniforms, a tall pale Sikh priest with long theatrical beard, a Catholic priest and nun, a trio of Anglican chaplains that included a husband and wife and a colleague in youthful trainers, and small tidily framed imam with apologetic hands that open at the start of every sentence . . . Off stage, as it were, are a rabbi, two monks, another Sikh and a Methodist preacher, all out at work. The atmosphere, however, is uncompetitive—no one is going to be thrown out of the balloon—indeed, it's extremely cordial. 'We all believe in God, so it's easy for us to work together,' Bhai Hajirinder Singh explains . . .
>
> While Christian groups use the chapel, other faith groups use the prayer room upstairs, the small memorial garden or even just the corridor and anteroom to the chapel itself. 'There'll be 60-80 Muslims here for Friday prayers and sometimes this means they spill into the general areas,' says Imam Ovaisi. The hands make a cup and close gently.
>
> Jewish prayers, led by Rabbi Hershi Vogel, are also held in the general spaces and everybody is very careful not to tread on one another's toes. The prayer room, reached at ground level, is a simple structure: a triangular room tapering to a point just off the direction of Mecca . . . No figures or symbols appear in the room. Each faith group has its own religious accessories, and these are tidied into separate cupboards at the end of every prayer session.
>
> 'How has the post-11 September climate changed things?' I ask Imam Ovaisi. 'O dear,' he sighs. 'We came here all together on 14 September to say words of reconciliation. It was very important. The Muslims working at Heathrow felt very keen to dissociate themselves from that kind of thing.'
>
> 'But the whole thing is very relaxed now, though,' Fr Paschal Ryan soothes. 'You'll occasionally find Sikhs, Muslims and other faith groups all praying in the prayer room at the same time. And if I'm giving a service in the chapel and a Muslim comes in to pray, we don't ask anyone to leave. It's the same if anyone approaches any one of us while we're going round the airport. Our first question isn't to ask what faith they might be.'
>
> This ecumenical flavour is all very well, but doesn't this submersion of difference, this easy accommodation of other faiths, ever make them wonder if religious doctrine is itself rather pointless? 'Wow, that's a heavy one,' exhales Fr Ryan, wiping his face with his hands as if washing the mere thought away. 'We may all seek a vision of God but we do so in our own way,' chips in the Sikh. This is an attractive rejoinder but I'm not sure that the question isn't one that some of the clerical staff here haven't asked themselves before.
>
> Have any of them felt pressure from their own congregations outside the airport to turn the heat up a bit and to proselytise a little bit more? 'For a start, Sikhs don't try to convert and Jews don't either,' says Bhai Harjinder Singh, who is quickly interrupted by Fr Ryan and Major Thompson, who both try to assure me that conversions at Heathrow aren't the done thing. 'We're not here to provoke, but to act like a propeller and move things forward,' says the imam, waving his hands in delight at his own analogy.
>
> He and his colleagues are part of a worldwide network of airport chaplains, so, as you sit back in your seat, pondering the frailty of humankind as the plane soars heavenwards, remember that wherever you land, there'll probably be a team of religious quietly at work. (Mark Irving: 'Prepare for take-off,' *Tablet*, 18/25 December 2004)

What is happening at Heathrow is very much a part of today's pluralist society. None of the participants have abandoned their faith to take part in various acts of prayer or to minister in what is virtually a single space. There is more hope for the world in Heathrow's chaplaincy than there is in the church down the road where Particularism prevails and the congregation have decided that—despite their faithful service to Christ through the church over many years—they should make life as difficult as possible for Freemason members.

Heathrow Airport chaplaincy may offer one solution, but Freemasonry has offered another for almost 300 years. A mason is not required to give up his faith, but to accept that others of different faiths may occupy the same space at the same time, and enjoy themselves in an evening of ceremony, speechmaking and good food during which prayers are said to acknowledge God's presence, but without any person being able to question the appropriateness of another's presence on religious or political grounds.

Hans Kung offers a prayer in his new book *Der Islam* (Piper Verlag, Munich) which he has written so that Jews, Christians and Muslims might say it together. Its 27 lines include:

> Your will be done, wherever men exist.
> Living and benevolent God, hear our prayer:
> Our misdeeds have grown immensely.
> Forgive us, children of Abraham, our strife,
> Our enmities, our trespasses against one another.
> Redeem us from all needs and give us peace.
> (translated by Roland Hill, *Tablet* 17/25 December 2004)

So it is not only Freemasons who believe that human beings of differing faiths can offer valid prayer together.

UNDIVIDED LOYALTIES

Another potential problem of ecclesial reports is that they are by and large prepared by clergy. The minister of a church has the church's welfare entirely at heart. Every daily activity is directed at the honouring of God. Even their family life must be seen as part of a God-given vocation. Occasionally they might have a time-consuming hobby like carpentry, lawn bowls or stamp collecting, and this is rationalised in terms of providing a balance. Even Rotary or Soroptimist membership might be seen as a means of making contacts that will be beneficial for ministry, either leading to conversions or to meeting people who can facilitate church business.

This one-track approach to life makes it very hard for the clergy to understand why it is that some church members do not attend every Sunday morning, fail to attend mid-week Bible studies, and are not keen to devote their Saturdays to polishing the church brass. Surely, they think, the priority of the faith and the church is so important that every Christian ought to be in church every Sunday, rise early every morning for a 'quiet time', and mention Jesus to everyone at work pretty well every day.

The reality in which the laity live is very different. It is necessary to rise bleary-eyed early in the morning to catch a train for the London commute. Sunday is the only day that the young son can go to rugby training. Wednesday night is ballet class and mum must take her daughter to that, meaning that dinner is later than usual and the church Bible study must be missed. All this means that the laity are constantly juggling their priorities, and that sometimes the church must miss out. The moderately devout will simply say that there is no time to fit in churchgoing this week, we'll try next week instead. The more devout say that the whole of life is the Christian life, and so everything that is done—rugby, ballet, Rotary, Soroptimists and all—must be fitted into a set of priorities which on an overall basis is living a full Christian life to the glory of God. When the minister asks why he or she is not in church, it is a Christian's duty to stand firm and say that the priorities have been properly worked out.

But not all of these events give an opportunity for direct witness. A person who spent his son's rugby lessons witnessing to other parents on the touchline about what Jesus meant to them would soon find himself being avoided, and the other person would soon go and chat to someone else about the quality of tackling by the backs. In fact, even when a minister attends Rotary or the Soroptimists, they would soon find the same thing. The best witness to Jesus is the quality of membership, and soon the other members will say that the vicar is quite a decent chap, and the minister is a caring lady. The other members will soon establish whether or not a lay person is a practising Christian, with the same results.

All the adverse reports seem to live in a world apart, where a Christian, lay or ordained, has nothing to do but to be in church and tell others about Jesus. There is no sense of the need to juggle priorities, and no feeling that in that process, masonry can fit as easily as ballet classes.

PATERNALISM

There is an unfortunate paternalism about church reports and other anti-masonic literature. The poor man or woman who has been a contented mason for twenty years or more and who has not heard a thing against faith or society is told that the church had appointed a committee which met half a dozen times and discovered from perusal of a few books that Freemasonry is unChristian and that they should resign membership. The fact that he or she, after a great deal of masonic activity, may have become a member of, let us say, the eighteenth degree is exploited to suggest that there are dire things going on somewhere higher up, in the thirtieth degree or whatever, of which that person is unaware. Yet in that mason's many years of experience no dire thing has been suggested, let alone actually happened, and they have been perfectly prepared to take the benign nature of the 'management' on trust. After all, those who hold responsible positions in masonry are not isolated from the membership, and the most junior of masons will meet them at normal lodge meetings and find them to be upstanding and fine persons in whom trust can be placed.

Dire warnings, after a period of superficial study by an *adhoc* church committee or a commercial journalist, that regular masonry involves heretical belief and insidious motivation, fail to persuade the vast majority of masons. The committees and outside authors involved in anti-masonic pronouncements cannot by definition have entered into an understanding of the spirit of masonry, and their claim to superior knowledge which enables paternalistic advice to be proffered rings hollow.

31
Hardship

INTRODUCTORY

The case of the Marquess of Ripon, described on p108 of this book, shows that a high-ranking mason can be forced out of masonry simply because his religious superiors have decided that he may not remain a member, even though he himself as a mason had never experienced anything 'against Altar or Throne'. The relatively minor problems experienced by this author as the result of uninformed and irrational prejudice against Freemasonry have been given in the Preface to this edition. It nevertheless resulted in my leaving the Craft, with a residual feeling of dull resentment against the fellow Christians who caused it.

There is no central organisation which catalogues examples of hardship and prejudice against masons by their churches. No Grand Lodge has to my knowledge set up any receiving mechanism for such bad news. In most individual cases the problem is simply avoided, by masons moving to a less prejudiced church, quietly resigning from the Craft, or ceasing to attend church. I know a Roman Catholic mason of considerable seniority in the Craft who chooses an understanding confessor from the many available. But the overall result of increasing Christian prejudice over the past few years is that many Freemasons have retracted into their shells and literally keep their lodge membership secret, especially from fellow church members. This must be regarded as a bad thing both from the point of view of masonry which is anxious to adopt a more open profile, and from that of the churches whose ministry to mason members becomes constrained.

PREJUDICE IN METHODISM

The most consistent attempt by masons to record examples of prejudicial conduct by churches was conducted by the Association of Methodist Freemasons. This was set up in response to a Report to the 1985 Methodist Conference from the Faith and Order Committee called *Guidance to Methodists on Freemasonry*. Paragraph 22 stated, 'Consequently our guidance to the Methodist people is that Methodists should not become Freemasons.' It immediately went on to say, '23. We recognise that there are many loyal and sincere Methodists who are Freemasons, whose commitment to Christ is unquestionable and who see no incompatibility in their membership.' It advised Methodists who remained masons 'to declare their membership to avoid suspicion and mistrust', something that the prejudice subsequently displayed effectively reversed, and Methodist Freemasons and those in other negative churches have been forced 'underground'.

The Methodist Church of Great Britain claims an adult membership of some 600,000 with a considerable number of non-member adherents. Roughly speaking this means that there are or were some 20,000 or more masons within the Church.

The reaction of the many Methodists who were Freemasons is set out in their *Review* of October 1993 resulting from ten circuits having submitted memorials requesting a review of the *Guidance*. The submissions were largely ineffective and the Association of Methodist Freemasons was later disbanded. The hurt remains.

The Association listed known cases—no doubt the tip of the iceberg—where there were 'problems' arising from the *Guidance*:

The Secretary of the Association was pestered with rude, presumptuous and judgemental letters by a layman from Worthing on many occasions from June 1991 onwards.

A refusal by the Methodist Conference Directory of Nottingham and Derby to recommend publication of an advertisement for the Association in 1993, although it had carried the same advertisement the previous year.

An application form for the Lay Witness Movement which had a typed-in extra clause at the end: 'The management Committee would prefer that Freemasons did not apply to be witnesses.'

The 1986 Newsletter from the President of the Association in which he referred to 'quite a bit of hate mail' which he had received including one letter starting 'Dear Satan-worshipper', with the comment that that was not the worst!

A letter from a lifetime Methodist who had held the highest of lay offices reporting a meeting with his circuit minister who had said, 'I will not be happy until you and all other Freemasons are excommunicated from the Methodist Church.'

A summary of 22 cases in which Freemason Methodists had 'resigned all Church Offices', those who were 'removed' from membership of their church, newcomers who decided not to apply for church membership, those who had actually resigned from Methodism, and so on. Some suffered family division as a result of the publication of *Guidance*, in two cases the husband and wife eventually resigning from Methodism together, and in the other the husband eventually and very reluctantly leaving his lodge.

A letter about a young man who was a local preacher and had all the qualifications for entry to Training College to become a minister, when he was suddenly told that he 'could not become a Methodist minister because he was a Freemason'. The appendix includes a copy of a letter from the General Secretary of the Division of Ministries in which it is clarified that, 'Methodism has not said that a person who is a mason cannot be a minister'.

He asks for evidence of this 'question of justice'. However, the would-be minister considered that he and his family had had enough aggravation.

A letter from the Stour Vale Circuit in which a candidate Local Preacher was congratulated on passing his exams. However, the writer had been 'distressed to learn' of an involvement with Freemasonry, and before proceeding further the candidate was required to read 'the Conference Statement on Freemasonry', with clear unwritten implications.

A typescript of a tape which was apparently circulated in Stour Vale, in which Derek Prince speaks on 'Healing and Deliverance' which asserts that Freemasonry is an 'invisible barrier to healing'. It includes much anti-masonic rubbish, but particularly disturbing to any sense of logic is a case of a young mother whose six-week-old baby would not feed, and asked for prayer. The preacher questioned her about masonry, and it happened that her husband was one. The people ministering to her prayed against 'the spirit of Freemasonry' and 'it came out' of the mother and baby together with a loud shriek. Six hours later the mother reported that the baby had taken three full bottles. Of course, this interpretation of medical matters is wholly archaic and pre-scientific, and no genuine medical evidence was offered.

(I do not recall that masons assembled in their lodges, despite a certain seniority in their average age, are any more bereft of the benefits of medical healing than are the older non-masons in my Sunday congregation. Our prayer requests book in my local church is filled with requests for prayers for healing from presumed non-masons.)

A letter from the Chairman of the Council of Newmount Methodist Church announcing to Derby South Circuit that Freemasons would not be welcome to preach there. This was apparently a disguised personal attack on two elderly local preachers.

This was followed by a letter from the Secretary of the Association to the Local Preachers' Office in London, reporting on a meeting of the circuit Local Preachers which had pronounced 'the rightness of their decision because the members were spirit-filled and Christ-like', and pointing out that this was self- righteousness and lacking in charity. The chairman (Superintendent) in return had pointed out that only he was authorised to decide appointments to preach. The Secretary of the Association asked that it should be clarified that *Guidance* should not be used in this way.

The Secretary for Local Preachers in London replied that he was saddened by the news, that he was the son, grandson and nephew of masons whose Christian lifestyle he respected, but that he could not interfere in the matter.

A reply to a similar letter was received from the Chairman of the Nottingham and Derby District, noting that the Superintendent was solely responsible for appointments, that he would not be dictated to by churches, but that he would have to be sensitive (implying that he would not appoint the mason local preachers to preach at Newmount).

A letter from Preston Methodist Church refusing a gift from a masonic source and enclosing a copy of a pamphlet from Diasozo Trust—this would have been a thoroughly ill-written pamphlet called *7 Reasons why Freemasonry is not of God*.

This was followed by a letter from the Secretary of the Association to the chairman of the District noting that the offer of a gift had been accepted by the organisation on receiving an enquiry *before* the money was collected, and that refusal was embarrassing. He also objected to the pamphlet being issued, apparently to represent the Methodist viewpoint, which it most certainly did not.

The chairman responded saying that the charity concerned had the right to accept or refuse gifts. He thanked the masons for their generosity and goodwill towards a Methodist project. The letter had made 'unfounded assumptions' about the Conference statement (ie, *Guidance*) and the pamphlet which had been sent was not 'helpful or accurate'. The feeling of rejection which the masonic committee must feel was deeply regretted. But he could do nothing.

A letter from the former Property Steward of Warton Methodist Church in Carnforth, who had recently completed a successful church building development project. He was then approached by the Senior Steward about his masonic membership. It was put to him that unless he resigned from Freemasonry his position as Property Steward would be questioned at the next Council Meeting. He did not stand for office again, but continued to attend his church, feeling that he was regarded as a second class member. He hoped that the Faith and Order Committee would reconsider its *Guidance*.

A letter from a lifelong Methodist (48 years) and Freemason (34 years) who had reached the most senior lay positions possible in the Bristol District Synod. He had declared his masonic membership in his church and it seemed that this was accepted. He and his wife had helped in a Christian bookshop for four years, but had been told that he must 'consider his position' or he would no longer be allowed to work as a volunteer in the shop. He had long since considered his position, and it was that Christianity and Freemasonry were compatible, so he and his wife ceased to assist the shop.

The writer also mentions an Anglican example—see below—and also unspecific cases of the clergy alienating Freemasons from attendance, on the basis that 'the church doesn't want us and as I have no intention of giving up Freemasonry, there is no place for me in the church'.

A potential President of the Jersey Council of Churches was nominated by the Methodist Superintendent, supported by the Dean of Jersey and the senior Roman Catholic priest. The vote was unusually divided, and it was realised that those against thought that the candidate's masonic membership disqualified him. He decided to withdraw rather than cause division.

The Masonic Hall in Jersey (with its museum dealing interestingly with masonry during the German occupation) had issued invitations to various bodies offering to show them around the premises, such as Women's Institutes, Guilds, and various churches and their clergy. Appreciation had always been expressed at the 'openness' of the fraternity. Evangelical Methodist and Anglican churches had been notable for their absence.

A Methodist who presented a memorial to the Derby South District Circuit Meeting asking for a review of *Guidance* was subjected to orchestrated intimidation, including a specially prepared pamphlet issued at the door to all delegates. The person who handed out the tract, a Local Preacher, said during the meeting that he would not accept that the allegedly offensive word Jah-bul-on had been eliminated from the Royal Arch ceremony 'unless he can hear testimony from a Royal Arch Mason who has recently left Freemasonry under the guidance of the Holy Spirit'. This refusal to accept the truth of a clear statement from a fellow Methodist was particularly upsetting to the Secretary of the Association.

An interesting piece of evidence that it is the Church which has changed its stance is a copy of the petition for the formation of Epworth Lodge submitted in 1916. This included:

> The object of the petitioners is to unite together in Masonic fellowship Freemasons of the Methodist Churches throughout the world, by means of a Lodge held at the Buildings which are now recognised as the Headquarters of the Methodist Church . . . [A] number of Methodists of position and influence, not yet Masons . . . have manifested a keen interest in the project. The name Epworth is peculiarly associated with Methodism, that Town having been the birthplace of the Founder of Methodism, whose father was the Rector of the Parish.

The petition was sent from Central Buildings, Westminster.

I am of course aware that some Christians who read of Methodists resigning from their Church or its committees will see this as proof of the insidious power of Freemasonry over people's lives. How could it be possible for a genuine believer to rate his faith so lightly? Surely the persons involved must at best have been nominal Christians, attending out of social convention rather than Christian conviction. But it would be possible to read too much into a resignation: the mason may just have moved to a sympathetic church down the road. And it would be wrong to assume that those who resigns were not committed. The offence caused when a central body issues edicts which seem to bear little relation to reality may well lead to indignant resignation by a person whose masonic activity fitted well into his life as a believer. It must not be assumed that those left behind are any more committed, as the vast majority will not have been put to the test.

Above all, the majority of Christians do not see commitment in black and white terms, but in terms of nurture and growth. An unenthusiastic church member may be suddenly transformed by an experience which leads to a deeper commitment; but equally there must always be a slow process of transformation taking place. The person who is forced out of his church by a decision about Freemasonry has been deprived of that experience. Obedience is a Christian virtue, but the leaders 'are keeping watch over your souls and will give an account' (*Hebrews* 13:17). This accountability applies as fully to those who have forced others out as it does to those who been over-protective of those who remain in.

PREJUDICE IN THE ANGLICAN CHURCH

In the Church of England, there was very little open reaction to the passing of the report on *Christianity and Freemasonry—Are They Compatible?—a contribution of discussion* for further discussion, at least in terms of creating that discussion. Instead it has had the effect of making anti-masons believe that the Church had decided that the two *are* incompatible, even though it did nothing of the sort. It was clear from the recorded discussion at the Synod that several members voted in favour of the adoption of the report simply because they wanted more discussion. An attempt by Bishop Hugh Montifiore to re-start discussion a couple of years later by an article in the *Church Times* was met with deadly silence. By my reckoning, there have been only two other mentions of Freemasonry in the *Church Times* over the intervening years, one an enquiry as to the present stance of the Church and the other a misguided critique, both of which were answered by me.

This writer managed to persuade the Dean of Hong Kong—not a mason—to host a discussion on the subject shortly after the Synod adopted the report. The format was to be a presentation by me followed by open questions. The meeting was plagued by a young lady who rudely insisted on praying out loud in tongues throughout my presentation, thereby indicating that she intended to disrupt rather than listen. In the end it transpired that an over-enthusiastic newly converted layman was intent on attacking the Dean for his sympathetic approach to homosexuals, and the meeting ended with a shouting match between the two. Masonry was not considered in a rational way, and in fact gained in the eyes of the unprejudiced onlooker by the display of two non-mason Christians in combat.

The Dean later refused to permit a normal unamended Evensong in his Cathedral as a part of the celebration of the centenary of the founding of the District Grand Lodge of Hong Kong and the Far East, and it was held in another Anglican church nearby.

The Methodist evidence included a letter from Jersey explaining that the priest in charge of St Aubin's Church had refused to allow Freemasons to take part in Bible readings. Another document from Jersey repeats this case. The offer to take part in the reading of *Genesis* 1:1 to *Revelation* 22:21 over several days as a fund-raiser *for the church* had been made by the whole resident membership of St Aubin's Lodge No 958.

Again, the Methodist evidence records that, prior to 'Mission Jersey 1990', a communicant Anglican was appointed its honorary treasurer, but was asked to resign when it was realised that he was a mason.

A fellow student of mine at Oak Hill College returned from a mission to Devon called 'March of a Thousand Men' convinced that their work had been rendered less effective because Devon was very strong masonically and that the masons had been praying against it. I assured him that Devon was no stronger than average in masonic terms, since I had studied this a few years previously and found that the 'strongest' English counties were Surrey and Lancashire. Further, it was inconceivable that lodges would summon meetings to pray about anything, let alone against a mission, since prayer in lodge meetings uses brief formal wording and is solely for the meeting and the candidate. It was likely that some of the masons in Devon would be actively supporting his mission through their churches, although many would be indifferent.

The Dean of Norwich felt compelled to write in the *Cathedral Magazine*:

> I have been both surprised and deeply saddened by the outcry of some of my fellow Christians to a request that was made by a leading Anglican layman and an Anglican priest. They asked whether they, together with other Freemasons from this area, might come to their Mother Church to worship Almighty God. Quite clearly it would have been totally unthinkable to refuse—that is, as long as the worship formularies fell within the normal Christian tradition. In fact, these are brothers and sisters for whom Christ died, and we provided a shortened form of Evensong in the Cathedral as their act of worship. The prayers which were traditional Anglican ones had been submitted to my hawk-eyed scrutiny, the hymns were from New English Hymnal, and the readings were both from the New Testament—to wit, the Beatitudes and St Paul's hymn about charity in 1 *Corinthians* 13.
>
> Certain Anglicans have written to me suggesting that there could be some connection between occultism (or even Satanism) and Freemasonry. Quite frankly, I find this stretches credulity beyond reasonable limits. I have only to reflect that amongst my personal friends past and present, Archbishop Geoffrey Fisher and Bishop Westall of Crediton, together with the present Dean of St Albans, have all found no incompatibility between their Christian commitment as priests and their Freemasonry. You can understand that I am not prepared to accuse them of lack of intellectual honesty.
>
> Personally, I find it deeply offensive that they . . . should have their Christian integrity called in question. I myself have never been and do not intend to become a Freemason: but equally I know that I would be failing my Lord and Master most grievously were I to refuse to allow them to worship God in Norwich Cathedral . . . Were we to proceed down that road, then in honour bound we should have to conduct an inquisition into the theological views . . . of the Normandy Veterans . . . the Royal Norfolk Agricultural Association—not to mention the wide variety of bodies who hold carol services in the Cathedral at Christmas time.
>
> I don't believe that we can in honesty talk glibly about the Decade of Evangelism and yet at the same time seek to exclude those who have actually asked to come and hear God's word and offer him praise in his house. I notice that Jesus Christ was always inclusive . . .
>
> I have to say that I have found some of the wilder outbursts of certain of my fellow Christians against their Freemason brothers and sisters very hard to equate with Jesus' own words, 'By this shall all men know that you are my disciples—that you have love one for another'. That is why I am so deeply saddened by some Christian reaction to this act of worship. I certainly dare not adopt an exclusive outlook, because I know perfectly well that Jesus Christ would never have tolerated any such approach.
>
> *J. Paul Burbridge*, Dean

The letter has been shortened slightly. The full text was sent to the Methodist Conference with the Dean's permission.

Gradually, attitudes mellowed, and although stirred to an extent by American TV evangelists, the objection to Freemasonry at the turn of the millennium became an assumption that the Church of England did not approve of it, but that some men (and women) might be allowed a little indiscretion.

However, the ogre of prejudice suddenly raised its head in a brief article in the *Church Times* of 3 December 2004. The Bishop of Sodor and Man had held an informal meeting with the Provincial Grand Master of the Isle of Man over allegations that a Priest-in-Charge of a parish had said that he would ban Freemasons from the three churches of which he held the cure. The priest had then clarified his stance, saying that he would minister to all people without distinction, that he had not banned masons from office, but that he did not want 'ministers who are Freemasons' to serve in his parishes. He stated that, 'the difficulties encountered by Freemasons were the subject of a report by the Church of England House of Bishops some years ago'. He had clearly not read *A contribution* nor was he aware which body had adopted it. He was said to be further reconsidering his position in view of the meetings with the bishop. At the time of writing no resolution has been reported.

This nevertheless elicited a letter from a woman who had sent out a questionnaire to 'nearly 900 deans, archdeacons, rural and area deans and bishops advisors in the deliverance ministry'. To the question, 'Do you believe that Freemasonry is compatible with the priesthood?' the answers were currently 15.6% Yes, 66.5% No, and 17.9% Don't know. The question was not about *lay* masonic membership, and my own resignation was based on the call for openness in a lay ministerial position; a different proportion might have resulted from a different question. The correspondent concluded:

> It is to be hoped that the increasing openness shown by the United Grand Lodge of England over the past two years [sic, surely 'few years'] will encourage amicable discussions between Masons and non-Masons, leading to a greater understanding of the sensitive issues involved.

I can only respond with a hearty Amen.

Cases of hardship like those given above pale into insignificance when compared with what Christians suffer for their faith in many parts of the world as recorded in the work of organisations like Christian Solidarity Worldwide and the Barnabas Trust. But they ought not to be suffered at all in an open church in a civilized society.

32
Anti-masonic Literature

GENERAL COMMENT

A recent visit to the nearest branch of Wesley Owen to enquire what books they had about Freemasonry drew a negative response. They were sure that they had had some such books, but the shelf was bare, at least in that respect. Reference to the computer indicated that only three books had been recently available but were out of print. They indicated that they would have to go to American sources to find anything, and that they would phone me back. I responded that American sources were unreliable because they were largely funded by television evangelism and that extravagantly adverse claims, no matter how unreliable, produced greater donations to the TV evangelist. I was later contacted and offered a brief pamphlet and a book that might be reprinted at some future but unknown date.

This is very different from the situation fifteen years ago, when evangelical and Roman Catholic bookshops generally had a selection of up to a dozen books and pamphlets on the subject. Knight's unsupported fulminations were even available in the high street stationers WH Smiths, but this has ceased to be the case. This would seem to indicate that the witch-hunt against Freemasons has died down, but there are some indications that this is not altogether the case. As far as the anti-mason churchgoer is concerned, the situation has been clarified by most denominations and, once membership becomes known, Freemasons are generally unwelcome in church. It is assumed that the two are wholly incompatible and that is that. And as far as the churchgoing mason is concerned, he or she now keeps masonic membership even more secret than in the past.

This is not altogether true, and there is a dear old widow in my church who wears a masonic emblem as a brooch. I asked her if her husband had been a lodge member, thinking that she was making such a display out of respect for him. But she responded that it was *she* who attended lodge and was proud of it! But other masons that I know, mere males, make a great deal of effort to keep it secret in the church community.

Since anti-masonic literature is now virtually unavailable, this chapter is confined to a review of booklets and a pamphlet which are mentioned in the text of this part of this book. One thing can be said: apart from a pamphlet by Grove Books, not one of the respectable and responsible Christian publishers has within the last quarter century published an attack on Freemasonry. Such publications are the religious equivalent of 'pulp-fiction'.

ANKERBERG and WELDON'S THE MASONIC LODGE

This 48-page booklet, published in the same year as the first edition of *Workman Unashamed*, is quoted several times in the Southern Baptist study of Freemasonry, and so it seemed worth while to examine it.

The rear cover gives the qualifications of the co-authors. Ankerberg is host of a TV show which features bringing together members of Christian and non-Christian religions and secular authorities. He has master's degrees in divinity, church history and Christian thought. Weldon is an author with degrees in sociology, divinity, apologetics and comparative religion. This places them academically at about the same level as the author of this book.

The booklet cites as authority the statement of a single mason that the ritual (booklets detailing what happens in lodge meetings) is authoritative and the recommendations of the 50 US Caucasian Grand Lodges for masonic reading. The result of this survey was that nine books were 'recommended' by the 25 Grand Lodges that responded. The highest points went to *Coil's Masonic Encyclopedia* at forty-four per cent thus in effect being recommended by twenty-two per cent of the Grand Lodges only (p9). That was published in 1961, so it is now over 40 years out of date.

At the end of the booklet (pp45–48) there is a bibliographical list of 117 works, combined with reference numbers, some of which are starred as 'recommended'—but misleadingly this recommendation is not by the Grand Lodges but by Ankerberg and Weldon. A few of the references are to impartial encyclopaedias and published Bibles, but it is evident that some forty per cent of the citations are from anti-masonic sources. Some which appear from their titles to be masonic, such as the publications of Ezra A. Cook of Chicago, are exposés of ritual accompanied by virulently anti-masonic commentary. Far from trying to achieve a balanced picture, all but one of the *recommended* books are anti-masonic. Hence a jaundiced view must be taken of the assertion that what the booklet says is 'confirmed as accurate' by masons.

Despite the insistence on the Grand Lodge recommendations, the booklet immediately goes on to say that, although masonry teaches that a 'blue lodge' mason is complete and possesses the same essential knowledge as every other mason, 'some Masons' say that what really matters lies in 'the higher degrees'. Thus the authors immediately depart from their 'authoritative' texts by telling us what 'some Masons' think. (pp5–6)

Masons accept that in the past their history and teaching have been badly represented. Enthusiastic masons were far too keen to produce a false antiquity for the ceremonies, and an unacceptably high picture of their spiritual objectives. Anti-masonic activity in the past has been valuable in getting masons to think things through more logically. Hence what was written in the nineteenth century is generally historically inaccurate. What was written before the 1950s was generally suspect from a religious point of view, and the Baptist minister, the Revd Joseph Fort Newton, who had some very exotic ideas of the importance of masonry, is a typical case in point. This should have been sorted out by the US Grand Lodges in making their recommendations, but regrettably—in my opinion—they hold too dear the memory of their heroes like Albert Mackey and Albert Pike, who were great jurists and writers of the past but should not be cited as authoritative today. Needless to say, Ankerberg and Weldon specialise in quotations from such writers.

Apart from a brief historical excursion in Section 1, the booklet deals with only two questions. The second section is on 'Is Freemasonry a Religion?' followed by 'Where does Masonic Ritual Conflict with the Bible?'

One of the problems of dealing with fundamentalists is that they are unable to differentiate between authority and infallibility. Police officers have authority, but they are not infallible. Indeed, their rulings are frequently tested by the courts, and decisions made by juries or judges as to their correctness, but the juries and judges also claim no infallibility. Hence, despite the statement that the majority of masons and indeed some of those quoted (p12) do not believe that Freemasonry is a religion, Ankerberg and Weldon have found a single statement by one writer, H.W. Coil, that 'the fact that Freemasonry is a mild religion does not mean that it is no religion' (p15). This is from one of the list of books cited by twenty-two per cent of the American Grand Lodges as authoritative, and thus to Ankerberg and Weldon it must be infallibly correct. Thereafter they confuse 'religion' with the idea that an institution can be 'religious', whereas it should be obvious that an organisation like the Council of Christians and Jews is religious but it is not the property of any one religion. Its members are absolutely free to express their own preference and to practise their own religion, but the organisation cannot do so. Oxford University Press can publish books about many religions and hopes they will all sell well, yet Christians do not condemn it for joining religions together.

Their attitude to other faiths, despite Weldon having a degree in comparative religion, can be described as narrowly fundamentalist. They quote passages like, 'I am the Lord, that is my name; I will not give my glory to another' (*Isaiah* 42:8) in support of their exclusivity (p33). They are selective in their use of Scripture and have failed to see that there are other passages that offer a wider view of God as being able to be found by nations outside the covenant and the church. Many examples are given in chapter 30, but here are two, one from each period:

> From the rising of the sun to its setting my name is great among the nations, and in every place incense is offered to my name, and a pure offering; for my name is great among the nations, says the LORD of hosts. (*Malachi* 1:11)
> He made all the nations to inhabit the earth . . . so that they would search for God and perhaps grope from him and find him, though indeed he is not far from each one of us. (*Acts* 17:26–27)

Ankerberg and Weldon deal with dictionary definitions of religion, some quoted by masons in their writings, but of their own choice they use

Webster's New World Dictionary (p12). It is astonishing that two students of comparative religion should offer a definition which is so inadequate that it clearly excludes most Buddhists (because they do not believe in a Creator) as well as all Hindus and Shintoists (because they do not believe in a single god). Needless to say, the rituals of Freemasonry which evolved in the eighteenth century retain evidence of the attitude of mind which created the old definition, but its openness to persons of all faiths means that this is interpreted very liberally in practice.

Apart from the allegedly syncretistic word (or words) Jah-bul-on, amply covered in the original text of *Workman Unashamed*, the main topic of the last section is that Freemasonry offers salvation by works and without faith. To reach this position they ignore the fundamental question asked of every candidate at the beginning of his initiation ceremony—'In all cases of difficulty and danger, in whom do you place your trust?'—and pick out a few brief quotations which speak of 'upright conduct' and so on. The mason's answer to the initial question indicates that faith in God is taken for granted in all that follows. Nevertheless Ankerberg and Weldon attack any suggestion that good conduct leads to salvation:

> By many different symbols Masonry teaches a doctrine of 'works salvation'—that by personal merit and works of righteousness, the Masonic initiate will become worthy of salvation and eternal life. (p38)
> The following scriptures give the biblical position on how a man gains eternal life: 'For by grace you have been saved through faith; and that not of yourselves, it is the gift of God; not as a result of works, that no one should boast'. (*Ephesians* 2:8,9) (p39, similar examples omitted)

In fact, of course, the authors have selected passages from the Bible that support their own idea of human access to salvation. It would be equally possible to select:

> For he will repay according to each one's deeds; to those who by persistently doing good seek for glory and honour and immortality, he will give eternal life. (*Romans* 2:6–7)
> One of you says to them, 'Go in peace; keep warm and eat your fill', and yet you do not supply their bodily needs, what is the good of that? So faith by itself, if it has no works, is dead. (*James* 2:16–17)
> If you invoke the Father as one who judges all people impartially according to their deeds, live in reverent fear during the time of your exile. (1 *Peter* 1:17)

These brief passages come very close indeed to those parts of the ritual which Ankerberg and Weldon say contradict the Bible. It is not the intention of masons to interpret that Bible in a way that teaches justification by works, but a good case might be made out that the masonic ritual does not contradict the Bible, any more than the Bible contradicts itself. And every regular Grand Lodge will say that masonry does not offer any way of salvation.

Despite its being quoted several times, *The Masonic Lodge* was not convincing to the committee who wrote *A Study* for the Southern Baptists. It was clever of Ankerberg and Weldon to ask the American Grand Lodges for authoritative literature, but their purpose was clearly not an unbiased examination of the evidence, but a means of quarrying for proof texts that could be quoted against Freemasonry, whilst making the spurious claim that what they had produced was 'confirmed as accurate'. The picture they paint of Freemasonry is one that no mason would acknowledge.

7 REASONS

The pamphlet published by Diasozo Trust which was sent with an anti-masonic letter to a Methodist Freemason has the full title of *7 Reasons why Freemasonry is not of God*. It is still occasionally circulated in the form of xeroxed copies. Some years ago I did a rebuttal intended to be published in the format of a twice-folded A4 sheet and asked the then Grand Secretary if Grand Lodge would arrange for its publication. He felt that it would have the negative effect of drawing attention to the original pamphlet. It is reproduced here because of the continuing life of the original. Its contents can be judged from my responses.

1.

A review of
7 REASONS WHY FREEMASONRY
IS NOT OF GOD

An anonymous pamphlet published by
Diosozo Trust

[Publisher, etc]

Introduction

Diasozo Trust issues a number of fundamentalist tracts and books. The pamphlet under consideration is the same size as this response. There is no reference to copyright and the author hides in anonymity. As would be expected from the title, it has seven points, but these are preceded by a biblical quotation and followed by a conclusion and space for the 'issuing fellowship' to fill in an address.

The title is typical of the irrelevance of the argument. I suggest that Marks & Spencer, traffic wardens and Wimbledon tennis are human creations and would not claim to be 'of God'. But they have a very important place in practically everyone's lives, including devout fundamentalists. The fact that they are very much *of man* does not mean that they are not beneficial.

The pamphlet makes a direct comparison of Freemasonry with Christianity throughout, to the apparent detriment of the former. This is of course an invalid comparison, as it is comparing a men's club with its own rules about membership with a complete religion.

2.

Of course a religion is superior, and the United Grand Lodge of England is first to admit this in its official publications, insisting that a mason's first duty is to God.

1. *'The Oath of an Entered Apprentice.'*

The objection is to a 'blood curdling oath of secrecy'. Masonic 'obligations' — not oaths—used to include a physical penalty which was obviously symbolic, but this has been eliminated, so they cannot now be described as 'blood-curdling'. Oath taking is not forbidden by Christ in *Mat* 5:34, merely swearing by something else, an item absent from the obligation. Elsewhere in the New Testament, oaths are accepted, such as *Heb* 6:16. Mutilation has never been practised by masons, but see *Mat* 5:29 for Jesus' own symbolic usage.

2. *The 'Secrecy' of Freemasonry.*

Here the author quotes a shortened version of the text on the front cover (*Eph* 5:6–11) about 'unfruitful works of darkness'. What has this to do with secrecy which is commended by Jesus in *Mat* 6:4, 6 and 18? So how can the author say that secrecy is condemned in the Bible?

The official pamphlets of the United Grand Lodge of England state that the secrets of masonry are simply concerned with recognition, such as a special handshake and password, which were used in the old days before plastic membership cards existed to prove that a man was really what he claimed. These 'secrets' can be read about in exposures, notably those of Fr Hannah.

3.

3. *Masonry is 'not Genuine Fellowship'.*

The author objects that masonry is only for men who are free, reputable, literate and so on.

Surely Mother's Unions and Women's Aglow are not unChristian because they are for one sex! There are many clubs that will not admit children, and my church will not admit a person to its electoral roll unless they are eighteen.

And who today is concerned with the limitation of membership to free men—when did you last meet a slave who wanted to be a mason?

With his comment that it is for 'reputable people' and thus the well-off, he quotes the personal opinion of a mason as if it were a Grand Lodge rule. But is it wrong to charge a subscription? Many Christian societies to which I belong have subscriptions too, such as the Bible Society and SPCK.

Again, objecting to a modest requirement that an applicant for masonry must fill in a form in his own writing, and must thus be literate, is surely the grossest of nit-picking in these days of universal education.

He objects that 'mutilated or maimed' persons cannot 'ordinarily' be admitted. The requirement to which he refers was dropped from English masonry in 1815, 190 years ago!

He suggests that the rich and powerful are privileged in masonry. If that were true, is it not strange that masons call one another 'brother' in lodge, meeting in terms of fullest equality? Antient Charge IV starts, 'All preferment among masons is founded upon real worth and personal merit only.'

4.

4. *Freemasonry is 'a Federation of Religions'*

Our anonymous author quotes the personal opinions of two long-dead clergymen masons—the Revd J.F. Newton and the *Entered Apprentice Handbook* (which was by Bishop J.S.M. Ward)—to prove that this allegation is true. He has picked two masonic writers who are regarded as the least authoritative by modern scholars. Grand Lodge has officially stated that it is not masonry's task to 'join religions together'.

Another objection is that 'men of any religion may enter'. Does the fact that the Boy Scouts, the Post Office and the National Trust treat all persons as equal irrespective of their religion mean that Christians can have no part in them? Of course not!

5. *An alleged 'Composite God'.*

A reference to the Royal Arch degree as the 'seventh' indicates that the author knows nothing of English masonry, where it is the completion of the third. He says that in this degree there is a composite name for God which is 'Jabulon', which is similar to a word which used to be used.

Without justification he states that the first syllable is Greek for Jehovah, the middle syllable is the pagan god Baal, and the last is from an Egyptian mystery religion. This bears no relation to the explanation that used to be given to every Royal Arch mason, that the word describes four attributes of God—eternity, lordship, supremacy and Fatherhood.

But the issue is out of date, as the Grand Chapter of England dropped the word in 1989.

5. 6.

6. *'It is finally a worship of Satan.'*

Here the pamphleteer gives an alleged quotation from Albert Pike whom he describes as 'Sovereign Pontiff of Universal Freemasonry', an office of which I have never heard: he was Grand Commander of the Scottish Rite in the Southern USA. The quotation requires 'initiates of the higher degrees' to maintain 'the purity of the Luciferan doctrine . . . Yes, Lucifer is God.'

A thorough search for this quotation has been made in the archives of the organisation in Washington DC which Pike led, and in the Library of the Grand Lodge of England, to no avail. Pike's genuine writings refer to Lucifer as the evil opposite of God, making the quotation inconsistent. Its earliest occurrence indicates that it was invented in 1894 by a French anti-masonic writer, A.C. de la Rive. Our author is quoting false evidence.

The Grand Secretary has publicly stated that masons must believe in a *good* God. Thus the author's reference to 'the mystery of iniquity' from 2 *Thes* 2:7 is irrelevant.

7. *'Masonry is a Deception from Beginning to End.'*

He states that the new mason is told that he is in search of a secret, but that it is never found. He then states as a deduction from the wrong conclusion based on false evidence from para 6, that the unrevealed secret is that 'God is Satan!'

In reality, new masons are told that there are masonic 'secrets' and that they are recognition signs. They are revealed within a few minutes of admission and again in subsequent ceremonies. The secrets are revealed quickly and have nothing to do with Satan.

The inner pages of the pamphlet finish with isolated statements which are to me indisputable but irrelevant.

For example, 'Jesus sets men free', something which I fully believe; or 'Freemasonry ignores Jesus as Saviour', but then so do Marks & Spencer, traffic wardens and Wimbledon tennis. We support and accept their existence without Christian objections.

Supposed 'Conclusions'.

The author claims that his seven points progress to the conclusion that Freemasonry is incompatible with Christianity. Since each is to a lesser or greater extent in error, the conclusion must also be false. It is possible for a mason to live an uncompromisingly Christian life.

Thus the three steps which follow the conclusion are not relevant either:

> Since membership is compatible with Christian belief, there is no need to *renounce* it;
>
> Since it is not in itself sinful, there is no need to *repent* before God; and
>
> Since neither of the above is necessary, there is no need to *seek pastoral help*.

This is not to say that Freemasons do not need to renounce obstacles to spiritual advancement, to repent and to seek pastoral help, but their membership of the Craft can only be purely incidental to their general need for spiritual counsel in common with everyone else.

Finally, the pamphlet quotes part of the Ten Commandments, including 'You shall have no other gods before me' and 'You shall not take the name of the Lord your God in vain'. No explanation is given, but the presumption must be that Freemasons have transgressed them.

Bearing in mind the false quotations and outdated arguments used in the pamphlet, it is not surprising that it does not quote, 'You shall not give false testimony'. (*Ex* 20:16).

Several other pamphlets were also drafted by me at that time, but to reproduce them all would be irksome, since the arguments used against masonry are repetitive and tedious, and differ only in terms of the degree of gullibility exhibited.

Some success may be recorded in that the editor of Grove Books was sufficiently impressed by the errors pointed out in one of their publications that a decision was made not to do a reprint.

BERRY'S WHAT THEY BELIEVE—MASONS

This was the 'pamphlet' that Wesley Owen eventually produced, although it contains 53 pages, admittedly of small format, published in 1990, revised in 1999. The author claims to have been Professor of Bible & Greek at Grace University of Omaha, Nebraska, and it was published by Back-to-the-Bible Publishing. It may thus be assumed to be of fundamentalist provenance.

In true academic form the author gives references and footnotes. He has not subjected himself to the discipline of Ankerberg and Weldon in restricting quotations with a degree of consistency to books recommended by US Grand Lodges, and he thus moves at random through the personal opinions of authors who were masons (not one of whom is still alive). The only modern works which he mentions are anti-masonic, such as Ankerberg and Weldon's book, reviewed above, and a book by Jim Shaw and Tom McKenny called *The Deadly Deception: Freemasonry Exposed . . . by one of its Top Leaders*. This is quoted and referred to several times.

The basis of the book is that Jim Shaw claims to have been a Thirty-Third Degree mason and thus a significant masonic leader, able to paternalistically tell junior masons how wrong they are. Shortly after it was published, the *Scottish Rite Journal* of Washington DC investigated this claim and found that Jim Shaw was indeed a Scottish Rite member, achieving the 32nd Degree. There is no great credit in that, as all American members of the Rite reach this same point, in most cases having gone through all degrees from 4th to 32nd in a series of ceremonies held over a single long weekend. The diligent enthusiast will eventually receive what is colloquially called '32½', actually 'Knight Commander of the Court of Honour', and that is as 'high' as they can go. Exceptionally a KCCH member is elected by the 33 members of the 33rd Degree to make up the number when one resigns or dies, to join them in the autocratic government of the Rite; and equally exceptionally a very limited number are elected to honorary 33rd Degree status. The *Scottish Rite Journal* found that Jim Shaw was indeed a resigned member, but that he held merely the 32nd Degree and was under consideration for '32½' when he resigned. Thus his book was based on a lie and everything he wrote about the evil intentions of the government of the Rite was based on supposed exposés or a fertile imagination. But no matter, he would consider that God could be well served by a lie!

The booklet contains a list of seven recommended books (pp48–49), including of course Ankerberg and Weldon's and Jim Shaw's. All of them are anti-masonic. The references for masonic quotations specialise in antiquated masonic books, and the Revd Joseph Fort Newton, author of *The Builders*, is quoted as having been 'an Episcopal minister' (p13) when in fact he was a Baptist. When he advises his readers 'to examine the Masonic sources for yourself' (p39) he has of course given only those which support his viewpoint. To check them for accuracy would be pointless, they are typical of the old-fashioned masonry of the nineteenth and early twentieth centuries, with its pseudo-history and woolly thinking, which the Authentic School was founded to overcome (see chapter 33, 'Academia').

The booklet displays a few other inaccuracies, such as a statement that the 'U.S. Headquarters' of Freemasonry is at 'Alexandria, Virginia' (p46). There is no such thing, as each Grand Lodge in every US State has its own headquarters. It states that 'Freemasonry uses the Bible only in a "Christian" lodge; the Hebrew Pentateuch in a Hebrew lodge, the Koran in a Muslim lodge . . .' (p46) whereas, not uniquely, the United Grand Lodge of England lays down that the Bible must always be open in *every* lodge meeting, but that *in addition* a candidate from another faith may take the obligation on the book that is binding on his conscience. It states that 'The Entered Apprentice is told: "In his private devotions, a man may petition God or Jehovah . . ." ' (p32) but the quotation is not from a masonic ceremony but from a book expressing the opinion of its writer. Some of its statements apply mainly to America, such as a reference to 'a religious service to commit the body of a deceased brother to the dust' (p14), when the English masonic authority prohibits masonic funerals, stating clearly that the last rites of every faith are complete without additions or alternatives.

Towards the end Berry asks five questions such as, 'Do you believe that Jesus Christ is God?' and 'Do you believe that trusting in Jesus Christ as Savior is the only way to obtain salvation?' (pp41–42) and suggests that, 'A knowledgeable and committed Mason would have to answer no to all these questions if he is truthful.' I could certainly answer Yes to both, but not to some of the others, and I am not a mason. I suggest that only a fellow fundamentalist could answer Yes to all five, and there are many committed Christians who like myself are not masons who could not pass Berry's test. It is narrowly exclusivist and, for example, would be unacceptable to Catholics in its omission of the role of sacraments within the church.

This booklet displays to a high degree those faults which are enumerated in the chapter on 'Faults of Negative Reports'. Above all else, its fundamental stance is that, because Freemasonry is open to holders of all religions and cannot by definition offend any one of them, it cannot emphasise the uniqueness of Jesus Christ. Therefore it is not possible for Christians to be members. It is unable to see that persons who become masons are encouraged to bring their complete faith with them and not to compromise it in any way—but to accept it as a fact of life in a multi-faith society that Christians must coexist, and can enjoy doing so, with holders of other faiths.

TAPE RECORDINGS

The Association of Methodist Freemasons noted the bad effects of tape recordings being circulated amongst believers. A tape recording of a sermon or talk by the Revd David Pawson was widely circulated in the Christian circles in which I moved, and because I was *then* a mason I was about the only person who did not know of it! When I eventually obtained a copy, I realised that it was full of errors, made a transcript of it, and wrote to Pawson.

Eventually a pamphlet was produced by me without using Pawson's complete text, but the development up to that point was interesting and was described as follows:

> At that time [probably 1969, Pawson] accepted the possibility of error in what he said, and invited any mason present to correct any such after the meeting, but whether they did or not, the tape was circulated very widely. Its continued circulation means that, even if no masons spoke out at the time, its errors should be corrected now, rather than have Christians seeking the truth in this field further misled, albeit unintentionally. The tape is by now [1988] somewhat out of date, and some of the comments correct this, and are obviously no reflection on what David Pawson said then.
>
> I had originally intended to print the actual text of the tape, followed by my correctional comment, and wrote to Pawson, suggesting that I should do this and offering him the opportunity to react to my own comments. In response, he offered no comment except that some masons had said that he was more or less right, retracting nothing. By he also threatened to use the full force of the copyright law if I proceeded. It upset me considerably that he should so lightly regard the truth in this sensitive matter, all the more so because the tape sent to me originally by a well-meaning Christian was itself obviously a pirated copy. (p v)

The introductory 'How this booklet came about' continued:

> I have not sat under the ministry of David Pawson, but on the basis of what friends have told me, I am sure that he is inspired by the Holy Spirit. However, the Holy Spirit does not overrule, but takes men gently as they are, with their personalities, their education, their knowledge, even their prejudices, and gradually moulds them to the image of Christ . . . But if this process of moulding is a correct description, then the basis of carefully researched facts which we place at the disposal of the Holy Spirit and of other growing Christians is of extreme importance. Here it is that I find Pawson's tape to be lacking . . . (p vi)

Regrettably a pamphlet of this kind would not be read by those Christians who wish to believe what Pawson said, and, like him, prefer not to be confused by truth.

33
Academia

THE 'AUTHENTIC SCHOOL' AGAIN

In chapter 7 of this book (pp76ff) I have already mentioned the development of the 'Authentic School' of masonic history. After almost two centuries in which 'speculative' masonry meant not just non-operative working, but also non-factual history, two major landmarks occurred in the last quarter of the nineteenth century. The first was the founding of the Quatuor Coronati Lodge No 2076 in 1886, and the second, a few years later, the publication of R.F. Gould's monumental *History of Freemasonry.*

In the first, the members were determined to allow only papers which were based on actual research, and to discuss them critically in lodge, so that only the genuine facts would filter through. In the second, an excellent first attempt to produce a consistently factual history from the medieval operatives to the time of writing meant that the general public as well as masons might read how Freemasonry had developed.

That may all seem a long time ago, but Freemason-writers continued to write over-imaginative literature until well into the twentieth century. Much of their nonsense has been quoted by me to prove this point, and quoted by the churches against the Craft. This denial of rationality has been helped by non-mason writers who have produced much speculative but popular nonsense about the continuation of the Knights Templar in Scotland, the burial of the Ark of the Covenant in Provence, and equally tenuously recorded ideas, all somehow connected in the mind of the writers with Freemasonry. Each step of argument concludes with a possible solution, and the next chapter assumes the possibility to be a fact, and thus a house of cards is built on possibilities.

Some of this kind of literature has been responsible in part for the formulation of church reports on Freemasonry which take the view that for their flocks to be 'safe' the whole thing were best avoided, and to stop potential pollution by such ideas, masons should be kept out of church. Whereas this may seem to many to be excessively paternalistic—telling mature adults that they are in danger from something that they know to be perfectly safe—the absence in many masonic jurisdictions of official histories and the recommendations, especially by American Grand Lodges, of books that continue the old ideas, means that the churches often cannot be blamed for their naive and overbearingly negative reports.

THE NEED FOR ACADEMIC RESEARCH

One of the great and foundational books on the social history of operative masonry was Frederick Knoop and G.P. Jones' *The Medieval Mason,* first published in 1933. Knoop was a Freemason, and Jones was not, and they worked together on medieval manuscripts in the University of Sheffield to produce a book that will probably never be eclipsed. In fact, G.P. Jones was the first non-mason to deliver a paper to the Quatuor Coronati Lodge, which took place during a meeting, 'called off' to admit the non-mason, receive and discuss his paper, and then 'called on' again.

Although they dealt with operative masonry, this was perhaps the first sign that Freemasons and non-masons could work together on authentic masonic research, and that their work could receive the distinction of publication by a university press which prized academic integrity above all else. Indeed, to an extent it must be true that such collaboration may often be essential if the best of specialists are to work for excellence in their research. In 1969 the Oxford scholar John Roberts published an article in a prestigious historical journal pointing out that, while Freemasonry had been a major subject for historical research in Europe, professional historians in Britain have taken little or no interest in it. Frances Yates' *Rosicrucian Enlightenment*, published in 1972, has already been noted in this book (p74) as an early if not entirely satisfactory attempt.

Professor Andrew Prescott mentions some sad lapses in recent years. John Pine was a brilliant eighteenth century engraver who did the frontispiece of the first edition of *Robinson Crusoe*, an impressive edition of Horace, and Rocque's map of London. These are amply covered in the standard reference books on his life, but not one of them mentions that he was a Freemason, that he engraved the frontispiece of the first *Book of Constitutions* and the engraved lists of lodges between 1725 and 1741. The latter sounds rather uninteresting, but the lists are depicted as perspective drawings of what, in proportion to the human figures below, would be a huge noticeboard within a detailed classical frame, listing some fifty lodges, each lodge with its emblem, often that of the teahouse or hostelry where it met. Each engraving includes a crowd of masons standing at the foot studying it. None of this is mentioned in the 'secular' histories, and yet there is sufficient material for a substantial exhibition to have been mounted at Freemasons' Hall, London, open to the general public.

A similar lacuna exists in the major biography of the Duke of Connaught which fails to mention that he was Grand Master, and indeed any of his rich contribution to the masonry of his day.

THE SHEFFIELD RESEARCH CENTRE

In 2001 the Centre for Research into Freemasonry was established in the University of Sheffield, the first such in a British university. It is largely funded by masonic bodies such as the Provincial Grand Lodge of Yorkshire West Riding. Professor Prescott, a non-mason, heads it. At a recent address about its work to Grand Lodge the same procedure was adopted as for G.P. Jones many years previously—Grand Lodge was 'called off' so that his talk could be inserted in the agenda, and then 'called on' again.

Since its foundation the centre has had an active programme in which a wide variety of subjects has been explored, and he mentioned James Joyce, Unitarianism and medieval guilds. Audiences have consisted of local Freemasons, academics, and university students. Discussion between masons and academics has been very fruitful. A website with recordings exists for those who live further afield. A conference in 2002 was organised with the University's Centre for Gender Studies, on the influence of fraternal organisations in shaping the roles of men and women in society. Even more recently the theme of a conference organised with the Society for the Study of Labour History was 'Freemasonry in Radical and Social Movements'.

The Centre has provided an advisory role for media students from Salford and Newcastle making a film about Freemasonry, and work with architectural students measuring up an old Masonic Hall.

Professor Prescott is himself heavily engaged in research, and has for example found a use of the word 'Freemason' in English dating from 1325, half a century earlier than that previously thought the earliest. He has likewise, apparently for the first time, studied the 'electrifying' parliamentary debate which led to the passing of the 1799 Acts which required lodges to be registered. The Centre has made available in database form John Lane's *Masonic Records* of all lodges warranted by the English Grand Lodge between 1717 and 1894, and is extending this to the current time, funds permitting, as well as a CD-ROM of the multiple editions of William Preston's *Illustrations of Masonry*, a very influential educational work for masons at the turn of the eighteenth/nineteenth centuries, to enable comparisons to be made.

It is hoped that in 2005 the Centre will be in its own designated premises, and that this will be known as the 'Knoop Centre' after the local professor of economics who co-authored *The Medieval Mason*.

Why mention this at such length in a book on the subject of the churches' relationship to masonry? Because the atmosphere of calm academic consideration of the subject is so different from that exhibited by the churches in their frenzied attempts to condemn. Eventually the reports to synods and the like which have featured in this book will be looked back upon as a misguided blot on the history of the practical expression of the faith in the churches, not unlike that of the witch-hunts of the seventeenth century or the anti-Darwinist attacks of the late nineteenth. Repeated references to Satan-possession and exorcism owe more to the Dark Ages than to the last three centuries; they are wholly alien to the atmosphere of the Sheffield Centre.

THE CANONBURY MASONIC RESEARCH CENTRE

An organisation with similar objectives to the Sheffield Centre exists on a less academic basis in North London. It does not have the same university background or funding, but it nevertheless plays an important part in this new academic approach to masonry. It was established at the end of the last century, somewhat before the Sheffield Centre, with the enthusiastic support of the Marquis of Northampton, Pro-Grand Master of England. It has an annual 'international conference' and a programme of lectures roughly once a month.

The 'Sixth International Conference' was held in November 2004 over a long weekend, and I was able to attend as a non-mason. I did so because the subject was 'Freemasonry and Religion: Many Faiths—One Brotherhood'. This was the first on this subject. The other participants were an interesting mix: about a third were women, varying from one at least who shyly admitted to being a member of a woman's lodge that meets just across the river from my house, to senior members of the English mixed Grand Lodge, and the wives of a delegation of a half dozen Italian masons. There were a few clergymen, a number of female officials of United Grand Lodge such as the librarian and the custodian of regalia, as well as members of the Quatuor Coronati Lodge whom I knew from the past. Some younger persons included a student who wished to know more of masonry before applying for initiation and a young woman student from the School of Oriental and African Studies who was doing a dissertation on oriental influence in masonic initiation. The schedule was intense, and we had twelve full lectures and question sessions in two days.

Here are some of the topics covered:

Geoffrey Bissell: 'The Masonic Archbishop of Canterbury, Geoffrey Fisher.'
Dr Yuri Stoyanov: 'The Inter-relations between the Eastern Churches and Freemasonry.'
Professor Antonio Panaino: 'Zoroastrians and Freemasonry.'
Robert Gilbert: 'Paranoia and Patience—Freemasonry and the Roman Catholic Church.'
Professor Cecile Revauger: 'Freemasonry and Religion in 18th Century Britain.'
Dr Henrik Bogdan: 'Kabbalistic Influence on the Early Development of the Master Mason Degree of Freemasonry.'

These papers have been selected to show the breadth of subject matter. But what was equally important was the diversity of speakers at a high academic level from many countries. Their credentials included, a lecturer on Western Esotericism at the Department of Theology and Religious Studies at Lampeter; a holder of a doctorate from the University of Sofia who had done field work in the Balkans and Anatolia and written on the relationship between Christian and Islamic apocalyptic; the Professor of Iranian Studies at the University of Bologna; the Professor of English studies at Bordeaux University; an academic from the Department of Religious Studies at Gothenburg University; and a lecturer on British Intellectual and Religious History at the University of Szeged in Hungary.

One paper deserves special mention: one given by David McCready, a holder of degrees in theology from the universities of St Andrews and

Strasbourg and a master's degree in Irish History from Belfast. It was on 'The Theology of Craft Ritual as Demonstrated in Emulation Ritual.' This took as its start the principle of *Lex orandi lex credendi*, and sought to see if there is a theology in the prayers of the lodge. The paper appears prima facie to run counter to the assertion of United Grand Lodge that 'Freemasonry has no theology and because it will not allow religious discussion, permits no theology to develop'. Regrettably the paper was not available to take away for study, and it will take a while for the printed proceedings to be produced.

In the meantime, I would comment that there is a difference between Christian beliefs, doctrines and theology. It is possible to express a belief in a few words, to which the creeds bear witness. The moment that an attempt is made to explain a belief and look at its implications, it becomes a doctrine. But the development to theology is much more complex, because a theology, always singular, is a unified statement which co-ordinates multiple beliefs and doctrines into a single system. Hence Alister McGrath's 600-page *Christian Theology* is subtitled *An introduction* because he modestly and correctly sees it as not yet reaching the status of a full theology. He dwells at some length on sources of theology but then tends to cover uncoordinated doctrines in the second part of the book. On the other hand, a much harder book, John Macquarrie's *Principles of Christian Theology,* attempts in a mere 544 pages to set out what he wishes to teach within a single framework, and even if he claims only to write of 'principles', it is close to theology in itself because it is the principles that meld the doctrines into a unity.

But David McCready writes in synopsis:

> As far as the ritual is concerned, the doctrine of God it teaches may be summarised in several propositions: God is Creator, He is Governor, He is Revealer, He is Helper, He is the Source and Reward of Goodness. All these propositions may be said to mirror exactly the theology of Jesus Christ as expressed in the Synoptic Gospels. More controversially, one might give a 'Masonic' reading to the New Testament and see Jesus Christ as the Master Mason par excellence, the Builder and Constructor of a New and Perfect Temple.

Whether this view of Jesus Christ is right or wrong is not a question for this book. McCready is doing precisely what he would *not* be permitted to do in lodge, and that is to make doctrinal and even theological deductions from the very simple beliefs expressed in masonic prayer. He is permitted to do so in an open research centre where, provided it is academically sound, anything goes. He is a Christian developing beliefs about the God simply described in prayer along Christian lines. Jews, Muslims, Parsees or Sikhs might equally do so in their own minds, write them down at home and present them as a learned paper; but they are not permitted to speak of their insights to the assembled lodge members.

Thus although McCready appeared to be giving ammunition to the anti-masons who maintain that the Craft is a religion with its own theology, he was, on analysis, supporting the opposite view.

And the openness of the Canonbury Centre to mason and non-mason alike, and to both sexes, with the only provision that they must take an academic interest in the subjects under discussion, further points away from the fears of the churches. There is no secret religious doctrine in Freemasonry in competition with the Christian faith of the churches.

The genius of Freemasonry was to establish the process of taking a simple ceremony of admission into a craft guild and modifying it so as to appeal first of all to the wider audience of the middle class of the eighteenth century, and then to eliminate specific Christian references so that it might be the basis of a meeting ground for 'all good men and true'. In this it has long been ahead of the churches, which failed to develop any consistent doctrine of other faiths until the later twentieth century; indeed, it appears that some have still not done so. Even so, a reversion to Exclusivism or Particularism is evidenced the moment they attempt to face up to the existence of Freemasonry. This is not to suggest for a moment that the churches should emulate masonic ritual, but to point out that in a pluralist society the masons are only doing what in practice everyone does in order to coexist with members of other faith groups on an everyday basis.

GLOSSARY

BIBLIOGRAPHY

INDEX

GLOSSARY

As Freemasonry, along with any other society with specialist activities, uses a number of words in a technical sense, it seems sensible to provide a list of the more important of these. The reader will no doubt wish to refer to this section from time to time.

Ahiman Rezon: the name the *Antients* adopted for their *Constitutions,* probably intended to be Hebrew for 'Help to a Brother'.

Altar: see *Pedestal.*

Anno Lucis: Latin for 'the year of light', counting the calendar from the year in which God created light. This was calculated by Archbishop Ussher using the biblical genealogies as happening in 4004 BC, and masons have generally rounded this off to 4000, except in Scotland. Thus AD 1987 is given on formal masonic documents as AL5987, or in Scotland as AL5991. The purpose of this system would appear to have been to provide a calendar which did not favour one religion.

Antient: alternative spelling of ancient, with no special significance. Antient Charges, see *Charge.*

Antients: the nickname of a Grand Lodge in England founded in 1751, claiming to retain traditions forsaken by the original Grand Lodge of 1717, which they dubbed the 'Moderns'.

Apprentice: as it implies, the first step to becoming a qualified *Master Mason.* In full it is 'entered apprentice', a Scottish term originally meaning entered in the burgh books. The ceremonial of admission is called 'making' or 'initiation'.

Blue degrees/masonry: conferred or practised in a normal lodge, as opposed to 'red' degrees in a *chapter.* In Ireland this usage extends to 'green' masonry (Red Cross Councils) and 'black' masonry (Knights Templar), and so on. Seldom used in England. Based on the main regalia colour.

Ceremonial: see *Ritual.*

Chaplain: a lodge officer who says the prayers at opening and closing, and at the beginning of each degree ceremony, and before formal meals. When a priest, minister, rabbi, etc, is a lodge member, he often holds this office, but as often prefers not to do so in order to make progress and eventually reach the chair of his lodge.

Chapter: a common term for a masonic body conferring a *'higher' degree.* It normally connotes a *Royal Arch* Chapter unless otherwise differentiated, eg, Chapter *Rose Croix.*

Charge: a formal lecture delivered at the end of a degree ceremony, exhorting the candidate to virtuous behaviour.

The *'Old Charges'* are a series of over a hundred manuscripts and early prints from 1390 to 1750, which recount the history of masonry as seen by a medieval scribe, and lay down rules for behaviour. These are also called the 'manuscript constitutions'.

The *'Antient Charges'* are a very extensively revised version of the rules from the 'Old Charges', set out in the first *Constitutions* and more or less copied subsequently. Note, the 'Antient Charges' are less ancient than the 'Old Charges'.

The *'Summary of the Antient Charges'* is a rather different set of rules taken from both the Antient Charges and the *Constitutions* to which the new Master gives his assent prior to installation.

Charter: see *Warrant.*

Chivalric masonry/degrees of Chivalry: a general term for those *'higher' degrees* which are based upon the various orders of knighthood which were formed or developed during the Crusades. Membership is restricted to Trinitarian Christians, and is extended by invitation, usually to *Royal Arch* masons, rather than by petition. The best known such masonic Order is that of the Knights Templar.

Communication: the normal meeting of a Grand Lodge. Also used for all Irish lodge meetings.

Consecration: When a new lodge is formed or a masonic hall is built, it is consecrated (set apart for the purposes of masonry, not worship) and constituted.

Constitution: the governing body under which a masonic body works is identified by saying that a lodge is 'English Constitution'—it is under the United Grand Lodge of England. Americans would probably say 'jurisdiction' or 'Grand jurisdiction'. Canadians refer to the 'British Columbian Register' etc.

Constitutions: the book of rules for the self government of a Grand Lodge, and of the lodges under it.

Craft: usually, to do with lodges under *Grand Lodges*, and if so used, it is in contradistinction to the *'higher' degrees* and their governing bodies. Occasionally used for Freemasonry as a whole, or for masons as a body.

Deacon: a lodge officer who has a responsibility for candidates during their initiation etc. Various derivations have been suggested, in view of the senior officer of *operative* Scottish lodges having been so called: possibly from *decanus*, meaning 'in charge of ten men'.

Degree: the various steps by which a mason enters into and progresses within his lodge or any other masonic body. A ceremony lasting the better part of an hour, which combines impressive experience with formal teaching.

Diploma: Scottish term for a membership certificate.

District: see *Provincial.*

Fellowcraft: the second step to becoming a *Master Mason.* The ceremony involved is called 'massing'. In Scotland, often 'Fellow *of* Craft'.

Grand Lodge: a national or regional organisation administering all the lodges in the region under a uniform set of masonic laws. Normally, each Grand Lodge is formed by three or more lodges, which were either previously independent or were under the jurisdiction of a Grand Lodge outside the territory concerned. It is a democratic body consisting of representatives of each lodge in its jurisdiction.

Grand Lodge Above: used for the place of existence after death, but expressing no preference for the name of any one religion. Not used in an exclusive sense as a special Heaven for masons!

Hele: an old word meaning to cover.

'Higher' Degrees: degrees conferred in masonic bodies for which the qualification for membership is at least that of being a *Master Mason.* The word 'higher' is objected to as implying superiority, when the highest degree remains that of a Master Mason (completed by the *Royal Arch* in England)

and the highest office that of Grand Master. But no better general term has been popularised.

Initiation: see *Apprentice*.

Installation: the procedure by which a new Master is placed in his chair; the whole meeting at which this takes place, including the appointment/investiture of the other officers. Confusingly, in *chivalric masonry,* each new member is 'installed'.

Joining: when a mason applies for membership of a second lodge, he 'joins' it. In Scottish masonry, this is 'affiliation'.

Jurisdiction: the area of territory or group of lodges over which a Grand Lodge has control. See also *Constitution*.

Landmark: a term first used by James Anderson, which has come to mean an unwritten and unchangeable principle which is deemed essential to true Freemasonry. Since they are (or were) unwritten, they have been the subject of much debate, especially in nineteenth century America.

Lecture: in *Royal Arch* masonry, the equivalent of the '*charge*' of the Craft. In Irish masonry, an explanation of the preceding ceremony. In the English Craft, a series of catechisms which review the degree ceremony and add further explanations.

Lodge: the basic unit of masonic organisation, consisting of seven or more masons, usually subordinate to a national or regional Grand Lodge. Also called 'private lodge' in English, 'daughter lodge' in Scottish, and 'subordinate lodge' in Irish and American usage. Lodge has lost the meaning of a place where masons meet, but retains the meaning of the meeting itself. Some *'higher' degree* bodies are also called lodge, but usually with an additional title such as Ark Mariner Lodge, Lodge of Perfection.

Lodge of Instruction: a lodge attached to a normal lodge but with a degree of independence, which meets primarily to rehearse masonic *ritual*. *Grand Lodge of Instruction:* the Irish authority on craft working.

Lodge of Research: a lodge which meets only to hear papers read, normally on historical subjects, but generally on any subject related to Freemasonry.

Mark: a degree for which a *Master Mason* is qualified, but essentially an expansion of the *Fellowcraft* degree. It is governed by a separate Grand Lodge in England, but in most countries it is a preliminary to the *Royal Arch* degree.

Master: The presiding officer of a lodge, elected for a period of a year at a time, by all the brethren present at the election meeting. He is often addressed as 'Worshipful Master' in the sense of 'worth-ship', although his office is defined simply as Master. In Scottish lodges, he is addressed as 'Right Worshipful Master'.

Master Mason: the third step in a normal lodge, by which a member becomes fully qualified to vote, for office, to attend *Provincial Grand Lodge* etc. In English masonry, the *Apprentice* has most of the privileges of membership already, with variants in Ireland and Scotland, but in America he has none until he becomes a Master Mason. The ceremony by which this is achieved is called 'raising'.

Moderns: the nickname for the Premier Grand Lodge, founded in 1717, given by the *'Antients'*, qv.

Mystery: the trade secrets of a working man. Applied by present day masons to their recognition signs and words. Nothing to do with religious mysteries or gnosis.

Operative: related to the craft of building in stone, generally prior to the eighteenth century, cf *'speculative'*.

Order: used imprecisely to mean *regular* masonry as a whole, masons within one organisation, or one of the *'chivalric'* orders.

Pedestal: the base of a pillar, used to refer to the box-like table in front of the principal officers of a lodge.

Principal: the three senior officers of a *Royal Arch Chapter* are its First, Second and Third Principals. They are also known by the personages they represent in the degree, the First Principal being Zerubbabel. In Irish masonry, he is the King, and in America the High Priest, due to differences in the traditional history.

Provincial/District Grand Lodge: an intermediate organisational grouping of lodges, within a Grand Lodge and formed by the Grand Master. In practice, it is a small version of a Grand Lodge under a Provincial/District Grand Master. In the British Isles, a masonic Province is usually based upon a county, but is sometimes several together as in Wales, or further divided as in Lancashire. In English and Scottish masonry, a *District* is an area overseas. Many other jurisdictions divide their administration into small Districts of two to ten lodges.

Pure Antient Masonry: a phrase occurring at the beginning of the English *Constitutions*, which limits this concept to the *Craft* and *Royal Arch*. An equivalent limitation in Scotland is to the Craft and *Mark*, and in Ireland to Craft, Mark and Royal Arch. It implies relative modernity and limited significance for the *'higher' degrees*.

Regular: masonically, this almost invariably means conforming to the law. Masons are regular when they are made in a lodge which is recognised as part of a *Grand Lodge* which practises masonry that conforms to the original *speculative* principles set in eighteenth century England, and has not permitted atheists to be initiated, religion and politics to be discussed in its meetings, etc.

Regular meetings/*communications* are those held at dates specified by the lodge by-laws, as distinct from special or emergency meetings.

Rite: masonically distinct from *'ritual'*, a rite is a connected series of degrees conferred in a single or co-ordinated organisation. Hence the Ancient and Accepted *Scottish Rite* is a series of thirty degrees starting with fourth (the lodge confers the first three) and ending with an administrative degree, the Thirty-Third. The York or American Rite is ten degrees conferred in three groups by *Royal Arch* Chapters, Cryptic Councils and Templar Commanderies. Perhaps the most exotic was the Egyptian Rite or the Rite of Memphis and Misraim, consisting of ninety-six degrees and now happily extinct except for a very small irregular body in France.

Looser usage occurs, and Crossle has used 'Irish Rite' to mean the variant local form of masonry in all its degrees which exists in Ireland, and Hughan the same for England. Apart from the Ancient and Accepted Rite in the British Isles and the Cryptic Rite in Scotland, the term is uncommon in Britain, where there is a tendency to have a separate governing body for each group of a few degrees.

Ritual: the words (and in practice, actions) to be used in a masonic meeting, usually consisting of a formal opening, degree ceremony, and closing. Also called 'working'.

Also applied to a book containing a printed version of the ritual with rubrics for the actions, and to the variant workings sponsored by *Lodges of Instruction* or Ritual Associations, such as Emulation Lodge of Improvement and Taylor's Ritual Association.

Rose Croix: the eighteenth degree of the Ancient and Accepted or Scottish Rite, conferred in full in chapters in the British Isles.

Royal Arch: a degree for which a *Master Mason* is qualified, regarded in England as the completion of that degree. In most countries, it is part of a series of two to four degrees conferred in a Royal Arch *Chapter.* It is governed by a *Supreme Grand Chapter,* which in England is very closely linked with the Grand Lodge.

Scottish Rite. See *Rite.* Nothing to do with Scotland, having been invented in France and organised in its present form in America. In England and Ireland it is simply called 'Ancient and Accepted Rite'. In the British Isles, candidates must be Christians, but this is not so in most countries. The term 'ecossais' became an eighteenth century misnomer equivalent to *'higher' degree* today.

Speculative: means theoretical, referring to modern Freemasons who are not required to have practical knowledge of building in stone; cf *Operative.*

Supreme Council: the governing body of the *Scottish Rite* within each national jurisdiction. Autocratic bodies whose members, holders of the Thirty-Third degree, elect their own new members for life.

Supreme Grand Chapter: see *Royal Arch:* its national governing body. A democratic organisation consisting of representatives of each chapter.

Symbolic masonry/degrees: used for the first three degrees, with no apparent logic, as the 'higher' degrees are also symbolic.

Temple: strictly speaking, the room in which a lodge meets, by analogy with the Temple of Solomon, symbolically under construction during its meetings. Often misapplied to the masonic hall as a whole, giving it religious overtones which are not appropriate.

Tyler: a lodge officer who stands outside its door to keep off non-masons. (In Irish masonry, he is not regarded as an officer.) Possibly derived from the duty of an operative tiler to cover a building. Generally a retired person, often the resident caretaker of a masonic hall, he is known to fellow masons for his kindly instruction to candidates before they enter.

Warden: a lodge officer who shares duties in part with the Master. Each lodge has a Senior and Junior Warden.

Warrant: the document from a Grand Lodge authorising a lodge to meet. Outside England and Ireland, called the lodge's Charter.

Working: see Ritual.

BIBLIOGRAPHY

The Aldersgate Royal Arch Ritual. London (Lewis) 1978.

The Alternative Service Book 1980. London (Clowes/SPCK/Cambridge UP) 1980.

Anderson's Constitutions, 1723 and 1738. Facsimile Edition. London (Quatuor Coronati Lodge) 1976.

'Anglo-Catholic': *Reflections on Freemasonry*. Breaston, Derby (Freedom) 1930.

Ankerberg, John and Weldon, John: *The Facts on the Masonic Lodge*. Eugene, Oregon, Harvest House, 1989.

Association of Methodist Freemasons: *A Review of Information Assembled by the Association . . . about the Effects of the 1985 Conference Report about Freemasonry,* probably Manchester 1993.

Barr, James: *Fundamentalism*. London (SCM) 1981.

Old and New in Interpretation—A Study of the Two Testaments. London (SCM Press) 1982.

Barrett, David B (ed): *World Christian Encyclopedia*. Nairobi, OUP, 1982.

'Basic Principles for Grand Lodge Recognition' in *Information for the Guidance of Members of the Craft*. London (United GL) 1978.

Batham, C. N.: 'Chevalier Ramsay—a New Appreciation' in *AQC* 81. London (QC Lodge) 1968.

Berry, Harold J: *What they believe—Masons*. Lincoln, Nebraska, Back-to-the-Bible Publishing, 1999.

Bevan, Edwyn: *Symbolism and Belief*. London (Collins/Fontana) 1962.

Bierce, Ambrose: *The Enlarged Devil's Dictionary*. Harmondsworth (Penguin) 1971.

Blanchard, President J: *Scotch Rite Masonry Illustrated—The Complete Ritual of the Ancient and Accepted Scottish Rite, Profusely Illustrated . . .* Chicago (Ezra A. Cook) 1972.

Book of Common Prayer—with Additions and Deviations Proposed in 1928. London (Oxford UP) ND.

Brault, Eliane: *La Franc Maconnerie et l'Emancipation des Femmes*. Paris (Dervy-Livres) 1967.

Brown, Francis et al: *The New Brown-Driver-Briggs-Gesenius Hebrew and English Lexicon*. Peabody Mass, Hendrikson, 1979.

Brown, Raymond E: *The Churches the Apostles Left Behind*. London (Chapman) 1984.

The Epistles of John—Anchor Bible, vol 30. New York (Doubleday) 1982.

Bruce, Sinclair: 'The Deacons' in *AQC* 98. London (QC Lodge) 1986.

Bultmann, Rudolf: *Primitive Christianity in its Contemporary Setting*. London (Thames and Hudson) 1983.

Burns, Revd George A: 'For the Good of Freemasonry' in *The Philalethes* vol XL No 3, June 1987. Des Moines, Ia (Philalethes Society).

Cadogan, Andrew: 'When pagan rites entwine with Christian practice' in the *South China Morning Post Christmas Magazine*. Hong Kong (South China Morning Post) 1985.

Carpenter, William A: *The Exemplar: A Guide to a Mason's Actions*. Philadelphia (GL of Pennsylvania) 1985.

Carr, Harry: *The Freemason at Work*. London (Lewis) 1976.

'Freemasonry before the Grand Lodge' in *Grand Lodge 1717–1967*. London (United GL) 1967.
'The Obligation and its Place in the Ritual' in *AQC* 74. London (QC Lodge) 1961.
Cavendish, R. (ed): *Man, Myth and Magic*. London (Purnell/BPC) 1971.
Ceremonies of the United Religious and Military Order of the Temple and of St John . . . London (Great Priory) 1965.
Clarke, J. R: 'The Change from Christianity to Deism in Freemasonry' in *AQC* 78. London (QC Lodge) 1966.
Clausen, Henry: 'A "Retort Courteous" to Mason-bashing' in *The New Age* vol xciii No 12 for December 1985. Washington DC (Supreme Council, SJ)
Coil, Henry Wilson (eds: Brown, William Moseley and others): *Coil's Masonic Encyclopedia*. New York (Macoy) 1961.
Comay, Joan: *Who's Who in the Old Testament—together with the Apocrypha*. London (Weidenfeld & Nicolson) 1971.
Constitutions of the Antient Fraternity . . . London (United GL) 1979
Constitutions and Regulations for . . . the Order of the Secret Monitor . . . London (Grand Council) 1969.
Corriden, James A., Green, Thomas J. and Heintschel, Donald E. (eds): *The New Code of Canon Law: Text and Commentary*. London (Chapman) 1985.
Crow, W. B: *A History of Magic, Witchcraft and Occultism*. London (Aquarian) 1968.
Cryer, the Revd N Barker: 'The De-Christianizing of the Craft' in *Ars Quatuor Coronatorum* vol 97 for 1984. London (QC Lodge).
Freemasonry and the Churches. Typescript. ND. *How did the Royal Arch Legends Develop?* Typescript, York. ND. *The Churches' Involvement with Freemasonry*. Typescript, York, 2004.
Cryptic Degrees. Edinburgh (SGRA Chapter of Scotland) ND, c1970.
Cupitt, Don: *The Sea of Faith*. London (BBC) 1984.
de Blank, Joost: *Call of Duty—Church Membership Considered*. London (Oxford UP) 1956.
De Haan, Kurt E: 'How do you get into Heaven?' in *Our Daily Bread* for June-July-August 1986. Grand Rapids (Radio Bible Class).
de Poncins, Vicomte Leon: *Freemasonry and the Vatican: a Struggle for Recognition*. London (Britons) 1968.
'Deism 'in *The New Caxton Encyclopaedia*. London (Caxton) 1966.
Dewar, James: *The Unlocked Secret—Freemasonry Examined*. London (Kimber) 1966.
Digest of Rulings for the use and guidance of Grand Lodge Office-bearers . . . Edinburgh (Grand Committee) 1949.
Dillistone, F. W: *The Power of Symbols*. London (SCM Press) 1986.
Douglas, J. D. and others (eds): *New Bible Dictionary* 2nd Ed. Leicester (Inter-Varsity) 1982.
Draffen of Newington, George: *The Triple Tau*. Edinburgh (SGRA Chapter of Scotland) ND.
Duncan, Malcolm C: *Duncan's Masonic Ritual and Monitor or Guide to the Three Symbolic Degrees* . . . New York (David McKay) ND.
Dyer, Colin: *The history of the first 100 years of Quatuor Coronati Lodge No. 2076*. London (QCCC Ltd) 1986.
'Some Thoughts on the Origins of Speculative Masonry' in *AQC 95*. London (QC Lodge) 1983.
Symbolism in Craft Freemasonry. Shepperton (Lewis) 1976.

Emulation Ritual as demonstrated in the Emulation Lodge of Improvement, 1st ed. London (Lewis Masonic) 1969.
Evangelical Alliance: *Christianity and Other Faiths—An Evangelical Contribution to our Multi-Faith Society.* Exeter (Paternoster) 1983.
An Exhibition on the History of English Freemasonry (pamphlet). London (United GL) 1986.
Finney, Charles G.: *Power from On High—a Selection of Articles on the Spirit-Filled Life*. Fort Washington, Pa (Christian Literature Crusade) 1984.
Ford, J. Massyngberde: *Revelation—Anchor Bible,* vol 38. New York (Doubleday) 1975.
Freemasonry and Christianity. London (United GL) 1986.
Freemasonry and Religion. London (United GL) 1985.
Gay, Peter: *Deism: An Anthology*. Princeton (van Nostrand) 1968.
Glick, Carl (ed): *A Treasury of Masonic Thought*. London (Robert Hale) 1959.
'Gnosticism' in *The New Caxton Encyclopaedia,* vol 9. London (Caxton) 1966.
Golka, F. W: 'Universalism and the Election of the Jews' in *Theology* for July 1987. London (SPCK).
Grand College . . . of the British Commonwealth of Nations and their Dependencies: Ritual I. Newcastle upon Tyne (General Board) 1963.
Grand Constitutions of Freemasonry, 1762 and 1786, Ancient and Accepted Scottish Rite. Manila (Supreme Council) 1978.
Grand Lodge: 1717–1967. London (United GL) 1967.
Gratton, F M & Ivy, R S: *The History of Freemasonry in Shanghai and Northern China*. Tientsin, Masonic Bodies, 1913
Haffner, Christopher: *The Craft in the East*. Hong Kong (District GL of HK and the FE) 1976.
'Freemasonry as a Cult' – A summary of . . . a tape recording by the Revd David Pawson with comments . . ., Hong Kong, Paul Chater Lodge and Lodge Cosmopolitan, 1991.
'Masonry Universal—a Geographical Study' in the *Transactions* of the Paul Chater Lodge No 5391. Hong Kong, 1978.
'Regularity of Origin' in *AQC* 96. London (QC Lodge) 1984.
'Structure in Freemasonry' in *Chater-Cosmo Transactions* vol 5, Hong Kong (CCT) 1984.
Haggard, Forrest D: *The Clergy and the Craft*. Missouri (Missouri Lodge of Research) 1970.
Hamill, John: *The Craft: a History of English Freemasonry.* Wellingborough (Crucible) 1986.
Handfield-Jones, R. M: *The Origin and History of the United Religious and Military Orders of the Temple and of St John of Jerusalem . . .* London (Grand Master's K.T. Council) 1973.
Hannah, Walton: *Christian by Degrees—Masonic Religion Revealed in the Light of Faith*. London (Britons) 1984.
Darkness Visible: a Revelation and Interpretation of Freemasonry. Devon (Britons) 1975.
Heino, Harri: *Freemasonry and the Christian Faith*, Tampere, Research Institute of the Lutheran Church in Finland, c1987.
Hayward, H. L: 'Freemasonry and the Bible' in *Holy Bible—Masonic Edition.* Glasgow (Collins) 1951.
Higham, M. B. S: 'From Craft to Tolerance' in *Masonic Square* for March 1986. Shepperton (Lewis Masonic)

Hoekema, Anthony A: *The Four Major Cults*. Exeter (Paternoster) 1963.
Horne, Alex: *King Solomon's Temple in the Masonic Tradition*. London (Aquarian) 1972.
Home Mission Board, SBC: *A Study of Freemasonry* (with separate synopsis and summary for the vote). Atlanta, Southern Baptist Convention, 1993.
Hughan, William James: *The Old Charges of British Freemasons*. London (Simkin Marshall) 1872.
History and Origin of the Masonic and Military Order of the Red Cross of Constantine . . . London (Grand Imperial Conclave) 1971.
Information for the Guidance of Members of the Craft. London (United GL) 1978.
'Investigation by the Presbyterian Church in Ireland into "The Beliefs and Practices of Freemasonry" ' in the *Annual Report 1991* of the Grand Lodge of Ireland, Dublin 1992 and same title in *Annual Report 1992,* ditto, 1993.
Irish Freemasons' Calendar and Directory for the Year A.D. 1979. Dublin (GL of Ireland) 1979.
Irish Ritual, unofficial. Hong Kong (Irish L of Instruction) ND.
'Irreconcilability between Christian faith and Freemasonry' in *L'Osservatore Romano* for 11 March 1985. Vatican City.
Jackson, Brig A. C. F: *Rose Croix—the History of the Ancient and Accepted Rite for England and Wales*. London (Lewis Masonic) 1980.
'Rosicrucianism and its Effect on Craft Masonry' in *AQC* 96. London (QC Lodge) 1984.
'Sir Charles Warren, G.C.M.G., K.C.B., Founding Master of Quatuor Coronati Lodge, No 2076' . Offprint of paper presented to QC Lodge on 11 September 1986, to form part of *AQC* 99, 1987.
Jones, Bernard E: *The Freemason's Book of the Royal Arch*. London, Harrap, 1957.
Keeley, Robin (ed): *The Lion Handbook of Christian Belief*. Tring (Lion) 1982.
Knight, Stephen: *The Brotherhood—The Secret World of the Freemasons*. London (Granada) 1984.
Kung, Hans: *The Church—Maintained in Truth*. London (SCM) 1980.
Lasky, Irving I: 'The Martyrdom of Galileo Galilei' in *The New Age* vol xciii No 12 for December 1985. Washington DC (Supreme Council SJ).
Lawrence, John: *Freemasonry—a religion?* Eastbourne (Kingsway) 1987.
Lepper, John Heron and Crossle, Philip: *History of the Grand Lodge of . . . Ireland*. Dublin (L of Research) 1925.
Lindsay, Robert Strathern: *The Royal Order of Scotland*. Edinburgh (Executive Cttee) 1971.
Littlefair, Revd David: 'No road for a Christian' in the *Evening Herald* for 7 August 1984. Plymouth.
Macoy 1982, Catalog 108. Richmond, Va (Macoy) 1982
Mackey, Albert G: *Encyclopaedia of Freemasonry*. New York (Macoy) 1946.
(rev Clegg, Robert Ingham): *Jurisprudence of Freemasonry*. Richmond Va (Macoy) 1953.
Masonic Year Book 1985–86. London (United GL) 1985.
MacBride, A. S: *Reprint of the . . . Ritual*. Glasgow (Kenning) 1947.
McBrien, Richard P: *Catholicism: Study Edition*. Minneapolis (Winston) 1981.
McCormick, W. J. McK: *Christ, the Christian & Freemasonry*. Belfast (Great Joy) 1984.
McGrath, Alister E: *Christian Theology—An Introduction*. London, Blackwell, 1997

Mackey, Albert G., rev Clegg, Robert I: *Encyclopaedia of Freemasonry*. New York (Macoy) 1946.
McLeod, W: 'A Lost Manuscript Reconstructed—The Ancestor of One Branch of the Old Charges', in *AQC* 94. London (QC Lodge) 1982.
Macquarrie, John: *Principles of Christian Theology*. London, SCM Press, 1977
The Old Gothic Constitutions. Bloomington, III (Masonic Book Club) 1985.
Meeking, Basil and Stott, John (eds): *The Evangelical—Roman Catholic Dialogue on Mission: 1977–1984: a Report*. Exeter (Paternoster) 1988.
Mellor, Alec: 'A Letter to "Die weisse Lilie",' in *Chater-Cosmo Transactions* vol 7. Hong Hong (*CCT*) 1986.
Middleton, Carl L. Jr and Craig, Robert P: *Teaching the Ten Commandments Today*. Mystic, Ct (Twenty-Third) 1977 pa
Morison, Frank: *Who Moved the Stone?* London (Faber) 1958.
Mudditt, B. Howard (ed): *Christian Worship*. Exeter (Paternoster) 1975.
Naudon, Paul: *La Franc-Maçonnerie Chrétienne*. Paris (Dervy-Livres) 1970.
Neill, Stephen: *Crises of Belief: the Christian Dialogue with Faith and No Faith*. London (Hodder) 1984.
The New English Bible with the Apocrypha, Oxford Study Edition. New York (Oxford UP) 1976.
Newton, (the Revd) Joseph Fort: *The Religion of Masonry: an Interpretation*. Richmond, Va (Macoy) 1969.
Nicholls, Bruce: 'We all believe something' in *The Lion Handbook of Christian Belief*. Tring (Lion) 1982.
Official Ritual—Heredom of Kilwinning and Rosy Cross. Edinburgh (GL of the Royal Order of Scotland) 1950.
Packer, James: 'God: from the Fathers to the Moderns' in *The Lion Handbook of Christian Belief*. Tring (Lion) 1982.
Panel of Doctrine of the Church of Scotland: *The Church and Freemasonry*. Edinburgh, St Andrew Press, 1990.
Pawson, Revd David: *Freemasonry as a Cult*. Tape recording, c1969.
'Pelagianism' in *The New Caxton Encyclopaedia*. London (Caxton) 1968.
The Perfect Ceremonies of the Supreme Order of the Holy Royal Arch. London (Lewis Masonic) 1956.
Pick, Fred L. and Knight, G. Norman: *The Freemason's Pocket Reference Book*. London (Muller) 1965.
The Pocket History of Freemasonry. London (Muller) 1969.
Pike, Albert: *Morals and Dogma of the Ancient and Accepted Scottish Rite of Freemasonry*. Washington DC (House of the Temple) 1969.
Poole, Revd Herbert (rev): *Gould's History of Freemasonry*. London (Caxton) 1951.
Pound, Roscoe: *Masonic Addresses and Writings of Roscoe Pound*. New York (Macoy) 1953.
Prescott, Professor Andrew: 'The Centre for Research into Freemasonry at the University of Sheffield' in *Quarterly Communication holden . . . 8th day of September 2004*, London, United Grand Lodge of England, 2004.
'Presentations for the CMRC International Conference 6th and 7th November 200, Freemasonry and Religion—Many Faiths One Brotherhood,' London, Canonbury Masonic Research Centre, 2004.
Proceedings of the Church of England Synod, Fourth Day, Monday 13 July 1987. Typescript.
Race, Alan: 'Christianity and Other Religions: Is Inclusivism Enough' in *Theology* for May 1986. London (SPCK).

Ratzinger, Cardinal Joseph and Hamer, Fr Jerome: 'Declaration on Masonic Associations' in *L'Osservatore Romano* for 5 December 1985. Vatican City.

Read, W: 'The "Extended" Working of the Board of Installed Masters' in *AQC* 84. London (QC Lodge) 1972.

'Let a Man's Religion . . . be What it May . . .' in *AQC* 98. London (QC Lodge) 1986.

Religion and Freemasonry. London (United GL) 1985.

'Report on the Panel of Doctrine of the General Assembly of the Church of Scotland' in *Proceedings of the Grand Lodge of Scotland,* 1989-1990 No 3, Edinburgh 1990.

'Response to the Report of the Doctrine Committee of the Presbyterian Church in Ireland . . .' in *Annual Report 1992* of the Grand Lodge of Ireland, Dublin, 1993.

Ritual No 2—The Masonic and Military Order of the Red Cross of Constantine . . . London (Grand Imperial Conclave) 1968.

Ritual of the Irish Chapter (unofficial, no title or date).

Ritual of the Supreme Grand Chapter of Scotland (no title). Edinburgh (SGRA Chapter of Scotland) nd.

Robinson, John J: *A Pilgrim's Path – One Man's Road to the Masonic Temple.* New York, M Evans, 1993.

Rogers, James R: 'Albert Pike—the Freemason' in *The New Age* vol XCIV No 4 for April 1986. Washington DC (Supreme Council SJ).

Ronayne, E: *Chapter Masonry, being The Opening, Closing, Secret Work . . .* Chicago (Powner) 1901.

Royal Arch Ritual Changes and Explanatory Leaflet, Annexes (A) and (B) to the Paper of Business for Grand Chapter for 10 February 1988. London (Supreme Grand Chapter).

Rules and Regulations for the Government of the Degrees from 4th to 33rd Inclusive . . . London (Supreme Council) 1972.

Rumble, Dr L: *Catholics and Freemasonry.* London (Catholic Truth Society) 1955.

Sanders, J. Oswald: *Heresies and Cults.* London (Lakeland) 1969.

Schaeffer, Franky: *Addicted to Mediocrity—20th Century Christians and the Arts.* Westchester, Ill, Crossway, 1981.

Seven [7] Reasons why Freemasonry is not of God (Anonymous). Erith, Diasozo Trust, ND.

Sheehan, The Most Revd M: *Apologetics and Catholic Doctrine.* Dublin (Gill) 1959.

Sherill, John and Elizabeth: *The Happiest People on Earth.* Old Tappan NJ (Spire) 1975.

Sheville, John and Gould, James L: *Guide to the Royal Arch Chapter, a Complete Monitor . . .* Richmond, Va (Macoy) 1867.

Stone, Nathan J: *Names of God in the Old Testament.* Chicago (Moody) 1944.

Stubbs, Sir James: 'The Government of the Craft' in *AQC* 95. London (QC Lodge) 1983.

Swedish Synod of Bishops: *Decision in case no 5/1984,* typescript, Uppsala? 1984.

Tan, Thomas Tsu-wee: *Your Chinese Roots—the Overseas Chinese Story.* Singapore (Times) 1986.

Taylor, Harmon R: 'Christians and Freemasonry—Mixing Oil and Water' in *The Evangelist* for June 1986.

Thornhill, Raymond: *The Mystical Lecture*. Typescript, probably 1988.
Tuesday Call: Tellex Report on Freemasonry. Typescript. London (Tellex) 1984.
van Ginkel, Frank and Haffner, Christopher: 'The First Japanese Freemasons' in *Chater-Cosmo Transactions* vol 2. Hong Kong (CCT) 1981.
Van der Veur, Paul: *Freemasonry in Indonesia from Radermacher to Soekanto, 1762-1961*. Athens, Ohio U Centre for International Studies, 1976.
Viewpoint – Baptists and Freemasonry, Edinburgh, Baptist Union of Scotland, c1988.
'Vindex': *Light Invisible. the Freemason's Answer to Darkness Visible*. London (Britons) 1964.
Wade, Paul: 'Freemasonry—an Investigation' in *Chater-Cosmo Transactions* vol 4, radio programme transcript. Hong Kong (CCT) 1983.
Walker, G. E: '. . . *Who must otherwise have remained at a perpetual distance': 250 Years of Masonry in India: a Study in Resolved Discords*. London (private) 1959. (see also *AQC*).
Walkes, Joseph A, Jr: *Black Square and Compass. 200 Years of Prince Hall Freemasonry*. New York (Writers Press) 1979.
'A Word from the President' in *The Phylaxis* vol xiii No 1—1st Quarter 1987. Kansas City (Phylaxis Society).
Ward, Lt-Col E: 'Anderson's Freemasonry not Deistic' in *AQC* 80. London (QC Lodge) 1968.
Ward, J. S. M: *Freemasonry and the Ancient Gods*. London (Simkin Marshall) 1921.
Watts, Robert B. (ed): *A Presentation Concerning the Ancient and Accepted Scottish Rite*. Washington DC (House of the Temple) 1978.
What is Freemasonry. London (United GL) 1985.
'Why ban masonry?' in the *Lafayette Sunday Visitor*, probably March 1986. Lafayette, Indiana.
Whymper, Henry Josiah: *The Religion of Freemasonry*. London (Kenning) 1888.
Wilkerson, Maj-Gen H. Lloyd: 'A Survey of Attitudes Toward the Masonic Fraternity' in *The New Age* vol XCIV No 5 for May 1988. Washington DC (Supreme Council SJ).
Working Group established by the Standing Committee of the General Synod of the Church of England: *Christianity and Freemasonry—Are They Compatible?—a contribution to discussion*. London (Church House) 1987.
'World Church & Mission Department – Appendix 2 – Freemasonry' in *General Assembly 1986*, [no details of place available], United Reformed Church, c1987.
Worley, Revd Dr Lloyd: 'The Truth about Freemasonry' in *The Philalethes* vol XL No 2 for April 1987. Des Moines, Ia (Philalethes Society).
Yates, Francis: *The Rosicrucian Enlightenment*. London (Routledge) 1972
Year Book of the Grand Lodge of . . . Scotland. Edinburgh (GL) 1986.
Young, Davis A: *Christianity and the Age of the Earth*. Grand Rapids, Michigan (Zondervan) 1982.
Young, Robert: *Analytical Concordance to the Holy Bible*. 8th ed. Guildford (United Soc for Christian Literature) 1939.

INDEX

BIBLICAL REFERENCES
in Protestant Bible order

NEW TESTAMENT

* 9 7 8 0 8 5 3 1 8 5 8 9 5 *
BV - #0092 - 051225 - C0 - 240/150/19 - PB - 9780853185895 - Gloss Lamination